The Legacy of
Anne Frank

The Legacy of
Anne Frank

Gillian Walnes Perry

PEN & SWORD
HISTORY

AN IMPRINT OF PEN & SWORD BOOKS LTD.
YORKSHIRE - PHILADELPHIA

First published in Great Britain in 2018 and reprinted in 2019 by
PEN & SWORD HISTORY
an imprint of
Pen & Sword Books Ltd
Yorkshire – Philadelphia

Copyright © Gillian Walnes Perry 2018, 2019

ISBN 978 1 52673 104 3

The right of Gillian Walnes Perry to be identified
as the Author of this Work has been asserted by her in accordance
with the Copyright, Designs and Patents Act 1988.

Typeset in Times New Roman 10/12.5 by
Aura Technology and Software Services, India

Printed and bound in the UK by TJ International Ltd, Padstow, Cornwall.

Pen & Sword Books Ltd incorporates the imprints of Pen & Sword
Archaeology, Atlas, Aviation, Battleground, Discovery,
Family History, History, Maritime, Military, Naval, Politics, Railways,
Select, Social History, Transport, True Crime, and Claymore Press,
Frontline Books, Leo Cooper, Praetorian Press, Remember When,
Seaforth Publishing and Wharncliffe.

For a complete list of Pen & Sword titles please contact
PEN & SWORD BOOKS LIMITED
47 Church Street, Barnsley, South Yorkshire, S70 2AS, England
E-mail: enquiries@pen-and-sword.co.uk
Website: www.pen-and-sword.co.uk

Or
PEN AND SWORD BOOKS
1950 Lawrence Rd, Havertown, PA 19083, USA
E-mail: Uspen-and-sword@casematepublishers.com
Website: www.penandswordbooks.com

Contents

Acknowledgements vii

List of Photographs viii

Prologue   Anne Frank is Here in the World x

Chapter 1   Anne Frank 1

Chapter 2   Otto Frank 19

Chapter 3   'Anne Frank in the World' is Launched 31

Chapter 4   The Anne Frank Trust is Born 36

Chapter 5   Anne and Eva Schloss – the Girl who
Became her Stepsister 45

Chapter 6   Anne Frank's Role in the Transition
from Communism 54

Chapter 7   The Woman Who Gave a Personal Pledge
to Otto Frank 73

Chapter 8   Anne Frank in Latin America 78

Chapter 9   Anne Frank and Audrey Hepburn 95

Chapter 10   On the Road with Anne Frank 99

Chapter 11   Anne Frank and the Children of Bosnia 110

Chapter 12   Anne Frank and Nelson Mandela 120

Chapter 13   Anne Frank and her Protector Miep Gies 128

Chapter 14   Anne Frank goes into British Prisons 137

Chapter 15   Anne Frank and Stephen Lawrence 145

Chapter 16   Anne Frank Helping to Make Peace in Ireland ... 151

Chapter 17   Anne Frank and her Secret Hero 155

Chapter 18   Anne Frank and Daniel Pearl 160

Chapter 19   The Anne Frank Declaration 163

Chapter 20   The Anne Frank Trust is Growing 173

Chapter 21   Who Betrayed the Frank Family? 188

Chapter 22   Anne Frank is Educating Millions 194

Chapter 23   Inspired by Holocaust Survivors 207

Chapter 24   Anne Frank and the Girl who was Kidnapped by
              Sardinian Bandits 219

Chapter 25   Anne Frank in the Far East 223

Chapter 26   Anne Frank was a Real Person 237

Chapter 27   Anne Frank in the Indian Subcontinent 247

Chapter 28   The Strange Circle of the House
              on Blaricummerweg 262

Chapter 29   Anne Frank and her Fear 269

Chapter 30   Anne Frank and the Future 272

References 281

Index 284

Acknowledgements

I truly want to thank everyone I have encountered or heard about in the world of Anne Frank for their dedication and for being an inspiration to me. But sadly I can't, or this chronicle will span a further 300 pages. So here are my thanks to a few of the key players in a story that relates the lives and activities of hundreds of fascinating people and spans a period of thirty years.

To all my wonderful colleagues, past and present, at the Anne Frank Trust, the Anne Frank House, the Anne Frank Fonds and throughout the Anne Frank family of educators and activists around the world. Too many to mention I fear, but they all know who they are.

To Hans Westra, Rabbi David Soetendorp, Eva Schloss, the late Bee Klug, Jan Erik Dubbelman, Dienke Hondius and the late Buddy Elias for the faith they placed in me all those years ago. I followed an unforgettable path with them, and they have guided my life with wisdom and love.

To Penguin Books, to Michelle Rosenberg and to Jon Wright, Laura Hirst, Stephen Chumbley and the team at my publishers Pen & Sword who have so ably and supportively helped to realise this dream.

It has been a true privilege to have worked with you all.

To my late husband Tony Bogush, who was behind me every step of the way from the start and left a huge mark on the Anne Frank Trust.

To my children Joe and Tilly, who lived throughout their teenage years with the Anne Frank Trust taking over their family home. Having survived the experience, they grew up to make me the proudest mother in the world from their remarkable achievements and a doting Nana to Ewan, Emily and Jonah.

Finally, to my amazing husband Elon Perry, who brought his talent and many years of experience as a celebrated Israeli journalist, writer, poet and editor, to help bring the manuscript into such shape that the publishers had no need for editing. Also, for his love, devotion, endless cups of tea, beautiful Sephardic meals, and his support along the way.

List of Photographs

1. Cover image: Anne Frank aged eleven in April 1941. Photograph taken at the Frank family apartment on the Merwedeplein, Amsterdam. Photo courtesy of the Anne Frank Fonds – Basel via Getty Images.
2. Happy and normal family life. Edith Frank takes seven-year-old Margot and three-year-old Anne on a trip to Frankfurt city centre in March 1933. Hitler has been in power for two months, and life for Germany's Jews is about to change. Photo courtesy of the Anne Frank Fonds – Basel via Getty Images.
3. In May 1941, the photographer Frans Dupont took a series of exquisitely posed studio images of eleven-year-old Anne. Photo by Frans Dupont/Anne Frank Fonds – Basel via Getty Images.
4. (a) The front cover and (b) inside of Anne's original diary with photos she pasted inside it. From the Anne Frank House collection.
5. The first Anne Frank traveling exhibition *Anne Frank in the World 1929-1945* was monochrome and huge in scale. Here it is on show in Glasgow in 1990. From the Anne Frank House collection.
6. Otto Frank and his wife Fritzi visiting Audrey Hepburn at her home in Switzerland, circa 1957. A copy of this photo was given to me in Los Angeles by Audrey's son, Sean Hepburn Ferrer. It was taken by his late father, the actor Mel Ferrer.
7. Anne Frank's cousin Bernd 'Buddy' Elias reads the Anne Frank Declaration to United Nations General Secretary Kofi Annan at UN headquarters in New York in January 1999. Those watching include (from left) footballer and UN Ambassador John Fashanu; my late husband Tony Bogush; the UK's Ambassador to the UN Sir Jeremy Greenstock; Eva Schloss; myself and at back right, Barry van Driel, who composed the Declaration. Photo: UN photographer, from the Anne Frank Trust collection.
8. A very special memory of attending the 1996 Academy Awards in Hollywood with Miep Gies. Jon Blair, the writer and director of the Oscar winning documentary feature *Anne Frank Remembered* is at the back on the right. Photo: Jerome Goldblatt.
9. Anne Frank House International Director Jan Erik Dubbelman greets Japanese children coming to the exhibition in Tokyo in 2010 Photo: Aaron Peterer, Anne Frank House collection.

10. Latvian and Russian teenagers performing together in *The Dreams of Anne Frank* Riga, 1998. For some it was their first opportunity to interact socially. From the Anne Frank House collection.

11. Student peer guides in the South African township of Orlando West with Aaron Peterer of the Anne Frank House education team (centre right back). Photo: Gift Mabunda, 2009 from the Anne Frank House collection.

12. Eva Schloss with a prisoner guide (face obscured) at Wormwood Scrubs Prison in London. On the right is Steve Gadd, the Anne Frank Trust prison tour manager. Photo: Mark McEvoy for the Anne Frank Trust.

13. Dutch Foreign Minister Maxime Verhagen (with red tie) is shown around the *Anne Frank, A History for Today* exhibition at the CEU Paraisopolis School in Sao Paulo, 2010. His enthusiastic and knowledgeable guides are as young as ten and eleven. Photo: Riccardo Sanchez for the Instituto Plataforma Brasil.

14. Anne Frank Ambassadors show schools and members of the public around the *Anne Frank + You* exhibition at Bradford College in West Yorkshire in 2013. With thanks to Bradford Metropolitan District Council and the Anne Frank Trust.

15. Anne Frank peer guides at the Forest Gate School in London. From the Anne Frank Trust collection.

16. After the thirty-year-long Sri Lankan civil war, the *Anne Frank, A History for Today* exhibition gave students in Jaffna an opportunity to reflect on their recent past and future. From the Anne Frank House collection.

Prologue

Anne Frank is Here in the World

'We're all alive, but we don't know why or what for; we're all searching for happiness; we're all leading lives that are different and yet the same'.
Anne Frank, Thursday, 6 July 1944

Some time in the late winter or early spring of 1945, a 15-year-old girl lay on a cold and bare wooden bunk in Bergen-Belsen, the near-abandoned Nazi death camp situated on the icy and windswept Luneberg Heath in Northern Germany. Beside the girl lay her older sister, trying to find the physical strength to continue breathing. But the older girl was so fragile, she toppled from the bunk on to the hard concrete floor and not having the strength to withstand the shock, died immediately. A few hours later, the younger sister also gave up her struggle to stay alive. Their emaciated bodies, already looking like skeletons from the hunger these young girls had endured, were carried out of the barrack and thrown into a pit serving as a mass grave. Eventually the pile of bodies was set alight.

The physical Anne Frank was no more.

Annelies Marie Frank was gone, but her spirit and her story is still echoing all around the world through a little red-checked notebook that she had used as a diary, a personal journal which she had kept while in hiding from the Nazis in rooms above her father's business in Amsterdam. Her diary was published as a book in June 1947 and became one of the world's most widely read and most admired chronicles of the Second World War. Even people who cannot quite recall who she was, and what happened to her, are familiar with the name Anne Frank.

But what is not so well-known is the story of a thread Anne Frank has woven around the world over the past thirty years. Not just through her diary, but through the world's most popular and enduring travelling exhibition and the educational programmes carried out in her name. These were not for commercial success nor for glorification or sanctification of her name, but purely for the noble cause of trying to make this fractured world a bit better.

This is a story of people from radically different places and circumstances who share a commonality. All their lives have been affected by Anne Frank. They are remarkable educators who have travelled to the far reaches of the globe or challenged the establishment for the betterment of their own community, they are young people brought up in deprivation or violence, they are brave human rights defenders who have risked their lives, or those who will become our next generation of influencers and change-makers.

This thread travels through the past three decades of some of the most seismic events in recent world history and into post-conflict arenas. It brings with it a platform for open and honest discussion between former enemies, or those from opposing cultures and communities who had never before had an opportunity to spend time together.

By bringing about productive and fruitful partnerships with local human rights organizations, social welfare groups, cultural associations, youth agencies, embassies and diplomatic missions, the Anne Frank exhibition and education programmes have left behind strong legacies that have been seized and built upon.

Most importantly, through implementing a peer-to-peer method of educating in some of the most challenging areas, it has empowered a generation of young people to consider themselves as our future leaders and influencers. Many of these young people live in the world's toughest societies, where violence, poverty and persecution are taken for granted.

This remarkable story is one of hope, inspiration and aspiration. It is an enactment of Anne Frank's dreams of making a better world and the embodiment of her father Otto Frank's vision of a force for good in his daughter's memory.

What follows is a collection of stories of people who found themselves living through turbulent times. The Anne Frank connecting thread over the past three decades has linked children in the townships of the newly post-apartheid South Africa, to those in post-civil war Sri Lanka, to those in gang-ridden cities in Guatemala and Brazil, to the follower of a murdered Russian priest, to the daughter of a young woman thrown from a plane during the Argentinian dictatorship, to a terrified little Jewish boy pushed forward by a hero-worshipping crowd towards Hitler, to a teenage girl who testified against the soldiers who murdered her family in Kosovo, to a boy killed on a London street whose family went on to challenge racism in the police.

The thread links leaders of countries going through great changes, such as Nelson Mandela, stars such as Audrey Hepburn, Luciano Pavarotti and Angelina Jolie who have offered their celebrity for the benefit of the less fortunate, or those who have found themselves in the wrong place at the wrong time, such as the idealistic American journalist Daniel Pearl. They are those who have survived the near impossible, such as Malala Yousafzai and Zlata Filipović, and inspirational Holocaust and genocide survivors. This story links world statesmen and presidents, British prime ministers and leaders of all the world's major religions with those who knew Anne Frank and hold memories of the real person and things she said and did.

So how did this thread come about? How and why did the world's most popular, enduring and effective travelling exhibition start? An exhibition that has so far been staged over 5,000 times in 95 different countries, and has to date been visited by over nine million people.

Thanks to Otto Frank, the Mayor of Amsterdam and a small group of friends, in May 1960 the building at 263 Prinsengracht in Amsterdam where the Frank family had sought refuge opened its doors to the public as a museum. It was known in Dutch as the 'Anne Frank Huis'. Although its first visitors had to ring the doorbell to be allowed in, by the 1980s the museum was receiving over 400,000 people a year.

One morning in 1984, after watching the very long queue of visitors standing patiently in the cold in front of the 'Anne Frank Huis' museum, staff member Bauco van der Wal approached the Director Hans Westra with a novel idea to create a 'touring Anne Frank House'. The Director warmed to the idea and tasked the museum's historian Joke Kniesmeyer to create an exhibition showing Anne Frank's life and times on panels that could be displayed in external settings.

Little did these three realize the impact this 'novel idea' was about to have on the world.

Chapter 1

Anne Frank

But first, who exactly was Anne Frank? It is a name well-known around the world, and across seven decades, because of her diary, written over the course of twenty-six months. From being drawn into its pages we get to intimately know a young girl, who is describing how it felt to have her very existence continually threatened by the irrational persecution of adults.

Over the past seventy years since her diary was first published as a book, Anne Frank's words have touched the hearts and minds of millions. She has inspired an unending stream of biographies, artistic interpretations of her story, academic analyses of her literary prowess, children's poetry and even pubescent obsessions. Anne's diary chronicled a fun-loving and intelligent girl's fears and frustrations in having to hide to save her own life. The complex personality leaping from its pages resonates with children and adults, male and female, with all who are in the process of going through, or have already been through, a time of emotional upheaval and physical changes to both mind and body.

But to millions of people around the world, Anne is even more familiar to them by what she looked like. This is thanks to an unusually large collection of black-and-white photographs taken by her father, Otto Frank, who was the proud owner of a classic 35mm Leica camera. He snapped his daughters Margot Betti and Annelies Marie spontaneously or in carefully posed situations. His twin passions became his beautiful little dark-eyed girls and his hobby of photography. He liked to experiment visually, and some of his photos (which have been referred to as the 'shadow pictures') even contain his own elongated and ghostly shadow in the foreground.

Otto Frank's family photographs have formed the basis of the Anne Frank travelling exhibitions, as well as many of the displays in the Anne Frank House and other Holocaust museums around the world, and have played a large part in visitors' understanding of the lives of the two girls that were lost.

I have come to know many of those images as intimately as if they were of my own children, through the twenty-eight years I worked closely with the Anne Frank travelling exhibition. The photos show Anne and her sister enjoying what we would describe as normal childhood activities – playing with friends, attending birthday parties, going on shopping trips in town with their mother, visiting the seaside or even the Swiss mountains.

I have looked on as adults and children have gazed at Anne Frank and her family, who in turn stared back at them from the Anne Frank exhibition panels. I have seen parents drawing their children closer to them in a protective gesture of understanding of the dreadful position Anne's parents, Otto and Edith Frank, found themselves in; older adults recollecting their own wartime experiences or those told to them by their parents; teenagers and children identifying with Anne and her friends enjoying themselves in situations surprisingly familiar to them.

Thus I will attempt to describe Anne's first thirteen years through some of the most memorable and affecting black-and-white photographs, most of them carefully directed by Otto.

Annelies Marie Frank was born in Frankfurt-am-Main in Germany on 12 June 1929 to a German-Jewish couple, Otto and Edith Frank. The family lived on a prominent street in the city centre called the Marbachweg. They had married in 1925 and their first daughter Margot Betti had been born on 16 February 1926, during the time that Germany was already suffering immense economic hardship after its defeat in the First World War. Anne arrived in the world just four months before the Wall Street Crash was to reverberate throughout the international community.

We first get to meet baby Annelies, whose name was soon shortened to Anne, one month later in a photo. She is being held on the lap of a rather prim-looking and clinically-dressed middle-aged woman called Mrs Dassing, who was brought in as a nanny to help Edith Frank in the aftermath of her confinement. Three-year-old Margot Frank, now assuming the role of big sister, is standing alongside Mrs Dassing, staring down towards her own feet, dressed in a summery light-coloured vest and shorts, and with her eyes almost closed. Little Margot is clutching something tightly, but we cannot make out what it is, whether a doll or a comfort blanket, as she has shaken it just as Mr Frank clicked the shutter and thus it is blurred. The baby Anne, however, swaddled tightly in a knitted blanket and with dark hair already visible, has her eyes wide open, as if she has been attracted by something on the ceiling. It is as though Anne's curiosity about the world and its workings have already been fired. A birdcage sits on the table behind baby Anne, although we cannot identify a bird, and a large plant has been placed on the windowsill behind the table. Looking rather like an incongruous hair bow attached to Mrs Dassing's head, there protrudes from behind her a pinwheel toy, a simple wind-driven mobile for children that is as popular now as it was then.

The baby was then handed to her doting mother for a photo. As Edith cradles her baby girl against her shoulder, Anne's eyes are still open, this time firmly fixed on her big sister Margot. Many of the photos taken by Otto during this period focus on his firstborn Margot, already growing into a very attractive child. One of the next photos of Anne is perhaps one of the most poignant. It is 1932 and she is not yet three years old. The National Socialists, the Nazi Party, are gaining in popular appeal, offering jobs and free holidays to the German people. Anne is sleeping peacefully and soundly in her bed. There she lies in her innocence, her dark hair now thick and luxuriant, her eyebrows defined and her lips full and dark. This girl needs neither her thumb nor a comforter while she sleeps, she is content with her world and unaware of the political catastrophe unfolding outside the walls of her home.

Family come to visit the Franks, including paternal grandmother Alice Frank and cousins Stephan and Bernd Elias from Basel in Switzerland and maternal 'Grannie' Rosa Hollander from the city of Aachen on the German border with Belgium. As well as a loving family, Margot and Anne also have local children to play with. These happy times are all recorded by Otto's camera.

The normality and security of the Frank girls' early childhood in Frankfurt was to change dramatically from January 1933, when Adolf Hitler and the Nazi Party came to power. Their vicious anti-Semitism was about to be given free rein. Under Hitler's leadership, the state became known as the Third Reich, 'Reich' meaning the realm of an empire. The First Reich had been the time of the medieval Holy Roman Empire, which lasted from Charlemagne in 800 until 1806. The Second Reich was the German Empire under the Kaisers Wilhelm I and II, lasting from Germany's unification in 1871 until Kaiser Wilhelm II's abdication in 1918 after defeat in the First World War.

By the end of March 1933, the victorious Nazi Party had brought in the Enabling Act, giving the German Cabinet – in effect Chancellor Adolf Hitler – the power to enact laws without the involvement of the Reichstag, the German parliament. This act, along with the Reichstag Fire Decree after the arson attack on the Reichstag building, abolished most civil liberties and transferred state powers to the Reich government. Just two months after his election by the German people, Hitler's government had been transformed into a legal dictatorship.

With the powers they had bestowed upon themselves, the Nazi government set about suppressing all political opposition. They soon started imposing sanctions and limitations on the Jewish community to make it hard for them to lead a normal life. Within a period of less than a year, more and more draconian measures were targeted against the Jews of Germany.

On 10 March 1933, the Frank family paid a visit to the bustling central Hauptwache plaza, on what could have been a trip for shopping or perhaps to a café. Otto's camera came along too, as he recorded the outing. It is obviously still wintry as his wife and daughters are wearing coats and hats. Edith smiles proudly towards the camera, Margot is holding her mother's arm and looking a little wistful. She is in a coat, beret and shiny Mary Jane shoes of a similar style to her mother's. Anne is in a white furry jacket, white gloves and leggings extending over her shoes, and with her head slightly bowed, scowling at the camera. This may have been a last family outing into the city as a normal life for Jews was becoming more difficult.

Otto Frank, whose family had emerged from the Frankfurt ghetto and had progressed to own their own bank by the late nineteenth century, and Edith, whose father had been a wealthy and successful businessman in Aachen, were about to make the painful decision to leave everything they had known and emigrate to the Netherlands. Like many fleeing Jews, they considered the Netherlands to be a safe haven, the country having remained neutral throughout the First World War.

Later that year, Otto left his homeland and went on ahead of his family to look for a business in Amsterdam. Thanks to an introduction by his brother-in-law Erich Elias, who worked for a company called Opekta in Switzerland, Otto was able to set up a new branch of Opekta in Amsterdam. Opekta manufactured and sold pectin, a setting agent for jam, which many people in those days made themselves at home. Later, Otto opened another company called Pectacon, which dealt in spices that were popular for sausage-making. His first Amsterdam business premises were at 400 Singel (in 1940 the business moved to 263 Prinsengracht). Edith, and then Margot, who was brought by her uncles, followed him to Amsterdam a few months later. Anne arrived in February 1934, brought by her maternal grandmother and playfully announced as a 'present' for Margot's eighth birthday.

In Amsterdam the family lived on the Merwedeplein, a new development in the south of the city where many other German-Jewish refugees from Nazism were settling. The apartment blocks had been built around a central triangular-shaped green where the residents' children would gather after school to play in safety. Both Margot and Anne soon made friends, their play captured in many of Otto's photos over the following years. Anne is often shown with her best friend Susanne 'Sanne' Ledermann, holding skipping ropes or dolls, Anne looking immaculately turned-out and the tomboyish Sanne with her socks invariably rumpled round her ankles, or with her taller fair-haired friend Hannah 'Hanneli' Goslar, who later became known as 'Lies' in Anne's diary.

In 1935 Anne had started to attend the local kindergarten. It was then called the Sixth Public Montessori School, but has now been renamed the Anne Frank School. A class photograph shows Anne's teacher Miss Baldal and her twenty-six pupils. The photo demonstrates the Montessori approach to learning that encourages children's independence and freedom, while still retaining a sense of order. Otto and Edith Frank, like many other Jewish refugee parents in Amsterdam, had chosen the Montessori school as they believed in a modern and progressive education. Miss Baldal's class are not seated in formal rows of desks, but at small tables around the room, each containing a game or activity. Some of the children are kneeling by their wooden games on the floor. Towards the back of the room, five-year-old Anne sits on her wooden chair in a white dress, short dark socks and white shoes, her small feet dangling as they do not quite reach the floor. Five years later Anne would be forced to leave the Montessori school, but not because of any misdemeanour.

In September 1935, Otto took his younger daughter Anne to visit their family in Switzerland. Together they journeyed to the idyllic lakeside resort of Sils Maria. He photographed six-year-old Anne in a dark sun dress sitting in the long scrub-like grass, leaning a little forward towards the camera, her body bathed in sunshine and radiating a smile to match the carefree day. Clearly, the Frank family were enjoying the freedom afforded by their new lives in the Netherlands, reassuringly far enough away from the growing anti-Semitism of their former German homeland.

There were many photos taken of Anne and Margot on the beach. Zandvoort has long been a popular seaside destination for Amsterdam residents as it is only

24km from the city. The Frank girls are shown in 1938 on a warm July day, but it is clearly a windy one too, as deckchair canvases are seen to be billowing fiercely outwards from their frames. The girls are wearing identical dark floral halter-neck tops over tartan check shorts, the ensemble connected by a tasselled rope belt. They would still look extremely stylish if they hit the beach today in these outfits. In one of their father's photos they are facing the camera and staring into it. Then in an artistic flourish, they are also shown from the back, standing together at the edge of the sea looking out towards the horizon. This strikes a particular chord with all who see this image with the hindsight of history. It seems almost as though the two girls were contemplating their future lives and what they would hold. The poignancy of this is almost unbearable.

In June 1939, Anne celebrated her tenth birthday. She invited eight girl friends to join the celebration and there they are pictured in the street in their best party dresses. The nine girls stand in a line closely packed together with their arms around each other. To give balance to the line-up, Otto has directed the tallest girl, Juultje, to stand in the middle. Some of the girls, such as Hannah, have bows in their hair, and Susanne Ledermann's socks are unusually tidy. Anne is positioned second from the left, wearing an Empire-line floral dress adorned with white buttons and collar. She is smiling as if in pride at her bevy of friends, most of whom were non-Jewish classmates from the Montessori school. On that happy sunny afternoon, who could have suspected that the parents of the cute little blonde girl on Anne's right were to become active and enthusiastic members of the Dutch Nazi Party the following year?

In August 1940, Margot and Anne were photographed by Otto on the Merwedeplein apartment building roof. By now, the older girl Margot is clearly pubescent, the top of her fashionable two-piece bathing suit framing a developing bust. She has lost some of the striking beauty of her childhood, her large dark eyes are now obscured by regulation spectacles, and her hair is scraped severely back from her forehead. In a separate photo, Anne is slouched into a deck chair with her lower legs almost protruding out from the front of the photo. Yet again Anne is scowling at the camera, her head tilted down, her eyes surrounded by dark shadows, appearing almost like those of a painted clown. Half of the right side of her body is off the edge of the photo – we are not sure if this is by Otto's artistic design or by accident, as photographic errors could only be discovered once the roll of film had been developed and printed.

Perhaps the demeanour of the girls on this sunny rooftop terrace reflected the new status quo in their adopted country. Three months earlier, and after the Frank family had spent seven years in the perceived safety of Amsterdam, the most feared, but still unexpected, calamity had happened. On 10 May 1940, Germany had invaded the Netherlands after five days of brutal air bombardment of the port city of Rotterdam. The Dutch Queen Wilhelmina and her family, the Dutch Prime Minister and key members of his government all fled to London. After a few months of relative calm, by October 1940 the German occupiers were starting to introduce measures targeted against the country's Jews. All Jews in the Netherlands were required to be registered and by May 1942, they were forced to attach a yellow cotton Star of David to their outer upper garments to publicly identify their religion. Now the word on it in bold black letters was not the German 'Jude', but 'Jood', the Dutch for Jew.

Two years on, in June 1942, Anne was to describe the process of the implementation of the measures in her newly-received diary. She shows how every aspect of her own life was affected:

> After May 1940 the good times were few and far between: first there was the war, then the capitulation and then the arrival of the Germans, which is when the trouble started for the Jews. Our freedom was severely restricted by a series of anti-Jewish decrees: Jews were required to wear a yellow star; Jews were required to turn in their bicycles; Jews were forbidden to use trams; Jews were forbidden to ride in cars, even their own; Jews were required to do their shopping between 3.00 and 5.00 p.m.; Jews were required to frequent only Jewish owned barbershops and beauty salons; Jews were forbidden to be out on the streets between 8.00 p.m. and 6.00 a.m.; Jews were forbidden to go to theatres, cinemas or any other forms of entertainment; Jews were forbidden to use swimming pools, tennis courts, hockey fields or any other athletic fields; Jews were forbidden to go rowing; Jews were forbidden to take part in any athletic activity in public; Jews were forbidden to sit in their gardens or those of their friends after 8.00 p.m; Jews were forbidden to visit Christians in their homes; Jews were required to attend Jewish schools, etc. You couldn't do this and you couldn't do that, but life went on.

In the winter of 1940, Anne is pictured at her desk at the Montessori school. An ordinary black-and-white photo that will become not only significant, but one of the most symbolic photographs taken during the years of 1939–45 when telling the story of the Second World War. In the photo, Anne has pencil in hand, poised as though it is in mid-sentence. Her dark hair is long and thick and her face is already showing signs of maturity. She gives a half smile and gives such an air of maturity that she could be an 11-year-old, which she is, but she could also be taken for an 18-year-old. She is surrounded by the paraphernalia of school work: sheets of paper, a pair of scissors and an inkwell from which to refill her fountain pen.

The following year, she is snapped by her father sideways-on at a writing desk at home. This is Otto Frank's study area in the couple's bedroom, the double bed is visible, as are filing cabinets and document containers. Anne's pencil is in contact with the page but she has turned her face towards the camera, and her eyes have drifted even further to the right of the lens. It is posed but spontaneous at the same time.

In the same month of May 1941, a local photographer called Frans Dupont took a series of posed close-up photos of Anne standing against a plain-coloured interior wall. They show a confident girl who was discovering her attractiveness to boys and leadership among girls. She clearly likes what she is wearing, a high-collared dress with an embroidered yoke, and an open knitted and embroidered cardigan over it. Her glossy dark hair reaches below her shoulders, parted on her left and with a side clip pulling it back on the right. The stunning images Dupont took of Anne that May day, one month before she would turn 12, strike us with their modernity – they could have been taken of a twenty-first century girl last week.

Anne is then photographed with 15-year-old Margot, whose by now full bosom is covered by a ribbed sweater. The sisters are both in profile, looking off camera to their right, probably instructed by the photographer. Unlike the previous photos of Anne taken that day, this one is mournful and atmospheric. One can only wonder at the series of conversations between the girls on that day as anti-Jewish measures are starting to bite hard into their lives. The girls were, however, unaware that their father had been desperately trying to get exit visas for his family to the US. His attempts proved unsuccessful as by the late 1930s America was already operating very strict quotas for Jewish refugees from Europe.

In late 1941, Anne was forced to leave the Montessori school. As part of the Nazis' isolation process, Jewish children could only attend Jewish schools, so along with Margot, Anne had to move to the Jewish Lyceum. Anne soon developed a reputation at the Jewish Lyceum for being a very talkative girl, among both friends and teachers. Her 'old fogey' maths teacher, Mr Keesing, despaired of getting Anne to quieten in his lessons, and for the third consecutive punishment he meted out for her constant talking in class, he ordered her to write yet another after school essay on the topic of chattering. After exhausting two shorter titles on the theme of chatterboxes, for this one he chose the title 'Quack, Quack, Quack, Said Mistress Chatterback'. Despairing of finding more to write, at the helpful suggestion of Susanne Ledermann, Anne wrote a piece in comic verse about a family of ducks. The class roared with laughter when it was read out and even Mr Keesing saw the joke, leading to an improvement in their relationship in class.

But outside her classroom things were getting more serious. In the same year Jewish-owned businesses were compelled to become 'Aryanised', i.e. their Jewish owners had to hand them over to non-Jews. Otto Frank divided up his companies, Opekta and Pectacon, and handed them to his trusted business associates Johannes Kleiman and Victor Kugler respectively. Pectacon became known as Gies and Co, taking the name of its new co-director Jan Gies, the husband of Otto's office administrator Miep Gies. Behind the scenes, Otto was secretly very involved in the running of the companies, seeing all the account books and offering advice where needed.

By 1942, Jews between the ages of 16 and 40 were being called up to report for work camps in Germany. Otto and Edith were terrified that 16-year-old Margot would be among those taken. They were right to be terrified; hardly anyone returned alive from this supposed 'workforce' project. The Frank family were trapped in the Netherlands with no escape. Otto was prompted by this threat of a call-up for his older daughter to prepare a hiding place. He shared his plan with his colleagues

Johannes Kleiman, whom he had known for fifteen years, and Victor Kugler. It was Kugler who first suggested that the unused series of rooms above and behind the old building of the Prinsengracht offices would make an ideal hiding place.

On 12 June 1942, Anne celebrated her thirteenth birthday. One of the presents she received was a notebook covered in a red and white checked fabric. This gift was not in fact a complete surprise. She had spotted it in the window of a neighbourhood bookshop when she had been out walking with her father not long before her birthday. Just as teenagers today will drop unsubtle hints about the latest-style trainers or techie devices as birthdays or Christmas approach, Anne had given a large hint to her father that she would rather like this notebook. Probably its main attraction was that it had a brass lock, essential for safeguarding intimate thoughts and gossip.

Anne started writing in her notebook on the day she received it. Her first words were, 'I hope I'll be able to confide everything in you, as I've never been able to confide in anyone, and I hope you'll be a great source of comfort and support.' She had no idea on that day that in three weeks' time the diary was about to indeed become a vital source of 'comfort and support'.

She goes on to describe her birthday party and all the other gifts she received, and over the next few days she shares her privately held views about her school friends. On this matter, she doesn't hold back, using adjectives such as 'stuck up', 'sneaky' and 'vulgar' for some of her unfortunate targets. By 20 June, Anne has given her new paper confidante the name Kitty, after one of the characters created by her favourite author Cissy van Marxveldt. Kitty is to become her friend, a surprising confession from a girl who says she has about thirty friends and a throng of boy admirers, who 'can't keep their eyes off me'. But with her human friends she feels the talk is superficial and about ordinary, everyday things. Kitty will be her 'true friend', paper will be her intimate confidante. And anyway, no-one is ever going to read it.

Three weeks after Anne had started her diary, on the afternoon of Sunday, 5 July, the doorbell on the Frank family's apartment unexpectedly rang. It was a postman delivering the dreaded notice for 16-year-old Margot to report at midnight for transportation to 'a work camp'. According to the notice, she would be permitted to take a number of specified items in a single suitcase which had to have 'first and last name, date of birth and the word Holland' written on it. In a foreboding of the true fate of the deportees, this was explained to be 'important because the owner's suitcase would be sent by a separate train'. The hindsight of history gives us a grim insight into these bureaucratic instructions. By this time, not only Auschwitz, but Belzec and Chelmno concentration camps, were fully operational in carrying out the extermination of Jews.

The very next day, early on the morning of 6 July, Otto, Edith and Anne left their Merwedeplein home together and trudged in the pouring rain across the city to the Prinsengracht offices of Opekta/Gies & Co. They were each wearing several layers of clothing and carrying one satchel, plus another bag laden with essential items. The city was still dark and people were scuttling about to get out of the downpour, so no-one would have taken much notice of the sodden group of people who were leaving their home for good. Having escorted Margot, Miep Gies had already arrived by bicycle at the Prinsengracht office to help with the moving in. To reach the stairs to the hiding place involved slipping through a door that had been carefully concealed by a strategically-placed wooden bookcase. The bookcase had been filled with the normal office paraphernalia of document folders so as not to arouse any suspicions from Mr Frank's office workers. Even to this day, all visitors to Anne Frank's hiding place access it by stepping behind this bookcase.

Perhaps the Frank family thought on 6 July 1942 that by the following summer they would be returning to their home on the Merwedeplein. But the months in hiding stretched on and on. Over the course of the next two years and one month the Frank family remained within the confines of the $70m^2$ of stuffy rooms above 263 Prinsengracht. One week after moving into the hiding place, they were joined by another endangered Jewish family. This was Hermann and Auguste van Pels and their 15-year-old son Peter, refugees to Amsterdam from the German city of Osnabruck. Hermann van Pels was also a business associate of Otto Frank who had worked for the sister company of Pectacon. He had done his share in helping Otto and Johannes Kleiman with the preparation of the hiding place, knowing it would be for his own family's use too.

One cannot relate the experiences of the Frank family and their friends during their time in hiding without explaining the critical role of those who risked their lives to help them, bringing moral support and vital supplies. This was a small group of Otto Frank's loyal office workers comprising Miep Gies, who was the general administrator; the aforementioned Johannes Kleiman and Victor Kugler; Bep Voskuijl, the young secretary; and also Jan Gies, Miep's husband. It was actually Johannes Kleiman who had come up with the idea of building a bookcase to conceal the door, and Bep's father Johannes Voskuijl who had built it. Over the course of two years, those in hiding relied totally on the courage and enduring goodwill of this group of people, who had to keep their dangerous secret from their own families, colleagues and the shopkeepers from whom they inveigled extra supplies.

In December 1942, Miep asked Mr and Mrs Frank and Mr and Mrs van Pels whether they would be prepared to let another endangered Jew join them. The person in question happened to be her dentist. Fritz Pfeffer was, like the van Pels and Frank families, a refugee from Nazi Germany, which he had fled in 1938 along with his Catholic fiancée Charlotte Kaletta. Before doing so he had managed to send his young son Werner to safety in England. After the arrival of Pfeffer, the social and physical claustrophobia caused to these eight people, by being in the unremitting presence of each other, started to take its toll, and judging by her writing, none more so than on the teenage Anne. In her first entries written from the hiding place Anne describes every room of 'our lovely Annexe' in excited detail as though they were on holiday 'in some kind of strange pension'. But after only three months, the boredom and despair have already set in, as she makes a retrospective addition to one of these earliest entries describing how upset she now feels about never going out.

What has given Anne's diary such enduring and universal appeal? Anne Frank was not the saintly figure of her portrayal in some of the sentimentalized dramatic interpretations that have appeared over the decades. She was a real teenager, lashing out in frustration at the failings, as she perceived them, of the adults hiding with her and the powerlessness to stop the wicked persecution inflicted on her. Perhaps it's also how her writing fluidly juxtaposes the profound and the prosaic.

The adults she is confined with are driving her mad. They are exasperating and interfering. Added to which, there are petty disagreements between Otto and Edith and Hermann and Auguste, two married couples accustomed to running their own homes and lives. In April 1943, Anne reports that 'the house is still shaking from the after-effects of the quarrels'. One can almost see her eyes rolling upwards as she writes this.

Fritz Pfeffer, Anne's roommate by necessity, is portrayed in her diary as an old buffoon, her resentment of the poor man compounded by the fact that she has to share her precious writing desk with him. Fritz was actually a handsome and athletic man of 53 when he joined the hiding place in 1942, proven by the photos kept by his beloved Charlotte. He was desperately lonely in hiding, being the only person there without any of his own family.

Anne feels that her mother is favouring Margot too much, and taking her sister's side in arguments because there is more of an affinity between them. Anne's affection is undoubtedly focused more on her father, whom she regards as wise and fair, and who has taken the role of home tutor while in hiding. Because possessions are so hard to replace, they are more treasured. Auguste van Pels is distraught when her husband gives her precious fur coat to Miep to sell for food. Anne writes an entire chapter in her diary entitled 'Ode to my Fountain Pen' after the pen she loves to use, a gift from her grandmother for her ninth birthday, has accidentally been thrown on the fire and destroyed.

Anne created fictional stories too, letting her vivid imagination fly out of the sealed and blacked out windows of her enforced imprisonment. Poignantly, in some of these stories she imagines being 16, the age she almost reached in real life but didn't, and in some she becomes Anne the adult, visiting Hollywood for an acting audition or revising her views on the boringness of old people when she engages in conversation with an elderly couple during a train journey from Amsterdam to the town of Bussum. Her stories often contain an indication of her growing ethical beliefs, despite her own terrible circumstances, such as the story 'Give!' which is an entreaty for us to help others less fortunate. In it she writes:

> Everyone is born equal, we will all die and shed our earthly glory. Riches, power and fame last for but a few short years. Why do we cling so desperately to these fleeting things? Why can't people who have more

than enough for their own needs give the rest to their fellow human beings? Why should anyone have to have such a hard life for those few short years on earth?

There is so much yearning for the previous life that the chimes of the nearby Westerkerk church clock and the snatched glimpses of the chestnut tree at the back of the building give Anne some degree of comfort. This young girl, whose previous interests revolved around boys, movie stars and clothes, writes of her longing to 'ride a bike, dance, whistle, look at the world, feel young and know that I'm free'. She re-evaluates her attitude to nature, something that once would not have interested or captivated her, and she even finds herself staying awake very late one night just to get a good look at the moon.

Soon, there is another type of longing. After Anne has turned 14 in 1943, she is more aware of the changes that are occurring in her body. Her sexuality is being stirred and Peter van Pels becomes the object of a typical adolescent obsession. Together they climb the wooden steps up to the dusty and unfurnished attic in the eaves of the old building, spending time alone together, discussing everything from religion and why the Jews have been so unfairly persecuted, to the inner workings of the female sexual organs.

She writes of her yearning for Peter, 'I long for him to kiss me but that kiss is taking its own sweet time'. In the intimacy of the attic, they do eventually share sweet kisses and embraces. By the late spring of 1944, Anne has tired of spending time with Peter and replaces her ardour with, as she describes to Margot, 'sisterly affection'. She finds Peter easy-going, but feels he has been hiding his inner-self too much from her. Meanwhile, Anne has meanwhile become busy with another project.

On 28 March, Gerrit Bolkestein, the Dutch Education Minister who was in exile in London, clandestinely broadcasts to the Dutch people that after the war he plans to make a collection of diaries and letters written during the German occupation of their country. Anne is fired up. How interesting it would be if she were to publish a novel about the 'Secret Annexe'. From then on she is writing feverishly, adding new entries to her diary while simultaneously editing the previous twenty-two months of writing, with her eye fixed on its publication.

Those who have read early versions of Anne's diary or seen productions of the 1955 play about her story may not be familiar with the names I have used of the other adults in hiding, or of their helpers. In her revised version of her diary entries after she began editing them in April 1944, Anne decided to give the main characters aliases, so Hermann and Auguste van Pels became Mr and Mrs van Daan, Fritz Pfeffer became the unfortunately-named Albert Dussel ('Dussel' being German for idiot) and Jan Gies became Henk van Santen. Victor Kugler and Jo Kleiman morphed into Mr Kraler and Mr Koophuis; Bep Voskuijl became Elli Vossen. On the publication of the diary in 1947, Otto Frank followed Anne's wish to retain the real names of her immediate family. Writing for possible publication becomes her focus, and on 5 April, she describes how she feels about the gift of writing:

> I don't want to have lived in vain like most people. I want to be useful or bring enjoyment to all people, even those I've never met. I want to go on living even after my death! And that's why I'm so grateful to God for having given me this gift, which I can use to develop myself and to express all that's inside me! When I write I can shake off all my cares. My sorrow disappears, my spirits are revived! But, and that's a big question, will I ever be able to write something great, will I ever become a journalist or a writer?

The craft of writing was in fact in the young girl's genes. On her father's side, she had come from a family of inveterate writers. Thousands of letters, stories and poems, dating back through several generations of Otto Frank's family, had been discovered in the attic of Otto's mother's house in Basel and lovingly curated into an archive by Gerti Elias, the wife of Anne's cousin Buddy. Many of these formed the basis of the Frank family saga published in 2011, entitled *Treasures from the Attic*.

On 11 April 1944, Anne lays out a plan for her future life, tempered by the knowledge of the fragility of her survival:

> I'm becoming more and more independent of my parents. Young as I am, I face life with more courage and have a better and truer sense of justice than Mother. I know what I want, I have a goal, I have opinions, a religion and love. If only I can be myself, I'll be satisfied. I know that I'm a woman, a woman with inner strength and a great deal of courage! If God lets me live, I'll achieve more than Mother ever did, I'll make my voice heard, I'll go out into the world and work for mankind! I now know that courage and happiness are needed first!

After nearly two years in the hiding place, Anne's vulnerability spills over into despair. At the end of May she writes:

> I've asked myself again and again whether it wouldn't have been better if we hadn't gone into hiding, if we were dead now and didn't have to go through this misery, especially so that the others could be spared the burden. But we all shrink from this thought. We still love life, we haven't yet forgotten the voice of nature, and we keep hoping, hoping for . . . everything. Let something happen soon, even an air raid. Nothing can be more crushing than this anxiety. Let the end come, however cruel; at least then we'll know whether we are to be the victors or the vanquished.

The poor food supplies they have to get by on also become a focus of Anne's descriptive writing. Potatoes are eaten at every meal, including breakfast, and all foodstuffs, even bread, consist of brown beans. The high point of the week is one slice of liver sausage and a scrape of jam on a slice of unbuttered bread. They can't use a flushing toilet during the day in case it is heard by the workers below, talk is in whispers and coughs and sneezes have to be suppressed.

And so the tedium of their cramped existence continues. That is until Tuesday, 6 June 1944. D-Day, the Allied invasion of Normandy. Anne writes, 'This is THE day. The invasion has begun!' Her excitement is palpable, 'It fills us with fresh courage and makes us strong again. We'll need to be brave to endure the many fears and hardships and the suffering yet to come. It's now a matter of remaining calm and steadfast, of gritting our teeth and keeping a stiff upper lip!' At the end of this diary entry, the girl who was often in trouble with her teacher and disdainful of lessons, is happily speculating that she might be able to return to school by that autumn.

Otto Frank started to plot the Allied advance across northern Europe by sticking pins into a small map he attached to the wall. Visitors to the hiding place can still see it displayed in the same place, but now protected under glass from millions of passing hands. Hopes were at long last building that the long months of hiding would soon be at an end. Anne was in turmoil, there was hope, but would their liberators reach Amsterdam in time? As food and necessary items were becoming scarcer in the Netherlands after more than four years of occupation, Dutch collaborators were betraying Jews for a few guilders.

On 15 July Anne sat and poured out her heart to her paper friend Kitty in one of her longest diary entries, seesawing between her hope for the future and fear of the reality. 'It's difficult in times like these: ideals, dreams and cherished hopes rise within us, only to be crushed by grim reality. It's a wonder I haven't abandoned all my ideals, they seem so absurd and impractical.' But by the end of the entry hope has prevailed. She is determined to hold on to her ideals, believing that perhaps one day she will be able to realize them.

On the warm and bright summer morning of 4 August 1944, the Frank family, the van Pels family and Fritz Pfeffer were arrested. A car pulled up outside the front door of 263 Prinsengracht and two officers, Karl Joseph Silberbauer, an Austrian Nazi, along with a Dutch policeman, calmly entered the building. In an instant they had appeared in the office where Miep Gies, Johannes Kleiman, Victor Kugler and Bep Voskuijl were working. Pointing a pistol towards them, the officers signalled towards the bookcase, which, with a heavy heart, Miep pulled open. The two men climbed the stairs towards the eight people above who were unknowingly going about another day in hiding. As they gathered their captives together at gunpoint, the officers spotted Otto Frank's briefcase and emptied its contents to use it for gathering up any perceived valuables. Anne looked on in shock as her diary, so meticulously edited for its possible publication, lay discarded on the wooden floor.

The eight petrified people were told to gather a few items for their journey and were led downstairs through the building and out into the busy Amsterdam street. Blinking their eyes in the sunlight, the eight newly-captured Jews were pushed into a police van. Victor Kugler and Johannes Kleiman were taken too, as helping Jews was a crime punishable by death. The van headed off towards the Gestapo headquarters in the south of the city. As it crossed the city streets, eight pairs of eyes, who had been for so long isolated from a normal street life, were pinned to the windows. Would this be the last they would see of this beautiful city they had all come to love? For seven of those eight it would.

After they were taken to the Gestapo headquarters in the south of the city, the petrified group of eight were loaded onto a regular passenger train with its doors bolted shut to prevent escape. The train steamed its way out of the city to Westerbork, the transit camp located in the north-eastern part of the Netherlands. There they would be awaiting certain deportation to the death camps they had so feared. In Westerbork they were assigned to Block 67, the 'punishment block' for prisoners who had tried to evade arrest by hiding.

Rootje de Winter, another inmate from Amsterdam, recalled that Anne had seemed almost happy while she laboured in Westerbork's industrial area doing the dirty job of dismantling aeroplane batteries. Anne was relishing the company of people other than those she had spent the past two years with, although she did choose to spend time in Peter van Pels's company.

The Allies were still battling their way through northern Europe, could they soon get to the Netherlands? On 3 September, the Allied armies reached Brussels, and it seemed that the liberation of the Netherlands could be imminent. But after failed airborne landings near Arnhem, the Allied advance came to a halt at the mighty river Rhine, and there it stagnated through the winter. On the very day the Allied forces had reached Brussels, the Frank family's names were announced for the feared deportation to Poland. By early morning on 3 September, a long line of cattle trucks stood in the centre of the camp, ready to transport over 1,000 people to Auschwitz. Unknown to the inmates, the train had sidled in to the camp during the night, and there it was 'waiting motionless like a masked executioner concealing his bared axe', according to one unnamed witness. The Frank family climbed together into the stinking, blisteringly hot cattle truck packed tight with other terrified Dutch Jews who were painfully aware that they were about to experience their very last journey. At 11.00 a.m. the whistle blew and the trucks started to move.

As the Franks' co-travellers started to die along the route from exhaustion, hunger and thirst, their bodies thrown out of the truck at each stop, did anyone on board, apart from the innocent small children, have any hope they would be kept alive once they had got to the dreaded destination? Several museums around the world have displayed empty cattle trucks in order to show the barbarity of that journey, but none could convey the pervading fear, the stench, the cries of hunger, thirst and despair of the real people who were huddled inside. Interviews with Holocaust survivors have often centred round their memories of the journey rather than their experiences once in the camp, so traumatic were those terrible days of travelling.

The train finally steamed in to the railway ramp of Auschwitz. Amid the shouted orders of the uniformed guards, the screams of mothers being separated from their children, and the barking of the fearsome dogs, Otto Frank was marched off in a different direction from his wife and daughters, he to the men's area of camp Auschwitz I and the women 3km away to Auschwitz-Birkenau. No longer could Otto Frank be a protective husband and father. The Frank family had been sent to their doom on the very last transport that left the Netherlands for Auschwitz. Had their arrest occurred just a few weeks later, they may all have survived.

During their time in Barrack 29 of Auschwitz-Birkenau, Anne became close again to her mother and they were inseparable. Their day-to-day struggle to survive was not the place for petty differences or squabbles. After one month in Auschwitz, despite surviving selections for the gas chambers by the feared Dr Josef Mengele, the Frank girls were in a bad condition. By the end of October, they both had scabies, a condition caused by lice burying under their skin. Edith was doing all she could to protect her daughters, trying to get any extra food to keep them going.

On 30 October there was a selection for transportation of some of the women to be taken out of Auschwitz-Birkenau to an unknown destination. Edith was selected to stay in Auschwitz-Birkenau. Her two daughters were called forward to be assessed by Mengele. With a quick nod and a flick of his finger, Mengele parted Edith Frank from her two girls forever. Again the two teenage girls boarded a train, along with 632 women. It was a freezing and tough journey, this time taking four days. The train crossed the Polish border and took Anne and Margot back to the land of their birth, Germany. Perhaps they thought that the cultured homeland of generations of the Frank family would be their ultimate salvation.

But their destination was Bergen-Belsen, a camp that would become synonymous with death by slow starvation and the world's first recorded encounter with walking skeletons. Once a former German army barracks and then a prisoner of war camp, by 1944 it was being used to contain sick Jewish inmates from other camps, with a plan that they may eventually be 'exchanged'. The camp was already in a severe state of neglect by the time the Frank girls arrived, with little sanitation, medicines, care or food supplies. Their survival prospects were extremely poor. Anne and Margot were first assigned to a tent and then to a barrack where they slept together on a wooden bunk by an open door, where the icy wind whipped in and around their bodies. The winter of 1944/45 was particular vicious and the girls' health had not been good when they had arrived due to the effects of scabies. Somehow they got through the worst of the winter months, but meanwhile getting ever thinner and weaker.

In February a miracle occurred. Anne met her old playmate from Amsterdam, Hannah Goslar, who had already been in Bergen-Belsen for a year, detained in the relatively more privileged block for 'exchange prisoners'. Hannah's father had been a German government minister prior to 1933, and the family were in possession of passports for Palestine. Hannah's living conditions were marginally better than those of the wretched ordinary prisoners, who included Anne and Margot.

One day in February 1945, Hannah happened to encounter Auguste van Pels. She was dumbfounded when she heard from Mrs van Pels that her close friend Anne had been in the very same camp throughout the winter. It had been widely believed around their group in Amsterdam that when the Franks suddenly disappeared from the Merwedeplein in July 1942, they had fled to the safety of neutral Switzerland, even though Hannah had worried that the family may have been arrested at the Swiss border. Mrs van Pels promised to bring Anne to Hannah. Some minutes later, there was Anne standing immediately on the other side of the barbed wire fence. This was no longer the vivacious, chatty and fun-loving Anne Frank, as Hannah later recalled the furtive whispered conversation between the two teenage prisoners. Despite being dark, the girls were aware that a German guard was watching them from the nearby watchtower, and even in the darkness Hannah was shocked to make out Anne looking desperately thin and with a shaven head. As they knew they only had a few moments, Anne briefly described to Hannah about her two years of hiding and the family's arrest. The two girls both wept in pitiful sorrow as Hannah told Anne that her mother and sister had died and her father was sick. Anne then told her that Margot too was very sick, her mother was probably dead and that her father, at age 56, had undoubtedly been gassed at Auschwitz. So much had happened to the two girls, who just six years earlier had lined up in their prettiest party dresses and hair bows to mark Anne's tenth birthday.

Looking back on that conversation, the adult Hannah Goslar has expressed sadness that Anne had really believed she had no parents. In fact, unbeknown to the girl suffering on that barren and remote German heath, Otto Frank had already been liberated from Auschwitz and was slowly making his way back across Europe to Amsterdam. If Anne and Margot had been aware of this, maybe just maybe, it would have given them the fortitude to hold on to life for just a few more weeks.

Hannah and Anne arranged to meet again the following evening. Hannah was able to use her menial camp privileges to gather together a small parcel of food for Anne. She threw the parcel over the fence to the waiting Anne, but before Anne could reach the parcel it was voraciously grabbed by a starving woman. Anne was distraught. Hannah promised to try again a few days later. This time Anne was able to catch the small bundle of vital items.

Hannah never saw her friend Anne again. Hannah's father then died and she was in mourning for several days according to the observant Jewish tradition. Yet another outbreak of the deadly disease typhus was fast spreading through the camp. This was difficult for a person to survive without medication, let alone without the sustenance of food. When Hannah returned to the fence to search for Anne, the whole area on the other side, previously thronged with women prisoners, was empty. Hannah herself then succumbed to typhus, but managed to make it through to the camp's liberation, where as a 16-year-old orphan she found herself responsible for her small sister.

There were, however, two sisters from Amsterdam who were with the Frank girls after Hannah's last meeting with Anne. They were Jannie and Lientje Brilleslijper, who had been arrested and sent to Westerbork camp on the same train as the Frank family. Jannie, who was married to a non-Jew and had two small children but was nonetheless active in the Resistance, had been able to evade arrest until the summer of 1944. She and her sister had been on the same deportation from Westerbork to Auschwitz as the Frank family. Then they were selected for Bergen-Belsen along with Anne and Margot, where they found themselves in the same barrack.

After his return to Amsterdam in the summer of 1945, Otto Frank came to visit the sisters during his desperate search for news of his missing daughters. Sitting together in the calm and safety of a sun-filled sitting room, Lientje quietly described to him in harrowing detail the final days of his daughters.

> Jannie and I were assigned to another barrack. We asked Anne and Margot to come with us but Margot had terrible diarrhoea and had to stay in the old barrack because of the risk of stomach typhus. Anne took care of her as well as she could. We visited them during the next few weeks and now and then we were able to bring them something to eat. When the snow had melted, we came to visit them again but they weren't in the barrack anymore, we found them in the sick house. We told them they mustn't stay there because whenever you give up hope the end was near. Anne said, 'Here we can both lie on one bunk, we are together and it's peaceful.' Margot could only whisper. She had fallen out of the bunk and was barely conscious with high fever. Anne had a fever too, but she was friendly and sweet. She said, 'Margot will sleep well and when she wakes up I won't need to get up again.' A few days later we found their bunks empty. We knew what that meant. We found them behind the barrack, wrapped their thin bodies in a blanket, and carried them to a mass grave. That was all we could do for them.

A total of 107,000 Jews had been deported from the Netherlands to concentration camps. Only 5,000 of these people had managed to survive. Otto Frank, the Brilleslijper sisters, Hannah Goslar and her little sister were among that small number. Edith Frank had died of starvation, illness and despair in Auschwitz on 6 January, no doubt desperately worrying about her girls until her last breath. Hermann van Pels had been gassed in Auschwitz in the autumn of 1944, having seriously injured his thumb, making him unfit for work. The athletic Fritz Pfeffer had died of illness, deprivation and exhaustion in Neuengamme camp in Germany in December 1944. After a brutal death march from Auschwitz to Austria, 18-year-old Peter van Pels died in Mauthausen, one of the most notorious of all the camps, just a few days before its liberation. Auguste van Pels was viciously thrown under a train by Nazi guards on the last transport to Theresienstadt. She died on the spot.

On 18 July 1945, the deaths of Margot and Anne were confirmed. There on a list at the Amsterdam office of the Red Cross Otto Frank saw in black and white the names Margot Betti Frank and Annelies Marie Frank, each name followed with a cross indicating their fate. Miep Gies was present when a letter from the Red Cross also arrived at the Prinsengracht offices with additional confirmation.

As the almost skeletal Anne lay on the freezing wooden bunk with her fifteen years of life ebbing away, one wonders if she gave more than a passing thought to the little red-checked notebook and the stories she had left behind in Amsterdam, callously thrown on the floor of the hiding place by the arresting officers.

What would she make of the million and a half people each year who wait patiently in line by an Amsterdam canal to be in the very rooms where she wrote her diary, to touch the same walls she brushed against, to gaze upwards to the dusty attic where she went to escape the adults? What would she make of the fact that millions of people around the world have come to know her through movies, plays, documentaries? And the fact that in every continent of this planet she has changed lives irrevocably?

Chapter 2

Otto Frank

'The task that Anne entrusted to me continually gives me new strength to strive for reconciliation and for human rights all over the world.'
Otto Frank

One cannot tell the story of Anne Frank's legacy without that of her father Otto Frank. It is his post-war vision of a better future that has brought about all the worldwide interest in, and educational work about, his younger daughter. It is Otto's vision that inspired me, my co-founders of the Anne Frank Trust UK, my colleagues at the Anne Frank House and all our international partners and associates.

In the Anne Frank Trust's early days, I received several calls from teachers who told me they had been motivated to go into the vocation of teaching by seeing a 1976 interview with Otto Frank on the BBC's popular children's programme *Blue Peter*. The show's presenter Lesley Judd had held the original copy of Anne's red and white checked diary, while the white-haired and balding Mr Frank, looking like anyone's kindly grandfather, spoke in a soft Continental accent about the hatred that had killed his daughters. Lesley addressed Mr Frank in a gentle and almost reverential tone as she stroked the pages of Anne's diary. Years later, the show's producer Lewis Bronze told me that the interview with Otto Frank was far and away the most requested item to be repeated of that year.

I have often referred to Otto as the polar opposite of Adolf Hitler, two men born three weeks apart in the same year, in the same region of Europe, and who both fought on the German side in the First World War. Both were individuals who were able to influence the hearts and minds of millions. One went on to wreak death and destruction throughout the continent of Europe, the other went on to encourage millions to create a better world so that other children would not have to suffer as his own two beloved daughters had at the hands of the former.

Otto Frank was born in the city of Frankfurt am Main in Germany on 12 May 1889 to Michael and Alice Frank. He had two brothers, Robert and Herbert, and a younger sister Helene, who became known as Leni. Germany had not long been a nation, its regions having become unified in 1871, just sixteen years before Otto's birth.

The Frank family had emerged from the Frankfurt Jewish ghetto, the Judengasse ('Jews' Alley') in the late eighteenth century; Otto Frank's great-grandfather Elkan Juda Cahn had still lived in the ghetto as a young man. By the late nineteenth century, Otto's father (and Anne's grandfather) Michael Frank was so assimilated into Frankfurt life that he did not simply work in a bank, he actually owned one – the Michael Frank Bank, which specialized in security exchanges and foreign currency.

In 1908, Otto went to study economics at Heidelberg University where he became friendly with an American student called Nathan Straus. This friendship resulted in Otto being invited to New York and being given a work placement at the Straus family's department store, the same Macy's which we still see in all major shopping streets and malls throughout America. Otto's happy time in New York was cut short in September 1909 when his father Michael Frank died suddenly and without warning at the relatively young age of 57. Otto returned to Frankfurt to help run the family bank.

This he did until the First World War broke out in August 1914. Otto Frank fought as a patriotic German, on the opposite side to his French cousins Oscar and Georges Frank, who were both killed. After his part in the fearsome battles of the Somme and Cambrai, Otto was promoted to the rank of lieutenant and was awarded the Iron Cross. At the end of the war, fatigued and battle weary, he did not return directly home to his anxiously awaiting family. Instead he took a lengthy detour, to act in what he believed to be the honourable way and return a horse he had borrowed as a soldier from a farmer. Back in civilian life, he resumed his role running the Frank family bank until its collapse in the aftermath of the Wall Street Crash of 1929 and the dire economic situation in Germany.

Otto married Edith Hollander in September 1925. Edith was the daughter of a wealthy industrialist from Aachen, whose family roots, as one would suspect from their name, went back to Holland. Although Otto Frank was not to be considered a wealthy man by the mid-1920s, the Frank family was still highly regarded in Frankfurt. The main concern of Edith's family was that her new husband, although suitably Jewish, was not at all religious. After honeymooning in San Remo on the Italian Mediterranean coast, Edith and Otto lived in Frankfurt where their first daughter Margot Betti was born on 16 February 1926. Three years later, on 12 June 1929, along came Annelies Marie, whose name was soon shortened by the family to Anne.

As related in the previous chapter, after Hitler's accession to Chancellor of Germany in January 1933, life was very soon becoming difficult for German Jews such as the Frank family. By late 1933, Otto had left his homeland for Amsterdam to create a new life for his family who would soon follow. For a seventh generation Frankfurt Jew it was a hard decision to grapple with. In his book *The Pity of It All*, the Israeli writer Amos Elon reflected on the German Jews and their one-sided love affair with their homeland. He says, 'Before Hitler rose to power, other Europeans often feared, admired, envied and ridiculed the Germans; only Jews seemed actually to have loved them. . . . No other group of European Jews tried so hard to become a part of their host country.' The attachment to Germany, the country he had fought for less than twenty years earlier, is true of Otto Frank. A decade later, in the confines of their hiding place, Otto had heard his daughter Anne railing against the wickedness of 'The Germans'. According to their helper Miep Gies, he had corrected her that it was not 'The Germans' as a whole but 'These Germans who are wicked'.

In 1938 Otto had actually attempted to get his family out of Europe to America, but a visa was refused, despite his connection to the wealthy Straus family. In December 1941, a visa was eventually granted for him to come to Cuba, but it was for him alone without his family, too late and too restricted, and as it was after Germany had declared war on the United States, it is not known if Otto ever received it.

Otto's cousin Millie Stanfield, who was living in England at this time, also wrote to Otto and Edith suggesting the girls come to live with her in Surrey. Otto and Edith could not bear to part with their beloved daughters, which gives an understanding of the unbearable dilemma of those parents who did give their children up to the safety of British families through the Kindertransport children's rescue missions. I had lunch with Millie in New York in January 1999, as she had emigrated to the US after the war. We celebrated her forthcoming 100th birthday with cake and champagne. It was a happy and convivial occasion, but quietly she told me that she had begged Otto to send his daughters to her in England, and he had had to live with his decision for the rest of his life.

Anne's relationship with her father was complex and veered between adoration, frustration and anger. She loved him as a sensitive, caring father, who would always lend a listening ear to her problems, and as an intellectual from whom she had inherited a thirst for learning more about the world. Otto Frank made sure that the long days the family was in hiding between July 1942 and August 1944 were put to good use. He instructed the three teenagers, Margot, Anne and Peter van Pels, in the lessons they would have had at school, including the sciences, maths and languages. School textbooks had been packed along with other essentials for the period of hiding. The adults had also brought books and study courses to help while away time and keep brains alert and distracted from the daily fears.

Anne had a pet name for her father, 'Pim', and certainly in the earlier days of the hiding sought out his company and comfort. She admired him as a respected leader, as a shrewd and successful businessman and someone whose wise counsel had been sought by fearful members of the émigré German-Jewish community in Amsterdam who had frequented their Merwedeplein apartment in the months before going into hiding. On the other hand, the feisty and opinionated Anne felt that her father undervalued her views and her judgement in the intense situations that arose in the crowded, claustrophobic hiding place. She also felt that her father had sometimes unfairly taken the side of her mother during their frequent confrontations.

Towards the end of the time in hiding, Anne's relationship with her father hit its lowest point, when she felt he had mistrusted her. Anne and 16-year-old Peter had often climbed up the rickety wooden ladder together to the bare dusty attic to spend time away from the adults. From the tiny attic window the two entrapped adolescents could look upwards to the precious sky, glimpse the top of the nearby Westertoren clock tower, and be aware of the seasons changing by the upper branches of the adjacent horse-chestnut tree.

Anne and Peter's relationship had fluctuated from companionship and solace to teenage infatuation, which the pubescent Anne wrote about as 'spring rising within her'. Many of her entries in the spring of 1944 talk about her feelings for Peter, as well as describing their conversations held when alone in the attic. By mid-1944, Anne's ardour had dampened and she viewed Peter's intellect with disdain. Nonetheless, her parents had obviously discussed their understandable concerns about the two hormonal teenagers spending so much time alone together, although Otto understood that if the worst should happen and the group were captured, this would have been Anne's only romance in life. Otto took it upon himself to talk to Anne privately about his concern at how close she was becoming to Peter and her parents' fear of her becoming pregnant.

Despite being in her father's constant presence, Anne put her well-used pen to paper and on 5 May 1944 wrote him a candid and angry letter pouring out her feelings about not being trusted by her own father. She also mentioned that she felt she was becoming independent from her parents. The letter inflicted pain on Otto and subsequent guilt on Anne. In 2006, this letter became the centrepiece of an exhibition at the Amsterdam Historical Museum called 'Anne Frank, Her Life in Letters'.

Anne justified writing the letter in her diary entry dated 15 July 1944, a particularly long piece where she compares the difficulties experienced by the young people in hiding to the relative simplicity of being an adult.

> Why didn't Father support me in my struggle? Why did he fall short when he tried to offer me a helping hand? The answer is this: he used the wrong methods. He always talked to me as if I were a child going through a difficult phase. It sounds crazy, since Father's the only one who's given me a sense of confidence and made me feel as if I'm a sensible person. But he overlooked one thing: he failed to see that this struggle to triumph over my difficulties was more important to me than anything else. I didn't want to hear about 'typical adolescent problems' or 'other girls,' or 'you'll grow out of it.' I didn't want to be treated the same as all-the-other-girls, but as Anne-in-her-own-right, and Pim didn't understand that.

Three weeks after this entry the family were arrested.

Otto came close to death in Auschwitz and, had the Soviet army not arrived on 27 January, he would not have lasted many more days. He weighed just 115lbs (52kg), having weighed 150lbs (68kg) even during the privations of hiding. He later described the miracle that saved him.

One day in Auschwitz I became so dispirited that I couldn't carry on. They had given me a beating, which wasn't exactly a pleasant experience. It was on a Sunday, and I said: 'I can't get up'. Then my comrades said: 'That's impossible, you have to get up, otherwise you're lost'. They went to a Dutch doctor, who worked with the German doctor. He came to me in the barracks and said: 'Get up and come to the hospital barracks early tomorrow morning. I'll talk to the German doctor and make sure you are admitted'. Because of that I survived.

After his liberation from Auschwitz, followed by the long tortuous journey across still war-torn Europe and eventual arrival back in Amsterdam in early June 1945, Otto went to stay with Miep and Jan Gies. He had been told by a liberated camp inmate he met on the homeward journey that Edith had died in early January from despair and starvation, but he was still in hope that his two daughters had survived. Miep was surprised when he asked to stay with them. His response was, 'I prefer to stay with you Miep. That way I can talk about my family when I want to.' Miep recalled that he never really did speak about them, but she understood what he meant.

A visit by Otto to the home of two sisters who had come back from Bergen-Belsen resulted in him hearing that Anne and Margot had died of typhus and malnutrition, probably within one day of each other. But still there was no official notification of the news he had dreaded. In her biography *Anne Frank Remembered*, Miep later recalled what happened next.

> Mr Frank held high hopes for the girls, because Bergen-Belsen was not a death camp. There were no gassings there. It was a work camp – filled with hunger and disease, but with no apparatus for liquidation. I too lived in hope for Margot and Anne.
>
> One morning, Mr Frank and I were alone in the office opening mail. He was standing beside me, and I was sitting at my desk. I was aware of the sound of a letter being slit open, then a moment of silence. Then, Otto Frank's voice . . . 'Miep . . . Miep.' My eyes looked up at him. 'Anne and Margot are not coming back'. We stayed there like that. Struck by lightning which burned through our hearts. Then Mr Frank moved to the door . . . 'I'll be in my office' he said. I sat at my desk, utterly crushed. Then I heard the others coming into the office . . . 'Good Morning' greetings . . . coffee cups.

Unbeknownst to Otto, after the arrest Miep had rescued something belonging to Anne, in the hope she could return it in person to her. Miep continued to describe the morning Otto Frank had the terrible news confirmed. 'I reached into the drawer, on the side of my desk, and took out all Anne's papers, placing the little red-orange checked diary on top, and carried everything into Mr Frank's office. I held out the diary and the papers to him. I said, "Here is your daughter Anne's legacy to you".'

Otto spent the next few days reading the personal journal and slowly realized he had never truly known and understood the inner depths of his younger daughter. All the frustrations, confrontations and disagreements with Anne came back to him and began to make sense. The fears and tensions of hiding and protecting his family had obscured the innermost thoughts, strong values and moral framework of Anne, the girl he had perceived as an opinionated, often disrespectful, hormonal adolescent.

Otto later said, 'For me, it was a revelation. There, was revealed a completely different Anne to the child that I had lost. I had no idea of the depths of her thoughts and feelings.' Interviewed for Jon Blair's 1995 documentary (also called *Anne Frank Remembered*), Miep asked those she imagined would be watching her on their TV screens, 'Can you imagine this poor man? He lost his wife. He lost his daughters. But now he had the diary.'

Otto did not know what should become of Anne's diary. On the one hand it was a private teenage journal, and on the other he knew Anne's dream was to have become a published writer and journalist. Otto showed the diary to many people to seek their opinion and advice. Should it be kept private, or given a wider audience and published as a testament to the suffering of millions? I was told by the Anne Frank Trust's co-founder David Soetendorp that when Otto showed it to his own father, Amsterdam rabbi Jacob Soetendorp, Jacob had offered these words of practicality to his bereaved friend: 'Dear Otto, I understand its importance. But who on earth would want to read Anne's diary?'

Eventually the historian, journalist and literary critic Jan Romein was passed a copy of the transcript by his wife Annie, whom Otto knew. Romein wrote an article about it, entitled 'A Child's Voice', and this was published in the Dutch *Het Parool* newspaper. From the interest the article created, Otto found a publisher, a small Catholic publishing company called Contact. They agreed to publish it with much of what was deemed 'unsuitable' for wide readership removed. Otto also removed sections where Anne had not written well of her mother and the others in hiding, and in fact five pages where she speculated on the genuineness of her father's love for her mother were entrusted to a friend, Cornelius Suijk, for safekeeping. These became known as 'The Five Missing Pages' and have never been published.

By 1952, Anne's diary had been reprinted three times in its original Dutch version, had appeared in German, French and Japanese editions, and in the UK and US. The revered American former First Lady Eleanor Roosevelt had written a powerful forward to the US edition. The Belgian-born aunt of the British Labour politicians David and Ed Miliband, Nan Keen, had worked for the British publisher Vallentine Mitchell at that time, and been involved in the translation and publishing of Anne's diary.

In 1953, at the age of 64, Otto rebuilt his shattered life and remarried. Elfriede 'Fritzi' Geiringer was, like Otto, a survivor of Auschwitz, who had lost her husband and teenage son in the final days before liberation. Otto and Fritzi spent the second part of their lives happy together and equally devoted to spreading the message of Anne's diary. In the 1950s, before teenagers felt they could share their adolescent turmoil with their parents, they started to open up to Mr Frank, whom Anne had painted as a worldly open-minded man. 'Mr Frank' became to some extent a universal agony uncle. Otto and Fritzi worked closely together, painstakingly answering every letter they received on a typewriter and taking the trouble to stamp and post them.

This dedication undoubtedly provided a form of therapy, in the days before psychological intervention, for both Otto and his wife. David Soetendorp, who had followed his father's vocation to become a Reform Rabbi, described in a moving address at the Anne Frank exhibition at Lincoln Cathedral in 1992 how as a young boy he would ask his father after each visit to their home by Otto, 'Daddy, why is Mr Frank always crying?' In his post-rabbinical career as a psychotherapist, David would definitely have the answer.

In 1960, like those former warehouses around it, the building at 263 Prinsengracht was becoming very dilapidated. By then it was already the object of pilgrimages by tourists visiting Amsterdam who had read Anne's diary. Buoyed by the success through the 1950s of Anne's diary, Otto approached the Mayor of Amsterdam and other friends and together the funds were found to open the building as a museum, known in Dutch as the 'Anne Frank Huis'. A governing body, the Anne Frank Foundation, was also created.

The rooms would remain bare and unfurnished at Mr Frank's explicit request in order to give a sense of the loss of those vibrant, opinionated people who occupied those spaces. Even now, as the thousands of visitors a day work their way slowly through the rooms, if you happen to be standing in a lower room and hearing the creaking of the old wooden floors above, it gives a shuddering sense of the ghosts of seven decades ago.

Otto Frank's vision was clear: 'I think it is not only important that people go to the Anne Frank Huis to see the secret annexe, but also that they are helped to realize that people are also persecuted today because of their race, religion or political convictions.' Otto's vision for the Anne Frank Huis was that it should not be a traditional historical museum, but more a centre of education, reflection and understanding. He also planned it as a venue for international student conferences. Just fifteen years after he had suffered so much at the hands of his countrymen, Otto Frank also determined that some of the first participants to be invited to the youth conferences should be German.

Michael Swerdlow was a 16-year-old boy in Liverpool in 1960 when he spotted a small but intriguing advertisement in the personal column of the *Sunday Times* newspaper. It was an announcement by the newly-created Anne Frank Foundation in Amsterdam. Although over fifty-six years later Michael cannot recall the exact wording, it referred to 'The first ever international youth conference by the Anne Frank Foundation for young people to get a greater understanding of being and working together'. There would be four participants from Britain and in order to be one of them you were invited to write to the Anne Frank Foundation and explain why you thought you should be.

Having had an interest in the running of youth clubs and activities since his early teens, Michael lost no time in writing and posting off his submission to Amsterdam. Although he had read Anne's diary, he had no strong emotional attachment to the book, but he had been born in 1943 at the height of the Second World War in Liverpool, the most-bombed British city apart from London. He had grown up conscious that he, as a Jewish kid, could so easily have been deported and murdered if the Germans had invaded.

To Michael's huge excitement he was informed he had been selected to attend the conference and his recollection gives us a helpful insight into those very early days of Otto Frank's educational mission. Carrying his carefully-packed precious cine camera (another teenage passion of his) and a small suitcase, young Michael boarded a plane from what was then known as London Airport, as there was actually only one international airport serving London in 1960. Apart from a school trip to Belgium, it was his first time travelling away from home completely on his own, let alone to a foreign country.

Arriving at the Amsterdam canalside building on the Prinsengracht, young Michael tentatively rang the doorbell. The door was opened by friendly Dutch members of staff of the Foundation who greeted him in English. Michael was told that the building was not yet open to the public although they were soon going to open its doors as a museum. He was given an escorted tour of the building, which was still in its original state, and could feel and smell the evidence that it had been a warehouse. There was a small exhibition on simple boards of photographs, not of the Frank family, but of the round-ups of Jews in Amsterdam.

Michael was given a set of keys and told that during his time there he could have the run of the building to explore as he wished. He was then shown to the building next door which was the Amsterdam University students' residential hall, recently completed and with all its facilities brand spanking new. This would be the participants' accommodation. The first meeting of the international conference was to be held that evening, and knowing there would be a packed agenda over the coming days, he set off with his camera to indulge his hobby by filming the streets, buildings and people of Amsterdam.

Michael then returned to 263 Prinsengracht. Initially nervous, he was shown to a small room down in the basement of the building where he was introduced to around thirty other participants. They were from the Netherlands, France, Spain and Switzerland, and to his great surprise also from West Germany. 'We were mainly teenagers but there were a couple of them who were in their early twenties. This was my first exposure to people from other countries and because we all spoke in English, we bonded as a team and got along well. We were all enthusiasts, and in those days of polite reserve and hand-shaking, we hugged and kissed each other when we left.'

Otto's friend and confidant Rabbi Jacob Soetendorp was a friendly father figure to the group, and activities were run by his oldest son Avraham, who had been hidden with a Dutch farming family as a baby, Avraham's fiancée Sira, a child survivor, and two other members of the fledgling staff of the soon-to-be Anne Frank House. Michael had expected all the seminars to cover the Holocaust and the Second World War but this wasn't the case. He recalled, 'The topics we discussed were current affairs, politics, the arts, culture and how we could work together. I discovered that LSD stood for Lysergic Acid Diethylamide as drugs was also an issue we covered' (LSD had recently arrived on the streets of Amsterdam).

On the third day of the conference Mr Frank came to meet them. Michael recalls spotting a slim and sprightly man who was striding up the street carrying a small briefcase. As he approached the building he was smiling (which he continued to do throughout his visit). At that point out came Michael's cine camera for the first time during the seminar as he had felt that filming during the previous sessions would have been intrusive and disruptive. His film of the arrival of Mr Frank at the first-ever international student conference, along with footage of Amsterdam as it entered the 1960s, is now in the Anne Frank House archive.

The group went downstairs to the basement room and crowded around Mr Frank, asking him questions and hanging on to his answers, which were in very good English (Otto had been at work improving his English during the years in hiding). Mr Frank gave the impression that he was very proud of his team and what they were doing to implement his ideas about bringing young people together.

The next day was also one that influenced Michael's life. It was termed 'Art Appreciation Day' and the group were taken to both the Stedelijk Museum, where Michael discovered the work of Mondrian for the first time, and then on to the Rijksmuseum. There, in front of Rembrandt's magnificent 'Night Watch' a professional curator demonstrated to the students how to use one's 'inner eye' to truly appreciate what an artist is trying to convey, something Michael says has never left him, and guides his appreciation of paintings to this day.

The only reference to the Holocaust was as the students left the conference and they were given a booklet listing all the concentration camps in Europe. This was an eye-opener in terms of the young people's awareness of the number of camps that were set up throughout Western and Eastern Europe, and contained many names which were little known in 1960, such as Majdanek and Belzec, words that now fill us with horror at their very mention.

The conference, his time at the Anne Frank Huis and his meeting with Otto Frank affirmed to Michael, a good friend of mine, that youth work is where he wanted to be. Along with his business activities, he has spent his life engaged in voluntary youth work in Liverpool.

The Anne Frank Huis, or Anne Frank House, as I shall refer to it in the rest of this book, officially opened its doors on 10 May 1960. As difficult as it is to imagine now, when in peak periods people from all over the world can wait in line for up to two hours, the first visitors rang the doorbell to be allowed into the building.

But as the popularity of Anne's diary grew, increased by the 1955 American play and 1960 movie *The Diary of Anne Frank*, so did the visitors. Otto Frank remained determined the Foundation should speak out and educate about other issues of racism and discrimination and abuse of human rights around the world.

In 1963, Otto Frank created a second organization based in Basel where he lived. Known as the Anne Frank-Fonds, it would own and administer the rights of Anne Frank and other close members of her family, be responsible for handling copyrights and distributing the royalties from the diary, and be a distinct entity from the House. The Anne Frank-Fonds promotes projects in the spirit of the message of Anne Frank, helping in disseminating Otto Frank's wish of better understanding between societies and religions. Over the past two decades the House and the Fonds have oftentimes been at legal loggerheads over copyrights pertaining to documents, artefacts and photographs, a fact that would undoubtedly have saddened Otto Frank, who had created the two organizations with so much good intention.

Indeed the Anne Frank House and its founder Otto Frank did not always see eye to eye. In the early 1970s the House staged a series of three consecutive summer exhibitions in the temporary display space called 'Nazisme in Zuid Afrika'. Otto felt that the Anne Frank House were overstepping the mark in making a direct comparison between Nazism and apartheid. By that time Otto had retired from the Board of the Foundation but was concerned about any politicization of the Anne Frank House, which was not in line with what he had in mind in setting it up. Otto complained vociferously to the then Director Dr Hans van Houte about the exhibition but to no avail. The creator of the display, South African exile Berend Schuitema (who had also been wary of the name and inference of the exhibition but had acceded to the views of other members of staff), recalled that Otto Frank told him gently but firmly that 'nothing can compare to the Holocaust . . . Frank's view was that he wished to see the main function of the Anne Frank Foundation as a contribution to reconciliation and peace which is what Anne, his daughter, wished. Anne, after all, was not a Rosa Luxemburg but a young, innocent girl for whom admiration crosses all boundaries, including political.' The banners that had particularly offended Otto Frank were taken down by the Director, Dr van Houte. However, the most radical members of staff were angry about the interference of the by-then elderly Mr Frank, and called for a vote of no confidence in the Director. It must have resulted in a highly volatile working atmosphere as those who opposed Otto Frank's wishes were fired and van Houte resigned not long afterwards.

Until he became too infirm, Otto and Fritzi travelled the world meeting people and helping to promote Anne's diary as a force for good. In 2002 I found myself as a tourist at the synagogue on the small island of Curacao, a former Dutch colony in the far west of the Caribbean. My hosts proudly showed me a photograph of Otto and Fritzi's visit. The couple also spent many happy times in London with Fritzi's daughter Eva and her growing family, Otto becoming a doting and wise grandfather to Eva's three daughters.

Looking back on his commitment to promoting the diary and answering all those letters, Otto explained, 'Anne's diary was a great help for me in regaining a positive outlook on the world. With its publication, I hoped to help many people, and that proved to be the case.'

Otto and Fritzi lived a simple life in their home in Basel, eating sparingly and whenever possible forgoing taxis for public transport. Well known and admired in his own right, whenever he was asked to sign a copy of Anne's diary he refused to do so, shaking his head and politely stating that it was not actually his work. There were difficulties to deal with, notably the attacks on Anne's diary by Holocaust deniers describing it as a forgery that had been created by her father after the war to make money. This was forensically proven to be untrue by both the Netherlands Institute for War Documentation (resulting in the scholastic publication the *Critical Edition of the Diary of Anne Frank*) and a West German court, but sadly not until after Otto's death. Attacks on the authenticity of Anne's diary continue to this day, from right-wing extremists and also from Middle Eastern countries as a way of delegitimizing the state of Israel.

There was also the 'Meyer Levin case'. Otto Frank was sued for $1,000,000 (a huge sum in those times) by the American writer and journalist Meyer Levin for what he considered a broken promise concerning who would write the script for a stage play based on Anne's diary. Initially having verbally promised approval to write the play to the impassioned Levin, Otto and the Broadway producers felt Levin's script had made the story too Jewish and it would not get performed, except perhaps to a limited audience in the very Jewish city of New York.

The play that actually opened on Broadway in 1955, and which is still being performed all over the world, was written by a Gentile husband-and-wife team, Albert Hackett and Frances Goodrich, whom the writer Lillian Hellman had introduced to Otto. In Hackett and Goodrich's hands, the persecution of the Frank family became universalized for a time when there was less interest in racism and anti-Semitism and America's most pressing concern was about Communist infiltration. Levin believed the original idea for a play had come from him, had been shared with and approved by Otto and Fritzi Frank and accused Frank and the producers of plagiarism and infringement of his version. After many years of litigation, during which even Eleanor Roosevelt tried to mediate, Otto Frank was ordered by the American court to pay Meyer Levin a minimal amount of $15,000 to stop the ongoing litigation and recognize that it was Levin's idea to create a play. Otto Frank had effectively won the case but it weighed heavily on him for many years. It also did on Meyer Levin, who in 1973 wrote a book about this deeply felt experience. He titled his book *The Obsession*.

Otto and Fritzi Frank continued their mission to promote Anne's memory well into their twilight years. Engaging with people kept them focused and active, and like many Holocaust survivor educators as they have neared the end of their lives, they became even more driven. In 1979, on the cusp of his tenth decade, Otto Frank declared, 'I am now almost 90 and my strength is slowly failing. Still, the task I received from Anne continues to restore my energy: to struggle for reconciliation and human rights throughout the world.'

Otto Frank lived to be 91 and died in Basel on 19 August 1980. Many of the Holocaust survivors I have met over the years have had similarly long lives, I am sure partly due to the strength of character that helped them survive what was intended to be unsurvivable. Fritzi continued to live in their home in Basel until she too became frail. She came to live in London with her daughter Eva, until she passed away aged 94 in 1998.

I recall Fritzi, who became one of the Anne Frank Trust's founder patrons, at the launch of the exhibition 'Anne Frank, A History for Today' at Southwark Cathedral in 1997. She was still a handsome woman, but at the age of 93 her memory had faded and she was clearly struggling with being in a large crowd of strangers. At one point Fritzi was being photographed in front of a panel showing a large image of Otto in the 1970s. She happened to glance behind her and her piercing blue eyes lit up. Her finger extended out towards the photo, then she smiled back at us and said proudly, 'That's my Otto'.

Chapter 3

'Anne Frank in the World' is Launched

'Anne Frank in the World, 1929-1945' was the name given to the Anne Frank House's first travelling exhibition, touring the world and soon becoming an international phenomenon. The driving force behind the international success of the world's most enduring and popular travelling Anne Frank exhibition has, for the past thirty years, undoubtedly been due to a man called Jan Erik Dubbelman, the International Director of the Anne Frank House.

The exhibition was first launched on 12 June 1985 to coincide with the day that would have been Anne's 56th birthday. The venue chosen for this auspicious event was the Westerkerk, situated adjacent to the Anne Frank House, a Protestant Reform church built in the 1620s during the age of Amsterdam's seafaring and trading supremacy. The Renaissance-style Westerkerk, with its imposing gold-adorned clock and bell tower known as the Westertoren, has long been a feature of the city, reflecting Amsterdam's commercial importance. Anne Frank wrote about the chiming of the Westertoren bells several times in her diary, describing how the 'dearly beloved bells' gave her comfort in her isolation from the world. Certainly, it was an appropriate choice of venue. On my first visits to Amsterdam in the late 1980s I would stay in a hotel just along the Prinsengracht and hearing the sound of the Westertoren bells gave me an ethereal bond to Anne.

Queen Beatrix of the Netherlands was guest of honour at the exhibition launch and the keynote speech was to be given by former West German Chancellor Willy Brandt. This choice was somewhat controversial to some members of the Amsterdam Jewish community, many of whom were Holocaust survivors or those who had been hidden. There had been suspicion that West Germany under Brandt's chancellorship had failed to protect the Israeli athletes who had been slaughtered at the 1972 Munich Olympics, despite a prior tip-off to the West German government that the Palestinian terrorist group Black September had been planning an attack. On the other hand, Brandt had been the first West German Chancellor to offer contrition for the Holocaust. In an act that came to be known as the Warsaw Kneefall (Warschauer Kniefall), Brandt had prostrated himself as an act of silent atonement at the memorial to the Warsaw Ghetto. The Amsterdam Jewish community's concern proved unfounded and Brandt gave a warmly-received speech to declare the 'Anne Frank in the World' exhibition open.

The panels of 'Anne Frank in the World' reflected a time when the only accessible photographs of the rise of Nazism and the Second World War were in stark black-and-white. Printing and image-scanning processes were pre-digital and the exhibition, designed to travel, comprised thirty heavy-duty aluminium frames which held white PVC display panels (not unlike shower curtains) with the black-and-white images accompanied by black text. Designed by the Dutch, a nation of tall people, the first version of the travelling exhibition showed panels some 2.5m high, which required long ladders to erect and the craning of necks by visitors to read the higher-positioned content.

Dienke Hondius is an Associate Professor of History at the University of Amsterdam and author of many respected books on the social history of the Netherlands, specializing in documenting its waves of immigration and how Dutch citizens reacted to these. In the early 1980s, Dienke had been part of Amsterdam's radical activism scene, including being a proud member of the 'Squatters' Movement' who would use empty buildings as temporary homes. In line with her ideals and years ahead of the eco movement, when I first knew Dienke she jointly owned a car with a friend to help cut down on carbon emissions. As a newly-graduated historian, in the mid-1980s Dienke happened to be using the Anne Frank House archive to study neo-Nazism in order to help her activist movement to challenge it. The Anne Frank House historian Joke Kniesmeyer asked the willing and knowledgeable young graduate to help her in the creation of the panels for the planned new mobile exhibition.

Dienke recalled some of the thinking that drove the content. 'One aspect that we consciously included in the historical part was the topic of anti-Nazi resistance within Germany on the one hand, and that of pro-Nazi collaboration within the Netherlands on the other hand. We wanted to oppose the outdated idea, particularly in the Netherlands, that all the Dutch had been in the resistance, and that all the Germans had been Nazis.'

The narrative of the exhibition was written in the present tense, giving the reader, who understands where it is leading, a feeling of history playing out in the here and now. Dienke explained this rationale, 'As a general rule, the present tense has the effect of bringing historical events closer to us; we imagine more easily how things happened when we read about it in the present tense. Bringing history closer to our lives here and now was one of the main objectives of making "Anne Frank in the World".'

The exhibition started by introducing visitors to the Frank family, Otto Frank in the Great War, his wedding to Edith Hollander and the births and early childhood of their daughters, and it then took its time in building the context of the persecution of the Jews and the Holocaust. Panels showed the freefall of the German economy after the First World War, the rise from nowhere of Adolf Hitler and the National Socialist party and how every section of civil society was sucked into propagating its ideology. There were panels about German universities, where young anti-bourgeois students were some of the most fanatical and avid book-burners, and about the corruption of the justice system and the judiciary. The exhibition also showed how the German people, still recovering from the trauma of the Great War and the economic crash, were seduced by cheap Volkswagen cars, paid summer and skiing holidays (under the 'Strength Through Joy' programme) and the offer of jobs building autobahns and in armaments factories. There was a panel on school life and how children were taught their gender differences – boys encouraged to fight for their nation and girls to cook and to produce Aryan children. A strong-faced woman was shown proudly wearing a large medal, awarded by the state for being a productive Aryan mother.

The Wannsee Conference of January 1942, when senior Nazi leaders met to ratify the Final Solution to the Jewish Question, was not shown until well into the exhibition. From then on the Frank family's increasingly dangerous situation as Nazi measures against the Jews intensify resulted in their fleeing into hiding when Margot was summoned to be deported. The eventual arrest and fate of the eight people in hiding, the publication of Anne's diary and Otto's later life and mission closed the historical section of the exhibition. The final panels gave a snapshot of northern Europe in the mid-1980s with neo-Nazi movements on the rise. One of the most memorable images was of an enraged middle-aged woman in Sweden hitting a neo-Nazi demonstrator with her handbag. She was comical and heroic in equal measure. Dienke explained, 'This was one of the parts of the exhibition where we wanted to zoom out from the "Dutch" and "German" and "Frank family". Here, too, the aim was to stimulate discussion and to show connections between "then & there" and "here & now".'

After its much-publicized launch at Amsterdam's Westerkerk, German- and English-language copies of 'Anne Frank in the World' opened in Frankfurt and New York respectively. The New York event proved to be very expensive as, because it was early days in the exhibition's life and still an unknown quantity, verbal promises of sponsorship mostly didn't materialize. When hearing about the costs that had been incurred in New York the Board members of the Anne Frank House put their foot down. They unanimously agreed that 'There is no future in a travelling exhibition', echoing projections about the future of motor cars, TV and telephones – and even Anne Frank's own question as to whether 'anyone will wish to read the musings of a thirteen-year-old girl'. The Dutch-language exhibition, opened to great fanfare by the Queen of the Netherlands just a few months before, was already languishing in storage in a back room of the Westerkerk 'covered in pigeon poop', as recalled by Jan Erik Dubbelman, the man who was to be the saviour and driving force behind the Anne Frank exhibition.

Jan Erik had joined the Anne Frank House in January 1982 working in Information and Documentation. At that time a new extreme right-wing party was emerging in the Netherlands and as a challenge to this anti-Fascist committees were springing up throughout the country. From his desk at the Anne Frank House, and having access to relevant documents and articles, Jan Erik started to support these committees by providing useful information. He also helped to organize a large anti-Fascist demonstration in the centre of Amsterdam, which he believes put the Anne Frank House on the map as an organization that was addressing contemporary issues as well as educating about the past.

Jan Erik was in fact a draft resister. The Netherlands, a country that had suffered the dire consequences of Nazi occupation, continued active conscription to the armed forces up until 1995. Dutch conscription dated back to its introduction in the early nineteenth century by Louis Bonaparte, who had been installed as King Lodewijk I of Holland by his older brother the Emperor Napoleon. Many of the Anne Frank House staff up until the mid-1990s were similarly draft resisters as the last conscripted soldiers were not demobilized until 1996. Jan Erik chose to resist the draft, despite strongly believing that 'there are times in history when there is a real justification for going to war'.

Jan Erik was appointed Head of the International Department in 1989, not long after I first met him in Bournemouth, and set about growing the Anne Frank exhibition into the global force for good that it has become. He has spent most of his life since 1989 in a bright canalside office, either on the phone, receiving and sending faxes and after the mid-1990s responding to hundreds of emails a day, inspiring his growing team of equally dedicated staff, or boarding planes and trains to ensure the Anne Frank project happened. He has met thousands of people along the way in all parts of the world, setting up the projects, and then convincing others to fund it. Having known him for thirty years, I like to remind Jan Erik that he is personally responsible for bringing Anne Frank's story to many millions of people. Highly intelligent, charismatic and with an impish sense of humour, Jan Erik is nonetheless imbued with a quiet modesty. Never comfortable as a public speaker, he was always happy to take a back seat at the openings he had made happen, watching successive Anne Frank House directors, Hans Westra and then Ronald Leopold (and myself when fortunate enough to be sent by the Anne Frank House), give the keynote speech at each international launch.

Nonetheless, Jan Erik believed in a future for taking the story of Anne Frank out to the world. He flew to London and met with representatives of the Greater London Council (abolished by Prime Minister Margaret Thatcher in 1986), community leaders and anti-racism activists. 'Anne Frank in the World' duly opened in February 1986 at the Mall Galleries, just along the road from Buckingham Palace in central London.

Successful as the Mall Galleries event was, Jan Erik wanted to ensure that Britain maximized the use of this specially-created English/Dutch language copy of the exhibition. He came to live in London for three months in the autumn of that year, living in one room in the East End, cycling around the city and getting to know England and Scotland by train. He made connections in those weeks which resulted in twelve cities taking the exhibition over the next two years, while raising £75,000 to kick the programme off – no mean feat in those early days.

From its inception 'Anne Frank in the World' was something special and unique in its transformative power. Whether being shipped across oceans from Amsterdam to countries where people knew little about the horrors of Nazism or were emerging from their own painful histories, or going to communities riven by division, suspicion and sectarianism, there has never been a travelling event that has been such an empowering force for good.

In the following pages you will read about some unforgettable people from all over the world and learn about Anne Frank from a new perspective. But before we go on that adventure, I will explain what happened next in Britain.

Chapter 4

The Anne Frank Trust is Born

In 1986, following the opening of the first Anne Frank exhibition in Britain, Jan Erik Dubbelman from the newly-formed International Department of the Anne Frank House had come to live in the East End of London to help ensure the exhibition continued. Using the traditional Dutch means of transport, a trusty bicycle, to get himself around the city, he started building a network of local and then national connections, mostly from the more sympathetic left wing of British politics.

This was around the middle period of Margaret Thatcher's government, which saw the rise and influence of young testosterone- and cocaine-fuelled City traders. The term 'yuppie' was being used as an acronym for 'young urban professional' – particularly those who worked in a well-paid job and had a luxurious lifestyle. These outputs of Thatcherite Britain were satirised by a new wave of comedians such as Ben Elton and Harry Enfield. Shoulders became wider on male and female clothing due to 'power padding' (referencing popular culture such as the American TV series *Dynasty* and British bands such as Duran Duran and Spandau Ballet). On the other hand, the Live Aid concert in July 1985 heralded a new era in which young people felt they could and should take responsibility for the iniquities and inequalities of the world.

The UK was becoming a very polarized country by the mid-1980s. In the post-industrial north of England the coal industry was dying following the crippling year-long miners' strike. At the opposition Labour Party's annual conference in Bournemouth, the party's leader Neil Kinnock had made a damning speech about the Militant wing of his party, and in particular Liverpool's left-wing council. This was considered the finest speech made by Kinnock, and is cited as a historic turning point in the history of the Labour party – leading to its thirteen-year period of government between 1997 and 2010.

An hour before the speech, David Soetendorp and I had sat with Kinnock in a nearby hotel lounge discussing the plight of Soviet Jewish 'Refuseniks' (to our delight we later heard him refer to their plight in his speech). As we were leaving the meeting Kinnock took us over to a group of men in animated discussion. He introduced us to the black man who seemed to be leading the conversation. The man looked up at us, politely smiled and said a friendly hello. 'This is Oliver Tambo,' Kinnock said casually. We smiled back and waved hello.

We were greeting the exiled President of the African National Congress, after whom Johannesburg International Airport is now named.

Meanwhile, during these times of social upheaval, Jan Erik and his wife Dienke managed to arrange a meeting with the Conservative government's Schools Minister Angela Rumbold. Unlike later meetings with government ministers that he and I came to experience, Jan Erik recalled being surprised that it was the Minister without the attendance of any advisers making notes and action points. There were pleasantries and supportive words over a cup of tea, but no government support for the Anne Frank exhibition to continue its work was forthcoming.

Despite this, Jan Erik's determination proved to be successful and between 1986 and 1990 there were bookings for the 'Anne Frank in the World' exhibition by twenty British cities, including Manchester, Glasgow, Liverpool, Barnsley and Bradford. It was an important time in the evolution of formal Holocaust education with the creation of the Holocaust Educational Trust and its campaign for Holocaust education to be a part of the History curriculum in secondary schools; the 1988 'Remembering for the Future' conference organized by the respected Holocaust historian Dr Elisabeth Maxwell (the French-born wife of the disgraced tycoon Robert Maxwell) and the publication of the Auschwitz teaching pack by the Inner London Education Authority (which ceased to exist in 1990), the first-ever comprehensive Holocaust teaching resource produced by a governmental body in the UK.

One of the people Jan Erik and his partner, the exhibition's co-creator Dienke Hondius, had met while planning the Manchester exhibition was a young historian called Tony Kushner. To give an indication of the lack of Holocaust education in British schools prior to the mid-1980s, a decade earlier Tony had chosen History for his O-Level and A-levels. For both exams he had studied Nazi Germany but, despite the excellence of his teacher, there was astonishingly no mention in the curriculum of either Jews or the Holocaust.

Tony's interest was first sparked by watching the episode on the Nazi genocide of the ITV flagship series *The World At War* (first screened on 27 March 1974). 'My mother was disabled and my brother was blind. I remember thinking how incredibly vulnerable we would have been under the Nazi regime, let alone being Jewish.' He decided he wanted to be a social historian and went to Sheffield University, the only faculty with a course on Social History. Sheffield, home city to the headquarters of the National Union of Mineworkers, was known as the 'Socialist Republic of Sheffield' during the mid-1980s and the atmosphere was highly charged politically. After completing his PhD, Tony went to work at the newly-created Manchester Jewish Museum, where he worked on an exhibition called 'Before the Holocaust' about Jewish refugees from Nazism who had settled in the city. 'At that time, Holocaust survivors were not as prominent as they are now and their stories were more unknown than those of the refugees to Britain.' In 1986 Tony moved to the University of Southampton where he set up the highly esteemed Parkes Institute for the Study of Jewish-Christian Relations. He has also written several books connecting Britain and the Holocaust.

In the summer of 2016, Tony and I sat in the café of the University of Southampton. He reflected back on those times when the Anne Frank exhibition was just starting out on its journey throughout the UK.

> If you had said to me in 1989 that Holocaust education would become part of the school curriculum, there would be War Crimes legislation in two years, that the Imperial War Museum would have a Holocaust exhibition larger than its World War II exhibition, and that there would be a national Holocaust Memorial Day, I would have laughed at you at the improbability of it all.

In the summer of 1988, I had received the telephone call that was to change my life forever. It was from my good friend Rabbi David Soetendorp. He had just come home from paying a pastoral hospital visit to a congregant. During the conversation, she had mentioned to him casually that there was an exhibition travelling around Britain about Anne Frank and that her daughter had seen it in Bristol. On the phone to me David sounded excited. 'Was I was aware that his Dutch father Rabbi Jacob Soetendorp and Otto Frank had been good friends? Would I be interested in helping him bring this exhibition to Bournemouth?' Yes, David, I would.

David contacted the Anne Frank House, where there is an education room named in memory of his late father. He then called a well-known philanthropist called Bertha Klug, who divided her time between her homes in London and Bournemouth. Bertha, known to all since childhood by her nickname of Bee, invited us to her apartment overlooking the sweep of Bournemouth Bay. When I walked into the room, already sitting round the laden tea table was David, happily conversing in Dutch with Jan Erik Dubbelman, Dienke Hondius and Cornelius 'Cor' Suijk, Otto Frank's friend who was the Emeritus Director of the Anne Frank House and a roving international ambassador for the organization. I later learnt that Cor, who died in 2014, had belonged to a group of Dutch Resistance heroes during the Second World War who had saved the lives of thirteen Jews.

We sat around Bee's table and were all equally inspired by the enthusiasm of Jan Erik, Dienke and the much older Mr Cor Suijk. After tea had been served, Bee left the room and returned carrying a framed photograph. She proudly pointed out her son Brian, a young man in the midst of a large group of smiling men and women. Bee then explained that this was Brian in the 1960s, attending one of Otto Frank's international student conferences. And there, on the right hand side of the group, was an unmistakeable young David Soetendorp. David recalls that, 'This certainly led to a very good outcome from that afternoon. Bee wanted, there and then, to become the principal backer of the exhibition.'

Bee and her businessman husband Sid generously offered to sponsor the cost of staging the 'Anne Frank in the World' exhibition in Bournemouth, in those days £5,000 to cover the transportation and build costs. A strange customs anomaly meant that in those days the exhibition had to travel back and forth from Amsterdam to the UK for each staging. Also back and forth across the North Sea came a pair of gung-ho exhibition builders led by Joost Dekkers, who drove it to each venue in a large truck.

We set up a voluntary committee of local educators and activists to plan and stage the exhibition in Bournemouth. I can't recall what my exact role was on the group – probably David's 'Girl Friday' – but I remember it took up my every waking moment for the following nine months.

Our first task was to find a suitable venue. After doing the rounds of local churches and civic facilities, we were offered a large room at Bournemouth College of Art which, although on the outskirts of the town, was perfect. A competition was held among the art students to design the event's publicity materials, which long before Apple Macs and whizz-bang computer graphics and technology, were rather naively amateurish.

On a sunny April morning in 1989, I stood in anticipation outside the college and watched as a large truck, containing the panels and frames of 'Anne Frank in the World' as well as the two waving and smiling Dutch exhibition builders, drove up the road towards the building. Anne Frank and her story had arrived in our town. I was overcome with emotion and tears welled up in my eyes watching the previous nine months of activity and excitement come to fruition.

Inside the empty exhibition space a team of five teenage boys doing Community Service for petty criminality were waiting around with their supervisor to help our Dutch friends. It was my first of many future encounters with young offenders. The boys had no idea of who Anne Frank was, let alone what had happened to her, and they set about their building task in a nonchalant, sometimes even petulant, manner. As the panels took shape one by one and the story unfolded, each of the boys seemed to quieten down and start to take an interest in what they were doing. Their work ethic seemed to change too. At the end of the build, Joost Dekkers presented each one with the exhibition catalogue in appreciation of their hard work, and as a further learning tool.

Eva Schloss, in the early days of her journey as a Holocaust speaker and educator, came from London to launch the exhibition. I felt the excitement at her visit as so many have done in the subsequent thirty years of her remarkable travels and lectures. She was 59 on that evening of our first meeting and as I write is approaching 90, but is as active as ever.

The 'Anne Frank in the World' exhibition was on show for three weeks in that fateful spring of 1989. Over 10,000 people from Bournemouth and its neighbouring towns came to see it. At the end of the three weeks I felt bereft at its leaving but managed to obtain a large metal road sign advertising the Anne Frank exhibition which I kept on the inside wall of my garage as a souvenir.

I was restless that summer and couldn't leave the experience of the Anne Frank exhibition behind. In September, I took a plane across to Amsterdam for a further meeting with Jan Erik and Dienke, who introduced me to the Anne Frank House Director, Hans Westra. I convinced Hans that the tour of the Anne Frank exhibition had to continue in the UK – it was essential – and that they needed someone who was based in that country to manage it.

That road sign sitting in my house became a metaphor for my future career. I was duly appointed by Hans as the 'British Representative of the Anne Frank House' that autumn and was tasked to promote the exhibition in the UK. I would receive a percentage of the hire fee for each exhibition I brought to fruition. I immediately set to work with huge drive and motivation, partly because I was in the sad process of separating from my first husband Peter Walnes, had two growing children and needed an income.

Several further meetings in Amsterdam followed. In the spring of 1990, it was agreed with Hans and the Anne Frank House's Managing Director Kleis Broekhuizen that a charitable trust should be set up in the UK to help groups of volunteers and community activists around the country who wished to bring the exhibition to their town or city. The Anne Frank Educational Trust, as it was first known, was duly born. I was to be its Executive Director.

To apply for charitable status we now needed a Board of Trustees and a Chair of that Board. In Hans Westra's office we decided to invite David Soetendorp, who had such close links to Otto Frank, to be the Founding Chair, to which he naturally and readily agreed. Eva Schloss was asked to be a Trustee and Jan Erik suggested others from around the country he had worked with. The first Board included Shirley Daniel, head teacher of a high-achieving Asian girls' school in west London and Professor Tony Kushner, whom Jan Erik and Dienke had first met in Manchester but was by now director of the Parkes Institute for Jewish-Christian Relations at the University of Southampton. Otto Frank's widow Fritzi was appointed as a Founding Patron. As an elderly and always supremely elegant white-haired lady she attended a couple of our first Trustee meetings brought along by Eva, but Fritzi's English was not very good so her venerable presence in the room was more motivational than practical.

Once our charitable status was achieved, we started to plan the official launch of the Trust. By then I had a part-time administrator, Janey Mitchell, whose other job was as a news presenter on the local Dorset radio station. We worked together in the study of my Victorian house in the historic Dorset town of Wimborne, ten miles north of Bournemouth. Thanks to our new colleagues at the Holocaust Educational Trust, it would take place at the House of Commons in November 1991. Bee and Sid Klug, generous as ever, kindly agreed to host the event but were rather surprised when more than 300 people turned up, politicians, educators and activists – all curious about the new Anne Frank Educational Trust. The proceedings were chaired by the recently retired Speaker of the House of Commons, Lord Tonypandy, who to our delight called for 'Order, Order' in his booming and very distinctive Welsh accent. Coming just two and a half years after I had watched the Anne Frank exhibition truck roll into Bournemouth Art College, sitting on the speaking panel in that parliamentary setting was perhaps the first, of many times, I have said to myself, 'How the hell did we get here?'

But I had a reason for such strong motivation. I was born in 1951, just six years after the end of the Second World War. Though I wasn't really aware, my father Harry Goldblatt went away to do his obligatory National Service when I was a small child and my rather glamorous mother, Eileen, was still struggling to 'make do' from the post-war rationing. It's odd that when I look back to those 1950s childhood days, I see everything in black, white and various shades of grey and beige. Maybe it's because the few cars we saw around the streets as children were mostly black. An exception was our brightly flower-bedecked rear garden, my father's labour of love each Sunday,

My father came from a large Polish émigré family, indeed my grandparents Rebecca and Abraham Goldblatt spoke with thick Polish accents, so much so that when my father started his primary school, his teacher called him Eric for a few weeks. Eventually one afternoon he burst into tears and wailed to the teacher that his name was really Harry. She apologized to the distressed child and explained that his name Harry had sounded so much like Eric when his Polish mother had introduced him to her, that she took this for his name. My grandmother used to swear and curse in Yiddish if she ever heard mention of the Russian Tsar and his family, as it was intimidation by his Cossacks which had forced them to flee their town of Sziedlce, cross Europe and embark on a ship to London.

As a growing and curious child in the mid-1950s I soon became aware of family 'whisperings'. I vaguely understood in my childlike way that there had been some kind of catastrophe. I had no idea what the catastrophe was, or even what the word really meant, but eventually I discovered that this 'catastrophe' had affected our paternal grandparents' remaining family in Poland, both on my paternal grandmother's and grandfather's sides.

I was around seven or eight when I was told by my mother that my father was planning to take a trip to Poland to see if he could locate any family property and, even more importantly but more unlikely, any news about 'surviving' family members. I was really not sure what all this meant. However, my mother firmly put her foot down about this impending expedition as she was very worried she would never see my father again if he should disappear behind the impenetrable Iron Curtain.

I can't actually remember how old I was when I discovered what the catastrophe actually entailed. I guess for protective Jewish parents of that generation it was too difficult to sit a child down and tell them the truth. I do remember reading the French lawyer and diplomat Samuel Pisar's autobiography *Of Blood and Hope* as a young teenager, and then reading it again as what he described was so difficult to comprehend. Years later I met Samuel Pisar when he was a still handsome elderly man and was able to show him my torn and much-thumbed copy of his book. Pisar sadly passed away in July 2015.

Through the following years I read more, saw more in films, TV and articles, and heard more from others I encountered, as no Jewish family in Europe was untouched by the catastrophe. Although I have been asked in many interviews when I first read Anne's diary, I actually think it was many years later. The American TV miniseries *Holocaust* starring the young actors Meryl Streep and James Woods, was a watershed, and many adults, astonishingly including British Jews, told me they had only really learnt about the Shoah from that series, made in 1978.

In the early 1980s, as a young mother myself at home with my two small children Joe and Tilly, I decided I wanted to become involved with human rights issues. I think having children does that to you – you have the need to make the world better for your own children's future, and indeed many of the Anne Frank Trust's most passionate activists have joined us when they have become new parents. I joined my local Amnesty International branch, but found its global human rights mission too all-encompassing. I soon felt I would be a small cog in a very big wheel that was trying to change too many of the ills of the world. Years later I was in fact to work closely with Amnesty International again on several projects, including the development of a joint Amnesty International and Anne Frank Trust teaching pack called *Writing in Impossible Circumstances*.

In early 1981, I was invited to attend a talk in Bournemouth being given by Avital Sharansky, who was travelling the world, telling the story of her young husband Natan, then known by his Russian name of Anatoly. Sharansky had been a charismatic and influential leader of the Jewish movement to leave the Soviet Union, and along with the renowned physicist Andrei Sakharov, was calling for greater human rights in his country. Of course he could not be allowed to do so for long, and in 1978, in a show trial reported on throughout the free world, Sharansky was sentenced to nine long years in the Siberian gulag. He and Avital had been married for just one day when he was imprisoned, and she was exiled soon after.

Hearing Avital speak, I was overcome by a feeling of 'this could have been me'. I joined the Bournemouth Committee for Soviet Jewry and, for seven years as its Chair, the cause became my passion and mission. Our very active campaigning group wrote supportive letters to 'Refuseniks', but these were usually intercepted on arrival in the Soviet Union and not delivered to their intended recipients. 'Refuseniks' was a term given to Soviet Jews who had applied to emigrate but had had their request refused by the authorities (very few requests were actually approved). Our little group also lobbied those with power in the West to put pressure on Leonid Brezhnev, and then Yuri Andropov, the hardened and intransigent Soviet leaders, to allow the Jews who wished to leave the Soviet Union to do so. Bournemouth was a well-known conference town so we were fortunate in being able to get to meet powerful political leaders, including Margaret Thatcher, and we were constantly thinking up sensational new ways to attract media coverage for our cause. One time, when Presidents Mikhail Gorbachev and Ronald Reagan were due to hold a summit in Reykjavik in 1986, we had sticks of Bournemouth seaside rock candy specially made for us in a local factory with the words 'Let Our People Go' printed inside. They were duly delivered to the Soviet and US embassies in London with a request to be sent on to Iceland in advance of the summit meeting.

Many of the campaigners went on missions to the Soviet Union, travelling as 'bona fide' tourists with Intourist Travel, the Soviet travel company. We visited beleaguered Refusenik families, many of whom had a family member in a labour camp, taking them much-needed supplies, as once they applied to leave they were denied a means of work, medical treatment and essentials to live on. This is how the word 'Refusenik' came about – refused emigration, and as a consequence of applying to leave, then refused work and benefits. The term 'Refusenik' had been coined by a London activist and Russian speaker called Michael Sherbourne, and has gone on to be universally used by the media in describing people who doggedly reject the status quo.

In advance of my first trip to the Soviet Union in 1982, I started to learn Russian and sailed through the first few lessons as it is such a lyrical language to speak. My confidence grew with my ease of reading the Cyrillic text, that is until my teacher started on all the exceptions to the grammatical rules I had learnt. The exceptions started to outnumber the rules, and I decided that Russian is a language best to be learnt from early childhood.

By the late 1980s, our dynamic campaign was losing its momentum. Mikhail Gorbachev had introduced Glasnost and Perestroika and the door of emigration for our plucky 'Refuseniks' was creaking open. I was starting to feel bereft. But then I received the call from David Soetendorp and less than two years later I was running the Anne Frank Educational Trust.

What a different world it was at that time in so many areas, social, political, technological and demographic. In 1990, the most innovative technical device in the Trust's office was a fax machine, which spewed out shiny cream-coloured paper that had to be read and noted within three weeks before the type faded away. I struggled with a basic computer and the Locoscript programme (no Windows, Word, Macs or tablets in those far-off days). The internet was yet to take over our lives, and we conducted our business through posting and receiving letters, or for urgent matters, using the fax machine or making phone calls.

On a more serious note, many Holocaust survivors were just in the process of 'coming out' in a public way about their experiences, having suppressed their personal stories for many years while rebuilding their lives and bringing up well-adjusted children. Once they had taken the courageous step of speaking publicly, many survivors found a vocation and mission to educate, and went on to become superb educators and role models for young people.

When we started the Trust, Stephen Lawrence was a bright South London schoolboy with hopes of becoming an architect, and terrorism was something associated most usually with the 'Troubles' in Northern Ireland. Britain was a member of the European Union, but along with just eleven other countries. Immigration from European countries was the exception rather than the norm. Immigration to the UK was much more from former Commonwealth countries, such as India, Pakistan, Bangladesh and the islands of the West Indies. British

Asian-born or Asian-heritage women, were depicted in their colourful saris. Muslim women's headscarves and burkhas were not often seen around our city's streets, except on Arab tourists in the West End of London.

There have been waves of refugees arriving to our shores in the ensuing years, reflecting the world's unrelenting conflicts and persecutions, Rwandans, Kosovans, Liberians, Zimbabweans, Somalis and Sudanese, Afghanis, Iraqi Muslims and Iraqi Kurds, and most recently Syrians. Many young refugees have been involved with our work as educators, been recipients of our Anne Frank Awards for Moral Courage and spoken at our fundraising events. One young man who came to speak, the son of a murdered doctor, had fled for his life from Guinea Bissau, a country I had hardly even heard of until we were told his terrible story.

Over the past ten years the Trust has changed the way it works, from one major travelling exhibition that visited a city for a month, to more intensive work in individual schools for a two-week period. From its humble beginnings in my own home, the organization now has over 30 staff members, educating over 30,000 young people a year about the damaging effect of prejudice. Later I will describe how it grew from one person to the flourishing organization it has become.

Chapter 5

Anne and Eva Schloss – the Girl who Became her Stepsister

As a refugee child in Amsterdam, Eva Geiringer Schloss had played with Anne Frank before both their families were forced into hiding for their lives. One of the girls managed to survive and the other didn't. Their lives crossed again when Eva's mother married Anne's father Otto. Eva became Anne's 'posthumous stepsister' and many years afterwards she became a co-founder of the Anne Frank Trust UK.

I first met Eva in March 1989, when she came to Bournemouth to open the 'Anne Frank in the World' exhibition, the first I had been involved in. I was a little in awe of the prospect of meeting Anne Frank's 'posthumous stepsister', but little did I know how our paths would conjoin for the following three decades.

Eva had only 'come out' three years earlier about the pain she endured in the Holocaust. It took her a full forty years after her liberation to be able to speak publicly about things she had buried deep in the recesses of her mind, and this was not something she had volunteered to do. Like so many Holocaust survivors I have met, after the terrible times she had been through, she chose to lock the door of that compartment in her mind and throw away the key. Eva had a busy post-war life, relocating to London where she studied photography, met and married a young man called Zvi Schloss, brought up her three daughters Caroline, Jackie and Sylvia, and then made a successful and fulfilling business from her passion for antiques. After four decades of silence about her early life, Eva had finally opened her wounds to her husband and children. She had spoken about the separation and deaths of her father Erich Geiringer and teenage elder brother Heinz. 'I left feeling that I was walking on a precipice between my current life and the one I had left behind,' she recalls in her memoir *After Auschwitz*. 'Suddenly my mind was full of memories of Pappy and Heinz, our life in Amsterdam, the terrible train journey to Auschwitz, and saying goodbye on the ramp. I remembered how cold and dirty it had been in Birkenau, the frostbite cutting into my toes and the pain of starvation.' She had 'let the story tumble out' and couldn't stop the memories even if she had wanted to.

It happened in an unplanned way in March 1986 at the Mall Galleries in central London, located along the tree-lined avenue that leads to Buckingham Palace. The occasion was the VIP and media launch of the very first British showing of the exhibition 'Anne Frank in the World'. As she entered the crowded room with her mother Elfriede 'Fritzi' Frank, Eva, who at the age of 56 had never been in the public eye before, was rather overwhelmed by being at such a high profile event. The two women were welcomed by Ken Livingstone, who was at that time the Leader of the Greater London Council and was acting as the chairman of the evening's proceedings. He had done his research and knew the women's close connection to the Anne Frank story, so cordially invited Eva and Fritzi to join him at the top table. Livingstone indicated to Eva to sit alongside him, which she duly did – even though she had no idea who he was. She explained that, 'In those days my world was around my family and my antiques business – I wasn't so interested in politics.'

During the evening, Livingstone asked Eva to tell him some more about her life and how her mother and Otto Frank had met. Leaving behind the warmth and comfort of that splendid room in the heart of springtime London, Eva's mind took itself back to the winter of 1945 and the days immediately after the liberation of the death camps of Auschwitz I and Auschwitz II/Birkenau. After the Soviet army had entered the camps and announced that the inmates were now liberated, some of the women who were still alive and strong enough made the 3km walk across the fields from Birkenau to Auschwitz I camp in search of any surviving male relatives. Forty-year-old Fritzi had been too weak, but 15-year-old Eva went in search of news of her father and brother. Entering one of the Auschwitz barracks, she had spotted a familiar face. There, lying on the top level of a wooden bunk, wrapped in a blanket and staring sadly in front of him, was the father of her Amsterdam playmate Anne Frank. Mr Frank raised himself up as Eva approached and she reminded him that she was Anne's playmate. But he had no news of Erich and Heinz Geiringer to give to Eva, he was awaiting news of his own wife Edith and daughters Anne and Margot. Eva shook her head to indicate she had not seen any of his family and left the barrack.

After three weeks, a group of survivors boarded trains out of Auschwitz, escorted by their Soviet liberators. Instead of taking those who had come from western Europe homewards, all the trains headed eastwards behind Soviet lines, as war was still raging further west. Although these transports were in fact open trucks, they were almost comfortable compared to the packed and sealed cattle trucks used to bring the prisoners to their fate in the camps. The journey home was long and tortuous, taking three to four months of travelling across eastern Europe. Every so often the train would stop, the passengers would get down and stretch their legs or relieve themselves and use the opportunity to mingle and search for news of loved ones. Eva recalled that people would come from the nearby villages to see who was on the train and would try to sell them items of food such as eggs and potatoes, but the newly-liberated prisoners had no money to buy anything with – except perhaps a woman's headscarf that could be traded for a few eggs.

On one such stop, Eva spotted Mr Frank again, looking forlorn and tired. This time she took her mother over to talk to him. The two adults had in fact met before in Amsterdam as they were near neighbours, and had similar-aged children. Standing on that remote railway line chatting, Otto, Fritzi and Eva all desperate for news of their families, who could have anticipated how close their three lives would become? Then the train's whistle sounded and all the passengers got back on board, each to their designated carriages, but Eva was about to have a new worry.

Somewhere further along the journey, on another stop, Fritzi had got off the train to relieve herself. Eva was back on board when the whistle sounded, but the train slowly started to move off before Fritzi could get back on. Some passengers in a similar plight were able to hurl themselves back on, but as the train gathered speed Fritzi was left screaming and waving by the railway track. The train continued its journey across Eastern Europe and days and nights slowly passed. Eva could not believe that, after all she and her mother had been through together and against all the odds come through, finally after their liberation they would be torn apart. The joy of freedom was replaced by utter despair, as 15-year-old Eva was alone in the world.

Eventually, after a week, when the train stopped in the city of Czernowitz (at that time in Romania but now in Ukraine), mother and daughter were somehow miraculously reunited. Fritzi had been doggedly determined to find the train from Auschwitz, and after days of travelling across former Austrian lands and staying with a returning Jewish family, a group of freed British prisoners of war had helped her find the Auschwitz convoy. Meanwhile, further along the same train as it pushed on towards Odessa on the Black Sea, Otto Frank had encountered another woman from Amsterdam, Rootje 'Rosa' de Winter. She had the sad task of gently telling him that she had been with his wife Edith when she had died on 6 January. Just three weeks later the Soviet army had arrived, but it was too late for Edith Frank, overtaken by starvation and worry about her precious daughters Anne and Margot.

As Ken Livingstone listened intently, Eva continued her story by describing the return to Amsterdam after the war in Europe had finally ended. Not long after their arrival, Mr Frank came to pay Eva and her mother a visit. He hoped that they might have any scrap of information that could lead him to news of his daughters. As the two adults eventually learnt of the terrible fate of their families, they became a support for each other and their friendship blossomed. Eva had finished telling Ken Livingstone her story and her focus returned to the present time of March 1986, the room full of people, the new Anne Frank exhibition being launched and the congratulatory speeches being made by the dignitaries.

As the formal proceedings wound to a close, Livingstone suddenly pushed back his chair and stood up. To her horror, Eva heard him announce to the audience, 'And now, just before we finish, Eva is going to say a few words to you.' Eva started trembling. There was nothing to be done. She nervously got to her feet and was handed a microphone. As if she were watching herself from a distance, she heard a stream of words coming out of her mouth. From not having had any previous desire to share her wounds publicly, it was as though, once the words had started to flow, they were continuing under their own momentum. The words themselves wanted to let the world know the true horror of the Holocaust.

Eva told the audience about her early childhood in Vienna, the family's flight to Amsterdam by way of Brussels, their happy times living in the Merwedeplein apartments, how she had got to know her contemporary Anne Frank, her family's enforced hiding from the Nazis, their betrayal and the horrors of the time in Auschwitz with her mother. She describes her anguish when her mother had been selected for the gas chamber and she thought she had been murdered. Thankfully a plea to the notorious camp doctor, Josef Mengele, by a cousin who happened to be a camp nurse saved Fritzi's life. But it was several months before mother and daughter were reunited, as Fritzi had been staying in the hospital block. So their separation during the post-liberation train journey across Europe had not been the first time they had been forced apart.

When Eva finished telling her story on that spring night in London, she sat down in shock at what she had done, contemplating what the response would be from her mother alongside her, and her daughter Jackie in the audience, who were listening intently. She need not have worried. A large crowd made up of family and strangers gathered around her, all telling her 'Well done', including Fritzi, whose own story had now been made public.

After this first spontaneous speech, Eva was asked by the Anne Frank House to speak at openings of the exhibition which was starting to travel around the UK. She and her husband Zvi worked together on writing her earliest speeches, and Eva recalls reading the first ones very nervously and badly. She admitted to me once that she actually took a tranquilliser to calm her nerves before these early speeches. Travelling with the exhibition to different cities, she became fascinated to learn about people's lives in the final years of Margaret Thatcher's government, and because the exhibition was attracting interest across the social and political spectrum, she saw for herself divided communities.

Ken Livingstone has been a controversial figure, most recently with his insistence that Adolf Hitler supported the idea of Zionism as a way of ridding Europe of its Jews, before he devised the 'Final Solution'. This has been particularly offensive to Holocaust survivors. However, Eva, as a Holocaust survivor herself, remains grateful to him for setting her on an irreversible path to educating tens of thousands of people about Nazism and the Holocaust.

I have not counted, but I have probably heard Eva speak over a hundred times. I have listened to her, and have often been asked to introduce her, in a wide variety of settings: exhibition openings in cathedrals and civic halls, in schools, colleges and prisons, and even at the Anne Frank Trust's fundraising events. In every speech she makes, she includes something different and I invariably get to hear a surprising new fact or insight. Eva tailors the account of her experiences to what she wants a particular audience to take away from it, as you will understand further on in this book when she has addressed prisoners at Wormwood Scrubs, a high-security prison in London. She believes in people taking all the opportunities and chances they are offered in a democratic and free society, and realizes that she is becoming more liberal-leaning and worried about social inequalities as she gets older. I have found her recently to be more pessimistic about the future and questioning as to whether we have indeed made the difference we educators, and her stepfather Otto Frank, had hoped to. I hope that when she reads the following pages it will help to alleviate that feeling.

Having lived for more than half of her life being shy and reticent, Eva in her later years does not hold back from sharing her views, most recently about governments accepting more refugees fleeing conflicts. In her role as a founder, Trustee, and now Life President of the Anne Frank Trust, she has been a vociferous and hugely valued advocate who has travelled all over the UK supporting the Trust with her presence, but has also proved to be a critical friend when she feels strongly about an issue or activity. When people hear Eva Schloss speak, they never forget the experience and still talk about it years later.

A few months after she had first started her journey as a speaker, a friend encouraged her to write her story down. Eva enlisted the help of Evelyn Kent, a teacher who was also the mother of a school friend of her daughter, and together Eva and Evelyn set about the task. *Eva's Story* was published in 1988 by W.H. Allen, and subsequently was self-published by Eva and Evelyn under the publishing imprint Castle Kent, Castle being the German for Eva's surname Schloss. Thirty years on, it is still a hugely popular book, translated into eight languages. Eva has subsequently written two further memoirs, *The Promise* published by Puffin Books in 2004 and *After Auschwitz* by Hodder & Stoughton in 2013, now in a Russian edition. *The Promise*, aimed at younger readers, focuses on Eva's older brother Heinz, a very talented artist, poet and musician. The book's title concerns a promise that their father Erich Geiringer made to his son while the family were all still living together before going into hiding, but in continual fear of their possible fate at the hands of the Nazis. In answer to Heinz's anxious question, 'Pappy, do we live on in any way after we die?', Geiringer decided that he could not give his teenage son an unrealistic belief in his survival, as the odds were so firmly stacked against it. He looked his beloved teenage son in the eye and told him gently that even if you died, part of you would always remain because of what you leave behind. This answer motivated Heinz to indulge his love of painting by creating many skilful canvases. Almost as if he knew his fate, Heinz managed to hide fifteen of his paintings under the floorboards of the apartment.

In 1998, the American writer James Still encapsulated Eva's story in a play called *And Then They Came for Me, Remembering the World of Anne Frank*. The play simultaneously tells the story of Ed Silverberg, who was born Helmuth Silberberg in Germany and emigrated as a refugee to Amsterdam, like the Frank and Geiringer families. Ed was Anne Frank's boyfriend before she went into hiding and in her diary was known by his nickname 'Hello'. Through assuming a false identity, Ed had survived the Holocaust and went to live in New York, where he married another survivor and died in 2015. The multimedia production, depicting young Eva, Heinz, their parents Erich and Fritzi Geiringer, Ed and his parents, a Hitler Youth member and, in the final scene, Anne Frank, continues to be performed around the world and is often used as a drama-in-education tool for schools. Eva is delighted at the diversity of the casting in productions of the play; she has seen her father Erich played by a black man and Anne Frank by an Oriental girl. Nic Careem, the Sri Lankan-born human rights activist who had helped promote the Anne Frank Declaration and the Trust's work in prisons in its early days, was very helpful in getting *And Then They Came for Me* performed in some influential settings, such as New Scotland Yard, the House of Commons, the Russian and Chinese embassies and eventually in China itself.

In July 2016, I visited Eva in her central London apartment, two weeks after her husband Zvi had passed away at the age of 91. We spoke about Zvi's philosophy of life. Born in Munich in 1925, he had also fled the Nazis and arrived in Palestine in 1936. Zvi's grandfather had been a very popular doctor, and was generous in giving free treatment to those who could not afford to pay. For this reason, he felt that nothing would happen to him, as there were surely many non-Jews who would protect him. It wasn't to be. After his wife was deported to Latvia in 1939, Zvi's grandfather killed himself, leaving no suicide note.

Eva had first met Zvi Schloss in London in the early 1950s. Zvi had come from Israel to study economics and Eva, encouraged by the keen photographer Otto Frank, was studying photography. It so happened that Eva and Zvi were both renting rooms in the same building. They spent a lot of time together, and eventually fell in love. Zvi duly asked her to marry him, but to his great disappointment, Eva turned him down. Much as she cared for him, she felt that after her apprenticeship she should go back to Amsterdam to look after her widowed mother. But then Otto Frank arrived in London to see Eva, and stunned her with some amazing news. Otto and Fritzi had fallen in love and were going to get married. Eva felt relieved. After so much sorrow, four broken lives fell happily into place. Eva and Zvi married in 1952, and Otto and Fritzi the following year.

Over a typical Viennese afternoon tea and cake on elegant china, our conversation on that July afternoon in 2016 turned to the Frank family and Eva's personal recollections of Anne. The Franks and the Geiringers had lived in the same development in the New South area of Amsterdam, known as the Merwedeplein. Built between the wars in a simple Dutch style, the Merwedeplein apartments had become popular with German and Austrian Jewish refugees who felt a comfort in living surrounded by their compatriots. The apartment blocks were built around a central grassy area where the children, Jewish and non-Jewish, played together and got to know each other. Eva recalls a very good-looking older boy who had a 'real Dutch look and we all fancied him'.

As the Franks lived at apartment No 37 and the Geiringers at No 46, and Anne and Eva were only one month apart in age, it did not take long for them to get to know each other. Eva remembers Anne as having been very popular with both boys and girls. Anne was into magazines, movie stars, and at 12-years-old was generally more adult than most of the other girls. Among their playmates, Anne was the one who had ideas and always insisted on things being done her own way. Eva surprised me by an insight into Anne's own view of herself, saying, 'I thought

Anne was very pretty. I am sure this was due to the fact that she was so lively and animated. Always talking, always laughing. But I know that Anne wanted to be prettier than she felt she was.' Susanne Ledermann, the pretty dark-haired girl with socks usually crumpled around her ankles in Otto Frank's photos, was very sweet and friendly according to Eva, who admits to even having a schoolgirl crush on 'Sanne', as she was known. The sweet and friendly Susanne was murdered in Treblinka in November 1943 on the day of her arrival at the camp.

When the Jewish children were forced by the anti-Jewish decrees to leave their mainstream schools, Eva's parents decided not to send their daughter to the Jewish Lyceum that they were instructed to attend. They didn't feel that Eva's Dutch was good enough. Instead, Eva and nine other Jewish children were taught privately in the home of a local Jewish teacher, Mr Mendoza, from the Amsterdam Sephardi community. Five centuries after his ancestors had fled the anti-Semitic persecution of medieval Spain, Mr Mendoza and his mother were deported by new persecutors and killed. Fritzi and Erich Geiringer visited Otto and Edith Frank to ask if they would like Anne to join this group, but the Franks declined, probably understanding full well how much their daughter thrived on the social interaction of school. Eva thinks this was the only time that the two couples spent any time together, the two couples who would eventually become one.

Eva then told me about the time she encountered Anne Frank in a dress shop. She had heard, from behind the dressing-room curtain, Anne's voice firmly instructing the assistant on what alterations were needed to make the coat she was trying on suitable for *her* taste. Eva compared this to her own 12-year-old self, far too involved in sporty and tomboyish pursuits to be considering the trimmings and hemline of a coat. This picture of Anne painted by Eva gives us an impression of a very self-confident, perhaps precocious, girl, and this has been verified by interviews with some of Anne's other friends, such as Hannah Goslar and Jacqueline van Maarsen.

After the war, despite her adoration for her lost father Erich Geiringer, Eva grew to have a deep love and respect for her stepfather Otto Frank.

> He helped me a lot as I was very miserable, full of hatred and mistrust of people. He told me that I mustn't go through my life hating everybody because I will be the one to suffer. He also told my mother that I had to go back to school because a good education was something nobody could take away from me. I went back to school but was very unhappy. I felt I was an adult because of all the terrible things I had experienced and I couldn't relate to the others in my class.

Eva looked wistfully out of the window and continued:

> After finishing school I didn't know what I was going to do with my life and didn't really care. Otto and my mother decided I should become a photographer and this is what I did. Otto gave me his beloved Leica

camera and my first commission was to take a photo of Miep and Jan Gies, with their baby son Paul and Otto. Otto, who was such a keen photographer, must have spotted something in me. He knew someone in London who had a photographic studio and so in 1951 I went off to London to become an apprentice.

Eva discussed differences she saw between Otto's first wife Edith and her own mother Fritzi. Although Fritzi had initially struggled with learning Dutch on her arrival in Amsterdam, she had persevered. Perhaps because of intense homesickness for Germany, Edith had not learnt to speak Dutch, unlike Otto who quickly mastered the language, and this possibly gave Edith an added sense of insecurity in her country of refuge. Fritzi Geiringer was a tall and handsome woman, confident and outgoing in men's company, whereas photos of Edith Hollander-Frank show a plainer and more simply dressed woman, even when her girls were babies and Edith would only have been in her twenties. Eva referred to Edith Frank as 'a dedicated housewife', comparing her to her mother Fritzi who enjoyed a range of other interests such as playing the piano.

I asked Eva about her recollection of Margot. Was she the quiet, deep-thinking and bookish girl overwhelmed by her vivacious younger sister as one feels from Anne's diary? Eva's older brother Heinz knew Margot better than Eva did, as they were the same age and were in the same class at the Jewish Lyceum. As they lived so close and were both studious, Heinz and Margot sometimes did their homework together at one or another's apartments. More than that she couldn't say.

Pouring another cup of tea, Eva then went on to recall the terrible days in the summer of 1945 when she, her mother and Otto, who frequently visited their home, had learnt of the fates of their respective families. She told me about one particularly day that unbeknown to her then would have a long-term effect on her life.

One day Otto arrived with a small brown paper parcel tucked under his arm. He opened it and showed us a red checked cloth notebook. It was Anne's diary. To our astonishment he said he was considering publishing it. At that moment I certainly didn't imagine what would follow, thirty million copies sold, the museum in Amsterdam, the hundreds of responses to children's letters my mother and Otto would write.

And then she looked at me with a half-smile and said, 'Otto found consolation talking with my mother about everything that was going through his mind.'

To the Nazis, Heinz Geiringer had been just another tattooed number – a young Jew to be tormented to his death in Mauthausen slave labour camp. But to his adoring little sister Eva, the loss of this talented artist and poet, gifted pianist, guitarist and accordionist, avid reader (lover of the world of Jeeves and Bertie Wooster), who while in hiding taught himself six languages but still found time to make his sister laugh, profoundly affected her whole life. Much of Eva's motivation for her long years of educating about the Holocaust was to have the opportunity to speak about Heinz. His spirit was with her when she was awarded an MBE at Buckingham Palace in 2012, given honorary degrees from the universities of Northumbria and York St John for her educational work and umpteen civic honours. It is with her when she speaks out publicly about the treatment by governments of modern-day refugees. Heinz is there in her metaphorical suitcase as she travels around the world, including to nearly every American state.

In 1945, after the Red Cross had confirmed by way of a short and formal telegram that both Erich and Heinz Geiringer had died in Mauthausen concentration camp, Fritzi and Eva decided to pay a visit to their former apartment. Otto Frank had received some comfort from being given Anne's diary and reading her words. Perhaps if they could find Heinz's paintings, they would receive some comfort too. When they rang the doorbell they found the flat to be occupied by a couple who were not surprisingly rather suspicious of them, but nonetheless they were able to convince the couple that their intentions were honourable. With their hearts racing, Eva and her mother found the very floorboard they remembered was hiding the cache of paintings, lifted it with trembling fingers, and sure enough buried underneath, there they were – all of Heinz's secreted paintings. Along with the paintings were 200 poems he had written too. Thanks to a vision by the South African Holocaust & Genocide Centre, images of these deeply-haunting paintings are now included in an international travelling exhibition, 'The Promise, A Holocaust Tale of Love and Hope' (the originals were donated by Eva to the Dutch Resistance Museum in Amsterdam). In line with the promise his father made to him, Heinz is becoming known through his own talent.

Eva remains determined to live her life to the full as though she is seeing and experiencing the world through the eyes of her lost teenage brother, the boy who was afraid of dying. In the summer of 1999 Eva (and perhaps with a vision of Heinz alongside her) soared above the Mediterranean Sea on a hang glider, quite a feat of daring for a 70-year-old woman, and one which she told me she is not planning to repeat!

Chapter 6

Anne Frank's Role in the Transition from Communism

In 1985 a wind of change began to blow in Moscow that would have dramatic ramifications on all the countries that made up the mighty Soviet Empire. The 54-year-old Mikhail Gorbachev was chosen to succeed the old school hard-liner Konstantin Chernenko as 'Chairman of the Presidium of the Supreme Soviet', in effect becoming the new leader of the Soviet Union. Following on from three elderly and traditionalist Soviet leaders who had died in quick succession, here was a relatively young, well-educated and pragmatic man who looked to the future rather than the prevailing status quo. Gorbachev had graduated with a law degree from Moscow State University and worked his way up through the ranks of the Communist Party.

Gorbachev was conscious that the days of hard-line Communism were numbered. The Soviet economy, much of which was geared to the nuclear arms race against the USA, had been stagnating since the late 1970s. In an era of new technology, the corrupting influence of Western satellite TV had the ability to be beamed uncontrollably into the Soviet Union. Gorbachev quickly set about introducing dramatic reforms. We soon came to hear of two new words that filtered into the languages of Western countries. 'Perestroika', which described the reform and restructuring of the Communist Party, and 'Glasnost', which meant more open and increased government transparency. US President Ronald Reagan held several meetings with the new Soviet leader to discuss arms control and the UK's Prime Minister Margaret Thatcher proclaimed that Mr Gorbachev was 'a man I can do business with'. A Soviet leader had become almost likeable and certainly less fearsome. The West nicknamed him 'Gorbie' and we soon came to associate the large and distinctive red birthmark extending down from the bald top of his head to his forehead with a map of the world he wished to reach out to.

And then the USSR, the Union of Soviet Socialist Republics, itself began to disintegrate as its diverse groups of peoples, Slavs, Serbs, East Germans, Croats, Poles, Lithuanians and others, sought to re-establish their nationhood. From Moscow, from where the tentacles of the Communist ideology had spread out seventy years earlier, to Poland and the Baltic States in the north, across the Eurasian Steppe, to Ukraine, Belorussia and Georgia, outwards to the central and southern European nations of Hungary, Czechoslovakia and Yugoslavia, and eventually the last bastion of hard-line Communism, Albania, country after country abandoned the Soviet yoke and Communist ideology and established themselves as independent nations. On TV screens all over the world, people watched in disbelief as events took place that were only recently unimaginable, including the Christmas Day 1989 execution by firing squad of the tyrannical and corrupt Romanian President Nicolae Ceauşescu and his wife, and finally in November 1990 the fall of the Berlin Wall. By 1991 the USSR had ceased to exist. The world order had changed and the old certainties of the Cold War were no more. Summed up in the words of Vladislav Zukov, Professor of International History at the London School of Economics, 'The collapse of the Soviet empire was an event of epochal geopolitical, military, ideological and economic significance.'

***

In those very early days of the dismantling of Communism and breakup of the Soviet Union, the Anne Frank exhibition became one of the very first cultural events to arrive in Russia from the West, and its presence had a profound impact.

From three venues in Moscow the exhibition went on to Ukraine, giving Holocaust survivors a platform to at last speak openly of their experiences for the first time in forty-five years. The project was helped by Anne Frank House International Director Jan Erik Dubbelman being introduced to a fearless Russian journalist called Elena Yacovitz, whose bravery Jan Erik was to witness for himself on one chilling evening in Moscow. Even though there had been seismic regime change, the old Soviet systems of repressive and paranoid bureaucracy had not completely disappeared, as I too discovered to my cost.

Since those early days of transition from Soviet authoritarianism, the Anne Frank exhibition has been playing an invaluable role in helping newly-independent countries throughout the former Soviet bloc address recent history and embrace pluralism within their borders. To this day, the Anne Frank exhibition continues its travels across the thousands of kilometres that shaped the map of the former Soviet Union – from the Baltic states of Lithuania and Latvia to Kazakhstan, from Poland to the former Yugoslavia – diverse regional histories and conflicts have been reassessed through the prism of Anne Frank.

Anne in Moscow

The 'Anne Frank in the World' exhibition had been invited to Moscow in 1990 through state-approved routes. It so happened that the internationally well-known Liberal Rabbi of The Hague, Avraham Soetendorp, had connections to a member of the Russian Academy of Sciences. Avraham was the brother of the Anne Frank Trust's co-founder David Soetendorp, and was as equally involved in the 1980s in the international support campaign for oppressed Soviet Jews as David and I were. It was Avraham's rather off-the-wall idea to take the Anne Frank exhibition to the rapidly-changing Soviet Union. After confirmation of the Academy of Sciences' endorsement of the planned project, the Dutch Ministry of Culture agreed to fund a tour of the Anne Frank exhibition to the Soviet Union.

Even though there was high-level support, Jan Erik described the project as 'extremely fragile', as there were no grassroots community groups or passionate individuals who could spread the word through their networks help as volunteers in the usual way. That is, until Jan Erik was introduced to the young journalist Elena Yacovitz via a Dutch correspondent living in Moscow. Elena certainly had the passion, even if not the background knowledge of the subject. On their first meeting to discuss whether it would ever be possible for the Anne Frank exhibition to come to the USSR, Jan Erik was shocked to discover that, despite being the daughter of Jews and a well-read and curious journalist who worked for an internationally-known literary journal, Elena had never heard the word 'Holocaust' until he had used it in their conversation. She was then able to relate this newly-discovered word to the talk of a European genocide she had heard from her parents' and grandparents' generation. Stirred by the prospect of the exhibition, Elena nonetheless questioned its probability with the blunt query, 'I feel the Anne Frank House is ready for Russia, but is Russia ready for the Anne Frank House?' However, as an intrepid young journalist who had lived through dangerous times, Elena loved nothing more than a challenge. She promised Jan Erik she would do all she could to make it happen through her own network of grass-roots contacts in Moscow. Jan Erik had the impression that there would indeed be a new welcoming atmosphere in the capital of the former Soviet Union.

After months of planning, in the summer of 1990 the Anne Frank exhibition was set to open in Moscow in a government-owned art gallery in the city centre. I was thrilled when Hans Westra, the Anne Frank House director, invited me to join the high-level delegation that would fly to Moscow to attend the opening. On a sunny morning in June, I arrived with my suitcase at the check-in desk at Heathrow Airport excited to be joining the first-ever delegation from the Anne Frank House to the former Soviet Union. The plan was that I was to hook up with the Anne Frank House delegation and a group of Dutch high-level dignitaries in Stockholm, where we would all change flights and continue on together to Moscow.

As the check-in attendant smiled and took my passport and ticket, I felt how different times were since my last visit to Moscow in 1986. Since then I had been refused entry twice as I was considered by the Soviet authorities as an unwanted troublemaker, due to my long-time activism in the campaign to help Jews leave the religiously-repressive Soviet Union. Armed with a precious visa that had been issued to me a few days earlier by the Russian Embassy, here was I about to see for myself a transformed post-Soviet Moscow.

All was not right, though. While I stood in front of her, the check-in attendant made a call, put down the phone and leaned forwards towards me. The smile had been replaced by a serious expression. 'I am sorry Mrs Walnes, but your visa to travel has been rescinded,' she told me. I was shocked and despondent. Even though so much had changed in Russia, and many of the people we had worked to free had finally been granted exit visas, clearly I was still considered '*persona non grata*' by the new regime and its Soviet-era data bank. An uncontrollably deep sigh left my body. The Anne Frank exhibition opening in Moscow was to take place without me.

Jan Erik recently recalled those heady days of the Anne Frank exhibition in Moscow, and nearly thirty years on he could still picture the dramatic scene of elderly Jewish attendees at the exhibition launch event openly and unashamedly shedding tears. This was their first experience of a public exhibition about the Holocaust. The reason for their emotional response was explained to Jan Erik as, 'Not just what you have brought here, but the very fact that this could happen at all'. It was an indication for them that times were changing for good, a definite and irreversible change that could not be turned back. What struck Jan Erik most was the growing realization in these people that they could perhaps now even travel abroad themselves if they wished to.

The Anne Frank exhibition was a catalyst for open discussions among Jews and non-Jews on whether there was still evidence of old anti-Semitism in the new Russia. Young people felt it was no longer an issue, even though in 1990 there were still restrictions in place on Jews attending university or getting jobs. They perceived anti-Semitism to be more about *violence* against Jews, rather than simply professional or academic doors being closed, explaining their feelings as, 'Anti-Semitism is when your life is in *real* danger'.

However, Jan Erik told me about a frightening incident that had happened when he and Elena Yacovitz had attended a meeting at 'The House of Writers'. This was in fact a group of intellectuals that regularly met in a room near Moscow University to talk about literature. Although the meeting was conducted in Russian, the vodka flowed freely and the assembled intellectuals had seemed welcoming. Jan Erik expected that writers, and this group seemed to be highly intellectual, would all be pro-democracy and liberal-leaning like Elena and her friends. However, he was surprised when the atmosphere in the stuffy and crowded room became increasingly heated, especially after Elena had posed a question. After their goodbyes to the group at the end of the session, Jan Erik and Elena started to walk back together through the dimly lit Moscow streets.

As they approached a road, Elena took a couple of steps in front of Jan Erik and he immediately spotted that there was something strange on the back of her coat, which she evidently hadn't noticed when she put it on. Puzzled by this, Elena removed her coat to see what it was and Jan Erik noticed that her whole body seemed to freeze. She slowly explained to Jan Erik what the message, scrawled in lipstick, was. Elena's coat had been daubed with a large circle surrounding a cross, like a target for shooting practice. It was not a joke and it clearly indicated violent intent. Jan Erik could see that Elena was clearly very shaken, but after a minute or so she shrugged, saying softly and calmly, 'It happens'. The incident was not spoken of again. Jan Erik recalled, 'This young woman was so amusing and fun to be with. Even since this deliberately threatening incident, she has continued to be outspoken in her journalism. This left a big impression on me of courage under pressure.'

What also struck Jan Erik about working in Russia in that momentous time was that he and the Anne Frank House team felt they were part of history, part of a changing world, where there was so much hope for, yet fear of, change. Jan Erik even underwent his own change in attitude towards a long-perceived enemy.

Jan Erik Dubbelman had been born in 1955, while the Netherlands was still recovering from the trauma of the German occupation and the privations it had brought. This was also a Europe where fear of Fascism had been replaced by fear of the Cold War. His recollections of a western European childhood are similar to my own, 'We children of the 1950s were terrified of the "H-bomb" being dropped on us and the threat of "Reds under the Bed", i.e. the spread of the Communist empire to our own country.' Jan Erik remembers being scared seeing movies where the Soviet Army were nightmarish armed aggressors in large grey coats and fur hats. But in Moscow in 1990 Jan Erik found himself chatting warmly to, and even embracing, the former Red Army officers he had so feared as a child. These were men who were now trying to help ensure people came along to the Anne Frank exhibition.

From the central art gallery, the Anne Frank exhibition moved to the Library of Foreign Literature, just outside the intimidatingly high redbrick walls of the Kremlin. This venue was at the invitation of the library's Director, another fearless Russian woman called Ekatarina 'Katya' Genieva. Katya's personal motivation for her invitation to the exhibition is extremely interesting and serves as another illustration of the turbulent and violent times as religion was re-emerging in the Soviet Union. Under Communism Katya Genieva had not been afraid to challenge officialdom. One example of her determination to be fearless was that as a student at Moscow State University in the early 1970s she wrote her dissertation on James Joyce's *Ulysses*, at that time a banned book in the Soviet Union.

Katya had been an admirer of the charismatic Russian Orthodox priest, theologian and writer Alexander Men. Among Men's vast canon of literary and charitable works, his book *Son of Man* served as the introduction to Christianity for thousands of citizens in the Soviet Union who had been brought up in the atheist state. He went on to baptize hundreds, possibly even thousands, of new Christians, and even founded an Orthodox 'Open University'. For all Alexander Men's altruism and spirituality, his earthly reward was to be murdered early on a September Sunday morning in 1990, just outside his home in the village of Semkhoz and while on his way to conduct a church service. It was a particularly gruesome and nasty killing by an axe-wielding assassin who was waiting for the priest on a secluded country path. Bleeding profusely, Men managed to drag himself back to his cottage, but died that day in hospital. He had not been robbed so the axeman was thought to have been from, or maybe paid by, the KGB. Alexander Men's influence in Russia and abroad is still widely felt and there have been calls for his canonisation.

Katya Genieva was so deeply affected by Men's brutal killing that she made a vow that to honour his memory she would never bow to pressure from the establishment. In what she felt was a positive and affirmative act, she made the approach to the Anne Frank House about hosting the Anne Frank exhibition at her

Library of Foreign Literature. She even invited Archbishop Vladimir Kirill, at that time a senior official in the Russian Orthodox Church to speak at the opening – no small step in such a supposedly egalitarian, but in effect hierarchical, society.

Archbishop Kirill agreed to attend and on the night his address started well when he spoke about Anne Frank as a brave girl. But then, from behind his thick white beard, and dressed in his flowing white ecclesiastical robes, Kirill went on to describe Anne's death in Bergen-Belsen as unavoidable, because the decision had been made by God and nothing could be learnt from it. Feeling he was doing a good deed by endorsing the event with his presence, the Archbishop had nonetheless placed Anne Frank and the Holocaust into his supremely conservative religious interpretation. This did not go down well with the Holocaust survivors in the audience who had faced forty-five years of Communist denial of their experience and were finally seeing an end to the suppression of their histories. A young Jewish man in their midst could take it no longer. He quietly removed his shoe and to gasps from the audience, threw it directly at the Archbishop.

Vladimir Kirill is now the Patriarch of Moscow and All Russia, the Russian equivalent of the Pope, and is respected by many. His conservative views have not lessened, recently describing the jailed rock band Pussy Riot as carrying out 'the work of Satan' and some fundamental human rights as 'contradictory to the Church and therefore heresy'.

Ilya's story

Another of Elena Yacovitz's promised contacts that she had brought in to help with the Anne Frank exhibition was the historian Ilya Altman. Ilya had been born in the same year as Jan Erik, but on the other side of the 'Iron Curtain' in a town near Kiev in Ukraine. Both Ilya's parents had been Red Army officers, real examples of those images that had given little Jan Erik his dramatic childhood nightmares. Ilya's parents had met in 1943, the year before the town was liberated from German occupation. Three thousand Jews had been murdered in that one town but miraculously all Ilya's family had managed to survive.

Ilya had grown up knowing he was Jewish, but not really sure what that meant. He did however learn about the massacres carried out by the Nazis at the nearby ravine of Babi Yar. Over 100,000 people – Jews, Russian prisoners of war, Roma and Communists – were shot at this notorious site. Ilya told me modestly that he wasn't considered a top student, but had excelled at football and chess. Nonetheless, he graduated from the Moscow State History Institute and published three articles in well-read historical magazines. In a time of anti-Jewish professional and academic quotas, he had personally encountered no opposition about studying for a doctorate, although another Jewish friend of his in St Petersburg had been forced to travel three hours each way every day to a different town in order to be allowed to lecture in his subject.

In the 1980s, Ilya had worked in the main Russian historical archive, at that time called the State Archive of the October Revolution. He even presented a

Soviet TV programme called *Lessons from History* which made him quite well known. Some time later he heard through other historians about the existence of an ominous-sounding document, published in Jerusalem in 1980 in Russian, that was known as *The Black Book*. This attracted Ilya's curiosity and he decided to find out more. He discovered that *The Black Book* had been compiled by Vassily Grossman and Ilya Ehrenburg, two Jewish journalists who had served as war reporters with the Red Army. From as early as 1943, these two journalists had started documenting the atrocities they had witnessed. Grossman and Ehrenburg were part of the unit that had entered Treblinka and Majdanek death camps and their testimonies had been used at the Nuremburg War Crimes Trials of senior Nazis. Under its full and explicit title, *The Black Book: The Ruthless Murder of Jews by German-Fascist Invaders Throughout the Temporarily-Occupied Regions of the Soviet Union and in the German Nazi Death Camps established on occupied Polish soil during the War 1941–1945*, their testimony was partially printed in the Soviet Union immediately after the war. However, when it came to the attention of the Soviet censors, the writers were pressed to conceal the anti-Semitic character of the atrocities and downplay the role of Ukrainian collaborators in the murders. Although translated copies did appear in the US and other countries, publication in the Soviet Union was forced to stop in 1948. Ilya Altman's discovery of the horrors that were contained in *The Black Book* started his mission to document the Holocaust, even within the restrictions of the last years of the Soviet regime. It resulted in his role in the eventual publication of *The Black Book* in Ukraine in 1991. Ilya's influence on Holocaust knowledge and understanding in the immediate post-Communist era cannot be underestimated.

Ilya told me that the 'Anne Frank in the World' exhibition that travelled around Russia in 1990 astonished visitors and project partners by the level and quality of its hardware, design and presentation of information. Looking back now, and comparing it to current digitally-produced and easily-transportable exhibitions, it seems like a technological dinosaur in its monochrome simplicity of heavy metal and plastic.

As a historian looking back over a quarter of a century, Ilya reflected that, 'At the time I was frustrated that the Russian authorities and museum curators in the various cities seemed much more interested in the partnership with a prestigious international organization than in presenting the facts about the Holocaust.' He continued, 'Now I understand more about the difficulties they were encountering just organizing such an event, and I believe the exhibition actually opened a new chapter in Russian understanding of the history of the Holocaust.'

Anne in Ukraine

After Moscow, the 'Anne Frank in the World' exhibition had then travelled 850km southward to Kiev in Ukraine. It was set up in no less an institution as the Museum of Lenin, with its vast rooms and high ceilings overwhelming the 200m^2 and 2m-tall

Anne Frank exhibition. In the entrance lobby stood a colossal and all-dominating 6m-high statue of Lenin, carved in white marble. Times were changing in Ukraine but some potent vestiges of Communist society still remained intact.

As the doors of the launch event were thrown open, a throng of chattering people entered the room, fascination and curiosity visible on their faces. During the course of the evening, and after all the formal speeches, Jan Erik was to make an astonishing discovery. Dozens of the people standing among the exhibition panels, which depicted the effect of the Holocaust on a Western European family, were themselves survivors of the brutalities carried out by the Nazis in the east of Europe. Jan Erik found himself talking to middle-aged women in their 50s and 60s who had hidden this traumatic chapter in their lives deeply within themselves throughout the intervening years of Soviet rule, but here at the Anne Frank exhibition were opening up about their experiences for the first time.

The 'Anne Frank in the World' exhibition displayed some distressing images of the mass shootings of Jews carried out by the 'Einzatsgruppen' execution squads in the forests and ravines of Eastern Europe. Set against the stark white panels, these blurred black and white images had a particular power to shock exhibition visitors. Men, women and children were photographed by their executioners as they stood terrified, arms in the air, in the full knowledge that their lives were ending and they would be joining the tangled masses of bodies in the open pits below their feet. One young woman in a dark dress and coat clutches her baby tightly to herself and, with an imploring look at her killers, prepares for their two lives to be extinguished. Men, women and children who just a few hours earlier had awoken from their night's sleep, and dressed themselves for the possibility of another full day spent alive. Their agonized pleas and screams have fallen silent as we look at the two dimensional images printed onto white plasticised panels, their pitiful faces carefully rolled up after each exhibition and transported on to the next venue.

Like many of us who have seen those images of highly-efficient firing squads, Jan Erik had not realized that there had actually been a small number of people who had survived them. One such person was Clara Vinakur, who told Jan Erik what had happened to her. Clara was just 12 years old when she crawled out of a mass grave that contained the bodies of all her family and hundreds of others. The young girl, despite the agony of bullets in her body, had the presence of mind to play dead until the men of the killing squad had left the scene, probably to spend the evening washing away the vision of the day with tumblers of strong vodka. But there was no vodka-soaked relief for little Clara who grew up with this memory seared into her mind. She had to wait over forty years, until she came to see an exhibition about a Dutch teenage girl, to tell others what had happened to her.

After Moscow and Kiev, the Anne Frank exhibition rolled onwards to the Ukrainian city of Nikolayev, then to St Petersburg and the Black Sea port of Odessa. While the exhibition was touring Ukraine, the Anne Frank House unexpectedly received a manuscript written by a survivor of a little-known concentration camp in nearby Moldova, where the inmates had been abandoned to rot away by their guards. No one from the Anne Frank House team had ever heard about the existence of this camp before. Jan Erik felt that, with the opening-up of the Soviet Union and the Anne Frank exhibition encouraging people to come forward and speak, this added to the feeling that 'we were entering a world of Holocaust experiences and testimonies that we in the West had hitherto no idea about. We were going into territory that nobody had really visited. It was a very special time.'

Following the Anne Frank exhibition's visit to the former Soviet Union in 1990, Ilya Altman and Elena Yacovitz were both invited to attend an international conference in the Netherlands. Coming from Communist Russia, they had spent their lives accustomed to waiting patiently in line for many hours to buy any item of food or household requisite, which I can verify from seeing these queues during my own visits to the Soviet Union in the 1980s. A long queue could form outside a shop simply if word spread of the arrival of a consignment of apples, potatoes, meat or even the scratchy regulation lavatory paper. Ilya described to me his first sight of the long line of people waiting outside the Anne Frank House in 1991 and how he had innocently asked Jan Erik, 'Are we shopping for food now?' That queue on the Prinsengracht is now an Amsterdam tourist attraction in its own right, just as the Soviet food queues were to bemused Western tourists three decades ago.

Seeing the huge interest from the public in visiting the Anne Frank House, a site of Holocaust significance, ignited Ilya's idea to have some kind of similar centre in Moscow. And this eventually did come to pass. For the first five years of its existence, the Russian Research and Educational Holocaust Centre was housed in Ilya's own apartment with just himself and his archivist wife as the staff. They avidly researched, published documents and created exhibitions, building the reputation of the centre, until eventually the Russian government gave them a space in a building near the Kremlin. The authorities even offered to pay the rent, and their centre became one of only ten organizations in Russia so supported by the government.

During the conference Ilya and Elena attended in the Netherlands in 1991, he had listened with some cynicism to the focus on the general issue of tolerance. 'This topic was far from my consciousness as a Russian historian and archivist. But step by step I started to understand the reality. This new understanding led directly to 2010, when I helped to stage a conference in Beslan on "Children as Victims".'

In 2004, the town of Beslan, in the autonomous Russian province of North Ossetia, had suffered one of the worst ever massacres of children in recent history. A group of Islamist militants from the Chechnya and Ingushetia regions broke into a local school on the first day of the new academic year, when it was packed with pupils and their parents. The terrorists held more than 1,000 people hostage within the school for three terrible days. The hostages included 777 terrified children and parents, kept in inhumane conditions. As Russian security forces attempted to retake the building, the terrorists' booby-traps began to explode. Seeing no way out, they opened fire on their hostages. In all, at least 385 people were killed, including 156 children, the youngest of whom was only two-years-old.

Ilya said:

> In our 'Children as Victims' conference, we applied the lessons from the Holocaust to what had happened so recently at Beslan. The idea of the 'culture of the memory' is the same. In the hell and terror of that school, three days was like three years in a Holocaust era ghetto. We conducted two forums and prepared a handbook for students. I know now that we can use methods we have learnt of educating about the Holocaust for other chapters in history. I realized this from working with the Anne Frank project and the Anne Frank House.

Anne in Lithuania

In 1998, the Anne Frank exhibition paid its first visit to one of the Baltic States, when it went to Vilnius, the capital of Lithuania. Ruta Puisyte had been working as a historian for the Jewish Museum in Vilnius when she received a surprise communication from the Anne Frank House. They were looking for help with bringing the exhibition to the city. The Lithuanian Jewish community is small (still numbering under 5,000) and its members tended to keep their heads down. The Jewish Museum were excited at the prospect of working with the prestigious Anne Frank House, but with a degree of ingrained fear at the same time, even though the dreaded KGB had by then been effectively dismantled.

Ruta's work in Holocaust education had come through an unusual route. She had been brought up as a good Soviet citizen, but in a Catholic family that celebrated the festivals of Christmas and Easter. This was done quietly in their own home so as not to put them at risk in a regime that promoted state atheism. Although religion was never formally proscribed in the Soviet Union, the official structures imposed a strong sense of social stigma on practising a religion. It was also generally considered unacceptable for members of certain professions (teachers, state bureaucrats, soldiers) to be openly religious. The baby Ruta had been baptised in a church, but in a different village from their own, as having the ceremony in your local church could result in being reported by your neighbours to the Soviet authorities. Nowadays Ruta freely can attend her church every Sunday.

Growing up, Ruta had naively believed that everyone in Lithuania was an ethnic Lithuanian. She was aware that Jews had written the Bible and lived in Israel but had no idea that Jews also lived alongside her in Lithuania and of their importance to towns and villages. That is until she started her studies at Vilnius University. Her history professor just so happened to be a Holocaust survivor who described to her in gruesome detail something he referred to simply as 'the catastrophe' (the term Holocaust was hardly used at that time in Lithuania). Ruta wanted to investigate more about this crime and discovered that there were Holocaust survivors volunteering at the Vilnius Jewish Museum. As an inquisitive historian she wanted to talk to real people feeling that, 'Paper will never argue with you. A human being, who lived through it, will.'

And so in the late 1990s Ruta, now working at the museum as a historian, found herself being asked to organize the visit of the Anne Frank exhibition. The exhibition arrived in Lithuania at a time of huge transformation, and Ruta considers herself a 'true child of that time'. As well as its informative Holocaust content, she wanted me to understand the broader context of the exhibition. Ruta's account echoed what Ilya Altman had said about the Anne Frank exhibition in Russia eight years earlier. She explained, 'For people in the newly independent Lithuania anything arriving from the West was like the "whole universe" was coming to us. We were a young nation, insecure and looking for an identity. We were so excited that foreigners were making the effort to come to us.'

After the capital city of Vilnius, the Anne Frank exhibition went on to tour nine more Lithuanian cities. Funding for the tour came mainly from the European Union's Comenius programme, along with support from the Dutch Ministry of Foreign Affairs. The Comenius pan-European schools programme, named after the seventeenth-century Czech educator John Amos Comenius, aimed 'to help young people and educational staff better understand the range of European cultures, languages and values'. The programme ceased in 2013, but had been a great source of financial support for the Anne Frank House's work in post-Communist Eastern Europe.

Norbert Hinterleitner of the Anne Frank House, who spent a lot of time working in Lithuania, felt that the Anne Frank project was sorely needed there at the time. He recalled receiving a letter from the director of one of the museums who was to take the exhibition in 1998 which started: 'Dear Anne Frank, We would very much like to show your exhibition . . .', demonstrating a lack of knowledge that proved to be endemic in the country.

Twelve thousand people came to see the Anne Frank exhibition on its first tour of Lithuania, demonstrating that there was certainly interest in knowing more about the subject matter. The Lithuanian tour was complemented by a series of teacher training sessions and drama workshops involving Jewish and non-Jewish teenagers working together, often for the very first time.

The success of the drama-in-education workshops can best be described by the words of one of the teenage participants who told Norbert, 'My parents always told me that Jews are a little . . . a little bad. Now I know that it's not really the case.' Another proof of the project's success were sweet romantic flirtations between some of the Jewish and Lithuanian teenage participants. Something Anne Frank would have most definitely approved of.

When Norbert recalled those days of 1998 in Vilnius, my mind travelled back sixteen years earlier. In 1982, I had visited Vilnius during my days of campaigning on behalf of Soviet Jews. Our group would travel to the Soviet Union to bring vital supplies and moral support to those who had been dismissed from their jobs and deprived of income after making the brave step of applying to emigrate to the West. Once they had done so and been refused a visa, and became what we termed 'Refuseniks', they lived in precarious limbo without any form of state security. Many were victims of trumped-up charges of treason and found themselves spending many years in labour camps.

I found Vilnius to have a different atmosphere from that of Moscow, with its street upon street of drab concrete Soviet-style apartment blocks. Vilnius had a more European charm, still retaining its Lithuanian language, historic squares and narrow cobbled streets. The women's clothes hinted at a more relaxed existence, the colourful and perky little berets worn by the young Lithuanian women noticeably different from the ubiquitous fur hats or matrioshka-like headscarves of Moscow women.

However, despite this facade of a more carefree society, Vilnius had another side. Our group of four travellers from Bournemouth visited the children of the few survivors among those Jewish families who had been marched to the suburb of Ponary between July 1941 and August 1944. There, close to the suburban railway station, 70,000 Jews, along with thousands of Poles and Russian POWS, were systematically shot by Einzatsgruppen commandos and their Lithuanian collaborators. In actual fact Lithuania and the other Baltic States became the first countries outside occupied Poland where the Nazis would mass execute Jews as part of the Final Solution. Ninety per cent of Vilnius's Jewish population was slaughtered.

I will never forget spending an afternoon in the tiny apartment of Carmela and Vladimir Raiz, who told us about the fate of their families during those terrible years, but also described their current oppression as Jews who had committed the crime of wanting to leave the Soviet Union. Actually they didn't tell us these stories in normal conversation. They wrote the key words of information on a child's 'write and swipe' pad so that what they shared with us could be immediately obliterated. The reason for this being that one afternoon when Carmela and Vladimir were out, KGB operatives had come to the block and laid the wires to enable the authorities to tap into their every word spoken to each other in the kitchen, reception room and even their bedroom. They had found this out because, despite the fact that mostly your neighbours were possible KGB informants, one of the neighbours had warned the couple about what they had seen being done.

One afternoon during our visit to Vilnius our group were told by our concerned Soviet tour guide that we had to present ourselves to an office on the fifth floor of our hotel. Unbeknown to most tourists, each large hotel used by the (only) Soviet tour company Intourist allocated a suite of rooms to the KGB, the Soviet secret police. These rooms were used for the surveillance operation the KGB routinely carried out on Western tourists to ensure they were not making contact with the local people during their stay. So concerned were the Soviet authorities about subversive influence that even at airports Western tourists were kept in separate screened-off waiting areas from those of the local travellers.

It was an unnerving experience on that afternoon waiting to be called in to the KGB office, but it was as nothing compared to the constant harassment of the 'Refuseniks', who at any time could be arrested. We knew that we could leave the country, but these courageous people that we had come to lend our support to, definitely could not. Once inside the cramped office, we, the two women and two men who found themselves a world away from our comfortable lives in Bournemouth, were directed by two burly KGB men to cease our activity of visiting Soviet Jews or we would be 'on the next plane out' of Lithuania. We happened to know that the next plane from Vilnius to Moscow was in two days' time, the day we were due to leave, so having ensured that Carmela and Vladimir and the others were comfortable with it, we continued to do what we had come to Vilnius to do. Perhaps this was the day that my name had been added to the Soviet computer system as a 'serious troublemaker', resulting in the cancellation of my visit to Moscow for the Anne Frank exhibition opening eight years later.

Anne in Latvia

After its tour of Lithuania in 1998, the Anne Frank exhibition then proceeded north to the neighbouring Baltic state of Latvia, a country which was moving out of Communism but into a new and harsh form of nationalism. During the late 1980s, Latvian nationalism had worked well as a liberating force for the people and mobilized the disillusioned Soviet-ruled masses. However, once the country had become independent from Moscow, Latvian nationalism spawned the introduction of notorious post-Communist policies, such as its Citizenship Law. This measure disenfranchised about a third of Latvia's people on the grounds that they were considered 'Russian remnants' of the Soviet occupation. Because of this, as well as other restrictive policies, Latvian nationalism became thought of as a classic example of 'ethnic nationalism', where efforts to protect what the government liked to call 'cultural uniqueness' in fact generated anti-democratic policies.

As well as the travelling exhibition, Norbert Hinterleitner and his colleagues from Amsterdam brought to Latvia the popular play about Eva Schloss's life, *And Then They Came for Me*. Building on the success of the previous initiative in Lithuania to bring Lithuanian and Jewish teenagers together, this time Latvian and Russian teenagers were invited to participate together in the production of the play, both as the actors and the audience. For Eva Schloss, this production in the country where her own husband's grandmother had been murdered by the Nazis was in her view 'perhaps the most extraordinary'.

In Latvia, not only was there even more mutual understanding between the teenage actors from the different ethnic groups, but there were again a few romantic flirtations, this time between Russian and Latvian teens. Norbert never found out if their parents knew about these and, if they did, how they would have reacted. For him it was proof that 'Ethnic division is an artificial human construction. It is weaker than the human desire for love and peace.'

Anne Goes Back to Ukraine

After its first visit to Ukraine in 1990, the Anne Frank exhibition returned in 2003. Ukraine had meanwhile become an independent state in 1991, formalized by a referendum at the end of that year. Like much of eastern and central Europe, Ukraine had a varied history in terms of its nationhood and identity. Western Ukraine had belonged to the Polish-Lithuanian Commonwealth until the end of the eighteenth century, although for a short time in the seventeenth century parts of the region had been absorbed into the Ottoman Empire.

Eastern Ukraine had a different history, having been incorporated into the Russian Empire in 1667. During the eighteenth century the Russian empress Catherine the Great had invited European settlers to come and cultivate the lands of Eastern Ukraine, and Poles, Germans, Swiss and other nationalities took up her invitation.

Fearing the rise of separatism, during the nineteenth century Russia started imposing limits on the Ukrainian language and culture, even banning its use and study. Some Ukrainian intellectuals left the Eastern Ukraine for the Western side, while others embraced a Pan-Slavic or Russian identity. Many well-known authors or composers of the nineteenth century that we consider as Russian were actually of Ukrainian origin, notably Nikolai Gogol and Pyotr Ilyich Tchaikovsky. These deep-rooted issues of national identity affect Ukraine even today, resulting in the Russian annexation of Crimea in 2014, pro-Russian unrest in southern and Eastern Ukraine, and the continuous deadly fighting between Russian-aligning and Western-aligning Ukrainians.

In 2000, Ukraine had been rocked by a scandal which became known as the 'Cassette Scandal', or 'Tapegate', thus named after the discovery of tape recordings of the then President Leonid Kuchma apparently ordering the kidnap and murder of Georgiy Gongadze, a popular journalist. A criminal investigation into the President's involvement in the murder was inconclusive, but the event dramatically affected the country's domestic and foreign policy. It eventually led to the so-called 'Orange Revolution', which was actually an election process rather than a revolution, which installed Prime Minister Viktor Yushchenko as the new President. The 'Revolution' was co-led by Yulia Tymochenko, who became the country's first woman Prime Minister, instantly recognizable for the thick blonde plait always wound tightly round her head. Mrs Tymochenko was at that time named in Forbes magazine as the third most powerful woman in the world, but this did not save her from being convicted in 2011 for an allegedly corrupt gas deal between Ukraine and Russia, for which she served three years in prison.

Against this volatile historic and recent backdrop, in 2003 the exhibition that had superseded 'Anne Frank in the World', the appropriately-named 'Anne Frank, A History for Today', was taken to Ukraine. The Anne Frank House team didn't shirk from addressing specific Ukrainian issues. The exhibition was accompanied by two smaller localized displays, one about the Holocaust on Ukrainian territory, curated by the Ukrainian Centre of Holocaust Studies. The other, called 'Sources of Tolerance', showed the stories of ten post-war Ukrainian heroes who had risked their lives for citizens' rights, and teacher and guide training sessions for this exhibition focused on the issues of co-existence with minorities in the present day. These Ukrainian-focused ancillary exhibitions helped to bring in even larger numbers of visitors than expected. Norbert Hinterleitner proudly told me that it was the first international project to do this in Ukraine. 'The Ukrainian organizers, and the visitors too, valued the fact that here was a prestigious *international* partnership really caring about their history by giving a public showcase to Ukrainian experiences and their national heroes. They couldn't thank us enough for this.' The project also left a legacy of helping some of the smaller, more fragile Ukrainian NGOs to acquire funding to develop themselves.

Young Ukrainians related the Frank family's experience in hiding to their own growing up in Soviet times. 'There were eight people hiding on two floors in Anne Frank's secret annexe in Amsterdam. But this is how we grew up here.' Young people also took part in a weekend-long training seminar about prejudice and discrimination, called 'Who are your neighbours?'. After the seminar they were asked to look for cases of intolerance in their own locality. Their findings formed the basis of self-created micro-exhibitions about the situation of minorities and discriminated groups in their hometowns, which were displayed in the schools.

The Anne Frank exhibition continued touring Ukraine for the next seven years and in that time, it visited all twenty-five provinces of the country.

Norbert's Story

Norbert Hinterleitner, who has spent many years running Anne Frank programmes in post-Communist Eastern Europe, explained to me what has driven his enduring commitment to the Anne Frank programmes. He traces the first steps towards his journey as a moral educator to 1986, when he was a 13-year-old schoolboy in Austria.

Kurt Waldheim had just been elected the country's President. During the Second World War, Waldheim had been attached to the Wehrmacht, the combined armed forces of Nazi Germany, and served on the Eastern Front, in Yugoslavia and in Greece. Even if they took no active part, Waldheim's units were close enough to civilian massacres and the deportations of the Greek Jews from Salonika to have been aware of them. However, in Waldheim's memoir entitled *In the Eye of the Storm*, published the year before he became President, there were omissions and discrepancies about his wartime service fighting for the Nazis. The controversy surrounding this became known as the 'Waldheim Affair', both in Austria and around the world. It was never proved that Waldheim actually took part in any atrocities – only that he had lied about his wartime activities.

During this period in Austria, politics became the topic to talk about. Norbert describes himself as belonging to the 'Waldheim Generation'. 'We were a teenage generation confronted with questions and we asked those questions. At this age we learned to be critical thinkers.' In his early twenties in 1996, Norbert joined the 'Gedenkdienst', the Austrian Holocaust Memorial Service (an alternative to Austria's compulsory national military service), as he wished to contribute to a movement with a clear and positive mission, that of the acceptance of responsibility.

Vienna was the city where the Anne Frank House had chosen to launch their new flagship travelling exhibition, 'Anne Frank, A History for Today', which had been created to replace the eleven-year-old and rather outdated-looking 'Anne Frank in the World'. Through the Gedenkdienst's involvement with the Anne Frank exhibition in Vienna, Norbert became a volunteer exhibition guide, one of the very first to show people around the Anne Frank House's brand-new flagship exhibition.

'A History for Today' had its international launch in September 1996 at Vienna's Town Hall, overlooking Heroes Square and opposite the Hapsburg Imperial Palace. It was on the balcony of this palace that in 1938 Adolf Hitler stood and proudly announced to the ecstatic crowds in the square below the German annexation of Austria, the country of his birth. After the defeat of Nazism in 1945 this imposing palace balcony was not used again for a public speech, even for Pope John Paul II's visit to Vienna. The first person to be invited to make an address from that balcony was the Holocaust survivor and Nobel Peace Prize winner Elie Weisel, but not until over half a century after Hitler had made his notorious 'Anschluss' (annexation of Austria) announcement. In February 1993, the 20-year-old politically-charged Norbert Hinterleitner was standing in Heroes Square below that same balcony for a mass protest against Jörg Haider, the leader of the xenophobic right-wing Freedom Party. Norbert smiled when he told me that the numbers in the square on that night, estimated to be 250,000, far exceeded the number of Hitler's followers who were there for the Fuhrer's 'Anschluss' speech in 1938.

After volunteering as an Anne Frank exhibition guide in 1996, he carried out the remainder of his Austrian Holocaust Memorial Service term in the International Department of the Anne Frank House. Pretty soon he found himself working with the Anne Frank programmes in post-war Bosnia, helping to make a difference to the lives of war-traumatized young people. He remembers thinking, 'Wow, these people at the Anne Frank House really know how to involve young people and give them meaningful activities to put their heart and soul into. That was the starting point of a journey that I hope will never end.'

When I first met Norbert in London in 1997, he was an idealistic young man with long dark hair flowing down almost to his waist. Twenty years on, his hair by now somewhat shorter, and with his head containing an encyclopaedia of educational experiences from across the continent of Europe, Norbert Hinterleitner's journey has not ended. The young schoolboy who was stirred into action by being one of 'Waldheim's Generation' is now the Head of Education at the Anne Frank House, running a team of sixteen educators and project managers.

Anne in Kazakhstan

One of the most recent and surprising countries the Anne Frank exhibition has visited is the Republic of Kazakhstan, the mysterious land of Genghis Khan. Straddling northern Central Asia and Eastern Europe, Kazakhstan is huge, covering an area of nearly three million square kilometres, and is actually the world's largest landlocked country. Although Kazakhstan is best known in the West for the inept unsophistication of its mythical 'famous son' Borat, the country's gas and oil and vast mineral resources have made it the economically-dominant nation of Central Asia, generating more than half of the entire region's GDP.

Kazakhstan has long borders shared with Russia, China, Kyrgyzstan, Uzbekistan and Turkmenistan, and although officially a landlocked country, actually even has a 'shoreline' around some of the Caspian Sea, the world's largest inland body of water. Such a vast country has a very varied terrain, which takes in flatlands, steppe, taiga, rock canyons, hills, deltas, snow-capped mountains, and deserts. Given its enormous area, its population density is low, at less than six people per square kilometre.

The lands of Kazakhstan have historically been inhabited by nomadic tribes. Genghis Khan made the country part of his Mongolian Empire, but following internal struggles among the conquerors, power eventually reverted back to the nomads. The Russians began advancing into the Kazakh steppes in the eighteenth century, and by the mid-nineteenth century, they nominally ruled all of Kazakhstan, treating it as part of the Russian Empire. In 1936, it was named the Kazakh Soviet Socialist Republic, part of the Soviet Union. Kazakhstan was the last of the Soviet republics to declare independence following the dissolution of the Soviet Union in 1991. Although Kazakh is the state language, Russian remains the official language for all levels of administrative and institutional purposes.

Yelena Shvetsova was an idealistic young woman who had come from Kazakhstan to work as an intern with the International Youth Human Rights Movement in the city of Voronezh in south-west Russia. This is a network of young adults from more than thirty countries, all sharing the idea that human rights and individual dignity are crucial values to be nurtured and supported. Participants must be young, either in their actual age or in their heart, and agree that different people, attitudes and methods should be appreciated; only violence, aggression and discrimination are deemed unacceptable.

In 2012, Yelena encountered the 'Anne Frank, A History for Today' exhibition at a school in Voronezh. As she stood in front of its powerful imagery, she made a vow to herself, 'I am going to make this happen in my home country of Kazakhstan.' It just so happened that Yelena's determination coincided with plans that were being laid by the Dutch Embassy in Kazakhstan. They had been organizing an annual Human Rights Day event in the Kazakh capital city of Astana each year, and were looking for a new way of presenting Human Rights issues. Grant proposals were duly submitted to the Embassy and in due course a Russian/Kazakh language version of 'A History for Today' was created.

The representative of the Anne Frank House for the Kazakhstan project was Sergiy Kulchevych, a young man who had first helped the Anne Frank House with the exhibition in Kiev while he was working at the Jewish Foundation of Ukraine. When he had first been told about the exhibition, he was sceptical about presenting another Holocaust story to the Ukrainian public, and having studied the rich Ukrainian Jewish history, felt irritated by this continued focus on the death and destruction of its community.

However, when he was invited to Amsterdam in 2008 to visit the Anne Frank House his views radically changed. Just like the Moscow historian Ilya Altman had found a decade earlier, Sergiy found the Anne Frank House philosophy of making the message of the Holocaust relevant to today an exciting ideology to apply to his own academic area, that of Jewish History with a focus on Philosophy. Sergiy returned to Ukraine and lost no time in applying to be an intern for the International Department of the Anne Frank House. In 2010 he became a paid member of Jan Erik's team, working on the Russian tour of six cities. This included the port of Murmansk far up in the icy polar region bordering northern Norway, which in the Second World War had welcomed British and American ships bringing weapons for the Soviets to fight the Germans.

And so with this experience, in 2016 Sergiy found himself being asked to take the Anne Frank exhibition to Kazakhstan, a country that, despite its economic muscle, has a reputation for human rights abuses and suppression of political opposition. The Kazakh President, Nursultan Nazarbayev, has been leader of the country since 1991 and controls society in what is deemed the 'Russian way'. The NGO Human Rights Watch reports that 'Kazakhstan heavily restricts freedom of assembly, speech, and religion'. Officially there is freedom of religion, but religious leaders who oppose the government are suppressed.

Sergiy describes Kazakhstan as 'Certainly a central Asian country but somehow it has a different feel from its neighbours Uzbekistan or Tajikistan. It's more multicultural than Poland and the Baltic states such as Lithuania.' Multicultural it certainly is. Kazakhs make up half the population, with the other half made up of Russians, Poles, Uzbeks, Ukrainians, Germans, Tatars, Uyghurs and over 100 other nationalities and ethnicities. In the south of the country there is a huge Korean community. Islam is the predominant religion, with Christianity practised by a quarter of the population. Many of these people are descendants of those who were exiled there by the USSR and those who had come during the industrialization campaign.

Any intolerance in such a diverse society is carefully hidden from public eye. There are no football hooligans or neo-Nazi groups in evidence and President Nazarbayev glorifies his country as a nation that is tolerant of differences. He is wary of not letting Kazakh pride in its history, and its towering statues of ancient kings that are found across the country, be seen as nationalism, the kind that brought civil wars to the Balkans after the fall of Communism.

NGOs who are funded by international money are regarded with suspicion both at national and local level. 'There is a kind of paranoia that foreign money may bring about a revolution,' explains Sergiy. His local Anne Frank project partner Yelena Shvetsova, the young woman who was doggedly determined to bring the Anne Frank exhibition to Kazakhstan, has adopted a straight-talking attitude to dealing with officials and has succeeded in creating her own Human Rights NGO called 'Wings of Liberty' but this, and a plan to bring TEDx Talks, have received a negative response from officialdom.

One of the Anne Frank exhibitions was staged at a Nazarbayev School, one of a network of elite schools named after the Kazakh president but open to all ethnic groups. The aim of the school is to create a new generation of Kazakhs who will be active thinkers, but although these schools are open to international projects such as the Anne Frank exhibition, it is not possible for foreign NGOs like the Anne Frank House to come and undertake the project in their usual way of encouraging open discussion about the political situation.

The exhibition was located in the Nazarbayev School's concert hall where alongside it stood a traditional Mongolian yurt-style tent containing carpets, pottery and artefacts that were all redolent of the days of Genghis Khan. Having been worried that students so far away from Anne Frank's Amsterdam both in time, in distance and in culture would not make any connections to her life and theirs, Sergiy was delighted to see a huge enthusiasm for Anne Frank by the young people in the school. He conducted an exercise about the incremental implementation of the Nazis Anti-Jewish Laws and the students themselves connected these to current threats to democratic values.

***

In trying to capture twenty-seven years of the Anne Frank House's work across the vast expanse and diverse nations of post-Communist Europe, there is so much of equal importance that has gone unsaid. But the selection of stories I have related of those astonishing times and of the work these remarkable educators, activists and students have undertaken, reflect the imprint that Anne Frank's message has left on thousands of people with hugely different histories, views and hopes for the future.

Chapter 7

The Woman Who Gave a Personal Pledge to Otto Frank

Bertha 'Bee' Klug was a co-founder of the Anne Frank Trust and its Honorary Life President until her death in 2012. She was devoted to the charity and its mission due to a personal pledge she had given to Otto Frank in the 1960s. Born in 1920, Bee's entire life had been influenced by witnessing the rise of the Fascist movements that swept across Europe when she was a young woman.

***

The year was 1968, and the Western world was being influenced by a new radical movement, but this time with more benign motives. In San Francisco, the previous summer had seen the zenith of the flower power movement and the 'Summer of Love', calling for civil rights and social justice for African-Americans and the end of the Vietnam War that had sent young Americans to their death over the far side of the world. The call for change led by young people traversed the Atlantic, and in 1968, Paris was in lockdown, first by factory strikes and then by university students protesting against capitalism, consumerism and American imperialism. Protests also took place in Germany and Japan.

Then it came across the Channel from Paris to London as Hornsey College of Art succumbed to striking students, and then down south to Bournemouth College of Art, where I was a willing student activist, enjoying taking part in several days of rowdy protest sleep-ins (although I don't actually recall getting much sleep).

It was during this turbulent time, when young people were finding their radical political voice, that Otto Frank and his wife Fritzi, along with Fritzi's daughter Eva and Eva's husband Zvi Schloss, were enjoying a convivial dinner at the London home of Bee Klug, along with Bee's husband Sid and the Klugs' four offspring, Harold, Tony, Brian and Francesca.

After the usual inconsequential dinner-table chatter of new social interaction, followed undoubtedly by a conversation about the spreading worldwide protests, the mood had changed to something more profound. Bee and her family listened very attentively as Otto Frank spoke about being a seventh-generation German Jew who had grown up feeling safe and secure in his home city of Frankfurt. He and his contemporaries had been initially contemptuous of Hitler's threats against the Jews, believing that such things could never happen in Germany. Bee nodded sympathetically, explaining that there had been the same complacency amongst the Jewish people in England at that time.

Otto then quietly described to the Klugs his family's experiences under the Nazis, the daily struggles to stay alive in Auschwitz and the terrible fate of his wife and children. Bee later recalled that, 'We talked about how we could prevent such things happening again. Not just to the Jews but to anyone. The obvious answer was education. We talked of this in detail and what stands out in my memory was when Otto said, "If I could see something in education in England in Anne's name, it would be some compensation." There and then I vowed to myself that I would try and get something started.'

How the Klug and Schloss families had first come to meet is an interesting story. In the 1960s, Sid Klug was a successful businessman building a property portfolio. He had gone to meet a banker at the London branch of the Israeli bank Leumi, in order to raise finance for a new venture. The banker he met was Zvi Schloss. Not being a party to the meeting, I am not sure how the professional conversation turned to family matters but in conversation Zvi mentioned that his wife was the stepdaughter of Otto Frank.

Mr Klug told Mr Schloss that his wife was besotted with Anne Frank and in 1962, not long after the Frank family's hiding place had opened as a museum, Bee had taken her children to see it. On her return, she had not only written a poem about the experience, which she entitled 'The Ballad of Anne Frank', but had also indulged her other creative passion of painting by putting brush to canvas and producing a portrait of Anne in oils, copied from a photograph she had seen in a book. Zvi asked Sid for a copy of the poem that he could show Otto, who was at that time collecting people's reactions to Anne's diary. The poem was duly sent to Otto who then requested a meeting with its author, much to the excitement of Bee. A born hostess, she immediately invited Mr Frank and his family to dinner at their home.

Everything Otto had told Bee on that memorable evening in her home resonated strongly with her. She was determined to help him do something in Anne's memory for Britain. 'I first read the *Diary of A Young Girl* shortly after it was translated into English in 1952,' she said.

> It was then that I was fully confronted with the three faces of man. The perpetrators – who appeared human but had been dehumanized; the victims – not just those in the camps but also those in hiding; and the third face – people like Miep Gies, her husband Jan and the three other helpers who for two years risked their lives to try and save the eight occupants of the annexe. Having known about the horrors of the Holocaust and met survivors, I was dedicating much of my time giving talks to groups young and old. I was also using my poem as part of the talk to encourage people to read Anne's diary.

Bee Klug was a person who, throughout her long life, once encountered was rarely forgotten. She was stunningly beautiful, petite but with a magnetic aura that drew people to her. As she grew older, and her hair whiter, her blue eyes seemed to shimmer even more. She had a colourful personality and equally loved to be surrounded by colour. Having left school at 14 to work for a West End couturier, she expressed her love of life through clothes. Each day, her outfits and accessories were colour-matched, even down to the umbrella often carried against the English rain. On the rare occasion she chose to wear black, it would be trimmed by a hand-sewn edging of gold ribbon or thread, as another of Bee's passions was embroidery. Her image and personality positively gleams out of the Anne Frank Trust's photographic archive – just look out for the lady often sporting white leather ankle boots, sometimes accompanied by a white trilby hat.

Bee's childhood was spent growing up in a period of recession, depression, unemployment, poverty and the rise of fascist movements in Germany, Spain, Italy and Britain. She recalls an incident at her school in 1929 when she was just nine-years-old.

> There were 35 pupils in my class, of which five of us were Jewish. Our teacher frequently made unpleasant comments about the Jews. One day she made a blatantly anti-Semitic remark which greatly upset me. However, I kept it to myself until my father noticed I was troubled. Eventually I broke down and blurted out the situation. My father went to the headmistress and as a result our teacher made a public apology. I learned two major lessons that day that have remained with me, influencing the path my life has taken – that prejudice and hatred don't only come from the poor and uneducated and that when you are confronted with it, you have to deal with it.

In 1936, aged 16, she witnessed the famous Battle of Cable Street. This was the British Fascist leader Oswald Mosley's plan to send hordes of his Blackshirt thugs marching through the East End of London (where most of Britain's Jews lived). It was thwarted when thousands of anti-fascist demonstrators turned out to prevent the march from taking place, declaring 'They shall not pass'. Between 1936 and 1939, the International Brigades were fighting against Franco in the Spanish Civil War to stop the rise of fascism in Spain. Had their campaign been successful, the Second World War may have been averted. 'We know that fear is usually the basis for prejudice and hatred, which so often eventually leads to world shattering events like the Holocaust and other genocides,' said Bee when she described to me those terrible events, 'but also in communities and even among families. If we can eradicate it maybe it will then remove the fear of "And then they'll come for me"' (she would often make references to the German Pastor Martin Niemöller's celebrated anti-Nazi poem, 'First They Came').

The Klug and Frank families parted after their 1968 dinner party, all seemingly delighted that thanks to this fortuitous meeting, an Anne Frank inspired educational organization might soon be established in London. However, soon afterwards, despite all her good intentions to help Otto, Bee became very seriously ill, with a digestive complaint that no doctors could correctly identify.

After many months of severe illness, when this vivacious, intelligent and beautiful woman became a shadow of herself, she was eventually referred to a naturopath, who put her on a strict vegetarian diet, consisting mainly of fruit, vegetables and a little protein. Slowly she started to recover, and thankful for her return to good health, she wanted others to receive the caring treatment she had received.

So Bee set up a charity she named the Wessex Healthy Living Foundation, and funded it with money she had earned from managing a hotel her husband had bought in Bournemouth. She then set about convincing alternative practitioners, homeopaths and other therapists to donate some of their time to the centre or to give treatments and consultations at heavily reduced rates. The centre opened its doors in March 1977, housed in a bungalow the Klugs had bought near the cliff top in the Southbourne area of Bournemouth. Bee was immensely proud of the fact that the Wessex Healthy Living Centre has treated thousands of patients with its range of complementary and holistic treatments, giving them a renewed sense of wellbeing and hope.

In July 1988, as David Soetendorp, Cor Suijk, Jan Erik Dubbelman, Dienke Hondius and myself sat having tea at her home to plan the visit of 'Anne Frank in the World' to Bournemouth, Bee's former sparkle had very much returned. That meeting around Bee Klug's tea table can be pinpointed as the day the seed was sown for what in 1991 was to become the Anne Frank Educational Trust. Not long after the Trust's launch, Bee took on the role of the Trust's Honorary Life President, which, in tandem with the Wessex Heathy Living Foundation, became the bedrock of her philanthropic life.

Bee led her life according to the ethics and responsibility for mankind instilled into her by her father in the tough times of the 1930s. She was a fount of wisdom, often peppering her speech – for Jews and non-Jews alike – with the Yiddish she learnt in her childhood home in the East End of London. When Bee believed strongly in something, this petite persona in elegant high heels became a turbo-charged Rottweiler. Her most famous Yiddish catch phrase, instilled by her into us all, was 'Brochs into Brochas' (turn troubles into blessings), personified by the time she nearly died but was saved by complementary medicine and went on to create a health centre for the benefit of others.

No black type words printed on a white background can truly express the colour and vivacity of this amazing woman who lived a long, productive and active life. She attended all our Anne Frank Trust events of importance, many of which she and Sid sponsored, even fetching up at 7.00 a.m. in central London to help physically load the truck taking sacks of letters to children in war-torn Bosnia. She always carried the treasured photo taken around her dining table with Otto and Fritzi, and when closing an Anne Frank educational event would wave it with a flourish, look skywards and shout in dramatic fashion, 'Can you see this Otto?' in the hope that he was looking down and watching the success of the event. (She once did this at an event attended by the then Metropolitan Police Commissioner Sir John Stevens, who immediately invited her for dinner at Scotland Yard).

In May 2012, Bee passed away at the age of 92. In her final decade she had been afflicted with blindness. She took it with equanimity, as her vision had been slowly deteriorating due to a freak accident in America many years earlier. (On a routine visit to a hairdresser in Florida, her retinas were damaged by a highly potent hairspray being negligently sprayed directly into her eyes.) Though frustrated that she could no longer write, nor indulge her lifelong passions for painting or embroidery, nonetheless she did not let it ruin her life. Classical music on the radio became her joy, while her flat on the Finchley Road became a mecca for lively and probing conversation, ranging from politics, to human rights and her personal cause célèbre of social justice. She also organized weekly poetry readings for the residents of her building and never missed an Anne Frank Trust event, hosting a reception and animatedly welcoming each of the 100 guests at the Chancellor of the Exchequer's residence at 11 Downing Street – just one week after a major operation. A few months before the cancer she was battling finally took her, she stood in for the Secretary of State for Education, Michael Gove, to present the Anne Frank Poetry Prize (which she had donated) at the National Association for Schoolmasters and Union of Teachers annual diversity awards ceremony. Her impassioned speech about the immense value of teachers in guiding people's future lives was more than warmly received by the UK's largest teaching union.

Her children continued in Bee's fields of interest. Harold Klug became an osteopath, Dr Tony Klug was very active in human rights, becoming special advisor on the Middle East to the Oxford Research Group and vice-chair of the Arab-Jewish Forum, and Dr Brian Klug a Senior Research Fellow and Tutor in Philosophy at Oxford. Her much-loved and mutually adoring American cousin Sharon Douglas became a Board member of the Anne Frank Center in New York. Bee was also particularly proud that when she received her MBE from HM The Queen in 2003 it was in the round of honours that immediately followed the honour of an OBE to her daughter Francesca, a professor who had helped to draft the Human Rights Act for the UK. She believed that this 'daughter, then mother' royal recognition may have been unprecedented.

In 1972, Bee encapsulated her remarkable life and experiences by publishing a collection of poems under the title *Reflections in Rhyme*. The rhyming verses are of a rather dated simplicity but the philosophy is motivational, a belief in getting up and getting on with it, in God and in the wonder of life.

> I will – treat each day as a lifetime
> I will – greet it with joy in my heart
> I will – balance the scales of life's problems
> I will – if hope fades, accept it in good part.

Those lines sum up this extraordinary woman, and I will end this chapter in her voice which stands as an epitaph: 'My words to everyone who reads Anne Frank's diary and learns of the terrible blot on human nature of the Holocaust and other genocides, is not to be complacent. Every single one of us is a possible victim of prejudice and hatred.'

Chapter 8

Anne Frank in Latin America

Between the teeming metropolises of Guatemala City and Buenos Aires there lies a distance of 4,000 miles – a vast expanse which takes in Central American rainforests, the Amazon river, the Argentinian pampas lands of gauchos and bulls, the Andes mountains to the west and the South Atlantic Ocean to the east.

Thanks to the work of many remarkable people, the voice of Anne Frank has travelled that long journey in the continent of South America since the beginning of the 1990s. The Anne Frank exhibition has proved to be an effective tool for learning and reflection in a vast land mass which comprises many diverse cultures and countries with little connection to the Holocaust. In the course of the late twentieth century, millions of Latin Americans suffered under brutal dictatorships, and were the victims of terrorism and violence, often related to the illicit drugs trade, and almost always to poverty. This is how Mariela Chyrikins and Barry van Driel, educators from the Anne Frank House, have described the impact of their work in Latin America: 'Anne Frank has a particular appeal to young people in Latin America who have suffered at some point from prejudice and discrimination. Her story is used as an example of a young person like them who demonstrated strength and resilience in very difficult and threatening situations.'

Climb aboard for a whirlwind tour of this huge and fascinating continent, visiting several diverse countries and their recent troubled histories, where Anne Frank has left behind an indelible mark.

Anne in Chile

The 'Anne Frank in the World' exhibition, staged in the beautiful post-colonial city of Santiago de Chile, opened its doors in September 1991. In a city of 330,000 people, one in ten of its population came to see it, waiting patiently in a queue that stretched around the block. Anne Frank House International Director Jan Erik Dubbelman told me, 'Sometimes it happens at just the right time, like when we worked in Germany just before and after the Berlin Wall fell, and sometimes the timing can be problematic. As it happened, the timing in Chile was fortuitous. It was also springtime in the southern hemisphere, an upbeat time of year.' The country was emerging from its difficult years of dictatorship under General Augusto Pinochet.

78

The exhibition was opened by the country's first democratic president for eighteen years, Patricio Aylwin, and several government ministers.

Two months later, in November 1991 we launched the Anne Frank Educational Trust at the House of Commons. I recall Jan Erik describing the Chile opening with such excitement as a large group of us sat having dinner in a London restaurant just a few hours after our Palace of Westminster launch. It was still the early days of the Anne Frank exhibition travelling to the farthest reaches of the world and Jan Erik shook his head in almost disbelief as he described the scenes of people standing patiently in line.

The location of the Santiago de Chile exhibition was significant and Jan Erik believed people came not only because of their curiosity about Anne Frank but also because it was an act of resolve for the future. The exhibition was on display in the foyer of the once-prestigious University of Chile but, as with any dictatorship, academia had been considered by the Pinochet regime as a threat, and indeed the university had in fact been a hotbed of anti-government resistance. Over the years of Pinochet's regime, 80,000 people had been arrested, 30,000 suffering torture and over 3,000 were then 'disappeared' (the verb being used in the active sense of being 'made to disappear', i.e. murdered). Jan Erik reflected: 'There was such a symbolic value to the exhibition venue, it was a story about the regaining of democracy.'

In December 1998, seven years after the success of the 'Anne Frank in the World' exhibition in Santiago de Chile, and across the other side of the world, there was an opportunity to reflect once more on those terrible years of Pinochet's rule of terror. The former President had arrived in London that October for a spinal operation at the exclusive London Clinic hospital, and in a watershed judicial procedure against a former head of state, was immediately served with an international arrest warrant by the British government. The legal wrangling continued for several weeks, involving the British government, extradition experts and teams of lawyers. After his operation, Pinochet was transferred from central to north London, to a private clinic in the suburb of Southgate. While he languished in his room under police guard, and lawyers and governments were debating his extradition to either Spain or back to Chile, less than a mile away Southgate Further Education College was welcoming the visit of the Anne Frank's Trust's new exhibition, 'Anne Frank, A History for Today'.

The irony of an exhibition about dictatorship and its consequences being on show just around the corner from one of recent history's most notorious dictators was not lost on any of the exhibition's visitors. Former Chilean torture victims and British human rights activists conducted a daily vigil outside Pinochet's clinic and would then pop around the corner to see the Anne Frank exhibition. Needless to say, the General's name cropped up in all the opening speeches on exhibition launch night and in many of the visitors' comments. Pinochet died in 2006, with 300 criminal charges still pending, some for tax evasion and embezzlement but most for violations of human rights.

On the day of his passing, Barry van Driel, Mariela Chyrikins and Aaron Peterer from the Anne Frank House happened to be conducting a three-day human rights seminar at the Villa Grimaldi, the notorious former detention centre operated by Pinochet's secret police. During the years 1974–8 thousands of people had been held and tortured within the villa's walls, hundreds of whom then disappeared. Just as the Anne Frank House team were wrapping up on the seminar's final day, having listened to harrowing stories of life during the dictatorship, someone came running into the room and announced breathlessly that Pinochet had just died. As if of one mind and sentiment, the people in the room started to cry, men and women alike. Aware that Villa Grimaldi was located in the pro-dictatorship suburb of Penalolan, Barry and his team started to feel very perplexed and uncomfortable. They tentatively asked one of the group why they were all so emotional. 'Because he has died never having had to face justice for what he did. We will never have the chance to confront him.'

That evening Barry, Mariela and Aaron were in the city centre as pro- and anti-Pinochet riots broke out. They found themselves in tears too. Barry explained that 'this was in fact because of the effects of tear gas, so we made a very quick exit.' In an ironic twist, the date of Pinochet's death, of his passing from this world, was 10 December, International Human Rights Day.

Anne in Argentina

Anne's birth happened in a city on the far side of the world, but the relevance of Anne's story is perhaps more powerful in a yellow-painted villa in Buenos Aires than anywhere else.

Located on a busy street called Superi is a charming yellow-painted villa, entered through a black decorated iron gate and along a paved path. Behind the villa is a garden with a reasonably sized lawn and several mature trees offering shade. It is owned by a Jewish businessman called Mauricio Szulman who had made money in the 1950s from food supplements. Mauricio was not a religious or even a culturally affiliated Jew. But in 2007 he was in a state of grief. Hilda, his wife of forty-five years, had recently passed away, his three grown-up daughters Gabriela, Patricia and Mariana had all fled the dictatorship that had gripped the country between 1974 and 1983, and what was once a happy home was bereft of people, laughter and good times.

In the way that serendipity and timing often occurs, motivated by the idea to create a memorial to his idealistic wife Hilda, Mauricio donated his house to serve the cause of the moral education of Argentina's young. Inspired by the book *Testimonies for Never Again – From Anne Frank to Our Days*, which combined discussion of the dictatorship with Anne Frank's story and modern-day experiences of youths with social, ethnic and religious discrimination, Mauricio approached the book's co-author Hector Shalom, who had previously been a volunteer for the

Anne Frank exhibition on an earlier visit to Buenos Aires. Following the exhibition's success, Hector was at that time looking for a venue to open a permanent Anne Frank education centre. Thanks to meeting Mauricio Szulman, Hector's plan was starting to fall into place. The Centro Ana Frank of Argentina, as the Szulman home became known, opened its doors as a museum and education centre on 12 June 2009, the 80th anniversary of Anne Frank's birth in Frankfurt. Since then, this once normal family home has served as a reminder of man's inhumanity to his fellow man.

Behind the villa's imposing shiny black front door, the ground floor now contains a large room with a black and white photographic exhibition of the world Anne Frank grew up in many decades ago. Here visiting groups of lively and chatty Argentinian schoolchildren settle themselves down on the polished wooden floor, ready to be guided through the panels in Spanish by teenage peer educators. After they have been shown the life and death of their Dutch teenage counterpart, they climb the house's wooden staircase and, as if transported by plane across the world to Amsterdam, they enter the home's former bedrooms, now three rooms decorated and furnished just like the hiding place on the Prinsengracht. But after the wonder of imagining being in Anne's bedroom and the rooms in which she spent her days in claustrophobic hiding, their visit to the home on Superi Street has more to share with them.

The Centro Ana Frank contains one of the first public exhibitions in Argentina about the years of the country's brutal dictatorship. The exhibition is called 'From Dictatorship to Democracy; the Observance of Human Rights', and it demonstrates how the mechanisms and procedures of Nazism were repeated in the dictatorship. One of the first visitors to the Centro Anne Frank was the congresswoman and president of the Argentinian Human Rights Commission, Victoria Donda. The photos of Anne's happy childhood in Frankfurt and Amsterdam had an added resonance for Victoria. In her speech to the assembled guests she described her own carefree childhood being brought up by loving parents. But in 2003, at age 26, Victoria's world fell apart. She discovered that the man she knew as her beloved father had in fact been a torturer for the military regime, and that she had been snatched from two of its victims, a married couple Cori and Jose Donda. Cori was arrested when she was five months pregnant, and soon after giving birth to her baby, she was drugged, put on to a Fokker military aircraft and thrown while still alive into La Plata River, the fate of many of her fellow political prisoners. Not surprisingly, Victoria Donda is still an avid supporter of the Centro Anne Frank's mission and work.

Hector Shalom, who had co-authored the very book that had so inspired Mauricio Szulman, became the Centro's director. Hector's own life was very closely affected by the murderous regime. He had lost close friends who were arrested and tortured. Hector explains that, 'A museum that works with the memory of something that occurred a long time ago and very far away is more comprehensive if it includes the state terrorism that happened closer to our time. Our exhibition guides' uncles, relatives and grandparents experienced the dictatorship.'

In warmer months, the visiting school groups, once they have completed their tour of the villa, and by now more subdued and reflective than when they had arrived, are taken into the Centro's peaceful rear garden. Sitting in the shade of the trees, they are invited to share their thoughts and feelings about what they have just seen. But were they aware that the walls of the house on Superi Street had even more to share? Before the full excesses of the 'Dirty War' became rampant, Mauricio and his wife Hilda had been hiding in their home a young journalist who had criticized the government and was in fear of arrest, when 'being a left-wing idealist journalist was not a good thing to be', according to Mauricio. The journalist, Andres Alsina, had been given shelter in the house with his wife, until Mauricio helped them flee the country in a 'semi-legal way.' Mauricio and Hilda had also subsequently sheltered a Guatemalan escaping his country's dictatorship in the 1980s. Like 263 Prinsengracht in Amsterdam, number 2647 Superi Street, now the Centro Ana Frank, was itself a house of refuge and hiding.

I spent an extraordinary week acting as an adviser to the Centro Ana Frank in April 2010, and saw first-hand the importance of the lessons Hector and his team were giving to Argentina's children. I happened to arrive in Buenos Aires on 24 March, the annual commemoration of the start of the dictatorship. On my first 'working day' at the Centro I spent time getting to know the staff and the young volunteer guides, sharing our common and different experiences, speaking to a journalist from the *Buenos Aires Herald* and then in the evening giving a talk to members of the public, most of whom had not visited the Centro before. I was introduced to a woman called Eva Eisenstaedt, who had been a Jewish child refugee from the German occupation of Amsterdam, and whose mother had taught Anne and Margot Frank gymnastics.

The next day over lunchtime empañadas (tasty little South American meat pastries), the team of teenage peer educators told me how they were making what happened all those decades ago to a European girl relevant to twenty-first-century South American children. But, as with similar young peer educators in the townships of South Africa, they understood completely what the common factors were in a country that had so recently endured a tyrannous regime.

On my return to Buenos Aires, I paid a visit to the headquarters of the Argentinian Jewish community, AMIA, the Asociation Mutual Israelite Argentina. On 18 July 1994, a car bomb had been detonated outside the AMIA building, which is housed in a densely-packed commercial area of the city. The bomb killed eighty-five people and injured hundreds and was Argentina's deadliest bombing ever. The noise of the bomb had woken 17-year-old schoolgirl Mariela Chyrikins who lived fifteen blocks away. It was the first day of the school winter holidays and she had hoped to have a lie-in. Over twenty years later, Mariela still recalls the two reasons for her personal sense of shock. Firstly, although around the world we are now on our guard against terrorist attacks, it was only the second bombing in Argentina, and the first on a civilian target (the previous bomb having been planted at the Israeli Embassy in 1992 killing twenty-nine people). Secondly, was that just one week before, Mariela's father and cousin had been in the AMIA building to record the death of her uncle. It was the AMIA bomb that set Mariela on a path that would lead directly to her bringing the Anne Frank exhibition and project to many countries in Central and Latin America.

Over the years, the AMIA bombing case has been marked by incompetence and ongoing accusations of cover-ups. All suspects in the 'local connection' (among them, many members of the Buenos Aires Provincial Police) were found to be 'not guilty' in September 2004. In 2005, the city's Cardinal Jorge Mario Bergoglio, whom we now know as Pope Francis, was the first public figure to sign a petition for justice in the AMIA bombing case. The finger is now firmly pointed at Iran and the Hezbollah terrorist organization, who jointly orchestrated the bombing. Anita Weinstein, the administrator whom I met inside the building on that spring day in 2010, told me she was sitting at her desk on one side of the room when her female friend and colleague called out from the other side, 'Anita, I'm just bringing you over a coffee'. A very normal working morning. But a few seconds later she saw her friend, coffee still in hand, blown to pieces.

As a memorial to the victims of the bombing, there is an arresting and fluid artwork created by the renowned Israeli artist Yaakov Agam. But there is also another memorial in the heavily-gated grounds of the building, this one a simpler plaque mounted on the wall within the heavily gated grounds of the organization. It is to commemorate the 1,900 members of the Argentinian Jewish community who were murdered during the years of the 'Dirty War' of 1974–83, or the 'Process of National Reorganization' as the military dictatorship described their work. The number of Jewish victims was hugely disproportionate to their population figure: it is estimated between 10 per cent and 15 per cent of those who disappeared were Jews. I was told that the Jewish victims of the regime's henchmen were tortured twice before their murder, 'Once for their political crimes and again for being Jews'. Recordings of Hitler's speeches were played during torture sessions. 'I remember when I was arrested in 1977 there was a giant swastika painted on the wall at the federal police central headquarters where I was interrogated,' Robert Cox, the British former editor of the English-language *Buenos Aires Herald*, recalled in an interview in *The Guardian* newspaper in 1999. Nazi ideology had indeed permeated and inspired the military and security forces during the country's dictatorship.

The first Anne Frank exhibition, 'Anne Frank in the World 1929-1945', had visited Argentina in 1992, having crossed the Andes following its presentation in Santiago de Chile. Thanks to the efforts of Mariela Chyrikins, its next incarnation, 'Anne Frank, A History for Today', came to Buenos Aires in June 2000. The AMIA bomb in July 1994 had both physically and spiritually woken Mariela. She had grown up aware that her family was Jewish, but as they were liberal Jews she had little Jewish education and was scared by any mention of the Holocaust. Her best friend's sister had read Anne Frank's diary and was talking about it, but Mariela determined she would not read it. One of the first things Mariela did after the bomb was to get hold of a copy of the diary of Anne Frank. She immediately connected with the similarly dark-haired Dutch teenager. 'I liked her so much that I just didn't believe she was going to die,' she recalled.

Mariela's fear of knowing more about the Holocaust was no doubt caused by her close family history. Her grandfather Noah Hirik had been born in Ukraine. When he was a teenager a pogrom happened in his village in the Podol province. As the executioners were seen entering the village, Noah and his brother ran and hid at the top of a barn, from where they watched in terror as all their family were shot. Between the two world wars, Noah became an anarchist and moved to the city of Kiev. One day in the library he noticed a book about emigration to Argentina. It sounded the sort of exciting adventure he needed, beckoning a new life. He made his way to Amsterdam where the ships sailed far down the world to Uruguay, and then made the short crossing over the Rio de la Plata to Buenos Aires. On the ship Noah had met the woman who was to become his wife and Mariela's beloved grandmother. And on arrival in Buenos Aires the immigration officer, just like those in London or New York who had anglicized unfamiliar Eastern-European names, gave Mr Hirik the more Spanish sounding name of Chyrikins.

In 1995, a year after the AMIA bombing, an economic crisis hit Argentina, caused by the country's fixed exchange rate against the dollar and President Carlos Menem's policy of heavy borrowing. By this time Mariela had left school and was working in her father's accountancy office. One day at home, she happened to find a 1970s leaflet about the Anne Frank House, kept as a souvenir by her parents of their visit to Amsterdam before she was even born. She was fascinated to read that many teenagers were writing to Anne's father, Mr Otto Frank, and he had actually replied to them. Despairing and frustrated at the slow pace of the investigation into the bombing, and the impunity given to the Buenos Aires police who had been shown to have assisted with the materials used for the bomb, Mariela decided she would write to Mr Frank about the anti-Semitism and discrimination she felt was happening in Argentina.

A courteous reply duly came back from the Anne Frank House. 'Thank you for your letter to Mr Frank. However, we are sorry to tell you that he sadly passed away in 1980.' But Mariela, though saddened, was not deterred by learning of this. Every March, the anniversary month of Anne Frank's death in Bergen-Belsen, Mariela sent her own report and videos about the latest on the AMIA investigation across to the Anne Frank House. And in 1997, having saved money from her accountancy job and armed with a determination to challenge the discrimination she saw in Argentina, Mariela made her way to Amsterdam, the city from where her grandfather had left the anti-Semitism of Europe for a new life in South America.

She met with the International Director Jan Erik Dubbelman and convinced him that she could make it happen for the Anne Frank exhibition to come back to Argentina. He believed and trusted her and a few months later 21-year-old Mariela Chyrikins found herself addressing a meeting of the Dutch Embassy and the 'rather conservative and totally male' leaders of the Buenos Aires Jewish community. By then Mariela was working for the university. In the days before scanning documents and digital correspondence were in common use, she used her salary to pay for hundreds of colour photocopies of the stunning image taken of the new exhibition 'Anne Frank, A History for Today' at its UK launch in the nave of London's Southwark Cathedral. Finally, after two years, her perseverance paid off and the funding was in place to bring the Anne Frank exhibition from her grandfather's embarkation port to his future home. The exhibition toured twenty Argentinian cities over the next two years.

In line with Otto Frank's philosophy, Mariela made sure there was a clear connection between the 'then and now'. 'My childhood had been affected by my father's fear of talking about politics, and that the dictatorship would come back. Because of what had happened to his father's family, the Holocaust was also too painful for him to talk about with us. But in the Shoah Museum in Argentina I met a lot of Holocaust survivors, and they were the same age as my grandmother whom I loved. Meeting them affected me greatly.' One of the Holocaust survivors, Sara Rus, was particularly inspirational for Mariela. Sara's son, who had been working on a government atomic programme, was murdered during the dictatorship. One day he had been arrested and simply became one of 'the disappeared'. Another survivor, whom I also met at the Centro Ana Frank, was Monica Davidowicz, who chose to hide a young fugitive from the dictatorship in her home.

During the Anne Frank exhibition tour in the first two years of the twenty-first century, Mariela felt that the dictatorship was a constant 'elephant in the room'. Teachers would make the connection for themselves and this would lead them in turn to making real connections with survivors of the dictatorship. Through the story of Anne Frank and the Holocaust, contemporary discrimination and human rights were openly explored.

At one of the exhibition openings, the Minister of Internal Affairs happened to ask if the Anne Frank House did anything to educate police officers. Jan van Kooten, the Head of Education at the Anne Frank House, was duly informed by his colleagues about this interesting enquiry, but was not convinced it was serious, as he thought to himself that the Argentinian police had very difficult problems to tackle. Two weeks later an official letter from the Ministry duly arrived on his desk, and he soon found himself on a plane to Buenos Aires. 'It turned out the police were serious about exploring new ways to police their society, including the way they handled football hooligans. The officers were notoriously aggressive and had no connection with civil society.' Jan described the first meeting they held where officers were brought together with community representatives to discuss issues of human rights in an open and candid forum. The meeting was attended by a group of women from the 'Mothers of the Plaza del Mayo' (the mothers and grandmothers of the 'disappeared' who, wearing symbolic white headscarves, conducted a weekly procession around the large square fronting the Presidential palace). 'I asked them why they were sitting in a room with the police, who had historically been their tormentors. One of the women told me that it was because the Anne Frank House had invited them. I realized at that moment the immense power of Anne Frank to bring people together.'

Jan van Kooten visited Buenos Aires four subsequent times and worked with police trainers and naval police, helping them to create a new training curriculum for effective policing in civil society. Twenty senior Argentinian police officers then visited Amsterdam to learn new ways of working with drug addicts. 'These were tough guys', said Jan, 'but some shed a tear in the Anne Frank House.'

Mariela said that there are now many other organizations in Argentina dealing with human rights and memory and also using young people as peer educators and she has no doubt it is because of the effectiveness they have seen by the work with Anne Frank. Each year the Centro Ana Frank receives over 35,000 visitors and also runs a training institute which offers five different courses.

And in a country with a tragic recent history of dictatorship and brutality, National Law 26809, implemented in 2013 by the Ministry of Education and twenty-four provincial authorities, has designated 12 June, Anne Frank's birthdate, as the Argentinian 'Day of Adolescents and Youth: for social inclusion, coexistence, against all forms of violence and discrimination in commemoration of the birth of Anne Frank'.

Anne Frank in Brazil

In April 2010 I arrived in Rio de Janiero, sent by the Anne Frank House to help in the planning of the first ever visit of an Anne Frank exhibition to the city. The following day, I had thrown off the jet-lag the night before, helped no doubt by a churrascaria barbecue dinner washed down by several caiparinhas (the fiery Brazilian national cocktail) and the pure excitement of being a two-minute walk from the famous Ipanema Beach.

My associate in Brazil was Joelke Offringa, a Dutch woman who had come to São Paulo in 1993 to study and practice architecture, the final push to follow her long-time dream having come from her dying father. Once she had settled in Brazil, Joelke became drawn to social projects, especially those linked to architecture and city planning. On her own initiative she set up an office for architecturally-based social work, which led to her creation of the Instituto Plataforma Brasil, a Brazil-Netherlands linked cultural association that encouraged young Brazilians to raise their aspirations through sport and cultural projects and thus promote Joelke's vision of 'human development and opportunities'. Having met Jan Erik Dubbelman and Mariela Chyrikins, who were impressed by her enthusiasm and range of activities, Joelke was asked by them to represent the Anne Frank House in Brazil.

On my first morning in Rio, Joelke and I paid a visit to the Dutch Consul. He was a charming man who originated from the Dutch Antilles island of Curaçao, situated in the western Caribbean, which I told him I had visited in 2001. Otto and Fritzi Frank had also visited Curaçao in the 1970s, marked by a photograph of them proudly displayed in the tiny local synagogue there (which happens to be the oldest in the western hemisphere). The Consul was enthusiastic, promised to do all he could to help the project happen in Rio and then kindly offered us a trip back to my hotel in his very comfortable diplomatic limousine.

As we drove back along the promenade with its five-star hotels and plush apartment blocks, I looked up at the overlooking hillside. It was shocking to see that the 'favelas', the notorious Brazilian slum areas which were rife with poverty, drugs and murderous gangs, actually overlooked the affluence of Ipanema and Copacabana. There was no way for each demographic to avert its eyes from each other's circumstances – tourists and residents on the seashore would sit on their balconies looking up at the slums and the poor had their noses rubbed in the overt wealth of the much more fortunate. Another unsettling sight was that the more affluent residences were fronted by high security walls and their windows by impenetrable iron bars.

The Dutch consul was as helpful as he had promised to be and the Anne Frank exhibition was staged in Rio a few months later. It was shown in three very different locations – one in the centre of the city, one on the outskirts and finally in one of the most violent gang-ridden favelas. After two days of meetings in Rio, I flew down to Buenos Aires and two weeks later came back to Brazil, but this time to the sprawling city of São Paulo which, with a population of twelve million people, is by far the largest city in South America. There I was to open and speak at the Anne Frank exhibition in one of the country's flagship community schools.

To get to the 'Centro de Educação Unificado Paraisopolis' we drove through the wealthy area of Morumbi, with large villas set amidst lush gardens, but as I had come to expect, protected behind heavily secured walls and gates. Suddenly, without a noticeable change in the surroundings, we were driving into a favela, with its slum buildings and crowded, noisy litter-strewn streets. As we entered the modern school building within the favela, there was a real air of excitement in the school's large entrance hall. The Dutch Foreign Minister Maxime Verhagen was to be the guest of honour at the opening and the peer educators, trained by Joelke and her colleague Adriana Rachman, were tasked to guide him around the exhibition. I was startled when I saw that these guides were as young as 11, and hoped that the Dutch Foreign Minister would not be patronising towards what I expected to be their limited knowledge.

Verhagen duly arrived, gave a speech, and then the microphone was handed to me. As with speeches I had made at many previous openings I had read and re-read it and timed it according to the minutes allotted by Joelke, who had explained I needed to factor in the time the interpreter would need to translate my words into Portuguese. I thought I had done this to perfection by simply reading through my speech and doubling the time. Half-way through making my speech, having flown across the world to make it, I saw Joelke pointing to her watch and making 'time to stop' gestures. On that day I learned a useful lesson: that when making a speech that needs an interpreter, you must allow at least three times the length of the speech, as the interpreter needs to (i) mentally translate your words, (ii) listen to make sure it is the right time to take over, (iii) pause to figure out the best way of presenting what you are trying to get across, (iv) take a breath, and (v) say what they need to say. When they have finished, you need to nod to show your approval, take a breath and then continue. Each of these actions takes up valuable seconds which substantially eat into the speech's allotted time.

After the speeches the crowds of students, teachers and dignitaries made way for the start of Mr Verhagen's guided tour. I will never forget one of the guides, a small and charming girl who was all of 11-years-old, confidently and patiently, and with no sense of adult irony, explaining the aftermath of the First World War in Europe, the subsequent economic crisis in Germany and the rise of National Socialism – to the Foreign Minister of the Netherlands, who was beaming in appreciation. I hope she has remained immensely proud of herself.

The other passion of Joelke and her institute was to promote confidence and personal growth in these challenged kids through sport, and the second half of the afternoon was devoted to an exhibition of Panna, a form of street soccer that is played throughout Brazil. Some of Brazil's greatest footballing World Cup-winning heroes, including Neymar, Ronaldo and Rivaldo, learnt their skill through playing Panna on the streets. Mr Verhagen, his inhibitions I am sure broken down by the charming Anne Frank peer guides, removed his jacket, tie and shoes, pulled on a football shirt and enthusiastically joined in.

For my last night in South America, Joelke and I met for celebratory drinks in the rooftop bar of the architecturally spectacular Hotel Unique, with a 360° panorama of the endlessly sprawling city of São Paulo. Joelke asked if she could bring one of the volunteers with her, an educationalist who was going to help develop an Anne Frank project for São Paulo schools that would recognize the Brazilian curriculum requirements. I of course agreed preparing myself to spend the evening with an earnest and worthy civil servant.

Marceo Camargo Oliveira turned out to be anything but, and the story he told me became seared into my memory. Marceo had come from a very simple background growing up in one of São Paulo's poorer areas. When he was a young teenager, after his school day had finished he would walk to the local brick factory and spend the evening firing bricks to earn some extra money for his family. One day he spotted a book that had been thrown into the kiln, and carefully retrieved it. Instead of the book being destroyed by fire, it lit a fire within him. The book was about education and he found himself drawn to the contents of the singed pages. This started Marceo's path to becoming a teacher of History and Philosophy and a member of the Board of the Instituto Plataforma Brazil.

In the rooftop bar Marceo told me how he was volunteering as a guide for the Anne Frank exhibition in São Paulo and once the exhibition had finished he planned to help Joelke explore the best way to introduce education about Anne Frank into the local state school system. This they duly did, but it didn't have the positive reception Joelke and Marceo had hoped for. Although several companies were willing to financially support the Anne Frank project, as they also believed it was a way to help diminish the alarming level of violence in state-run schools, the local education authorities were not so welcoming. The education authorities would normally employ one person to handle a project that would cover 1,000 schools. But to implement the Anne Frank programmes successfully, with the level of training needed to have a really positive outcome, the local education authorities realized it would require 12 people to cover 500 schools, and even that would just give a 10 per cent reach of the local schools.

Joelke decided that to be implemented, the Anne Frank schools' projects would require a bottom-up approach. So she started with a pilot project in six schools, creating a team of 'Anne Frank Pioneers' in each school, similar in nature to the UK's 'Anne Frank Ambassadors' scheme, whereby these young pioneers, aged between 11 and 18, would do local projects to help in their community.

Joelke said that

> . . . these youngsters can really take their lives in their own hands and are changing their own communities. It starts by them getting sensitised to Anne Frank's story and they reflect on how they see their own future. They connect their needs to what they want for their community. The 'Anne Frank Pioneers' are promoting projects in sport, education, and making connections to Pioneers groups in other schools, through a WhatsApp group. It is giving these young people the confidence to approach the authorities themselves with ideas for improvement – the local departments for Education, Agriculture, Sports and even the Police.

Another area that the Anne Frank Pioneers are tackling is that of climate change. Joelke told me that this is very much felt in daily life in Brazil, where the winters are getting noticeably shorter and the summers longer and hotter. As one of their first activities the Anne Frank Pioneers are taken into the woods together to engender a feeling of the importance of the natural world. In Anne's writing she too describes her wonder at the beauty of nature. On 23 February 1944 she wrote:

> The best remedy for those who are frightened, lonely or unhappy is to go outside, somewhere they can be alone, alone with the sky, nature and God. For then and only then can you feel that everything is as it should be and that God wants people to be happy amid nature's beauty and simplicity. As long as this exists, and that should be for ever, I know that there will be solace for every sorrow, whatever the circumstances. I firmly believe that nature can bring comfort to all who suffer.

Joelke feels that where Anne's story will continue to have perhaps the most relevance in Latin America is in motivating and empowering Brazil's next generation of change-makers to create a good living environment. Describing how Brazilian youngsters have engaged with the programmes, she concluded, 'No other voice has such an appeal for young people as that of Anne Frank.'

Anne Frank in Central America

Central America was a notoriously violent region in the later years of the twentieth century with bloody civil wars taking place in El Salvador, Guatemala and Nicaragua.

The civil war in the tiny country of El Salvador lasted for twelve years between 1980 and 1992, during which time 75,000 people were killed. The Archbishop of San Salvador, Monsignor Oscar Romero, had spoken out against poverty, injustice, assassinations and torture and in the early days of the war was himself assassinated while conducting Mass in the chapel of a local hospital. Romero had been a friend of the UK's Archbishop of York, John Sentamu, who, when Bishop of Stepney in 2001, spoke at the opening of the Anne Frank exhibition in London's Bethnal Green, proudly but poignantly wearing a large colourful wooden cross that Archbishop Romero had given to him. In 2015 Romero was beatified by Pope Francis as a martyr.

In neighbouring Nicaragua, what was known as the 'Nicaraguan Revolution' involved thirty years of bloody complexity. The revolution took several forms, from opposition to the dictatorship of Anastasio Somoza in the 1960s and 1970s, the campaign led by the Sandinista National Liberation Front (FSLN) to violently oust the dictatorship in the late 1970s, and the Sandinistas' efforts to govern Nicaragua from 1979 until 1990, during which time there was a war raging between the Sandinista government and the Contras, right-wing guerrillas backed by the US.

Guatemala suffered an even longer civil war between 1960 and 1996, in which over 200,000 people were killed by their national army. The conflict was between the government and various leftist rebel groups supported chiefly by ethnic Mayan indigenous people and Ladino peasants, who together make up the country's rural poor. According to a UN commissioned report of 1999, 83 per cent of those killed were Mayans. Human rights defenders were attacked and threatened and in the aftermath of the conflict young people increasingly became involved in gang activities. By 2009, one in six murders were being committed by minors.

The Anne Frank House's touring exhibitions and educational programmes in Guatemala, El Salvador, Costa Rica, Nicaragua and Peru that took place between 2007 and 2010 had clear hopes for some influence in countries with such tumultuous recent histories (only Costa Rica, a historically peaceful country of lush rainforest that does not even possess a permanent army, was spared from conflict). By the end of the tour it was hoped that, by bringing new educational resources and learning methods, there would have been reflection on the importance of democratic values, human rights and cultural diversity, and an awareness by the young people of the human rights violations that took place during the internal armed conflicts in Guatemala and Peru. Groups of partner bodies would have the opportunity to discuss and exchange different ways of addressing racism, discrimination, human rights and historical memory.

The programmes in Central America and Peru were co-ordinated by two Argentinian women working at the Anne Frank House, Erika Del Carmen Mendez Chinchilla and Magdalena Vieyra. Erika had herself come from a disadvantaged community, but nonetheless through her determination she had completed a university degree. She identified with the inequality and discrimination Anne Frank had faced, as Erika had also faced these as a child. Magdalena had an Armenian grandmother, so had a family connection to a historical genocide and a wish to help prevent such events in the future.

The Guatemalans carry a clear sense of their individual cultural identity, describing themselves primarily as Latino, Indigenous or Mixed. The indigenous people do not feel fully accepted in Guatemalan society, and there is no real space in their everyday lives to talk about these issues. When the Anne Frank exhibition arrived in Guatemala something remarkable started to happen. Mariela noticed a discernible feeling among the young participants of, 'Anne Frank talked about her identity, so maybe I can too.' 'Anne Frank was brave. I will be brave too.' The project seemed to be making a clear impact on self-esteem as well as cultural pride.

One of the reasons for the effective way the Anne Frank House has worked in the international sphere has been its involvement on an equal footing with local partners. In Guatemala their main partner was CALDH, the Center for Legal Action on Human Rights, and in Nicaragua it was CEPREV, the Center for Prevention of Violence. It is a win-win situation, one that has been replicated around the world, where the Anne Frank House have the benefit of local knowledge and connections, and the partner organizations widen their networks and engage young people.

In Guatemala, the Anne Frank exhibition provided a safe space for young people to reflect about the past and present, and to connect with the local issues, presented on complementary panels developed by educators in Guatemala City. Many youngsters became aware of the presence and impact of racism, discrimination and exclusion in their society, and some came to realize that they were being discriminated against by their peers from another district. Some exhibition visitors opened up and started to talk about the conflicts in their own communities and the need to build a culture of peace and human rights.

Anne Frank in Peru

In Peru there is the same shared past of violence as in the Central American countries of Guatemala and Nicaragua. In 2009, Peru's former President, Alberto Fujimori, was sentenced to twenty-five years in prison for ordering killings and kidnappings during his government's war against leftist guerrillas in the 1990s. The Peruvian establishment was unwilling to confront the country's recent past, even intimidating those who had reported to the Peruvian Truth and Reconciliation Commission set up in 2000. A monument, known as 'The Eye That Cries' and dedicated to the 70,000 victims from both sides of the conflict, was vandalised by Fujimori supporters on the day after he arrived back in Peru from exile to face charges.

In March 2010, Magdalena Vieyra and Mariela Chyrikins travelled to Peru to meet with local partners on the Anne Frank project and to discuss the concept and approach to the educational resources. The tour of the Anne Frank exhibition would be a prominent event to celebrate the thirtieth anniversary of the regional educational authority in Lima. Together, the Anne Frank House team and the local education authority agreed to include information about Nazism in Peru in the exhibition and its educational resources, and to produce further exhibition panels dealing with the internal armed conflict in that country. They would also develop a training method which could make a connection between the history of Anne Frank and Holocaust and Peru's internal armed conflict, with a focus on genocidal forms of discrimination and racism.

Because the victims of the years of killings had mainly been indigenous people, Mariela recalled that exhibition visitors made a strong connection with the Roma and Sinti as Holocaust victims. Teenagers expressed surprise that Anne was discriminated against as 'she looks white and European'. Mariela pointed out that, unlike in her own country of Argentina, anti-Semitism is very rare in Central and South American countries, where there are only small Jewish populations, as the people hardly know or think about Jews. The main source of anti-Semitism is from the Catholic Church which still deems Jews as the killers of Jesus.

She expressed sadness that there was a feeling among young people in these post-conflict areas that violence is a natural occurrence. There was no questioning about this, just a feeling of resignation that this was how it was in their society. However, Mariela found that after the Anne Frank training sessions, young people started to ask questions about why there was violence and what could they do to stop it.

Teachers were especially grateful to have a resource like the exhibition to help them bring up the topic of the internal armed conflict with their students, as there were little or no resources available on this very sensitive issue. A few of the comments from the young exhibition guides illustrate this, such as, 'If a girl like her [Anne] could change the world with her diary, we can as well' and 'She confronted violence, we can also do it by finding non-violent methods and by preventing further violence. By doing this, we can build a better society.' This feeling of wanting to do something extended to older members of the community. A well-dressed woman exhibition volunteer, who described herself as middle-class and non-political, started asking questions, in an increasingly vocal way, about why no justice had been done against those who perpetrated the conflict and the dictatorship.

One of the most interesting aspects of the Anne Frank exhibition in Peru's capital Lima was the social diversity of the visitors: both students from very poor areas as well as students from the most expensive schools in Lima. Three youngsters who were trained as exhibition guides in the previous venue of Ayacucho also came along to the Lima training session, allowing a very interesting exchange between guides from the city of Lima and the rural area of Ayacucho. They were not only able to transmit their experiences as guides, but also to share their experiences of the conflict, with many having relatives who had been killed or displaced during that time. In that sense, the exhibition helped to tear down some of the social barriers that are so prevalent in Peruvian society.

***

The work of the Anne Frank House and its partners in Latin America continues, especially through the Centro Ana Frank in Buenos Aires. Jointly summing up the continuing need for the work in Latin America, the Anne Frank House educators Mariela Chyrikins and Barry van Driel explained:

> While introducing the history of the Holocaust, many teachers and students start to make certain connections to their own history of human rights violations, especially if the lens of human rights is introduced either directly or indirectly. Holocaust education, in general, has the potential to make a major impact in Latin America because it functions as a 'mirror' on society. The history of Nazi persecution not only focuses on the erosion of human rights, persecution and mass murder, but also on histories of discrimination, racism and exclusion. These are not uncommon themes in Latin American history. The history of the Holocaust, as a 'distant European history', acts as a kaleidoscope where 'close and distant', and 'past and present' histories of discrimination, racism, antisemitism and intolerance dialogue with each other.

They continued,

> *The Diary of Anne Frank* occupies a special place in educational work about the Holocaust and related themes in Latin America. Anne was a gifted writer who not only wrote about the persecution of the Jews but about a variety of themes that young people then and now struggle with. She was a typical adolescent and found love in difficult times. She argued with her mother and dreamt of a better life safe from the dangers around her. Her reflections are deep and strike a chord with those trying to manoeuvre through adolescence. Equally important from an educational perspective is that she never stopped writing. She was a young girl with

an opinion and would not be silenced. Latin American youth, especially girls, are inspired by this.

The Anne Frank projects in Latin America build on this activist element of Anne's diary to empower local youth. By encouraging youth to write about their own emotions, fears and dreams a further connection is made between past and present, between distant and local histories. By developing an awareness of human rights and providing youth with opportunities to engage in human rights activities the life and times of Anne Frank serve as a catalyst for both reflection and civic engagement.

Through their wide range of experiences, Mariela Chyrikins and Barry van Driel have thoughtfully summed up the power and relevance of the Anne Frank work in Latin America.

It mirrors other more local histories and realities, yet provides the temporal and geographical distance to address issues that might otherwise be too controversial, painful or threatening. Anne and her family were migrants. She suffered discrimination and oppression and she suffered due to the violent actions of a dictator. She had to hide. This is why young people from minority groups and relatives of political refugees particularly relate to her life.

Chapter 9

Anne Frank and Audrey Hepburn

'As you grow older, you will discover that you have two hands, one for helping yourself, the other for helping others.' Audrey Hepburn

Eva Schloss and I were standing in Audrey Hepburn's dressing room at the Barbican, the concert hall and arts centre in London, talking to a woman dressed in black. Yes, it really was her. AUDREY HEPBURN! It was May 1991, the Anne Frank Trust was barely a few months into its life and its official launch was still six months away. I was completely star struck by this astonishingly beautiful woman. She had walked onto the stage a couple of hours earlier to read from Anne Frank's diary, which had been set against a musical accompaniment by the American maestro Michael Tilson Thomas. This first performance was a special concert in support of UNICEF. As she walked towards the centre of the stage, a black folder containing the readings under her arm, the audience let out a tangible gasp. Audrey was already 60 but glided into view like a black swan, graceful and sylphlike on that large stage.

Audrey has described what reading Anne Frank's diary meant to her:

Anne Frank and I were born in the same year, lived in the same country and experienced the same war. Except she was locked up and I was on the outside. Reading Anne's diary was like reading my own experiences from her point of view. I was quite destroyed by it. An adolescent girl locked up in two rooms, with no way of expressing herself other than to her diary. She was in a different corner of Holland but all the events I experienced were so incredibly accurately described by her. Not just what was going on on the outside – but what was happening on the inside of a young girl starting to be a woman . . . all in a cage. She expresses the claustrophobia but transcends it through her love of nature, her awareness of humanity and her love – real love – of life.

Once we had been introduced in her dressing room, Eva told Audrey that her stepfather Otto and her mother Fritzi had so wanted her to be the actress to play Anne in the 1960 George Stevens film, *The Diary of Anne Frank*. As they talked, both women pronounced Anne's name in the Continental way of 'Anna'. Audrey responded: 'Eva, you do understand why I couldn't play Anne, don't you?' 'Well, I assumed you had filming commitments,' Eva said. Audrey looked Eva directly in the eye. 'No,' she almost whispered. 'It wasn't that. It was just too hard for me. It was too close to my life for me to do.'

Audrey Hepburn had been born in Brussels on 4 May 1929, one month before Anne Frank was born in Frankfurt. Her birth name was Audrey Kathleen Ruston, her mother a Dutch aristocrat and her father a British businessman. Sometime later her father decided to add the ancestral name of Hepburn to all the family's names. Joseph Ruston Hepburn walked out on his family when Audrey was just 6-years-old and she bore the scars of that rejection throughout her childhood and adult life. Audrey's mother never remarried and moved her young family back to Arnhem in the Netherlands, where her own father had been Mayor of the city. When the Nazis invaded the Netherlands in May 1940 Audrey was 11. Her mother wisely changed her daughter's English-sounding name so as not to put any of the family under suspicion. Ruston Hepburn was reverted to the family's own very Dutch sounding name of van Heemstra, and Audrey became Edda. Early on in the occupation, Audrey's maternal uncle Otto van Limburg had been executed by the Nazis in revenge for a Resistance ambush. One of her half-brothers was sent to a labour camp in Berlin and the other went into hiding. As a strategic crossing-place of the Rhine, Arnhem was a difficult place to be, especially after the Allied advance into the Netherlands and the fierce battles for control of its bridges. The family moved to the grandparents' home in the suburbs. Like many Dutch children who were seen to be skipping or running through the streets, their playfulness masked a dangerous secret, as on some occasions Audrey was actually running errands for the Resistance, carrying secret messages in her shoes.

The Dutch suffered privations throughout the German occupation and war, but the final months of 1944 and into 1945, after the German blockade of food and fuel to the farms in the occupied areas of the Netherlands, became known as the 'Hunger Winter'. What little food was produced was sent to the Dutch troops. Around 20,000 civilians starved to death and others survived on eating raw tulip bulbs. It was a rare case of famine taking place in Europe in modern times.

After the liberation, 16-year-old Edda van Heemstra was one of the children helped by the United Nations Relief and Rehabilitation Administration, which was soon to become known as UNICEF. She described herself as 'not starving but severely malnourished'. Throughout the rest of her life, as her star ascended, Audrey Hepburn never forgot the help those kind and caring people from the United Nations gave her in those days immediately after liberation, when they were distributing food, clothes and health care.

In 1988, having decided to retire from making movies, Audrey was appointed a Goodwill Ambassador for UNICEF. Her first field trip was to Ethiopia which had suffered a terrible famine in the mid-1980s. On taking up her role she noted that: 'Since the world has existed there has been injustice. The more so as it becomes smaller and more accessible. There is no question that there is a moral obligation for those who have, to give to those who have nothing.'

Edith Simmons-Richner, who had helped me with the Anne Frank Children to Children Appeal for Bosnia in 1993, was also the UNICEF Information and Social Mobilization Officer in Ethiopia, and accompanied Audrey on her first mission as a newly appointed UNICEF Goodwill Ambassador. On a trip to the north of the country, they visited an orphanage where young children who had lost their families in the three-year famine between 1992 and 1995 were cared for. Edith described to me what happened there:

> It was lunchtime, and we watched the children queuing up in silence for their meal. Then Audrey left our group and sat, alone, on the ground, at a distance, watching the children. Suddenly, a little girl left the ranks and ran spontaneously towards Audrey hugging her and nestling on her knees. It was a totally impromptu and very moving moment as we watched this little girl, and Audrey Hepburn, both survivors of terrible famines, holding and comforting each other in silence. I shall never forget it.

Later, Edith received a letter from Audrey Hepburn in which she wrote, 'Ethiopia is in my thoughts every day sometimes nights! I have really fallen in love with that country and their people. I have gone halfway around the world since I saw you, talking and talking about Ethiopia. I pray that our efforts will make some difference.'

While the conversation between Eva Schloss and Audrey Hepburn was taking place in her dressing room at the Barbican, I was standing with Audrey's long-time partner and the love of her life, the Dutch actor Robert Wolders. Like Audrey, Wolders had also been living in Arnhem during the war, in another suburb of the city, but their two paths had never crossed until they finally met at a party in 1980.

'Is there anything Audrey could do for you?' Robert asked me. Without hesitation and employing the utmost chutzpah, I ventured forth, 'Well, would she consider becoming a patron of the Anne Frank Trust?' He smiled and nodded. Yes of course she would. And so with great pride the name Audrey Hepburn was added to our notepaper.

Less than two years later, on 20 January 1993, Audrey died from a rare form of abdominal cancer. She was still astonishingly beautiful at the age of 63. She had not long returned from a gruelling visit to Somalia in her role as UNICEF Goodwill Ambassador. Her terminal illness and the speed of its progress came as a huge shock to her and her family; doctors had assumed her severe stomach pains were from a temporary infection she had picked up while in Somalia.

Edith told me about the final project Audrey had undertaken for UNICEF in the autumn of 1992, after returning from her mission in Somalia, and already very ill and close to death. This was a radio announcement to be broadcast to all factions in the war in the former Yugoslavia and asking them to put down their arms for the UNICEF 'Week of Tranquillity', during which much-needed items could be distributed to children on all sides of the conflict before the harsh winter set in. Speaking as a UNICEF colleague Edith said, 'Wherever she went, Audrey Hepburn's efforts made a huge difference. Her death was a big loss for us all, and especially for suffering children worldwide.' In the words of Audrey's great friend and revered fashion designer Hubert de Givenchy, 'She was an enchantress, inspiring love and beauty, and fairies don't disappear altogether.'

In 2002, nine years after Audrey's death, my second husband Tony and I were in Los Angeles, and paid a visit to Audrey's son Sean Hepburn Ferrer at the offices of the Audrey Hepburn Children's Fund in Santa Monica. We were welcomed warmly. Sean gave me a signed copy of his newly-published biography of his mother, *Audrey Hepburn, An Elegant Spirit*, as well as a framed black-and-white photograph that he told me was so important to his mother that she had kept it on her bedside table until her death. The photo had been taken by his father Mel Ferrer in 1957 in Switzerland. It was of Audrey with Otto and Fritzi Frank.

Chapter 10

On the Road with Anne Frank

When I helped to organize that very first exhibition in my own southern coastal town in 1989, little did I know that for the following twenty-six years I would be travelling to nearly every part of the United Kingdom setting up Anne Frank exhibitions.

In the process of visiting so many cities, towns and regions, I have been a witness to the social, economic and demographic changes that have affected the entire country during the successive Conservative, Labour, Coalition and then again Conservative governments, and the new wave of immigration from former Communist countries as they became part of the European Union. I have seen towns deeply affected by post-industrial deprivation, by white and Asian communities living side by side but with no integration, and monocultural regions where racist attitudes are borne out of ignorance.

For many months of each year I would find myself stepping off a train, scouring the station platform for publicity posters with Anne Frank's vibrant face shining out and heading into town to the cathedral, library, town hall or museum that would be hosting the Anne Frank exhibition for the next few weeks. I travelled from the north coast of Wales, to the religiously-divided cities of Northern Ireland, to the Cornish toe of England, inner and outer boroughs of London, and the multicultural post-industrial cities and towns of the north of England.

How did the Anne Frank exhibitions happen? Although many of the visitors may have thought they had fallen from the sky, or indeed arrived directly from Amsterdam to their town, the process for an Anne Frank exhibition taking place was usually something like this:

I would identify a town, city or county council that had not previously held the exhibition, or had already done so but several years previously and would now have a new generation of pupils in their schools. In some cases, a council representative would make contact with me first, often when they had relocated from one town to another and had hosted the Anne Frank exhibition in their previous location. The same also applied with cathedrals, for example the late Dr Colin Slee, one of the Canons of St Albans Abbey in Hertfordshire, moved on to be appointed the Provost of Southwark Cathedral in south London, the highest position in the cathedral. He had hosted our exhibition at St Albans Abbey in 1993, and it had attracted large crowds from the whole of north London. Colin wasn't long in his new senior position before I was invited to come and see him. It was in the magnificent Gothic nave of Southwark that we launched the new version of the exhibition, 'Anne Frank, A History for Today', in January 1997.

Once initial contact had been made with a civic authority through the Mayor, Chief Executive or one of the council's other elected or professional leaders, I would visit the town to meet those senior decision-makers who could agree to fund the project, or in some cases, underwrite it pending attracting sponsorship from businesses, local trust funds or unions. Next I would meet the team who would become involved in the planning and organizing of each event, including the recruiting of volunteers from the community to help guide the public or man the exhibition book shop.

I really loved the first engagement with each new planning team – walking into a room full of interested, enthusiastic people and bouncing around ideas on how we could make each month-long visit of the exhibition even more impactful and unforgettable for the local community. The council's education team would offer to create some new teaching resources, often highlighting local issues such as an abusive, violent or murderous racist attack or a concerning growth of extremist groups, and would then set about ensuring every school in their area had an opportunity to visit the exhibition; the PR and marketing team would develop a publicity campaign sometimes extending to posters at bus stops and in high street shop windows; and the equalities or community engagement teams would ensure all the local ethnic and religious community groups would be informed, would supply a pool of volunteers and bring their families to see the exhibition. Over the ensuing months the local team and I would be in close contact leading up to the launch event, which I would nearly always attend to conduct media interviews, make a speech on behalf of the Anne Frank Trust, and offer advice on planned satellite events. Out of nearly 200 openings over the years, there were very few I didn't attend in person.

During the course of the month-long exhibition, friendships were often forged across previous community divides, and from what I have been told many times in different cities there was nothing like the Anne Frank exhibition for breaking down barriers and bringing people together. The exhibition often left behind unforeseen legacies, some of which I heard about only years later. Local people were prompted by the Anne Frank exhibition to set up a new interfaith forum as a long-term legacy of the event. Through Anne Frank, intergenerational connections were built, and even warm relationships fostered across the political and social divide (I am thinking especially of Northern Ireland).

I remember a group of religious Muslim women who volunteered at the exhibition at Gloucester Cathedral in the summer of 1997. They were so enthusiastic about spending their days at a Christian place of worship to tell the story of a Jewish girl in the Holocaust, that they prepared and cooked their family's evening meal at six o'clock in the morning, so as to be able to devote their day to Anne Frank.

A memorable incident, where images of Anne Frank made a mark that resulted in national news headlines, was the exhibition's visit to the beautiful medieval city of York in January 1998. The city council found an unusual way to use Anne Frank's story to atone for a sin dating back 800 years. In 1190, fleeing a baying mob, the Jewish population had desperately sought refuge inside the stone walls of Clifford's Tower, a fortification overlooking the city. Anti-Semitic feeling was running high throughout western Europe in the twelfth century, stoked by the Christian fervour of the Crusades, which had caused aggression and violence against Jews across England, France and Germany, as well as against Muslims in the Holy Land. The York mob's thirst for Jewish blood was incited by several of the local landed gentry, who saw a convenient way of eliminating their debts to the Jewish moneylenders (moneylending was pretty much the only career permitted to Jews in medieval Europe). Realizing they had no escape, the Jews decided to end their lives by their own hand, the men slaughtering the women and children, and finally themselves. Those that demurred and gave themselves up to the mob fared no better, and the entire Jewish population of York was wiped out.

The City of York Council came up with an unusual way of recognizing this blot on the city's history. The 'Anne Frank, A History for Today' exhibition was to visit the city and the title of the exhibition, linking past and present, proved to be apposite. Directly facing Clifford's Tower stands what was then the Stakis Hotel, now brought into the Hilton hotel chain. The council approached the Stakis Group's Managing Director, a man called David Michels, with an idea to light up the long Yorkshire January nights by projecting images from the Anne Frank exhibition on to the exterior walls of Clifford's Tower. Mr Michels agreed without hesitation and the Anne Frank 'lumiere show' became a traffic stopper, generating national media coverage and local interest in both the Anne Frank exhibition and the Clifford's Tower massacre.

I convinced myself that I had become an informal 'expert' on the architecture of Britain's cathedrals, having visited so many of them with the Anne Frank exhibition. From my first view of its exterior I could tell you if the building dated from the Norman, Gothic, Baroque or Modern periods. On entering the nave and looking at the arches and flying buttresses I could then confirm the difference between the softer, rounded Norman arches, and the more pointed and towering style of the later Gothic period. Unlike other European and Latin American countries, the only Baroque cathedral in Britain is actually St Paul's, and indeed this is the only example of having been designed by a single person, Sir Christopher Wren, the previous cathedral on the site having been destroyed in the Great Fire of London of 1666.

I was a Jewish girl who loved spending time in cathedrals, but was always sad to think about the great loss of life and limb that must have occurred in the building of these great edifices in the centuries long before we had any Health and Safety regulations. Cathedrals took decades, and sometimes centuries, to complete. I would think about the common labourers who lifted the stones into place, the more skilled stone carvers and glass makers, who would give so many years of toil and often not live to see the finished result. In rural locations like the flatlands around

Ely in Cambridgeshire, where the cathedral spire could be seen from miles away, I would imagine the power of that huge overwhelming structure during the years that no other building would have been higher than one storey. Housed in those great stone walls were the combined power of God, of the Church and of the ruling classes to inspire awe and submission in the masses.

The cathedral staff would be welcoming and enthusiastic about acting as hosts for the exhibition, although there was sometimes what I called 'the stroppy verger', who paced around the floor, huffing and scowling because the exhibition and the numbers of people it attracted were an unwelcome hindrance to his or her daily duties. We also occasionally encountered our 'stroppy vergers' in schools (unhelpful caretakers) and in prisons (a small number of the prison officers).

In Blackburn Cathedral in 2009, a key organizer was Anjum Anwar, who was in fact the only Muslim Dialogue Development Officer in an Anglican cathedral. As one would suspect, the launch of the Anne Frank exhibition at Blackburn Cathedral was a truly multi-faith affair, with the triumvirate of Dean, Imam and Rabbi present as well as Mrs Thea Hirst, a child Holocaust refugee to Britain, who like Anne Frank had also kept a diary during those traumatic years.

I always maintained that the further away from London the Anne Frank exhibition was held, the more appreciated it was by the local community. And the smaller the town, the bigger the event became. Examples were Rhyl, a seaside resort on the north coast of Wales which had seen more affluent times; a shopping precinct in Dudley, on the outskirts of Birmingham, where people queued the length of the shopping aisle to see the exhibition; and some of the border towns in Northern Ireland ('Everything exciting usually goes to Belfast', they would tell me). In these towns there was a real buzz about the event, and you would see posters of Anne Frank everywhere, including at bus stops, displays of Anne's diary in bookshop windows; and even overhear people talking about it on the streets.

I heard some astonishing stories of connection to the Frank family in the most unexpected places. At St Edmundsbury Cathedral, in the rural east of England country town of Bury St Edmunds, I was introduced to an elderly local woman called Julia Donovan. Julia had grown up in the Netherlands but married an Englishman after the Second World War. Her profession as a young woman in wartime Amsterdam happened to be as a midwife. It was Julia who had delivered the baby sister of Anne Frank's best friend Hannah Goslar, the same friend whom Anne had encountered again in Bergen-Belsen. Julia was looking after mother and baby when the Frank family had come to visit the new arrival. There among the stone pillars of an English country cathedral, the 90-year-old Mrs Donovan described to me her memories of young Anne, as she recalled a vivid, smiling and friendly little girl with very dark hair and eyes. With a twinkle in her eye, the elderly lady also divulged her dangerous night time activities in the Dutch Resistance, one of which was throwing the bicycles of Nazi soldiers into the canals.

There were also amusing incidents along the way that I still laugh about when recalling. As I sat in Truro Cathedral, in the most south-westerly county of Cornwall, the guests were waiting for the overdue arrival of the town's Mayor to open the exhibition. Around ten minutes after the formalities were due to start, the cathedral doors burst open and a rather agitated and dishevelled middle-aged Lady Mayor ran down the aisle to her reserved seat. Afterwards, I asked her politely what had detained her. 'Well,' she started to explain in a thick Cornish accent, 'You see, I have a Saturday job in Marks and Spencer's and the woman who was supposed to come and relieve me on my till didn't turn up. I just didn't know what to do. I couldn't leave my till, even for Anne Frank.'

Mayors often provided amusement, especially when grappling with facts on giving an opening address for the exhibition. There was one in a nameless seaside town who kept saying: 'Now this Anne Franklin . . .' with clearly no idea of her story. And another in a northern city, whose wife was complaining to me that 'He gets a good allowance to kit himself out with new suits for his year of office. But me, nothing. Not even the cost of a new hairdo.'

Some of the opening events themselves have been so memorable that I still run a video of them in my mind. In 1996, at the Dylan Thomas Centre in Swansea, a group of children sang a song about the Holocaust that they had written for the Eisteddfod that year. The song was sung entirely in Welsh but was so powerful that the tears were streaming down my face. It was also on that evening that I met the Holocaust survivor Ellen Davies, who told her story to a silenced audience. Silent because they had never heard a woman from their own town, and speaking in an authentic Welsh accent with no trace of European roots, describe how her parents and siblings in Poland were all shot dead by the Nazis, and how she, because of the 'Kindertransport' children's rescue mission to Britain, had been the only one to survive.

In 1996 the Anne Frank House created a successor to their first travelling exhibition 'Anne Frank in the World'. In January 1997, the English-language version of 'Anne Frank, A History for Today' was launched at Southwark Cathedral. The Anne Frank House had capitalized on the new historical material that was being made accessible after the fall of Communism across Eastern Europe. 'A History for Today' contained many 'stop you in your tracks' colour photos, which made the Nazi period seem all the more real. With its structure of five adjoined hexagonal 'pavilions' and domed roof sections, the exhibition was beautiful to look at, but because of the way each pavilion had to be slotted together, it was not easily adapted to different shaped spaces.

One of the first venues for 'A History for Today' was quite unusual – a large marquee in the busy tourist destination of Camden Market in London. It resided there for two months in the summer of 1997, alongside a second marquee which housed lectures, concerts and theatrical productions, including a week-long run of the play *Dreams of Anne Frank*. In Camden Market, the exhibition attracted a very diverse range of visitors, including one afternoon Oasis founder Noel Gallagher and his wife, but one unwelcome one – a small hole in the marquee's roof let in rain and a bucket was duly positioned under it. It was fun to be right in the heart of the action of Camden Market, but because of the practical problems of being in a marquee, not one we decided to replicate. On the final day of the exhibition, the last Sunday in August, Nic Careem, who had been very helpful in the organization of the exhibition, arranged a thank-you party for all the volunteers who had helped over the two months. Nic worked until very late the night before to collect and prepare all the food, a generous gesture to thank and celebrate the volunteers. However, on the day of the thank-you party the mood was very subdued. Princess Diana had died in the early hours of that morning.

By 2004, we were again in need of a new exhibition. The Anne Frank House agreed to work in tandem with the Anne Frank Trust to create it and I started the fundraising process. Funding came from the National Lottery Community Fund (now known as the Big Lottery), the Home Office, the Association of Jewish Refugees, the Claims Conference in New York, and many individual supporters. Jon Blair, who had made the Oscar-winning documentary *Anne Frank Remembered* led the team, working with award-winning design company Metaphor, and educators from the House in Amsterdam and the Trust in London. On its completion in 2005, the new exhibition 'Anne Frank + You' looked fabulous – unlike any other exhibition that was touring the UK.

'Anne Frank + You' was created for young people and the 'You' was about them and their lives, making strong and often surprising connections with Anne's writing. The exhibition's launch took place in June 2005 in the very hip area of Brick Lane in East London, attended by comedian David Baddiel, BBC foreign correspondent Fergal Keane and one of the UK's most recognizable artists, Tracy Emin, who happens to be a huge fan of Anne Frank.

'Anne Frank + You' comprised two distinct sections representing 'then and now'. The historical section on the life and times of Anne and her family, from her birth in 1929 until her death in 1945, was appropriately shown on panels of monotone shades of grey and black, broken up by the occasional coloured Holocaust-era images as well as bright red illuminated showcases housing the Frank family photo collection. From these panels visitors would progress through the intimidatingly dark 'Holocaust and Genocide' tunnel. This explained the fate of the Frank family, plus other images of the Holocaust. At the end of this tunnel visitors were confronted with the question 'Never Again?', the answer supplied on a screen with disturbing moving footage from the genocides that have occurred around the world since 1945.

Visitors then take a step into Anne's world, by entering an almost life-size reproduction of Anne's bedroom in hiding. In this empty space, children loved to spend time, sitting cross-legged on the floor and listening to the recording of a young actress reading from Anne's diary. Through a replica window on the far wall, they look at images of the inside and outside of Anne's hiding place.

The other half of the 'Anne Frank + You' exhibition focused on contemporary issues and expanded on five themes Anne wrote poignantly about in her diary. These were: Racial Hatred, Conflict, Inclusion and Identity, Moral Choices and Freedom.

These panels were in vibrant colours, predominantly vivid reds and yellows, and each panel contained integral filmed interviews with British teenagers about the particular theme it covered.

'Anne Frank + You' was large and looked dramatic. It took a team of five able bodied people at least two days to build. When it was shown in a busy shopping centre or a major tourist attraction such as St Paul's Cathedral, our Exhibition Manager Doug Palfreeman and his team would have to build it overnight, under tight pressure to have it completed by the morning's opening time. I am reliably informed by Doug that a night spent working at St Paul's Cathedral amongst the centuries-old tombs and below its famed Whispering Gallery is a disquietingly eerie experience.

Over the twenty-plus years I have been travelling the country with the Anne Frank exhibition, there has been no other exhibition that has had the power and ability to bring all sections of the community together like ours. People drive many miles to see it, and recall it so intensely that they often tell me that it was 'a couple of years ago', when in fact I know that it was many more. A fascinating phenomenon, that I have heard time and again over the years, was that children who came on school visits would bring their parents back to see it at the weekend or in school holidays.

In its three different incarnations, the Anne Frank exhibition has been seen by over three million people in the UK, that's approximately one in twenty of the country's population. In London I recently met a woman in her thirties who asked me how I had first become involved with the Anne Frank Trust. I told her the story, as I have done many times, about the exhibition's visit to Bournemouth in 1989 and what it had led to. As I spoke she was nodding her head and then said, 'Yes. I remember that exhibition too. I was on holiday staying with my grandparents in the town and they took me to see it. I was nine years old and have never forgotten it.'

Anne Frank and the Jewish Boy Shown Off to Hitler

'You can decide for yourselves if we were beautiful or not, but Aryan we certainly were not.' Herbert Levy

From 1991 and for the following twelve years, I had a co-traveller touring the country with the Anne Frank exhibition. His name was Herbert Levy, otherwise proudly known as the 'Anne Frank Trust's Principal Guide and Guide Trainer'. To be taken around the exhibition by Herbert, whether as a volunteer guide being trained by him or as a visitor, was an enlightening and unforgettable experience. Herbert used his own life story, and his love of amateur dramatics, to relate Anne Frank's life in a unique way. His soft, well-mannered English commanded respect, interest and authority.

As a boy of 9, Herbert Levy had arrived at London's Liverpool Street Station on a steam train used for the Kindertransport, the rescue mission for Jewish children. The little German-speaking boy stepped off the train in the midst of a crowd of other bewildered German-Jewish children, most of whom would never see their parents again. Thankfully, and unusually, Herbert Levy's parents were able to flee Germany a few months after their young son, in August 1939, just as the doors of escape were closing tightly shut.

Herbert had been born in Berlin in 1929, the same year as Anne Frank, during the time that the Nazis were on their rise to power. By the time Herbert was four, the Nazis were the ruling party and started almost immediately to harass German Jews. He recalled a frightening night time visit by the police who went through his father's papers and then left with a large amount of the family's cash.

Two years later, six-year-old Herbert was to have a frighteningly close encounter with Adolf Hitler himself. Walking home one afternoon, Herbert and his mother had turned a familiar corner and found themselves in a crowd who were excitedly waiting for the Führer's car to pass. On spotting the little blond Herbert, members of the crowd scooped him up and carried him aloft to the very front – to be shown to the Führer as an example of a fine Aryan child in their midst. Herbert could recall his own fear and that of his mother, but as Hitler's car passed him, the bright six-year-old had the wherewithal to make the expected 'Heil Hitler' salute. The 'Aryan' little boy was then passed back over the crowd to his very relieved mother.

Soon after Herbert's parents' arrival in the UK, the Second World War broke out. The refugee Levy family were interned by the British government on the Isle of Man, described as 'Enemy Aliens', and incredibly held alongside actual Nazis. On their release the Levy family settled in north London, living for many years in Hampstead among the German-Jewish refugee community. Despite having been interned by his new homeland of Britain in the early 1950s, Herbert went on to do his national service in the Royal Army Education Corps. In 1961 he married Lilian Davidson, who had been found as a five-year-old orphan in Bergen-Belsen on its liberation by the British army.

As a young adult Herbert assimilated well into British life, and with a great love of English literature, his dream was to have been an actor or theatre director. He described the stage as 'in his blood' as the relatives who had taken him in on his arrival in London were seasoned stage performers. Herbert set up an amateur dramatics group, putting on productions in his synagogue in Belsize Square, Hampstead, aimed at alleviating the trauma of the Continental refugee families who had recently lost so many of their loved ones in the Holocaust. In order to support his wife and two children, instead of pursuing an insecure professional life in the theatre, Herbert set up a successful hosiery business selling nylon stockings, which were in the 1960s replaced by the exciting innovation of tights. He never spoke willingly or publicly about his childhood in Germany, the trauma of coming alone as a child to Britain, or of his grandmother's murder in Auschwitz.

In November 1991 the 'Anne Frank in the World' exhibition was staged at Belsize Square Synagogue, an appropriate choice as it had been founded by German-Jewish refugees (Herbert's parents among them) and its first Rabbi, George Salzberger, had been a friend of Otto Frank in Frankfurt. Herbert was asked to be one of the team of exhibition guides, and was at first reticent and very nervous, feeling that this would be too emotional and painful for him opening up old wounds. In his memoir *Voices from the Past* published in 1995, he describes the 'right to put aside these things, to forget and live a new life without bringing up these memories of fifty years ago'.

But he then talks about the choice that he and Lilian made to go ahead with becoming a guide at that time. Later on, when he found himself educating students and prisoners, the matter of personal choices became a focus of his exhibition tour.

> There are many parallels and many choices. The Germans had a choice, the Dutch had a choice – it was the Jews who had very little choice . . . And today's children in their later lives will have choices to make. I hope that something of what they saw will remain with them, so that when the time comes to make their own choices, remembering this exhibition will help them make the right choice.

After that first experience of guiding at the Anne Frank exhibition in November 1991, Herbert never looked back. In the words of his wife Lilian, 'It was an absolute release for him'. Herbert Levy's theatrical ambitions were finally realized when I appointed him the Principal Guide and Guide Trainer for the exhibition, and even though by this time he was well into his seventies, he travelled tirelessly all over the UK on behalf of the Anne Frank Trust. He educated thousands of young people and teams of volunteer guides in his unforgettable style, adding dramatic flourishes where required to this tragic story.

While explaining to school groups the irrationality of the Nazis' race laws against Jews and Roma, and others not deemed to have Aryan blood, Herbert would hold up a black-and-white photo of two smiling young children, a boy with blond hair wearing leather shorts and an older girl with long blond plaits. It was actually Herbert's aunt Charlotte Mendelssohn who had taken this photo of her pretty daughter Ellen-Eva and her cute little nephew Herbert. When Mrs Mendelssohn went along to collect the printed photos from the local photographic shop in Berlin she was horrified to see this photo proudly displayed in the shop window. Underneath it was a sign that read: 'TWO BEAUTIFUL ARYAN CHILDREN.' For a number of weeks, the enlarged photo was displayed in this and several other shop windows around Berlin.

Decades later, Herbert would stand in front of the Anne Frank exhibition panel explaining the Nazi race laws and tell them the story of the photograph he was holding. He would then lower his voice and say to the pupils, 'Now it's up to you to decide if we were beautiful or not, but Aryan we certainly weren't.' After this he would explain to the often very multicultural groups of children the absurdity of the Nazi 'science' of race.

Despite his own experience of internment, Herbert spent much of his time as a guide trainer in prisons, giving prisoners knowledge and understanding to be confident exhibition guides for their peers. In January 1997, Herbert took Tony and Cherie Blair around the brand-new 'Anne Frank, A History for Today' exhibition at Southwark Cathedral. Blair was so moved by Herbert's guiding that he determined on that morning do all in his power to bring about a national Holocaust Memorial Day in Britain, should he become Prime Minister in the forthcoming general election of May 1997, which in both cases came about. Herbert later joked that he had also tried to convince Tony Blair to introduce proportional representation for British elections, but sadly that had not been so successful.

Even well into his seventies, Herbert was travelling the length and breadth of the country and we spent a lot of time travelling together. We were once trapped by an ice storm for eight hours at Edinburgh Airport awaiting a flight back to London. Having been sustained and emboldened by the whisky samplings in the airport shop, Herbert drew upon all his dramatic skills to DEMAND AS A DIABETIC that we were prioritized on the first flight down to London. It worked.

Lilian and I still laugh about the time I was staying in a hotel with my husband Tony. I looked across the breakfast table and said, 'This doesn't seem quite right, Tony.' He asked me what on earth I was talking about. 'Well I feel I should be looking across at Herbert!'

In 2009, Herbert returned to the Isle of Man. The Anne Frank exhibition was being shown at St German's Cathedral on the west coast – its first ever visit to the island. Herbert was to be a Very Special Guest at the opening ceremony. And he certainly was. At the end of the ceremony, and after Herbert had spoken, the Bishop of Sodor and Man summed up the evening by saying that 'In five, ten and twenty years' time, people will still be talking about the opening of the Anne Frank exhibition on the Isle of Man.'

But there were other remarkable things that had happened while Herbert and Lilian were visiting the island with the exhibition. On the afternoon of the opening, a reporter from the local radio station was conducting an interview with Herbert at the gates of the internment camp in which he and his family had been held during the war. An elderly man cycled by and saw the radio team interviewing someone, and stopped to ask what it was about. When it was explained that they were interviewing a man who had been in the internment camp as a child, the cyclist went over to shake Herbert's hand. He told Herbert that he, as a young boy, had witnessed the day of the opening of the camp and the first German-Jewish refugees being marched in. A local newspaper article about Herbert's return to the Isle of Man was spotted online in Israel by a distant cousin of the Levy family, who had been unsuccessfully trying to trace some of her relatives. She contacted the journalist who had the very pleasant duty of putting them in touch.

As a German whose family, like that of Anne Frank, went back many generations in Germany, Herbert took a particular interest in our young German volunteers who had come to the Anne Frank Trust through the peace organization Action Reconciliation Service for Peace. When Herbert passed away aged 85 in January

2015, I was so touched to see that three of our German volunteers had come all the way to London for his funeral. In the words of one of them, Immanuel Bartz:

> Our first encounter took place at his home in North London in the form of an invitation to dinner. We quickly realized that both our families originated from Berlin and that we also shared a great love of theatre. In the years following this first meeting a deep and heartfelt relationship developed. Herbert was a man full of passion, dedication and conviction. He strongly believed that each person is presented with choices and how we respond to these choices presents new ways to live a good and fair life.

Herbert Levy inspired and influenced people young and old throughout this country to be compassionate and free from prejudice. And that black-and-white photograph of little Herbert and his cousin Ellen-Eva taken in Hitler's Berlin is still, I am pleased to say, proudly displayed on a panel of the Anne Frank exhibition.

Chapter 11

Anne Frank and the Children of Bosnia

'We have no food, heating nor electricity, but these things we can bear. We just cannot bear the hatred around us. Anne Frank didn't live to see peace. Will we?' From a letter sent to the Anne Frank House in 1993 from children in turmoil in Bosnia during the war.

During the years of Communism, Yugoslavia had been firmly controlled by its leader Marshal Josip Broz Tito. As a 1950s child the name 'Tito', when I heard spoken by my parents, put me in mind of a cuddly teddy bear. Later I was aware through photographs of a military-uniformed, be-medalled and strong-faced man who ruled an Iron Curtain country located in the south of Europe. Tito was described by many in the West as perhaps the most 'benevolent dictator' of the Soviet bloc. But, as a former brave and ferocious partisan fighting against the Nazis, he ruled his country with an iron fist. Marshal Tito died in 1980 but it was not until Communism started falling apart, and the lid on the Yugoslavian pot was lifted, that the boiling ingredients contained underneath started to come to the surface and escape.

By 1990 Tito's former Yugoslavia had started to break up into many countries, Bosnia and Herzegovina, Serbia, Macedonia, Slovenia and Montenegro. In the turmoil following the disintegration of Yugoslavia, Bosnia and Herzegovina declared independence in 1992, backed by a people's referendum. The population of Bosnia and Herzegovina consists of Bosniaks (Bosnian Muslims who came to the region as a result of the Ottoman conquests in the fifteenth and sixteenth centuries), Bosnian Serbs (Orthodox Christians who have close cultural ties with neighbouring Serbia), and Bosnian Croats (Roman Catholics who have close cultural ties with neighbouring Croatia). Having been spurred on by a speech given in July 1989 at the 600th anniversary of the Battle of Kosovo by Slobodan Milošević, the President of Serbia, the Bosnian Serbs saw their future as part of 'Greater Serbia', and resisted the referendum. In early 1992, following conflict in neighbouring Croatia, violent incidents started breaking out in Bosnia and Herzegovina. By April 1992, this had escalated into a full-blown ethnic war which lasted until December 1995. Over 100,000 people were killed, 80 per cent of whom were Bosnian Muslims.

ANNE FRANK AND THE CHILDREN OF BOSNIA

In March 1993, as the war in Bosnia was raging, the Anne Frank House in Amsterdam received a letter sent by fax from a school in Zenica, Bosnia's fourth-largest city. For eighteen months, Zenica (pronounced Zenitsa) had been isolated from the rest of the world, suffering considerable civilian casualties from sniper fire, shelling and also hunger. Most of Zenica's people had no water or electricity, and with few food supplies, life for its inhabitants was becoming unbearable. The heartfelt letter, accompanied by a pencil drawing of Anne Frank writing at her desk, was from a fifth grade class of 12-year-olds. They had been reading Anne's diary in their English lesson and were profoundly affected by it. They wrote:

> Our teacher has told us about Anne Frank, and we have read her diary. After fifty years, history is repeating itself right here with this war with the hate and the killing, and with having to hide to save your life. We have no food, heating nor electricity, but these things we can bear. We just cannot bear the hatred around us! We are only twelve years old. We can't influence politics and the war, but we want to live! And we want to stop this madness. Like Anne Frank fifty years ago, we wait for peace. She didn't live to see it. Will we?

Barry van Driel, a close colleague at the Anne Frank House in Amsterdam, was not quite sure what to do with it, so he faxed it over to me at the fledgling eighteen-month-old Anne Frank Trust. Earlier that week I had been chatting to two women Holocaust survivors at the opening night of the play *Kindertransport*. The women were distraught to see children suffering in Europe again as they had done fifty years before, and asked me if there was anything the Anne Frank Trust could do. I explained that we were a small educational organization and what we could do was limited. Besides, our remit was education – we were not an aid charity.

Driving home from the theatre that night, the voice of one of the Holocaust survivors and the shocking fact she told me was echoing, 'To try to break the spirit of the children in the concentration camps, the Nazis told them that they were not wanted by their families anymore and that the only way out was up the chimney.' When I got home I couldn't sleep. I read the fax from Barry over and over again and then discussed it with my husband Tony. The thought that children were suffering from hunger *again* in Europe could not leave me and there had to be something to do about it. It's what Anne Frank would have wished. How could we allow this horror to happen again? I could see the desperation in the eyes of those two Holocaust survivors pleading for some help for the children of Bosnia. My heart could relate to that plea. I felt that through this conversation an opportunity had fallen from the sky to help the children of Bosnia. Perhaps we could run a campaign with an *educational* element to encourage the children of Britain to support the children of Bosnia. I was thinking of a way of how to harness the media to create public awareness. I was virtually a one-man band, with only the help of a part-time administrator, how could I get something started?

I knew Bradley Viner, the popular vet on the Good Morning TV (GMTV) breakfast show, and I asked if he could speak to the show's producer. I also knew a PR woman who had links to the editor of a national newspaper. Another contact knew someone at UNICEF. One week after pulling the Bosnian children's letter from the fax machine, armed with huge motivation and the spark of an idea, a meeting was arranged with representatives from GMTV, UNICEF and the PR contact in the Fleet Street office of the *Sunday People,* editor-in-chief Bridget Rowe. Sitting in that room, it was yet another of many situations where I thought to myself: 'How the hell did I get here?'

After two hours of exchanging thoughts and throwing ideas in the air, we came up with the 'Anne Frank Children to Children Appeal for Bosnia', the name of the campaign agreed by all in Bridget's office. The concept was simple: children in the UK would be asked to send a letter to the children of Bosnia who were trapped in the war, showing their care and support. There was a feeling hovering in that office that the spirit of Anne Frank was about to link children across Europe.

The 'Anne Frank Children to Children Campaign for Bosnia' was launched by an appeal on the GMTV Breakfast Show in March 1993. I sat on the sofa with the presenters Eamonn Holmes and Lorraine Kelly and explained how we were asking for every British child to send a letter of support to a child in Bosnia. I hoped that thousands of children would be watching as they tucked into their cornflakes before going off to school. And maybe some teachers too, who would take the idea into their classrooms. I instructed the children to write on the envelope the word 'ZDRAVO' which means 'Hello' in the Serbo-Croat language. I also suggested adding the Serbo-Croat words for, 'I wish you peace and I care about you'. Writers were asked to put their age on the front of the envelope so they could be delivered to similar-aged children, and if possible to include a small token, such as a hair slide, a page of stickers or a friendship bracelet, to remind the Bosnian children of normality – and childhood. However, I did explain that this was not a pen pal scheme and the British children should not expect a response from a child who was caught up in war and also that the letters would be delivered to children from all sides of the conflict, whether Serb, Croat or Muslim.

As the letters started to arrive and the plan was becoming a reality, it was all set up for the delivery to Bosnia to be undertaken by the Post Office. But to my horror, when I called the Post Office regarding the first batch of letters waiting to be delivered, I was told by a regional manager that the Post Office had just stopped all their deliveries into the war zone. This was a disaster. How could we disappoint the children of Bosnia, as well as the British children who were busy composing their letters of support? I had managed to expose the idea to millions of people all across the UK, and now they would be let down due to a logistics problem.

Suddenly the phone on my desk rang. I was not in the mood to answer any phone calls as I was so frustrated. Thankfully Ruth, my administrator, answered it. It was the UNICEF press officer on the line phoning for an update on the campaign. When I shared with her my frustration about the failure of delivering the letters to Bosnia, she made a brilliant suggestion to solve the problem by taking some of them on her next trip to Bosnia. She also offered to connect me with a group of gung-ho and fearless young New Zealanders who were driving supply trucks from London to Bosnia. Their set up was called 'The Serious Road Trip' and their missions were indeed serious. I went to meet them in their Camden warehouse and they agreed to collect all the letters and deliver them to Bosnia.

At 7.00 a.m. on a bright morning in May 1993 a group of people assembled on the South Bank of the Thames alongside the TV studios. We were to be filmed for GMTV loading the truck with boxes containing no less than 100,000 letters and gifts. We were joined by several school groups and our co-founder Bee Klug and her husband, both by then elderly but still passionately involved. Everyone helped them load the trucks. After making sure everything was properly loaded, the trucks were secured and our grateful goodbyes to the convoy were said, the engine revved up and the truck was off on its way, leaving long smoke trails behind as it slowly disappeared in the distance.

Travelling on the convoy was a young woman reporter for the *Sunday People* newspaper. Her name was Ruki Sayid, small but feisty and not overly bothered by the fact that as a Muslim she might be given a hard time at the Serb checkpoints and possibly even jeopardize her safety. The drive across Europe to Bosnia took three days, but once across the Bosnian border, driving into the city of Zenica took even longer, due to the interminable waits to get through checkpoints. All around they could hear the sounds of gunfire and shelling. As they approached the first Serb checkpoint, Ruki's cavalier attitude was deflated, and she felt her first real concern when the armed soldiers demanded to go through the trucks' contents box by box. But then when the soldiers saw the letters and colourful gifts crammed inside the boxes, they directed the trucks to a Serb village a few miles up the road so that these children too could receive some of the goodies. At each checkpoint, the contents of the trucks were scrupulously inspected by the Serb Army, and only when the soldiers were satisfied that they were not transporting guns or ammunition were they allowed to proceed. The first stop in Zenica was to be the school where the original letter from the class of 12-year-olds had been sent from. When the truck eventually arrived at the school, Ruki and the guys found to their shock it had been closed down and turned into a refugee centre. The class of 12-year-olds could not be traced. The children's question about whether they would 'live to see peace' may have in some cases been premonitory. The convoy left some of the letters and gifts for the children at the refugee centre and headed on towards the ravaged city of Sarajevo, which had just thirteen years earlier been the proud location for the 1980 Winter Olympics. When 'The Serious Road Trip' got to the city, the letters were handed over to the UNICEF team, who delivered a consignment to children in a hospital and then made an appeal on the local radio station for children to come and collect letters and gifts.

Edith Simmons-Richner was working as the Liaison Officer for UNICEF in the Former Yugoslavia. She was travelling regularly through Croatia, Serbia, Sarajevo and Bosnia-Herzegovina managing a wonderful project called 'I Dream of Peace', which encouraged children throughout the former Yugoslavia to draw and write about their situation in the war and their hopes for the future. (An exhibition of the 'I Dream of Peace' drawings and paintings was later shown at the Anne Frank House and a book published by UNICEF sold all over the world.) I had first been put in contact with Edith while she was in Zagreb and she immediately became enthusiastic about the Anne Frank letter-writing campaign. Edith described the situation in Sarajevo when the convoy with our letters had arrived.

> Sarajevo was under siege and, on top of daily bombings, people were also targeted by snipers from the surrounding hills; it was very dangerous. Children no longer went to school and many hid with their families in cellars because groups were easy targets. I often visited families, and especially children, in their cellars and in the hospital. Children missed school terribly and often asked me if I had seen their teacher. So, instead of children going to school, UNICEF facilitated teachers to visit children and teach in the cellars. When your letters arrived in Sarajevo, they were distributed along with vital distributions of food and other survival items.

Edith reminded me that the Anne Frank Children to Children Campaign had inspired the Holocaust Education Trust in Albany, New York State, to send a delivery of teddy bears for the children in Sarajevo hospitals to cuddle during their treatment.

The 'Anne Frank Children to Children Appeal for Bosnia' lasted three weeks. There was no internet, email, or social media in 1993 but nonetheless the idea of Anne Frank's spirit linking children across Europe captured the imagination of the country. We received over 100,000 letters and gifts, including one from Zimbabwe and ironically we even had a few from the Netherlands. Some envelopes said 'From a Mother to a Mother' or 'From a Teacher to a Teacher'. The Mars confectionery company sent a crate of chocolate bars to be distributed to the children. Penguin Books sent a box of fluffy toy penguins, one of which sat on the truck's dashboard on its journey across Europe, and I am sure its defiant presence helped dissuade any snipers from targeting the truck. The letters and gifts had meant so much to the Bosnian children and were so gratefully received that UNICEF asked if the Anne Frank Trust could continue the campaign. We were flattered to have been asked and willing to do so, but with the Trust at that time consisting of just me and Ruth, it was impossible.

Towards the end of the campaign Ruth and I paid a final visit to 'The Serious Road Trip's' Camden warehouse and took photos of each other sitting waist-deep in letters and parcels. I can't describe my feeling of joy that Anne Frank's letter appeal had so captured the imagination of children.

In the spring of 1993 the 'Anne Frank Children to Children Appeal' for Bosnia had managed to fulfil the plea of the Holocaust survivors with whom I had a conversation that had echoed in my head all that night. The campaign had achieved in three weeks what we had set out to do – to show British children that they can take responsibility for children caught in war in faraway places and most importantly to send a message to the children trapped in war that they are not forgotten and there are others who care about them. We wanted to ensure that the Nazi method of breaking children's spirit by telling them that they were abandoned would not happen again. Anne Frank had brought together the children who suffered and the children who cared.

Zlata Filipović – the Bosnian Anne Frank

The war in Bosnia and Herzegovina was characterized by bitter fighting, indiscriminate shelling of towns and cities, ethnic cleansing and systematic mass rape. By the end of the conflict over 200,000 people had been killed, injured or missing, including those who had died from hunger or exposure. The Siege of Sarajevo, the longest siege of a capital city in modern history, lasted even longer than the notorious Siege of Leningrad in the Second World War.

After being first besieged by the forces of the Yugoslav People's Army, Sarajevo was then besieged by the Serbian Army between April 1992 and February 1996. The city was encircled by 13,000 Serbian soldiers stationed in the surrounding hills, from where they continually assaulted the city with artillery, tanks and small arms. Ten thousand civilians, including 1,500 children, were killed in Sarajevo during the 46-month-long siege.

Sarajevo's people fought desperately to defend themselves against shelling, starvation and the loss of everything they knew. 'Sniper Alley' became a notorious street where desperate civilians ran to get food and supplies, darting from side to side of the road to avoid the bullets. An elderly man was captured on camera lying dead beside two loaves of bread he managed to buy for his besieged family. Thousands of children also found themselves trapped. They could not play in the streets or playgrounds, they could not go to school and they could not see their friends. The children could not understand the meaning of the term 'war'.

Eleven-year-old Zlata Filipović was one of those children. Up until the spring of 1992 Zlata had enjoyed an idyllic childhood, brought up in a comfortable professional family as an only child. Like Anne Frank she enjoyed holidays, in Zlata's case spent on the Croatian coast or skiing in the mountains. Zlata's father was a lawyer and she loved playing in his office. As an avid reader and writer she appreciated having this easy access to paper, pens and stationery. Zlata grew up with no knowledge of who happened to be Serb, Muslim, Croat, Jewish or Catholic and finding herself trapped in a war zone was totally strange to her. 'When I read Anne's diary, I thought that wars only happened in history, not in Europe anymore and certainly not in my home,' she told me when I first met her in London in 1995. Later on, Zlata described to me how she felt for the fate of that 'incredibly talented writer and beautiful person called Anne Frank'. Having read *Anne Frank, The Diary of a Young Girl*, Zlata decided to start writing about being trapped in Sarajevo as the bombs rained down. She was also inspired by a friend who kept a diary, who was three years older and she considered 'pretty cool'. Copying Anne Frank's idea, she then made a list of names for her diary, most of which were comical, but then settled on Mimmy, in honour of her recently-deceased goldfish of the same name. As Zlata started to put pen to paper, little did this 11-year-old realize that she would soon become known around the world as 'The Anne Frank of Sarajevo'.

The brutal war was difficult for Zlata's family, particularly the siege which was intolerable. 'Only those who were in it could understand the feeling of being under siege,' said Meric Sidran, a 23-year-old student who managed to flee Sarajevo. 'The feeling that you are alive but limited, capable but controlled by others, could freak the most relaxed person.' Zlata's handwritten notebook detailed her day to day life, her reaction to the war, her dreams of peace and fears for the future. Just like Anne Frank, Zlata dreams of going to the park again, playing with her friends and doing the things she used to. Anne Frank had hidden with her family in rooms above her father's workplace, and in a vertical reversal Zlata hid in the basement *below* the family's home in the centre of Sarajevo. Anne wrote poignantly about leaving her beloved cat Moortje behind when going into hiding, while Zlata writes about how her canary Cico died because they couldn't get enough food for him.

Zlata's diary was first published as a pamphlet by UNICEF and then picked up by French journalists. The manuscript was bought by a French publisher, who pulled all possible strings to evacuate the family to France. Recalling her escape twenty years later to the *Daily Telegraph* she said, 'It was bizarre. If you were wounded, or an orphan, or sick, you could never have got out of Sarajevo. But we did.' Leaving the besieged city in a UN truck, she remembers staring out of the tiny windows at the post office, her school and the city she grew up in as they sped away. After crossing the border, they first went to Paris, where Zlata started to settle in and recalls even fancying a boy, but then the family moved on to Dublin. As a student of English from childhood she found no problem in settling there and found the people warm and welcoming. She now speaks with a soft and distinctive Irish accent.

In a speech at the opening of the Anne Frank exhibition in Dublin in 2013, Zlata described her discomfort and embarrassment at the time with being described as another 'Anne Frank' as she knew that Anne's writing was much more advanced and mature than hers as an 11-year-old. But as a worldly adult she was pragmatic at the description. 'I guess that's what journalists do. There's an Anne Frank of Afghanistan (Latifa), of Pakistan (Malala), and probably now of Syria. But in my mind there's only one Anne Frank.' But recently she has confided in me an additional reason for her resistance to the comparison with Anne Frank. 'There were 900 bombs falling on the city of Sarajevo. I was a superstitious kid. I didn't want to be the Anne Frank of Sarajevo as I was terrified my fate would be the same as hers.'

Fig 2. Happy and normal family life. Edith Frank takes seven-year-old Margot and three-year-old Anne on a trip to Frankfurt city centre in March 1933. Hitler has been in power for two months, and life for Germany's Jews is about to change. Photo courtesy of the Anne Frank Fonds in Basel, via Getty Images.

Fig 3. In May 1941, the photographer Frans Dupont took a series of exquisitely posed studio images of eleven-year-old Anne. Photo by Frans Dupont/ the Anne Frank Fonds in Basel, via Getty Images.

Fig 4. (a) The front cover and (b) inside of Anne's original diary with photos she pasted inside it. From the Anne Frank House collection.

Fig 5. The first Anne Frank traveling exhibition *Anne Frank in the World 1929-1945* was monochrome and huge in scale. Here it is on show in Glasgow in 1990. From the Anne Frank House collection.

Fig 6. Otto Frank and his wife Fritzi visiting Audrey Hepburn at her home in Switzerland, circa 1957. A copy of this photo was given to me in Los Angeles by Audrey's son, Sean Hepburn Ferrer. It was taken by his late father, the actor Mel Ferrer.

Fig 7. Anne Frank's cousin Bernd 'Buddy' Elias reads the Anne Frank Declaration to United Nations General Secretary Kofi Annan at UN headquarters in New York in January 1999. Those watching include (from left) footballer and UN Ambassador John Fashanu; my late husband Tony Bogush; the UK's Ambassador to the UN Sir Jeremy Greenstock; Eva Schloss; myself and at back right, Barry van Driel, who composed the Declaration. Photo: UN photographer, from the Anne Frank Trust collection.

Fig 8. A very special memory of attending the 1996 Academy Awards in Hollywood with Miep Gies. Jon Blair, the writer and director of the Oscar winning documentary feature *Anne Frank Remembered* is at the back on the right. Photo: Jerome Goldblatt.

Fig 9. Anne Frank House International Director Jan Erik Dubbelman greets Japanese children coming to the exhibition in Tokyo in 2010 Photo: Aaron Peterer, Anne Frank House collection.

Fig 10. Latvian and Russian teenagers performing together in *The Dreams of Anne Frank* Riga, 1998. For some it was their first opportunity to interact socially. From the Anne Frank House collection.

Fig 11. Student peer guides in the South African township of Orlando West with Aaron Peterer of the Anne Frank House education team (centre right back). Photo: Gift Mabunda, 2009 from the Anne Frank House collection.

Fig 12. Eva Schloss with a prisoner guide (face obscured) at Wormwood Scrubs Prison in London. On the right is Steve Gadd, the Anne Frank Trust prison tour manager. Photo: Mark McEvoy for the Anne Frank Trust.

Fig 13. Dutch Foreign Minister Maxime Verhagen (with red tie) is shown around the *Anne Frank, A History for Today* exhibition at the CEU Paraisopolis School in Sao Paulo, 2010. His enthusiastic and knowledgeable guides are as young as ten and eleven. Photo: Riccardo Sanchez for the Instituto Plataforma Brasil.

Fig 14. Anne Frank Ambassadors show schools and members of the public around the *Anne Frank + You* exhibition at Bradford College in West Yorkshire in 2013. With thanks to Bradford Metropolitan District Council and the Anne Frank Trust.

Fig 15. Anne Frank peer guides at the Forest Gate School in London. From the Anne Frank Trust collection.

Fig 16. After the thirty-year-long Sri Lankan civil war, the *Anne Frank, A History for Today* exhibition gave students in Jaffna an opportunity to reflect on their recent past and future. From the Anne Frank House collection.

Zlata's Diary, A Child's Life in Wartorn Sarajevo had first been published by UNICEF in 1993 while Zlata was still living in Bosnia. It was then picked up by countries around the world and her name became internationally known. She was first given the title the 'Anne Frank of Sarajevo' by the American journalist Janine di Giovanni and then other journalists followed suit. She had not known at the time about the Anne Frank Trust's letter-writing appeal in 1993 as the family only used the radio once a day to preserve the batteries. She had received a letter from a school in America and she told me how much it had meant to her not to be forgotten by the outside world. When she heard that I had run the letter-writing campaign with the aid of one staff member and that it had generated 100,000 letters she gasped and profoundly thanked me on behalf of the children of Sarajevo. Even twenty-three years later, hearing this response from someone who had been on the other side was emotional and humbling.

The Anne Frank Exhibition goes to Bosnia

Mostar was a medieval city and the cultural capital of Herzegovina. The city got its name from the bridge keepers (*mostari*) who in medieval times guarded the *Stari Most* (Old Bridge) over the River Neretva, which had been built by the Ottomans in the sixteenth century. It was one of Bosnia and Herzegovina's most recognizable landmarks and considered one of the most outstanding examples of Islamic architecture in the Balkans.

In November 1993, like many of Mostar's bridges and over 2,000 of its citizens who were killed, the Old Bridge became a victim of the Bosnian war when it was destroyed by a Croatian army tank, effectively dividing the Muslim community on the east bank and the Croatian community on the west bank. The Bosnian war was officially ended by the signing of the Dayton Agreement in December 1995. Soon afterwards, the great Italian operatic tenor Luciano Pavarotti, along with artistes such as Brian Eno, U2 and others, used a series of concerts called 'Pavarotti and Friends', to raise funds to set up a music and arts centre to help heal the war-damaged children of the town, where there was 'too much trauma'. The Pavarotti Music Centre opened in December 1997 providing music education for young people, as well as dance classes and theatre performances. There was even a small recording studio.

The centre's trauma therapists decided the children needed to be introduced to a different history and so approached the Anne Frank House to bring the Anne Frank exhibition. The Holocaust had extended to Bosnia and Herzegovina, which was annexed by the Nazi puppet 'Independent State of Croatia' and 10,000 of the country's pre-war 14,000-strong Jewish community were murdered. During the more recent Balkans war, the tiny remaining Jewish community, who were not targets of the violence, had taken part in the relief effort.

In the summer of 1998, the Anne Frank exhibition arrived along with the educator and facilitator Barry van Driel, my colleague who had faxed the children's letter from Zenica to me in 1993. During his preparations for the event, Barry came to realize that although the war was over, the conflict was still very raw. The exhibition panels could not be flown directly into Bosnia so were flown to Split in Croatia, and then hidden under blankets in the back of a van, driven across the border and on to Mostar.

For Barry, who was in the back of the van with the hidden panels, it was pretty hairy. He had first visited the Pavarotti Music Centre while it was being built and had almost been killed by a falling beam. He lay in the back of the van considering what he was doing in such a dangerous place. But even on arrival at the Centre it was not all plain sailing. Barry's usual method of working was to start the project off with a teachers' seminar to discuss the level of knowledge and issues that needed to be addressed. The Pavarotti Centre was situated on the predominantly Muslim east side of the river and teachers from the west Croatian side refused to come and sit in the same room as the Muslims. And then Barry as a Dutchman became the subject of suspicion.

The year before, in July 1995, Dutch UN peacekeepers in Srebrenica had failed to prevent a massacre of over 8,000 Muslim men and boys that had been carried out by units of the Bosnian Serb army under their noses. It was described by UN Secretary General Kofi Annan as the 'worst crime carried out on European soil since the Second World War'. Waiting to start his workshop and training session, Barry was confronted by a participating teacher with the question, 'How can the Dutch *dare* to talk about human rights issues?' A long and difficult discussion followed and after some four hours, frustratingly cutting into the seminar time, Barry was able to convince the teachers that the Anne Frank House was a non-governmental organization with humanitarian aims. The group eventually became co-operative so he asked them to walk through the exhibition and reflect on its educational value. Their response was unanimous. In the Anne Frank exhibition in post-war Bosnia and Herzegovina they found a message of hope in learning about the reconstruction of Europe after the Second World War. One teacher said: 'We can rebuild our society as Europe did after the Second World War, and despite all the hatred we can do it again.'

Barry then met the young people themselves. He was shocked to find that many of the 13-year-olds were already hardened smokers, who brazenly told him that if they had the money for drugs they would take those too. 'Often these young people could not talk to their own parents, as they too were deeply suffering. I was surprised to see my colleague Henri (drama in education practitioner Henrietta Seebohm) having a smoke with them, but I realized she was finding a way for them to feel comfortable with us.'

In Sarajevo, Barry worked with two boys who were both called Adnan. The younger one, known as Petsa, or 'Little One', went on to inspire the words of the Anne Frank Declaration. The older Adnan was given the role of Otto Frank in the performance of *Dreams of Anne Frank*, a new play by London writer Bernard Kops. Older Adnan's father had been killed in the war and because of the stress he had

118

endured, Adnan was already suffering from a diagnosed heart condition. After the first performance, where he had given a wonderful portrayal of Anne Frank's beloved father, none of the team could find Adnan. He was discovered outside crying his eyes out. Sensing it was something the boy needed to do, Barry and the other children let him be. After two hours of continuous crying, Adnan came back inside. All through the performance he had felt the presence of his own father by his side and told an emotional Barry that he had dedicated his performance to his father. The Muslim Bosniak girl who played Anne thanked Barry and the team for 'letting her sleep again'. Being Anne Frank, even for such a short while, had helped her to process all that had happened during the war.

Thanks to funding from Spain, the spectacular Old Bridge of Mostar was rebuilt and re-opened in 2004. And in the city's community the Anne Frank project in 1996 rebuilt hope for the future.

Chapter 12

Anne Frank and Nelson Mandela

'Some of us read Anne Frank's diary on Robben Island and derived much encouragement from it. It is particularly relevant for the South Africa of today, as we emerge from the treacherous era of apartheid injustice.' Nelson Mandela on opening the 'Anne Frank in the World' exhibition in Johannesburg, August 1994

Just four months after becoming president of the country that had imprisoned him for twenty-seven years, Nelson Mandela opened the 'Anne Frank in the World' exhibition at the Museum Afrika in Johannesburg, South Africa. A small figure in a black-and-white geometric-design shirt, Mr Mandela took to the stage in front of the gathered dignitaries. For most it was the first time they had seen their new president in real life. They craned forward to hear his words. After the usual words of thanks to the organizers and sponsors, Mandela's tone changed. He recalled living through the Second World War as an African: 'My own memories of the Second World War revolve around the hopes of black South Africans that the defeat of Nazism would not only bring about the liberation of Europe but also the liberation of the oppressed in South Africa. But instead, after the War, apartheid triumphed in our country.'

Mandela then remarked on the strong connection between apartheid and Nazism which shared

> the inherently evil belief in the superiority of some races over others. This drove adherents of these ideologies to perpetrate unspeakable crimes and to derive pleasure from the suffering of their fellow human beings. But because these beliefs are patently false, and because they were, and will always be, challenged by the likes of Anne Frank, they are bound to fail. The Anne Frank exhibition is particularly relevant for South Africans as we emerge from the treacherous era of apartheid and injustice, exploring the past in order to heal, to reconcile and to build the future.

And then to the surprise and fascination of the audience, Mr Mandela explained that he had read *The Diary of Anne Frank* while incarcerated on Robben Island for eighteen of the twenty-seven years of his imprisonment. 'It kept our spirits high and reinforced our confidence in the invincibility of the cause of freedom and justice.' He said that he had first read Anne's diary even before he went into prison, but felt that what he derived from books he had read before his incarceration was totally different from what he received from the same book read while in prison.

> The lessons of that tragedy sunk more deeply into our souls and encouraged us in our situation. Her life was one on which young people could model their own lives. What we took away from Anne Frank was the invincibility of the human spirit which expresses itself in different ways in different situations. By honouring the memory of Anne Frank we are saying with one voice, 'never again'.

Mr Mandela went on to relate the astonishing story of what the prisoners had done at great personal risk to rescue Anne's diary when it had nearly been destroyed. In the 1960s, while kept in Robben Island prison, 12km off the coast of Cape Town and yet clearly visible to its residents, Nelson Mandela had set up what he has described in his autobiography *Long Walk to Freedom* as the 'Robben Island University', a learning forum for the prisoners to be well-equipped to continue the struggle for democracy on their long-awaited release. A group of political prisoners confined for decades in the harshest of conditions built a centre of learning not of bricks and mortar, but of intellectual debate.

Spearheaded by Nelson Mandela, the 'University' allowed prisoners to lecture on their respective areas of expertise and debate wide-ranging topics including homosexuality and Marxism. In a barren limestone quarry on a secluded island, lectures and animated discussions were carried out during the short periods of rest, despite the attentions of the warders who guarded the imprisoned men and oversaw their long days of labouring in the quarry. The lectures and debates took place in snake-infested caves around the quarry during the men's brief respite from breaking stones to take food and shade. One of the books they read and discussed had been Anne Frank's *Diary of a Young Girl*. It had somehow found its way into the collection of books in the small prison library. Mandela had encouraged the prisoners to read her teenage writing as a testament to the strength of the human spirit. After several years the little paperback book had been passed around and thumbed so much that its pages fell out and it became an incoherent and incomplete collection of papers. But the prisoners, avid for the message of hope for a better future that Anne envisioned, took turns to clandestinely copy out the pages by hand and collate them back together, so that the younger prisoners could continue to draw strength from Anne's words. This was a dangerous act performed secretly by candlelight in the various cells at night. What happened to this volume we do not know, but it is one of the most remarkable examples of the place in history of Anne's diary.

I had been told this story myself a few months previously by South African anti-apartheid hero Govan Mbeki. A co-defendant at the notorious Rivonia trial, Mr Mbeki had spent twenty-four years, eighteen of them along with Mr Mandela, as a political prisoner on Robben Island, and was one of the political leaders of the prison. Mr Mbeki and I, along with courageous and long-standing anti-apartheid politician Helen Suzman, were together as speakers at the opening of the exhibition in the city of Port Elizabeth, which was taking place just a few days after the first ever democratic election in the country. Mbeki, by then 84-years-old, with a shock of white hair and stooping from his years of hard labour, took me aside as I showed him around the exhibition and quietly told me the story about Anne's diary on Robben Island, and about his own many years as a political prisoner. Mbeki died in 2001, and lived long enough to see his own son Thabo succeed Nelson Mandela as the second President of democratic South Africa.

In 2008, I took the ferry boat across Cape Town Harbour to Robben Island, where former political prisoners from those terrible years act as guides for visitors. Looking into the small cell where Mandela had spent so many years of his remarkable life, I imagined Anne's diary secreted in a place only he would know where, emboldening him with the belief that things could one day change. Later that morning a coach took us to the infamous lime quarry, where the 'Robben Island University' had actually been held. There on the parched ground, I spotted an ominous-looking coiled and glossy black snake baking itself in the sun, a reminder that many of the prisoner labourers had actually died from the venom of snake bites.

The Important Role the Anne Frank Exhibition Played in Helping to Create the New and Free South Africa

The timing of the first-ever tour of the Anne Frank exhibition to South Africa in 1994 was accidental. But it proved to be fortuitous, as it played a role in the transition of the country from its difficult past to a new democratic nation.

Back in 1991 a dynamic ball of energy called Myra Osrin was visiting London from her home in Cape Town. Myra, who at the time was co-ordinating the Cape Town Holocaust Memorial Council, had heard about the Anne Frank exhibition that was touring the UK and that I was the person in charge. She was interested in bringing it to a fast changing South Africa. When Myra and I first met we both felt that the timing would be absolutely perfect. Nelson Mandela had been freed from incarceration just a year ago in February 1990, apartheid had been dismantled and the first democratic elections were by then just a couple of years away.

I knew immediately that Myra was going to make the Anne Frank exhibition happen. Her enthusiasm brought in many people who became major sponsors, including the Dutch Embassy and Nedbank, a bank with Dutch roots based in South Africa. After months of planning, many international phone calls and faxes, the first ever tour of the Anne Frank exhibition to Africa was about to happen and would take in Cape Town, Port Elizabeth, Durban, Johannesburg, Bloemfontein and Pretoria. To my huge delight I was asked by Anne Frank House director Hans Westra to open the exhibition in Port Elizabeth, planned for May 1994.

One of the reasons for my excitement was because I have my own personal connection to South Africa, but did not wish to visit this beautiful country during the years of apartheid. My maternal grandfather, Sidney Cohen, who was born into a family of impoverished immigrant Polish Jews in the East End of London, had found a job as a cabin boy on a ship sailing to Cape Town a year or two into the twentieth century and just after the Boer War had been fought. Despite the fact that young Sidney was just 13-years-old, he had devised a rather cunning plan. The ship sailed from London Docks, and a few weeks later as Table Mountain came into sight, he went around the ship's crew collecting money for their tobacco needs and kindly offering to go ashore to get their supplies. Once ashore, and with the money in his pocket, he fled. He hid in Cape Town until he saw the ship heading over the horizon to head back northwards up the coast of Africa. The young teenager managed to get a job taking him up-country peddling New Testament bibles in African villages. After several years working in customs and excise at Cape Town harbour, the adult Sidney came back to England, met my grandmother Kate and duly settled in Cardiff.

The months leading up to the opening of the Anne Frank exhibition tour coincided with the country preparing for its first democratic election and the expected transfer of power from white to black. Myra Osrin recalls:

> Before the election we were busy running Anne Frank workshops and for the first ever time black, white and coloured educators were in the same room and engaging with one another. This gave one of the most important sectors of the community, the educators, an opportunity to share with each other their experiences. I don't say the Anne Frank exhibition was the only thing to help with the transition of the country, but I do believe it was one of them. The project had two primary intentions. First, to educate people about the history of the Holocaust; second, to use the Holocaust story to teach people about the evils of discrimination and the importance of human rights.

The timing for me turned out to be perfect. I arrived in Port Elizabeth just a couple of days after the election on 27 April, and in time for the announcement that there would be a government of 'national unity'. The new multi-coloured flag reflected what Mandela hoped would become the rainbow nation. Mandela showed an estimable degree of pragmatism in putting the needs of the new nation first, over and above any feelings of bitterness towards his former oppressors, by including in his new government representatives of the previous white status quo who had much-needed skills and experience.

After spending a few days in Port Elizabeth training an enthusiastic team of volunteer guides, I flew to Johannesburg to meet up with Tony, as we were heading on for a holiday at Victoria Falls in Zimbabwe. We had been warned by concerned friends that we should cancel our Johannesburg leg of the tour, as there had been violence and bombings in the run-up to the election. I flew back from Port Elizabeth to Johannesburg and met Tony's flight at the airport. We arrived at the Sandton Sun Hotel, and had been in our room unpacking for barely thirty minutes when I noticed a note slipped under our door. It was from the hotel management apologizing for any disruption to our stay. The security would be very tight as they had forty-nine heads of state and presidents arriving at the hotel for the period of Mr Mandela's inauguration. Security, disruption – who cared? I certainly didn't.

Over the coming days you could not sit in the Sandon Sun hotel lobby without coming across a president, a head of state or maybe several in earnest conversation over coffee. I left a welcoming note with the hotel's friendly public relations lady addressed to Ireland's President Mary Robinson, who had opened the Anne Frank exhibition in Dublin the year before, and she promised me it would duly be delivered.

The following day, despite having checked out of the hotel, we had taken up our usual people-watching positions in the lobby when Tony spotted Mary Robinson, her husband Nicky and a woman aide heading for the lobby café. We caught up with the presidential party just by the café entrance and had a chat about Anne Frank touring South Africa and the President's memories of the Dublin opening. Just as we turned to leave, Mrs Robinson's aide told me, 'We got your kind note and I've responded to it. The President would like you both to attend her reception this evening.' It appeared the note had been delivered to the reception desk after we had checked out, so the desk staff had ignored it. Tony and I duly appeared at the Irish Ambassador's reception for his President, and started mingling with the predominantly Irish guests. When President and Mr Robinson arrived we were asked to form a line so the President could receive her guests. We felt somewhat like infiltrators as Brits in the long line of Irish people. As we approached the President she looked at us and said laughing: 'Ah you two! I have decided to make you both honorary Irish citizens.' To this day I am not shy about using this great 'honour' whenever visiting Ireland or meeting Irish people.

In that post-election period of May 1994 the atmosphere on the South African streets was electric and euphoric. Everyone we met, whether white, black, or mixed race, told us of their optimism for the future of the country and its new President.

We returned to Port Elizabeth for the 'Anne Frank in the World' exhibition opening at the King George VI Art Gallery. Now known as the Nelson Mandela Metropolitan Art Museum, the gallery is surrounded by lush tropical gardens where Athol Fugard had written several of his acclaimed books and plays. For the journey down to the venue from our hotel, we were crammed into a minibus with the courageous white fighter against apartheid, Helen Suzman. For some thirteen years Mrs Suzman, a petite English-speaking Jewish woman in an arena dominated by Calvinist Afrikaner men, was the sole white voice of conscience in the South African parliament, speaking out against the injustices and humiliations the black, coloured and mixed race people were subjected to. While some of her political enemies came to admire her, most loathed her, and tried to drive her from their presence. In Parliamentary sessions, they jeered her interventions with sexist, anti-Semitic and domineering abuse. She was often harassed by the police and her phone was tapped by them.

Like so many, I had long been an admirer of the fortitude of Helen Suzman. And now here was I in the spring of 1994, listening to this rather genteel looking elderly lady, in navy blue suit and pearls, venting her anger that so many black South Africans in the countryside had not received their ballot papers in time to vote. They had waited a lifetime for the democratic exercise that we in Britain take so much for granted. Mandela remained a long-time admirer of Helen Suzman, telling her 'the consistency with which you defended the basic values of freedom and the rule of law over the last three decades has earned you the admiration of many South Africans'. Helen Suzman died at the age of 91 in 2009, by then an Honorary Dame Commander of the Order of the British Empire, and I was honoured to receive an invitation from her daughter to attend her mother's memorial service in London. But I will never forget my feeling of enormous pride when this great lady came up to me on that evening in Port Elizabeth and told me how much she had loved my speech.

The Anne Frank exhibition tour of South Africa was remarkable. In Cape Town, children from the elite white private schools went around the Anne Frank exhibition together with children from the black townships. One day a busload of children arrived from the sprawling black township of Khayelitsha, on the outskirts of the city. At the end of the visit the teacher approached Myra Osrin to thank her. 'You will never know what it has meant for our students' self-esteem. For the first time ever they have seen that a person could be discriminated against if they don't have a black skin.'

The South African Legacy of the Anne Frank Exhibition

And what of the ball of energy and passion that was Myra Osrin? Did she take it easy after the gruelling months of the South African Anne Frank exhibition tour? Not a bit of it. Four years later, Myra went on to create the first Holocaust museum on the continent of Africa, the Cape Town Holocaust Centre, which opened its doors in 1999. In the small space that had been found for the centre, a beautiful exhibition was created, set up under the guidance of Dr Stephen Smith, who had created a similar exhibition in the heart of England, which had been Britain's very first Holocaust centre too.

In 2005 Holocaust education became a mandatory curriculum subject in South Africa. The government of President Thabo Mbeki wanted South African pupils to understand the value of human rights through learning about human experiences in the Holocaust. Under Myra's leadership the centre rose to the challenge, and also expanded operations by creating similar centres in Johannesburg and Durban. Myra understood that there was a huge potential for Holocaust education to help with the transformation process of the country. She realized that what happened a long time ago to other people could be a useful tool for educators.

The Anne Frank House International Department has continued working and playing a role in the new South Africa for many years after the Anne Frank exhibition tour of 1994 had left, particularly in underprivileged communities. Jan Erik Dubbelman and Aaron Peterer, an experienced Anne Frank House educator, visited the country many times to work with children in the townships, training them to become peer educators and empowering them to be part of South Africa's future.

Aaron, of mixed Indian and Austrian parentage, had first joined the Anne Frank House in 2001 as a volunteer for the Austrian youth and memorialization service, the Gedenkdienst. This organization deals with the causes and consequences of the crimes of Nazism and sends young volunteers to work with relevant organizations that help Holocaust survivors or are in the field of Holocaust education.

In 2008, as part of the international team, Aaron and Jan Erik visited Durban, the third largest city in South Africa, for the opening of the city's new Holocaust Centre and its dedicated Anne Frank section. This visit was of particular significance to Aaron, as his great grandfather had arrived in Durban from India in the early twentieth century. Durban was known as the largest 'Indian' city outside India, as from 1860 to the early twentieth century over 150,000 Indians had been brought to Natal to work as labourers in the sugar cane fields.

Also living in the same area of the city was an Indian lawyer called Mohandas Karamchand Gandhi, who was a regular visitor to Aaron's great grandfather's house. Gandhi had come to Durban in 1893 as a newly-qualified lawyer, sent on a temporary assignment to act on behalf of a local Indian trader involved in a commercial dispute. What was meant to be a short stay for the young lawyer turned into twenty-one years. By the time Gandhi left South Africa to return to India for the last time in 1914, he had already earned the title Mahatma (Great Soul) for his work in securing significant legal concessions for the local Indian population in South Africa. His strategy and form of action known as *Satyagraha* (truth-force), in which campaigners went on peaceful marches and presented themselves for arrest in protest against unjust laws, became one of the great political tools of the twentieth century, influencing the civil rights movement in the United States and the African National Congress in its early years of struggle against apartheid in South Africa.

Aaron and Jan Erik Dubbelman then went on to Johannesburg to set up educational workshops in advance of bringing a new Anne Frank exhibition to South Africa. Echoing what Myra Osrin had told me about the pre-Anne Frank exhibition teachers workshops of 1993, they started to bring children together who were neighbours but who would normally have never got to meet. These included children from the township of Soweto and those from elite private schools. To break down barriers of suspicion the workshops started with the kids sharing the latest music and dance moves.

Aaron recalled one particular township school they visited. The teachers were mostly drunk and the children sold their school books to buy cheap drugs. One drug they used was called Tuc. 'It was made from a cocktail of rat poison, bleach and HIV medicine, all of which the kids could acquire for free. In that place

13-year-olds looked like 50-year-olds. Even the police considered it a no-go area. The schools themselves looked like derelict fortresses with rusty barbed wire and broken windows.'

The deprivation was such that Aaron found 17-year-olds sucking their thumbs. He found out that this was to help stave off the hunger pangs felt during the day.

> For the workshops we brought in tons of cookies. But they didn't eat them – they collected them to take home and share out among their families. The Anne Frank House paid for a full lunch for the kids so they would have the mental energy for their learning. After the lunches two thirds of the kids would fall asleep on their desks – they weren't used to their stomachs being so full. It was really heart-breaking.

The Anne Frank House team partnered up with the Hector Pieterson Museum, named after the 13-year-old boy who was killed in Soweto by police in the 1976 school uprising against the introduction of English and Afrikaans as dual instruction languages in schools. The photo of Hector's lifeless body being carried by another student accompanied by his distraught sister was published all over the world and Hector became a symbol of the struggle against apartheid. Members of the Hector Pieterson Museum Youth Division were trained by Aaron to act as exhibition peer guides. One of these boys, Bhekithemba Melusi Mbata, subsequently wrote about what it had meant to him to guide at the Anne Frank exhibition for a writing competition sponsored by the US Embassy. He was one of two South African winners and was sent to the US as his prize to meet other youngsters. Bhekithemba has become a great success story. He is now at university and politically active, and still insisting that his work as an Anne Frank exhibition peer guide had set his life 'on the right road'.

Aaron summed up what he felt the impact of the Anne Frank work had been.

> Every time I take a workshop, I am more inspired and satisfied. I see multipliers who will become instruments of change in their own society. Especially in the Third World where being an Anne Frank guide can really change your life. In Europe kids have chances and opportunities to become critical thinkers. But in the Third World it is a battle for survival every day.

By 2010, Nelson Mandela was hardly ever seen in public, as his health had been deteriorating over the months. In December 2013, I was in New York when I heard the news that Nelson Mandela had passed away after his long fading from view. The world seemed a different place with his passing.

Chapter 13

Anne Frank and her Protector Miep Gies

Austrian-born Miep Gies worked for Otto Frank's Opekta business and was one of the five courageous people who looked after the Frank family and the four other people in hiding on the Prinsengracht from 1942 to 1944. She put her own life at serious risk every day for over two years.

'In a town of celluloid heroes, please meet a real one,' said the film director Jon Blair when he introduced white-haired Miep Gies to the glittering audience of the 68th Academy Awards in Hollywood, and to one billion television viewers around the world. It was 25 March 1996 and Jon had just been presented with an Oscar™ statuette for his two-hour documentary film *Anne Frank Remembered*. He was now in turn introducing the world to Miep Gies, the woman who had risked her life to help the Frank family while they were in perilous hiding. When the audience realized who the lady on the stage was, they rose as one to their feet, and the likes of Meryl Streep, Michael Douglas and Brad Pitt broke into rapturous applause. On that Oscars night in the spring of 1996, Miep was 87-years-of-age. She went on to live to be 100 and died in January 2010, just one month before her 101st birthday.

As a teenager Miep had kept a personal journal. I am sure this is why she felt so much empathy for Anne while watching her busy writing in the secret annexe, why she had been so protective of Anne's diary as she kept it safe in a drawer awaiting its owner's return from the camps, and why she could not bring herself to look into its pages until two years after she had handed it back to Otto Frank, the person who had originally purchased the little red-check notebook for his daughter.

Miep had arrived in Amsterdam as a young girl soon after the First World War, sent by her parents to an adoptive family so that she would not have to suffer the privations of a defeated Austria. The Netherlands was seen as a land of milk, butter and cheese, the proteins needed for a nutritious diet. As a young adult woman living in Amsterdam in 1933, Miep was looking for work. Her neighbour, a travelling saleswoman called Sientje Blitz, mentioned that there was a temporary vacancy for an office worker in the company where she worked, and offered to introduce Miep to her boss. It was a spice and pectin firm called Opekta, whose director was the German émigré Otto Frank. Miep was duly interviewed by Mr Frank and employed. History works in strange and unforeseen ways. If it had not been for Sientje Blitz's spontaneous suggestion to help a friend get work, Anne Frank's diary would probably not have been gathered up and protected by that same friend in August 1944. Sientje and her family moved to South Africa before the German invasion of the Netherlands and so survived the Holocaust. Her daughter-in-law Mary and Mary's own daughter-in-law Cara visited me at the Anne Frank Trust in 2013. In that same year Cara's 12-year-old daughter Tali paid a visit to the Anne Frank House with her London school and surprised the staff at the museum when she explained her close connection to Anne Frank's story through her great grandmother.

Pectin is the setting agent for jam and, as part of her role for Opekta, Miep became an expert on jam-making, advising Dutch housewives on how to use pectin for successful results. Visitors to the Anne Frank House can still see a short film clip of the young Miep demonstrating jam-making. In 1941, the year following the German invasion of the Netherlands, Miep married Jan Gies, a bookkeeper. Jan performed heroics in his own right as he was clandestinely working with the Dutch Resistance. Indeed, unknown to the eight people Miep and Jan went on to assist in the secret annexe, the young couple were for some of that time also hiding in their own home a young Dutch man who had refused to join the Nazi Party.

By the spring of 1942, Otto Frank started to make plans to prepare a refuge for his family. He called Miep into his office and shared his secret with her, which at that time neither of his young daughters knew anything about. When, in early July, the time duly came for Mr Frank to carry out the planned hiding, it was Miep and Jan Gies, along with Mr Frank's equally trusted staff members Johannes Kleiman, Victor Kugler and Bep Voskuijl, that he turned to. They did not let him down and for over two years shared the enormity of their actions amongst themselves.

On that fateful Friday morning of 4 August 1944, when the Gestapo and Dutch police came to arrest the Frank family and the other Jews in hiding, Miep had been working in the office. She recalled that it had started as a particularly beautiful sunny day and she had paid a visit to the hiding place above to collect a shopping list of requirements from Edith Frank. Just two months after D-Day, hopes were rising among the Frank and van Pels families and Fritz Pfeffer that the Allied armies would soon liberate the whole of the country and they would be free to continue their lives (in fact the first Allied forces did not enter the Netherlands until September and the country was not completely liberated until the following May). Downstairs in the office, as typewriters were tapping away, ledgers were being completed and other prosaic administrative matters attended to, Miep suddenly looked up and was shocked to see a man in civilian clothes standing in the doorway. He was pointing a loaded revolver at her and the staff. Speaking in Dutch, he told everyone not to move and then walked towards the back office where Victor Kugler was working. Jo Kleiman looked at Miep and said softly the words they had all been dreading, 'Miep, I think the time has come.'

After several conversations with Kugler and Kleiman, the Dutch Nazi sat down opposite Miep, picked up the telephone and chillingly called for 'a car to be sent to 263 Prinsengracht'. The Jewish families one floor above were still oblivious of what was about to happen to them. The arresting officers then signalled with their guns in the direction of the bookcase that for over two years had successfully concealed the stairs to the hiding place. The brave helpers knew at that moment there was no escape and no choice. Their care and protection of the eight Jews in hiding was over.

Miep had meanwhile recognized the German speaker's Viennese accent and told him that she too was from Vienna in the hope of some degree of leniency. His name was SS-Oberscharführer (Senior Squad Leader) Karl Josef Silberbauer, who had been stationed in Amsterdam. To Silberbauer it was incomprehensible that a fellow Austrian would wish to help save the lives of Jews. He asked her, 'Aren't you ashamed of helping Jewish garbage?' After threatening that he would arrest her husband Jan if she tried to run away, Silberbauer left Miep alone in the office while he went to get on with the business of rounding up the poor unsuspecting Jews upstairs. Soon she heard the shuffling footsteps of her friends Otto, Edith, Margot, Anne, Hermann, Auguste, Peter and Fritz slowly descending the stairs and then the revving of the police truck as they were taken away to start their journeys into the abyss. Miep sat at her desk in a traumatized state for many hours. Her colleagues Jo Kleiman and Victor Kugler had also been arrested. Bep, who was able to leave the scene, eventually returned with Jan and one of the workers from the warehouse who had been totally shocked to hear their former boss and his family had been living two floors above them.

They determined to rescue whatever they could from upstairs. Using Miep's duplicate key, they entered the empty hiding place, and saw a scene of ransacked drawers and objects overturned. In Mr and Mrs Frank's bedroom Miep's eyes lit upon Anne's little notebook lying on the floor, along with the single sheets of paper Anne had used to write on when the notebook had been filled. Acting with speed, in case of the officers' return and the expected arrival of the local Puls & Company removal firm (winners of the contract for the work in taking away the possessions of arrested Jews), Miep and Bep scooped up Anne's papers. They took them downstairs and placed them in Miep's desk drawer to be looked after in the hope of Anne's return after liberation. And then in the evening of what had started as a normal working day, the two women left 263 Prinsengracht and went home.

But Miep's heroics did not end on that Friday evening. She had heard that in that final summer of the war there was a possibility that the freedom of arrested Dutch Jews could be bought. She went around to those in the neighbourhood she felt she could trust and managed to raise a sum of money. With this fund she went to see Silberbauer at the Gestapo headquarters in the south of the city and explained what she wanted. He shrugged and told her to come back the next day to see his commanding officer with her request, which she did.

Again she approached Silberbauer and this time was pointed upstairs to another office. As she entered the room she saw a group of Nazi officers huddled round a table listening intently to a radio. She recognized English coming from it and realized they were listening to BBC 'Allied propaganda'. This was considered a treasonable act for the Nazis, and for Miep to have witnessed this herself was extremely dangerous for all involved. The German officers threw her out of the room and she left the building with the money raised to buy the Jews' freedom still in her purse. As those she had worked so hard and so perilously to protect were boarding the train to Westerbork camp in northern Holland, there was no more she could do for them. Tragically no more.

I was privileged to have spent time with Miep Gies on several occasions in the 1990s. Our first meeting was in November 1991 when Miep and her husband Jan came to London as special guests of Belsize Square Synagogue to open the 'Anne Frank in the World' exhibition. I recall Jan Gies as a tall, white-haired and rather shy man, who despite his own wartime heroism, was content to be the consort of Mrs Gies. He sadly died in early 1993 and Miep spent the next seventeen years a widow.

On one of my early visits to Amsterdam, I visited Miep in her own apartment. During our conversation, she suddenly got up from her chair and went to a drawer. She wanted to share with me her mementoes of the Frank family's time in hiding. She showed me the typed menu card that Anne had created for dinner on the one night Miep and Jan had stayed overnight in the secret annexe. It was actually Miep and Jan's first wedding anniversary. She later described her own feelings about spending just one solitary night in the secret annexe: 'I never slept, I couldn't close my eyes . . . the fright of these people who were locked up in here was so thick I could feel it pressing down on me. It was like a thread of terror pulled taut.'

The other item Miep had pulled from the drawer to show me was a pencilled shopping list Edith Frank had given her for one of her dangerous errands to acquire food for the eight people in hiding. Despite the strict wartime rationing, Miep went on these risky missions to acquire food for herself, her husband and the eight people she supported in hiding (not counting the boy in their home), not once or twice, but for over two long years. Two long years of the fear that must have been attached to each of these shopping trips, relying on the goodwill of suppliers who may well have suspected her but also chose to turn a blind eye. In July 1943 Anne wrote about these vital shopping expeditions, 'Miep has so much to carry she looks like a pack mule. She goes out nearly every day in search of vegetables, and then cycles back with her purchases in large shopping bags. She's also the one who brings five library books with her every Saturday. We long for Saturdays because that means books.'

Whilst I was looking down in wonder at the treasured menu cards and shopping list in the palms of my hands, Miep then disappeared into her bedroom and returned holding a pair of red suede shoes of 1940s style with block heels and thick platform soles. She asked me if I knew anything about these and I nodded as I recalled this evocative entry in Anne's diary:

> Everywhere I go, upstairs or down, they all cast admiring glances at my feet, which are adorned by a pair of exceptionally beautiful (for times like these!) shoes. Miep managed to snap them up for 27.50 guilders.

Burgundy coloured suede and leather with medium-sized high heels. I feel as if I'm on stilts, and look even taller than I already am.

I found myself stroking the shoes that Anne herself had worn. To be shown these items by Miep herself, and in her own home, was a special privilege that I shall always hold dear.

On another occasion I took Miep to the BBC's Broadcasting House in the centre of London to record an interview for *Woman's Hour*, the long-running and popular magazine show. Although much modernized and expanded now, in the 1990s Broadcasting House still had the feel of the Art Deco architectural icon it then was. As we walked through the maze of corridors to the studio, Miep told me that the BBC, and the radio broadcasts from London they had listened to clandestinely, became their lifeline during those terrible war years. Being in that building was something very special for her. In the taxi on our way back she spoke about her memories of Anne, sitting at a desk in hiding writing her diary. One day Anne had become angry that Miep's arrival had interrupted her train of thought and she shouted at her, 'You know Miep I am writing my diary. And you're in it!' (Miep had understood this was not complimentary.) However, Anne did truly understand the risk their helpers were putting themselves through. In January 1944 she had written about the bravery of the Dutch Resistance:

> It's amazing how much these generous and unselfish people do, risking their own lives to help and save others. The best example of this is our own helpers, who have managed to pull us through so far and will hopefully bring us safely to shore, because otherwise they'll find themselves sharing the fate of those they're trying to protect. Never have they uttered a single word about the burden we must be, never have they complained that we're too much trouble.

Miep also spoke to me at length about Edith Frank, and how worried and frightened Edith had been that there would be a terrible outcome. Many times as Miep had been leaving the hiding place Edith had followed her down the stairs as far as the exit concealed by the bookcase and asked her quietly to tell her 'woman to woman' what was really happening on the outside. Miep did. On other occasions the two women had sat on Auguste van Pels's bed and Edith poured out her worries and concerns that they were not going to make it.

Anne's impatience with her mother comes over strongly in her diary, similar I am sure to many private teenage diaries as adolescents are wrestling with their future independence and who they are going to be. Edith Frank-Hollander was the protective mother of two teenage girls, and she was also shut up for day after day with relative strangers she was forced to get along with. Only in her early forties at that time, the poor woman was probably having something of a nervous breakdown through fear.

Miep told me she had a special affection for Auguste van Pels, who was a sweet woman despite the unflattering description of her in Anne's diary. Miep found Auguste to be stylish and fun and showed me the dress ring she had given Miep in gratitude for the help she had been giving her and her family. She told me she never took it off, so that she could constantly look at it and remember Auguste. Only recently it has been discovered that Mrs van Pels did not in fact die in Theresienstadt camp as had previously been thought – she was deliberately thrown under a train by Nazi guards en route to the camp and was crushed to death beneath its wheels.

Miep continued to correspond with children who wrote to her almost up to her death, and had a special relationship with St Joseph's Roman Catholic Primary School in Highgate, north London, and their teacher Paul Sutton. Each year, over the course of several months, Paul would undertake a project on Anne Frank, to help the children deal with their concerns about their forthcoming transition to their much larger secondary school. The project involved art, poetry and prose, culminating in a public exhibition at the end of the school year and a visit to the Anne Frank House by the pupils. Over the course of several years Miep wrote to each new year-group to encourage their work and of course her letters were displayed too. Paul Sutton tragically died of a heart attack on his return from the annual school trip to Amsterdam in 2010.

I still treasure the letters Miep wrote to me, her distinctive signature remaining the same throughout the years. In 1999, she wrote to thank me for the birthday card I had sent her. To my enquiry as to whether she was still walking up her dangerously steep stairs in high heels, this 90-year-old lady responded, 'I regret to disappoint you that I am no longer in high heels.' Miep's fondness for high heels was well known, after all it was she who had introduced a thrilled 14-year-old Anne Frank to wearing them.

In one letter dated November 2008, just fifteen months before the end of her very long life, Miep wrote to me excitedly having learnt that an Anne Frank Award for Moral Courage was to be presented in her honour. SHE (Miep!) considered it a great honour to have her name attached to an award sponsored by her friend, the Anne Frank Trust's Life President Bee Klug. Miep was aware the award would be given to an exceptional candidate. She finished the letter with the words, 'My dear Gillian, I wish you with my whole heart good health, true happiness and continued success.'

Actually the winner of the Anne Frank Award in honour of Miep Gies was supremely deserving. Her name was Nicole Dryburgh. A pretty dark-haired girl of 20, Nicole arrived at the House of Commons where the awards were taking place in a wheelchair and with many members of her proud family alongside. Nicole had been diagnosed with a spinal tumour at the age of 11, and had lost the use of her legs. Then, aged 13, she was diagnosed with a brain tumour and lost her sight. Nonetheless, determined to continue her studies, she achieved high marks in her GCSE exams at 16, especially in English, as like Anne Frank, Nicole had a dream of being a journalist and having a career as a writer. Nicole's spirit was indomitable.

She raised over £110,000 for two London hospitals, including by abseiling down the side of a tall building. She wrote two books: *The Way I See It* and *Talk to the Hand*. Less than a year after receiving her Anne Frank Award, in May 2010, Nicole lost her long battle with cancer. In Nicole's obituary, the Anne Frank/Miep Gies Award was cited as a special moment in her life.

As long as I knew Miep Gies she continued to carry a burden of guilt for not being able to save the members of the Frank and van Pels families and Fritz Pfeffer from their terrible fate. Reflecting on it, she would sigh, look down and shake her head. But what she did, and the constant state of peril she put herself in for over two years, should be considered the noblest and most courageous of human endeavours.

On one occasion I asked Miep why she had chosen to risk her life to help others. Her answer was simple: 'Because Mr Frank had asked me to help.' It's a simplistic answer and I am sure did not reflect the moral dilemma she had to face when asked. Probably at the time she did not realize it would be for over two years. But her answer also demonstrated the enormous respect she had for Otto Frank, whom she continued to address as Mr Frank even when he came to live with Miep and her husband after the war.

I have been very privileged to meet other Holocaust-era rescuers. They all carry a humility and when offered any form of praise often give a discernible shrug of the shoulders as if to say 'It was nothing. What else could I do?' Sir Nicholas Winton was such a person. A British businessman who found himself in Nazi-occupied Prague, Winton single-handedly established an organization to help children from Jewish families at risk from the Nazis. He set up his office at a dining-room table in his hotel in Wenceslas Square. Through his intervention, no less than 669 mostly Jewish children were taken out of Prague on the Kindertransport trains, thus saving their lives.

Winton had kept his wartime exploits very much to himself and they were not publicly known about until February 1988. His exposure on the primetime Esther Ranzten TV show remains one of British popular broadcasting's most memorable moments. Sitting in the front row of the audience Winton was unaware that he was seated next to Vera Gissing, one of the very children he had saved. The moment of that revelation was emotional enough and the tear he shed was visible. But then Esther 'innocently' asked if there happened to be any others in the audience that Nicky Winton had rescued. Slowly, almost row by row to prolong the televisual drama, over two dozen members of the audience rose from their seats. Hearing the movement behind him, Nicky stood up and looked round. To his stunned amazement the children he had helped on to trains were surrounding him, by that time all middle-aged men and women. As he sat down he took out a white handkerchief from his jacket pocket and his tears readily flowed.

As his fame deservedly grew and he was bestowed with many honours and awards, Sir Nicholas Winton retained his humility and mockingly dry sense of humour. I called him in late 2009 to invite him to be a guest of honour at the Anne Frank Trust's annual fundraising lunch the following January. 'Well my dear, in principle it's a yes, but I suggest you call me again much nearer the event just to check I'm still here.' Fortunately, he made it to the event. When asked on arrival at 10.00 a.m. if he would care for a mid-morning drink (we had coffee in mind) he insisted on a glass of bubbly. Sir Nicholas Winton lived to be 106.

In South Africa in 1994, I met Cor and Truus Grootendorst, a couple who had worked tirelessly in the Dutch Resistance and had saved 200 Jewish children by taking them from their desperate parents to live with Dutch families. As we sat in their sun-filled Cape Town flat they described dark days and even darker nights of fear. One of their missions had not ended well. When Truus had gone to collect two children from a young Jewish couple in danger, the mother had pleaded with her to let the family stay together for just one more night. Truus was fearful as she knew the Nazis were closing in with their search for Jews hiding in the area, but reluctantly agreed as the mother was so distraught at the thought of never seeing her children again. When Truus returned for the children before daybreak, to her horror the family had been found and taken away. I asked Truus if she was alarmed about her own safety, but she simply said, 'No. But I regret to this day that I couldn't save those children.' To which I could only respond, 'But Truus, you and Cor had saved 200 others.'

Sometimes Holocaust survivors themselves went on to become helpers in post-war events. One evening during my visit to Argentina in 2010 I gave a talk, with an interpreter alongside, to a gathering of community supporters of the Centro Ana Frank. A charming elderly woman was introduced to me as a Polish-born Holocaust survivor called Monica Davidowicz. I subsequently discovered that Monica had in turn hidden people during the 'Dirty War', and that several other Holocaust survivors had done the same.

In an article 'We Are Stones: Anne Frank, the Diary and the Play' published in October 2015, the Canadian educator Len Rudner referred to a study done by Samuel Oliner, a child survivor of the Holocaust.

> He [Oliner] wanted to know how it was possible that in a Europe that was dominated by the Nazis, it was still possible for men and women to say 'no' to evil and stand up against the Nazis to help the victims. In his study, 'The Altruistic Personality', he found that the 'helpers' were individuals who were taught from a very early age that they were no different from anyone else. They were taught to look past external differences to see the common links that existed between city-dwellers and country-dwellers, between farmers and shopkeepers, between Jews and Gentiles. They were raised to ask questions and to think independently.

Rudner continued:

> These were the characteristics of those men and women who saved the persecuted during the time of the Nazi horror. I suspect that they have existed in every age and in every time of terror.

The stories of rescuers fascinate me. You read of people who saved friends and lovers, but also those who saved complete strangers. You read about rescuers who saved individuals who they didn't even like: ungrateful dependents who ignored rules of safety and exposed themselves and their protectors to detection and risk through thoughtlessness and plain stupidity. And yet the rescuers persevered. And when asked where they found the reservoirs of heroism to draw upon, they denied that they were heroes. And when asked why they did what they did, they often responded as if the question was too foolish to even answer.

As Anne Frank's biographer Melissa Muller notes, 'We know very little about what the helpers were feeling. They never liked to talk about themselves. On the one hand they did not want to portray themselves as heroes; they did what they did simply because they were who they were and could do no different.'

On the night Miep Gies died, 11 January 2010, by a strange coincidence Jon Blair's Oscar-winning film *Anne Frank Remembered* was being rescreened on the BBC. After spending the evening preparing an obituary for *The Independent* newspaper, I settled down to watch the film and think about the woman whom I had been lucky enough to know and had just been attempting to describe in words. As the two-hour film closes, Miep stares directly into the camera and says in her broken English how important she finds it to speak to children: 'Very interesting are the letters from the German children. They ask me everything, telling me that their father and grandfather didn't tell me anything about the war, saying "that's the past and it is over". But that's not true. The past is always with you your whole life and we must learn from that past.'

Chapter 14

Anne Frank goes into British Prisons

'Here in the prison we need to look out for and remember the humanity in everyone we meet in order not to lose the humanity of our institution. That's why we have had the Anne Frank exhibition here before, why we are so pleased it has been here this fortnight and why we look forward to its return to the prison once more in the future.' Governor David Redhouse, Wormwood Scrubs Prison, London, December 2014

The Anne Frank exhibition has been touring British prisons since 2002, visiting at least ten establishments each year. Hundreds of serving prisoners have been trained to be Anne Frank exhibition guides and Holocaust survivors have received immense satisfaction from telling their stories within prison walls.

All the Holocaust survivors who have worked with the Anne Frank Trust in prisons have felt it to be one of the most rewarding things they have done, and almost always ask to repeat the experience. When the prisoners see an elderly man or woman stand in front of them, declare in a genteel Continental accent that they were 'once in prison too', and then go on to tell their horrific story, the prisoners are given a new perspective on their own grievances against society.

It was the racist murder of a teenage prisoner that made the Anne Frank exhibition tour come about. In March 2000, 19-year-old Zahid Mubarek, born in London of Pakistani heritage, was murdered while he was sleeping by his cellmate Robert Stewart. Mubarek was a first-time prisoner being held in Feltham Young Offenders Institution in west London, and when he was killed he was just five hours from the end of a 90-day sentence for stealing a pack of razor blades worth £6. After the murder, Stewart etched a Nazi swastika on the wall of their cell with the heel of his shoe. Campaigners are still asking whether the teenage Mubarek's placement in the same cramped cell as a known racist was accidental, negligent or, worse still, deliberate.

Later the same year, which had seen several other racist incidents in prisons, Sarah Payne, the Regional Manager of Thames Valley Prison Service, happened upon the Anne Frank travelling exhibition on display at Portsmouth's Historic Dockyard. Sarah contacted Nick Leader, the Governor of Reading Prison, as she knew there had also been incidents of racism at Reading, not only by inmates but by prison officers towards inmates. Sarah had coincidentally also encountered the

Anne Frank Trust's adviser Nic Careem at a government event, and he convinced her about the impact the Anne Frank exhibition could possibly have in prisons. All consequently fell into place for the first ever visit of an Anne Frank exhibition to a prison establishment in April 2002.

Early in the morning on the first day of the exhibition's week-long visit to Reading Prison, Herbert Levy, the Anne Frank Trust's Principal Guide, walked in through the daunting prison gate to spend the morning training a group of the prisoners to act as the exhibition guides. Herbert understood incarceration, due to his wartime experience as a German-Jewish refugee child held in the interment camp on the Isle of Man.

Inside one of the prison's communal rooms, the 'Anne Frank, A History for Today' exhibition stood awaiting its mission; its stands and panels having been set up the evening before by a group of prisoners. Another group of curious prisoners, the future exhibition guides, were waiting for Herbert. They had already been provided with books and guide notes to read in advance of their training and had been shown a 25-minute film on Anne's life that had been created by the Anne Frank House. Herbert introduced himself, asked each prisoner his name and proceeded with the training session, which involved giving each prisoner the responsibility for learning and then describing three of the thirty-four panels. Herbert was mindful that in a few hours the group would be demonstrating their knowledge to the local Mayor, the prison's board of friends and other dignitaries.

Prisoner involvement on this prominent level was a radical innovation. It proved to be a format so positive in outcome that it has remained throughout the sixteen years the Anne Frank Trust has so far been visiting prisons. Governors of prisons, especially ones who are known to be effective, spend their careers being moved around the country from prison to prison, sometimes being called upon to help turn round problematic establishments. Reading's governor Nick Leader became a great advocate for the Anne Frank prison education programme, which he subsequently invited to several further establishments he was sent by Her Majesty's Prison Service to run.

After the positive response to our week at Reading Prison, we were invited to Her Majesty's Prison Durham, a Category A high-security establishment. In Durham there was a surprising additional element to the programme. The governor had heard that Eva Schloss was one of the Trust's founders and wanted her to come and speak to the prisoners about her experiences during the Holocaust. When Nic and I first visited Durham Prison to plan the event, we were very concerned at how Eva would react to seeing protective barbed wire around the intimidating high grey stone perimeter walls and the German Shepherd guard dogs used by the prison officers on their patrols. The prison had been built in 1819, during the pre-Victorian reign of King George IV, and was the site of many judicial executions on its gallows.

As I suspected, when I approached Eva with the idea of going in to a high-security prison, she was initially extremely wary. But never one to shirk a challenge, in the autumn of 2002, this courageous and determined lady boarded a train and travelled the 270 miles to Durham, in the furthermost north-east of England. She spoke first at the men's prison and was then taken to repeat her talk in the adjacent women's prison, where on a tour of its facilities, she spotted the notorious serial killer Rosemary West quietly sitting reading in the library. Soon after Eva's visit the women's prison at Durham was closed due to overcrowding and the high rate of suicides.

Eva later recalled about going to Durham; 'I thought the experience would upset me, but I realized I had a message for the inmates. This is a project I like doing because of the big impact it has on the prisoners. They can relate to my suffering and realize that they are not so badly off after all.' Eva has continued to speak at prisons around the UK, supporting visits of the Anne Frank exhibition. I have been present at many of these talks and have seen for myself how attentive and respectful the prisoners are towards her, even younger prisoners and those from abroad who may not catch every word of her still pronounced Viennese accent. At the end of her talk, often lasting over an hour, she concludes by reminding prisoners of the opportunities they are given during their time inside to study and to learn new skills that can help them with their future lives. Coming from a survivor of Auschwitz, where every future possibility was focused on extermination, this message of hope carries huge weight.

Many of Britain's prison establishments were built in the Victorian age. Although in those days prisoners were deprived of all human contact as a form of punishment the prisons were designed for each inmate to have their own cell, which today would be considered a luxury. Ironically, in the nineteenth century, young Zahid Mubarak's murder would have probably been avoided. As I write, Britain has the largest prison population in Western Europe and a report in February 2015 stated that 60 per cent of the country's prisons were overcrowded.

Wormwood Scrubs Prison in West London, or 'The Scrubs' as it is known, was built in 1875 by nine prisoners selected from other prisons. The bricks used were manufactured on the site. During the Second World War it was commandeered for the war effort and housed MI5, the British counter-intelligence agency. After the war it went back to being an overcrowded Victorian-era prison and by 1979, after IRA prisoners had staged a rooftop protest over visiting rights, its former governor wrote to *The Times* newspaper describing it as 'a penal dustbin.' In 1986, Charles Bronson, once described as 'Britain's most violent prisoner', attacked and nearly strangled the prison's governor and then in the 1990s, twenty-seven prison officers were suspended for brutality towards the prisoners.

In December 2014, Eva came along to speak on the final day of the Anne Frank exhibition in Wormwood Scrubs. *Jewish Chronicle* reporter Rosa Doherty came to hear her and her subsequent article covered a full double-page spread of the newspaper. Doherty wrote:

> Inside a 19th-century chapel, flanked by high-security walls, sat row upon row of hardened criminals. Ninety of them, clad in regulation grey

track-suits, waited for the most unlikely of guests to a high-security prison – an 85-year-old, 5ft 2in woman dressed daintily in cardigan, trouser-suit and shoulder-bag. For the next two hours, the Wormwood Scrubs inmates sat tall, hands clasped often at their chest, while not one of them spoke as Eva Schloss described in vivid detail how her family was betrayed, captured by the Nazis, and suffered at the hands of sadistic guards at the Auschwitz-Birkenau Nazi concentration camp. There was no sound other than the occasional gasp or a discreet shuffle as someone moved uncomfortably in his seat . . .

Eva spoke calmly of the time she was tortured and made to strip naked in front of male guards, and revealed how she and her mother were forced to join a line for 'work' while others were separated and sent to 'shower' – the Nazi slang for gas chambers. She witnessed friends being dragged from their queue to take their place among those destined for death. She told how her father's last words to her were ones of regret and failure at the thought he had been unable to protect his family from the horrors of the Nazis. These and other stories – such as how she had her hair shaved in the cold of winter, and no clothes to protect her skin in summer – visibly moved her tough audience. One of them, David (name altered), admitted that the way Eva Schloss had described her own father's reaction had reduced him to tears. 'I got chills. I was the same age as her father when I was sent to prison and that is how I feel about my family. I've let them down,' he said.

Michael, 23, who is serving a two-year term for possessing a replica gun, said: 'It made me cry to hear her story. I came to this country when I was very young. My wife and kids are British and I'm facing deportation, all because of my mistake. Even though it is nothing like what happened to Eva, I can relate to that feeling of being kicked out of somewhere you call home because people think you are bad. In the same way people say all Jews are this or all Muslims are that, not all prisoners are the same. We are still human beings. I'm young and I want the chance to change my life. Eva's story teaches us all about responsibility. The Nazis were responsible for their actions, and Eva was responsible for how she felt after.'

British prisoners have also enjoyed hearing the remarkably active nonagenarian Freddie Knoller. His story of fleeing from the Nazis in a race for his life across Europe, until his eventual betrayal by a French girlfriend he had met in a Parisian nightclub, always captures their interest.

During the first few years of the Anne Frank prison exhibition tour, when the Trust was still embryonic, I travelled to many of the prisons along with our guide trainer Herbert Levy, who was often assisted by a young volunteer from the German peace organization, Action Reconciliation Service for Peace (ARSP). ARSP volunteers spend a year in peace and social justice projects in several countries of the world, including the UK, the US and Poland, and are to be found working in many organizations that assist Holocaust survivors. We started working with ARSP volunteers in 1998, and have found them to be remarkable and deeply morally driven young people.

Together we three, Herbert, myself and the volunteer, travelled to all kinds of prison establishments: high security, remand, young offenders' institutions and open prisons. An open prison is mainly for white-collar criminals and those who are coming to the end of a long sentence. Prisoners are allowed outside to work during the day but must return by early evening. One such prisoner was Malcolm (name changed), who had been serving a long stretch for armed robbery. He was a charming and gregarious South Londoner and was the godson of one of Britain's most notorious gangsters. As an avid history enthusiast, he loved his role and responsibility as a guide at our exhibition. Once, I invited him to come to the Home Office's Diversity Week event in Westminster and he guided round two Labour government ministers, who were very impressed and appreciative.

Malcolm was on a high afterwards and with a large grin on his face, beckoned me over to the corner of the room signalling he needed to have a quiet word with me. 'Gill,' he said in his chirpy South London accent. He sounded excited yet earnest. 'Look, you know I'm going to go straight when I come out next month. But before I do, I'd like to do just one more armed robbery – because I want to raise funds for the Anne Frank Trust.' I smiled and thanked him, but at the same time politely declined his kind offer.

Steve Gadd joined the Trust in 2005 to take over the running and delivering of the prison project. A former rock guitarist, Steve had spent several years as a 'roadie' working for top music impresario Harvey Goldsmith. As well as providing the practical and logistical skills we needed to transport and erect the exhibition each time, the idea of educating prisoners appealed to him. Steve proved to be a natural, well respected by prisoners and prison staff alike. As well as conducting the guide training, Steve would organize writing workshops with the performance poet Leah Thorn, the daughter of a German-Jewish refugee from the Nazis. After one writing workshop a long-term prisoner told the Trust's Chairman Daniel Mendoza, 'This is the first time in fourteen years that my heart has been opened.'

On the closing day of each exhibition visit, and often after the talk by the Holocaust survivor, a 'Graduation Ceremony' is held, where the visiting speaker presents certificates and offers congratulations to the prisoner peer guides to thank them for their work. In many cases this could be the first time these men or women have received a certificate for anything. We have heard that some prisoners wear their 'Anne Frank Guide' branded T-shirts for months afterwards, as a badge of honour.

In Wakefield Prison in Yorkshire the prisoners wanted to say thank you to the Anne Frank Trust for coming to work with them, so in their craft workshop they created a wooden replica of the Anne Frank House. It was built exactly to scale and even contained a tiny hinged bookcase, stocked with miniature books and folders and able to swing open and closed, just like the one that concealed the entrance to the secret hiding place. It was so beautifully crafted that a second copy was made and shipped to South Africa to be shown at the Anne Frank exhibition at Constitution Hill, a former political prison in Johannesburg.

In November 2012 we visited HMP Belmarsh, a high-security prison on the south bank of the Thames, where some of Britain's most notorious criminals and terrorists are incarcerated. One long-term prisoner, who acted as an Anne Frank peer educator and was present when Eva Schloss gave a talk, followed up his experience by sending me a personally-addressed letter enclosing a donation of £50, as a Christmas donation for the Trust. This was a very large sum saved from his weekly remuneration for prison work, and we were deeply appreciative. Further research of the man's name showed him to be 'one of Britain's most notorious serial killers'. There is no doubt in my mind that the Anne Frank exhibition and hearing Eva had made him reflect on what he could give back to society.

A female prisoner whom we trained as a guide in HMP Holloway, a women's prison in north London, found herself fascinated by learning about the Holocaust. She had come from an African country and at school had not studied anything about European history apart from its colonial impact. On her release she told the ex-offenders charity who were helping her to find employment that her dream job would be to work at the Anne Frank Trust. Steve gave her a glowing recommendation and she duly came to work for the Trust where she became a very important part of our administration team for over six years. She even went back into Holloway prison to give motivational talks to other prisoners.

Alan Smith, a journalist for *The Guardian* newspaper, visited the Anne Frank project in HMP Wellingborough in 2011. He reported: 'Casey and Ian [two of the inmates] had thrown themselves into it. They had learnt the material, erected the stands, which were laid out in the chapel. The officer in charge of them said "This has brought the men back to life – they have been themselves. It has been an oasis and given them back their humanity".'

Prisons are very tough environments, but I have often said that the governors, staff and chaplains who initiate bringing the Anne Frank educational project into their prison are some of the most visionary, empathetic and enlightened people I have met. One such is David Redhouse, the Deputy Governor of Wormwood Scrubs, who spoke at the closing event of the Anne Frank exhibition's visit in 2014. The exhibition, along with its peer guiding programme, was invited into Wormwood Scrubs for three years running, and in each of those three visits Eva Schloss came to give the prisoners a one hour talk about her life. The visit in 2014 ended the most successful year to date for the Anne Frank exhibition; one in which it visited 16 prisons and trained 122 prisoners to be peer educators, who in turn educated over 3,000 prisoners.

Introducing Eva and knowing the powerful story she was about to tell, Steve Gadd lightened the proceedings by explaining to the prisoners that he was actually brought up in west London just a few streets away from the prison, within sight of its fearsome looking grey stone walls. His father would apparently point to the walls and threaten the young Steve that if he didn't behave he would end up behind there. Well, as he reminded the prisoners with a cheeky grin, he did, and on many occasion!

Governor Redhouse explained why he and the senior management of Wormwood Scrubs believed it was so important to have the Anne Frank programme in the prison.

> We are a very diverse community, both prisoners and staff. We have Rastafarians, Catholics, Christians Jews, Buddhists – members of almost any religion you can think of. With so many differences there is obvious potential for divides. Having the Anne Frank exhibition here has helped prisoners to better understand the basic human values. Telling stories by Holocaust survivors is how we remind ourselves that history is really about people, not inanimate places or dates. The awful tragedy of a story like Anne Frank's is what makes it possible for us to understand and engage with the true horror of the Holocaust instead of being lost in the incomprehensibly large numbers of those murdered.

Ali (name changed) was one of six prisoners trained by Steve Gadd to be a peer guide for the exhibition on that visit. After serving a thirteen-month sentence for fraud, he said he thinks the experience is going to change his life.

> I was, for want of a better word, a career criminal, hacking computers. But being a guide for the exhibition has been great. I've been able to impart a bit of wisdom on the other prisoners looking round it. As a Muslim, it has given me the opportunity to talk with them and challenge some of their ideas. They would say to me 'but you are Muslim you should hate the Jews'. This whole exhibition has taught them something different. I know there are more things that unite Jews and Muslims than divide us. It was a privilege to be part of the Anne Frank exhibition, it has made me think differently.

It is not only in adult establishments that the Anne Frank exhibition has been working. In Scotland, troubled teenagers, those who have broken the law and those who are at risk of placing themselves or others at harm, are sent to establishments known as Secure Units. In April 2012, the *Times Educational Supplement* sent its reporter Jackie Cosh to visit the Anne Frank project at the Good Shepherd Secure Unit, where she spoke to 17-year-old Yasmin, one of our peer educators. Yasmin was full of apposite questions such as, 'How did Hitler get people to believe all these things?' and 'Why did the Jews not just change religion?'. Jackie Cosh also found Yasmin contemplating on what she would do to protect her own child in that situation.

The Good Shepherd's programmes manager Rhona McLaughlin explained her motivation for bringing the project, 'The hope is that [the girls] will automatically start to question attitudes to prejudice. If you have that sense of injustice for Anne Frank, and others in the war, then hopefully you will have this for everyone. It plants the seeds for looking at other issues later on.'

Because of data-protection issues around former prisoners it has been impossible to track the future career paths of the thousands of prisoners who have been involved in the Anne Frank project. Consequently, it has not been an easy project to receive government funding for, as successive Home Office and Justice departments have looked increasingly to evaluating the success of the penal system through the incidence of reoffending. We have relied on the support of individual funders and foundations, who have come along to prisons to see for themselves what we have been doing, and have helped subsidise the programme for the cash-strapped prisons.

However, we know from prison staff and prisoners alike that, as well as the delivery of knowledge and understanding of the consequences of prejudice and racism to thousands of British prisoners, the Anne Frank project has given confidence and aspiration and an enhanced sense of self-worth to those we have trained to be peer educators.

One prisoner exhibition guide from HMP Redditch in the West Midlands summed up the mission and success of taking Anne Frank into prisons, especially with those who have been removed from society, 'What I knew before about Anne Frank was tiny compared to now but it's not just about the history. It's about learning confidence with the public, interacting with people, to approach, talk to and answer them.'

There are now thousands of former prisoners whose reintegration back into British society has been undoubtedly helped by learning the story of Anne Frank, and in hundreds of cases, by telling that story themselves. Many have also had a very privileged opportunity, that of meeting a Holocaust survivor in the flesh. Whenever I have closed the talk to prisoners by a survivor, I have reminded them that this privilege has also put a great responsibility on their shoulders – that of imparting this story themselves to their children and future grandchildren.

Chapter 15

Anne Frank and Stephen Lawrence

On a chilly November night in 2000, Doreen Lawrence was standing amidst the stone pillars of Durham Cathedral in front of the Anne Frank exhibition. She was staring wistfully at a series of photographs of her son Stephen. In one he was very young, dressed in his primary school uniform. Doreen pointed to it, turned to me and sighed, 'That day he came home from school and excitedly showed me his school photo. But you know what, I told him off for grinning widely at the photographer. He couldn't help it that he had lost the whole front set of his milk teeth and I thought it would spoil the photo.' She paused, sighed and turned back to look at her son's face and said, 'How could I have told him off?'

A normal occurrence in a normal family; the child not posing for a photo exactly as his mother would like. But this was not a normal school photo – it was one that was going to be seen by thousands of people in the years to come. The curly-haired boy staring out from the exhibition panel, grinning to the camera despite a large gap where his front teeth should have been, was the six-year-old Stephen Lawrence. The same Stephen Lawrence who, just twelve years later as an 18-year-old school student, would be brutally stabbed to death on a south-east London street by a gang of locally-feared racist thugs. His story would become intertwined with that of Anne Frank's.

Stephen was in the course of studying for his A-Level exams on that fateful night of 22 April 1993, but had gone out with his friend Duwayne Brooks for an evening off from studies. Later that evening, the pair were waiting at a bus stop in the south London suburb of Eltham, when suddenly a gang of threatening white youths appeared in the street, and like a packs of wolves coming upon their prey, ran towards Stephen and Duwayne. Duwayne heard one of them shout 'What, what, nigger!' before he pulled out a large knife and plunged it into Stephen's chest. With the bloodied knife as a trophy, the howling group of youths ran away down the road. Duwayne and Stephen started to run in the other direction, but after just a few yards, Stephen collapsed in the street, bleeding heavily and fighting for breath. Despite the help of passers-by, Stephen died from his wounds there on the cold, hard pavement.

What were his thoughts in his last moments as the life drained from his body, this much loved boy who was planning to be a professional architect? Stephen's death, and the long campaign for justice by his family, plays an important part in the recent history of Britain. The little boy had been born into a loving, religious and hardworking family. His parents Doreen and Neville had both arrived in Britain from Jamaica in the early 1960s. The couple had married in 1972 and were aspirational, especially for their three children, Stephen, Stuart and Georgina. Doreen trained to be a special needs teacher and Neville followed his love of carpentry.

Unbeknown to the original investigating police officers, their handling of the case would cause a maelstrom in the British police force. What was at first perceived as ineptitude in missing vital evidence was discovered to be, after a long judicial enquiry conducted by Sir William Macpherson, a manifestation of the deeply-rooted institutional racism in the Metropolitan Police. Years later, the corruption and deliberate hiding of crucial evidence by a key police officer also came to light.

The day following Stephen's murder, an anonymous note was left in a telephone box for the police giving the names of four local men who could have carried out the crime. The previous year a 15-year-old Asian schoolboy, Rohit Duggal, had also been murdered in Eltham. His killer, 17-year-old Peter Thompson, was given a life sentence two months before Stephen's murder. Thompson was said to be an associate of two of the gang members mentioned in the note.

A police surveillance camera was secretly placed in the flat of one of the gang, and sure enough the group were filmed wielding a knife while making extremely racist threats. Those who had been named in the anonymous scribbled note, David Norris, Gary Dobson, brothers Neil and Jamie Acourt, plus their friend Luke Knight, were duly arrested. But three months after Stephen's murder the charges were dropped due to lack of evidence. In 1994, the Lawrence family brought a private prosecution against the gang but this too foundered due to lack of evidence. Duwayne Brooks's identification of two of the gang was deemed to be flawed. Years later, George Gyte, the Director of Education for the London Borough of Greenwich, described to me the atmosphere of fear that pervaded the streets of the borough in those days of the early 1990s, largely due to the activities of that small group of violent racist thugs.

The diminutive Doreen and the gentle giant Neville were perceived by the public as grieving parents who acted with remarkable dignity, and over the coming months gained huge respect for their demeanour in terrible circumstances. Doreen, supported by local community activists and the family's lawyer Imran Khan, became increasingly frustrated by the continual use of the word 'dignity' to describe her demeanour in grief, while her anger was growing at the way the case had been treated by the police.

In 1996 as the Anne Frank Trust was working with the Anne Frank House in Amsterdam on the development of the new exhibition 'A History for Today', the Stephen Lawrence murder had been long overtaken in the public consciousness by other stories. Alan Dein, a social historian whom I had asked to write a set of accompanying panels on contemporary British issues, approached the Lawrence family to enquire whether we could possibly use Stephen's story to illustrate how racial hatred, the evil that had killed Anne Frank, was still very much alive in 1990s Britain. The Lawrence family agreed and the new exhibition was launched in January 1997 and opened by the Labour Party leader Tony Blair, just four months before the electoral landslide that was to make him Prime Minister.

Blair and his wife Cherie were guided around the exhibition by Herbert Levy and myself, and towards the end of the exhibition, waiting patiently by the panel we had created about her beloved son Stephen, was Doreen Lawrence. Herbert and I had the pleasure of introducing her for the first time to Blair, and she certainly made a strong impression on him. According to the former Home Office Minister, Paul (now Lord) Boateng, one of our founding Patrons who had arranged the Blairs' visit to the exhibition, it was on that morning at Southwark Cathedral that Blair made a silent vow to himself. If he should win the election, he would commission an official inquiry into Stephen Lawrence's murder. That summer in the new Labour government, Boateng became Britain's first ever black cabinet minister. In one of his first acts as Prime Minister, Blair commissioned the retired judge Sir William Macpherson to lead an official inquiry into Stephen's murder.

During the month that the new Anne Frank exhibition was on display at Southwark Cathedral, the Stephen Lawrence case once again became headline news. *The Daily Mail*, a politically right-wing newspaper, ran a deliberately provocative and unmissable front-page headline accusing the five acquitted gang members of the murder of Stephen. The editor Paul Dacre published their names and dared each of them to sue his newspaper, which would have resulted in a public court case. The reason for Dacre's interest in the case was a personal one. He had recently employed Neville Lawrence to do some decorating at his home and he had got to know and sympathize with the plight of the bereaved father. Not surprisingly the gang members did not take the *Daily Mail* to court.

Sadly, the stress and pain caused by Stephen's murder had taken a terrible toll on his parents and they divorced in 1999. Despite this, they still attended some of our Anne Frank Trust events together. In 2001, we took 'A History for Today' to Greenwich Town Hall, in the home borough of the Lawrence family. Prior to the opening Neville had been interviewed about the exhibition, and Stephen's inclusion in it, by the local Greenwich newspaper, the *New Shopper*. According to the report, Neville had compared and equated the murder of six million Jews in the Holocaust to that of his own son. This caused a furore which reached as far as several national newspapers. Neville was mortified by this attack on him, and at the exhibition launch he pulled me aside to tell me why he felt he had been so unfairly treated. I was amazed at what this Jamaican-born black man then told me. 'Gillian, I promise you, I would never have compared Stephen's death to the Holocaust. You see, my grandmother was actually a European Jewess.' Seeing my mouth opening in surprise he continued, 'She left Germany in the 1920s and arrived in Cuba. There she met my grandfather, a black man, and they married and went to live in Jamaica. I know all about the Holocaust – it affected my own distant family'. The revelation that perhaps the most well-known young black victim of murderous racism in recent British history was actually one-eighth Jewish and shared Ashkenazi DNA with Anne Frank rocked me to the core. Who really knows where they have come from, what heritage and blood and DNA? That equally applies to the racist gang who killed Stephen purely because they thought he was so different and, like Anne Frank, unworthy of the right to live.

Neville eventually returned to Jamaica, where he felt as a black man he could live out his life without the fear of racism. Stephen's body was laid to rest in a churchyard in Jamaica, where his parents felt his young bones could lie without the threat of harm. The Stephen Lawrence Charitable Trust was set up in 1998 to help disadvantaged young people who had a similar interest in becoming architects. The Stephen Lawrence Centre in Greenwich opened its doors in 2008 to work with communities and local government to ensure that the lessons of fairness and justice from Stephen's murder are acted upon.

Doreen continued the fight to bring her son's murderers to justice. Thanks to her courage and determination, on a Friday afternoon in January 2012, some nineteen years after a knife tore into the flesh of Stephen Lawrence at a bus stop, I sat in the public gallery of the Old Bailey criminal court, watching with huge satisfaction the two young men, Gary Dobson and David Norris, who were standing in the dock. In 2005 the British government had scrapped the 'double jeopardy' law whereby a person could not be convicted for the same crime more than once. Forensic science had similarly moved on in the intervening two decades since the case had been thrown out for lack of damning evidence. Two microscopic spots of Stephen's blood found on the jacket of Gary Dobson eventually resulted in life sentences for Dobson and Norris, with minimum terms of fifteen years and fourteen years respectively.

On the evening the two were finally found guilty of what the judge Mr Justice Treacy described as 'a murder which scarred the conscience of the nation', I received an email from Doreen Lawrence's lawyer Imran Khan. Imran had been a Trustee of the Anne Frank Trust for three years in the early 2000s. He was sitting in his office with Doreen when my email of congratulations had appeared in what must have been a burgeoning inbox. He immediately responded to say that Doreen sent her love and that being a Trustee of the Anne Frank Trust had been one of the most significant things he had ever done.

Doreen, whom both Bee Klug and I considered a friend and inspiration, is now Baroness Lawrence of Clarendon OBE and continues to make her mark on society as a Labour member of the House of Lords. Stephen's younger and admiring brother Stuart is a teacher and Georgina is a young mother. Had circumstances been different they would perhaps had a successful architect in the family too. Or, like the speculation that Anne Frank would have definitely pursued a career in writing, maybe Stephen as an adult would have changed his mind about architecture and chosen another career. We'll never know.

Like many of the parents I have met of murdered children, Otto Frank perhaps being the most globally influential, Doreen and Neville were determined that evil would not prevail and their child's memory would be a positive force for healing some of the ills of society.

On the morning of 7 July 2015, I found myself sitting in St Paul's Cathedral surrounded by the families of the victims of the London 7/7 bombings which had happened ten years to the day earlier. Looking around, the families seemed to me a collection of such normal-looking people, with no discernible differences from any of us: a cross section of those who could just happen to be in the cathedral to pray, who could have come inside as curious visitors or that we could have seen outside the cathedral grabbing a coffee on buzzing Paternoster Square.

I was sitting next to Mavis and Esther Hyman, mother and younger sister of one of the tragic victims of the Tavistock Square bus bombing on that terrible day, the 31-year-old artist Miriam Hyman. During the service, my thoughts turned to the ways families of murdered young people have coped with their devastating loss. Through my work with the Anne Frank Trust, a charity borne out of a grieving father's belief in the power of education to combat hatred, I have had the privilege of spending time with quite a few of these extraordinary people, all of whose normal lives became extraordinary because of acts of violent brutality.

As the 7/7 victims' families hugged each other, nodding in tearful support and shared understanding of their grief, I saw people who had all experienced how an ordinary day could turn into the worst possible nightmare of any parent, spouse or sibling. Esther Hyman told me that the tenth anniversary had very little emotional impact on her – it was just a day like the 3,649 tough ones that had gone by since 2005. However, she and her redoubtable mother had used the opportunity to talk publicly through media interviews about their beloved Miriam. They also spoke about the materials for schools which had been developed by the Miriam Hyman Memorial Foundation, encapsulating Miriam's vision of a diverse and respectful world. Those teaching tools will go on to do a vital job.

I have also spent time with Barry and Margaret Mizen, parents of 16-year-old Jimmy who was murdered by a violent bully while buying a cake in his local bakery; George and Debbie Kinsella, parents of Ben who was knifed to death on an Islington street while celebrating his exam results; Sylvia Lancaster, mother of Sophie, beaten to death in a park for offending a youth by dressing in Gothic fashion; Gee Walker, mother of schoolboy Anthony, murdered in Liverpool just for being black; and Winifred Delaney, whose 15-year-old son Jonny was set upon and left to die in the middle of a playing field for being from the Irish Traveller community. These remarkable people have all turned the most profound and unbearable tragedy, the senseless killing of their beloved children, into a tool for teaching young people about how to be empathetic and responsible human beings. Siblings have also taken up the mantle. Jonny Delaney's younger sister Nellie received one of our Anne Frank Awards for Moral Courage in 2008 for her campaigning work, and Ben Kinsella's actress sister Brooke received an MBE in recognition of her campaign against knife crime.

Ahmad Nawaz also has a story to share with others. His adored younger brother Haris was one of the 147 victims of the Peshawar school massacre in Pakistan in December 2014. Ahmad watched in stunned disbelief as his class teacher was burned alive in front of him, and then he too was shot and wounded. He was flown out of Pakistan to the UK, and to the same hospital in Birmingham that had treated Malala Yousafzai. In February 2016, Ahmad stood proudly in his new Harborne Academy school blazer as he described the events of that terrible day to students at the nearby Rockwood Academy, a secondary school located in a predominantly Asian populated area of Birmingham. He told them, 'I've heard many children from this country are going to Syria, I want to discourage them from doing that. I also want to convey the message that we should fight for our education. In this country, an education is a right, but in mine it is a privilege.'

Ahmad was speaking at the Anne Frank exhibition visiting the school and he spoke following Mrs Mindu Hornek, Birmingham's last living Holocaust survivor. Rockwood Academy had previously been placed in 'Special Measures' by OFSTED, the schools' inspectorate body, as some of its governors had tried to bring in an Islamicized curriculum. The newly-installed school principal Fuzel Choudhury had set about reforming the school and it was now, according to OFSTED inspectors, back on the right path. In one of his first reforming initiatives, Mr Choudhury had invited the Anne Frank Trust's education programme to the school. Twenty of his pupils became Anne Frank Ambassadors, taking the story out into their neighbouring schools and local community. One month previously Ahmad had come to London to light a memorial candle in memory of his brother Haris and all the Peshawar victims at our Anne Frank Trust fundraising lunch. Waiting to mount the rostrum in front of 600 business people, this brave boy who had suffered so much told me that his greatest wish was to be an educator against all forms of intolerance.

After the St Paul's Cathedral ceremony in July 2015, I told Mavis Hyman that what she was doing with the foundation in her daughter Miriam's name was truly wonderful. She looked at me, sighed and quietly said, 'It's the way I survive.' I can understand that sentiment. It is exactly the reason Otto Frank devoted the second half of his life to promoting his daughter Anne's diary as a force for good. With such good people, turning the worst into the best, we will all surely prevail.

Chapter 16

Anne Frank Helping to Make Peace in Ireland

In the summer of 1992, I was invited to take the 'Anne Frank in the World' exhibition across the Irish Sea to the Emerald Isle. I had been introduced to a man called Eddie Lawlor, an Anglo-Irish property developer and philanthropist. Eddie was looking for a new project to sponsor that could bring Catholic and Protestant young people together.

So one summer afternoon in 1992, I drove over to Eddie and his wife Ginny's beautiful home in the Essex countryside, where we sat in their idyllic tree-lined garden. Our conversation drifted very quickly to less peaceful parts of the world. Nationalism was growing all over Europe in the early 1990s, the first Iraq war had taken place the year before and Northern Ireland was still deeply affected by a violent sectarian war euphemistically known as 'The Troubles'.

Eddie was well known and hugely respected both in Ireland and the UK. The second eldest of twelve children of an impoverished Catholic family from County Carlow, as a second son he had been expected to take holy orders and become a priest. To his credit he studied for five years as a teenager under the tuition of the Holy Ghost Fathers but soon realized the strict and pious life intended for him would not fit his personality. He left Ireland and headed to England, with just a few Irish punts in his pocket.

After labouring in Suffolk, he managed to save a few hundred pounds and came down to London. Seeking a place to stay, he was shocked at his first encounter with racism, as in 1950s London it was permissible to display a sign in the window of rented accommodation stating 'No Blacks or Irish'. What happened in between merits a book in itself, but when I met Eddie Lawlor he was a multi-millionaire who owned a large property portfolio that included at one time the largest independent chain of petrol stations in the UK. After his only son's tragic death from a drugs overdose, Eddie's attention turned from making further wealth to putting it to good use, and his foundation was tackling youth poverty and drug abuse, as well as promoting peace initiatives in Ireland.

To my astonishment Eddie told me the Lawlor Foundation would cover the costs of a four-city tour by the 'Anne Frank in the World' exhibition of Northern Ireland and the neighbouring Irish Republic. He then introduced me to two linked organizations he also supported, Co-operation North and Co-operation Ireland, who were doing excellent community work on both sides of the border. These two organizations would be responsible for finding the venues and the staffing for the tour. I drove back from Essex with exciting plans.

On my first exploratory visit to Belfast I soon became very aware of checkpoints, watchtowers and barbed wire. The city centre hotel I came to often use in Belfast, the Europa, was known in those days as the most 'bombed hotel in the world'. Only a week after one of my visits, the hotel experienced one of its most damaging bombings of the conflict.

After two further planning visits to Ireland, many phone calls and faxes, in March 1993 the Anne Frank pan-Ireland exhibition tour was officially opened at the City Centre Library in Dublin by the President of Ireland, Mary Robinson. After I had shown her around the exhibition, she mounted the podium in the middle of the library floor, and with a look of serious intent she told us how, 'Anne Frank was important to me when I cried myself to sleep reading her diary in bed as a young teenager, and she is equally important to us now.' She ended her eloquent, and very personal, speech with the words, 'It is really all back to this teenager Anne Frank, who brought home to the world that it is out of ordinary circumstances and an ordinary population, that there can be sown seeds of hate, distrust, fear and the beginning of an exclusion of a certain group of people for certain reasons, that become more creditable as more people accept them.'

Also present at the launch was one of Ireland's most venerated elder statesmen, Dr Brendan O'Regan, considered to be the founding father of the global airport duty-free industry. Dr O'Regan had opened the world's first airport duty-free zone back in 1947 at Shannon, the airport serving the city of Limerick on the west coast. Ever since, he had been a great campaigner for the duty-free airport concept, Irish tourism and, most of all, peace. He once said, 'I will fight to the last breath helping to make peace in my country' and he strove for that end through founding the peace and reconciliation charity Co-operation North, plus his untiring work for the Irish Peace Institute. He also believed that airports should themselves be international centres of peace. Like many men of great achievement, Brendan O'Regan was a man of quiet humility, and during the evening of the launch I was asked by several different people proudly nodding in his direction, 'Do you realize who this is?'

The 1993 Anne Frank in Ireland tour criss-crossed the border covering Dublin, Derry-Londonderry, Limerick and finally Belfast, staged at Queen's University. As well as the sectarian divisions in Northern Ireland, it was also an opportunity to highlight discrimination against the traveller community, an issue that, unlike the 'Troubles', has not gone away.

Since the first visit in 1993, the Anne Frank Trust has visited the Republic of Ireland several times with different versions of the Anne Frank exhibition, but we have spent much more time working in the north. In 1997, the Anne Frank exhibition was invited to visit the small town of Omagh, seventy miles west of Belfast in County Tyrone. Richard Collins, a local architect, had a keen interest in the subject of the Holocaust and housed an impressive library of Holocaust-related books in his own home. He had called me in 1995 after watching Jon Blair's documentary *Anne Frank Remembered* on the BBC. Immensely moved by the film, he was anxious to do something for the Anne Frank Trust. I mentioned that we were planning to launch a new exhibition in 1997, to which he quietly pointed out that such a prestigious project was unlikely to visit a small town such as Omagh. 'Why not?' I immediately responded. In a serendipitous way, it fell into place. The town had a large modern library and the regional Education and Library Board had actually been looking for a prestigious project for its exhibition space.

'Up the main street, down the same street', joked one of the volunteers as she drove me through Omagh's tiny town centre in April 1997. All the Omagh volunteers were of a similarly cheerful disposition, with a keen and ironic sense of humour, something I grew to love when working in any part of Northern Ireland. The exhibition's launch event that evening was packed with people who had come from many miles around to hear for themselves the testimony of one of Northern Ireland's last living Holocaust survivors. It was unsurprising that the frail woman who came onto the stage to speak had a beauty and gentle elegance, but also an air of strength, about her. She was the former ballerina Helen Lewis, who had survived Theresienstadt, Stutthof and Auschwitz camps, had evaded two selections for death by the notorious Dr Mengele, had learnt of the murders of her young husband and mother in the camps, subsequently married an old friend, come to live in Belfast with her new husband and gone on to found the Belfast Modern Dance Group. Generations of Belfast's dancers had been taught their craft under her tutelage. Helen passed away in 2009 at the age of 93 and on Holocaust Memorial Day in January 2017 a plaque to honour her contribution to the arts was erected in Belfast by the Ulster History Circle.

Just over one year later, in August 1998, this town of charming and gregarious people was devastated. The Omagh bombing, cynically planned for a busy Saturday afternoon on the 'main street, same street', killed 29 people and injured over 200. It was carried out by the 'Real IRA', an IRA splinter group who opposed the IRA's ceasefire and the Good Friday Agreement, signed over the Easter weekend of that year. This was the highest death toll from a single incident during the entire period of the Troubles. Practically everyone in the town knew someone who was killed or injured, I was told when I phoned Richard Collins to offer condolences. The bomb had inflicted damage to the town as well as to its people, and in the months and years to follow, Richard's architectural practice would be heavily involved in the rebuilding of the bombed buildings.

In 1999, the Anne Frank exhibition visited the beautiful town of Armagh with its elegant Georgian terraces. My first planning visit was early in February, yet every green space was already vividly emblazoned with open-headed daffodils. This is the ecclesiastical capital of Ireland, where reside two Archbishops of Armagh, the Primates of All Ireland for both the Roman Catholic Church and the Protestant Church of Ireland. In ancient times, the nearby Navan Fort, built into a grassy hillside, was a pagan ceremonial site and one of the great royal capitals of Gaelic Ireland. Although its county town can cite centuries of spirituality, the southern part of the county, bordering the Republic of Ireland, became known during the Troubles as 'Bandit Country' due to the high number of IRA operations conducted there.

The visit of the Anne Frank exhibition inspired a marvellous initiative. For the first time in the city's sectarian history, children from two local schools, one Catholic and one Protestant, joined forces to produce a cross-community journal called *Anne's Legacy* in which they recorded their hopes for a more peaceful future.

Much had changed by the time we returned for an extended Northern Ireland tour in 2010. The city of Belfast was flourishing with flagships stores, exciting hotels, enticing waterside apartments and the Titanic Quarter, housing a world-class museum about the building in the city's shipyards, and subsequent sinking, of the ill-fated liner.

The exhibition visited several towns, the names of which had become so familiar during the time of the Troubles, including Strabane in the west, Lisburn, Newry and also Enniskillen, scene of the notorious Remembrance Day bombing of 1987 which had killed eleven people paying their respects at the town's Cenotaph. By 2010, the checkpoints and watchtowers had been dismantled and there was none of the discomfort I had felt in the early 1990s whatsoever. Former IRA leader, and by then Northern Ireland's Deputy First Minister, the late Martin McGuinness, even opened one of the exhibitions.

In Belfast, we were hosted by the Spectrum community centre in the Shankill Road, in the heart of Protestant Belfast, with some of its famous militant wall paintings still in taunting evidence. The event got off to a worrying start – the truck bringing the exhibition over from Strabane was in fact owned by the Gallagher Brothers, a clearly Catholic name that was emblazoned on the vehicle's side. Once parked outside the community centre a crowd of local Protestant Loyalists started to gather round it, and our Exhibitions Manager Doug told me he had never seen the exhibition unloaded so fast by a removal company. Then off down the road sped the Gallagher Brothers and their truck, hardly waiting to check that all had been properly unloaded. However, once it had been set up, the exhibition was proudly manned by volunteers, young and old, from both sides of the Belfast community. Such is the power of Anne Frank to bring people together.

Even as I write, two decades after the Good Friday Agreement, most communities still live apart, divided along religious lines. Despite excellent cross-community work, there are very few Protestant/Catholic integrated schools, so children can spend their entire school life in segregated schools, never meeting someone from the 'other side'. Communities live, work and shop apart. The Irish tricolour flag still flies in Catholic areas and driving round the province for several days in July 2010 during the Loyalist Protestant marching season, I drove through entire streets of towns and villages bedecked with the red, white and blue of the Union Jack flag.

In the spirit of *Anne's Legacy*, the school newspaper published in Armagh back in 1999, Anne Frank can perhaps still have a role to play in this sectarian society.

Chapter 17

Anne Frank and her Secret Hero

Anne's first cousin Bernhard ('Buddy') Elias was born in Frankfurt on 6 February 1925. He was the second son of Otto Frank's younger sister Helene, known as 'Leni', and her banker husband Erich Elias. Bernhard's name was soon shortened to Bernd, by which Anne always referred to him, but the world came to know him by his nickname of 'Buddy'. He was Anne's secret hero.

During her childhood Anne spent happy holidays with her cousin Bernd and his family in Switzerland. He is also seen, sometimes with his older brother Stephan, in many of the photos taken of Anne and Margot as young children sharing happy times in Frankfurt. The fun they were having together seemed to jump out of the black-and-white photos. On one memorable occasion he even accidently tipped baby Anne out of her pram by pushing it too fast.

The families were so close that when Anne's friends heard in July 1942 that the Frank family 'had fled to Switzerland to stay with the Eliases' (when in fact they were still in Amsterdam in hiding), this untruth was never questioned. According to Melissa Muller in her book *Anne Frank, The Biography*, Anne and Buddy were very alike. They were 'sassy, playful, imaginative and tireless. They were constantly thinking up new pranks and inventing new games.' The two loved playing hide and seek and years later Buddy reflected ironically that Anne 'was very good at hiding'.

Anne certainly admired older cousin Buddy for his bubbly personality and in particular his prowess at ice skating, a skill that was to shape his future life. Anne wrote to him from Amsterdam in January 1941, eight months after the German invasion, when anti-Jewish measures were rapidly increasing. She tells him excitedly how she is taking skating classes and is up at the local ice rink every spare minute. She ends the letter by saying: 'Bernd, maybe we can skate together as a pair someday, but I know I'd have to train very hard to get to be as good as you are.' By her next letter to Buddy a few weeks later, the ice rinks and other sports venues are forbidden to Jews so there is no further mention of her skating lessons.

After the post-First World War economic hardship in Germany and the Wall Street Crash, the Michael Frank Bank, which Erich Elias, the founder's son-in-law, had worked for, collapsed. Erich went to Switzerland, got a job with a company called Opekta, and in 1931 when he was ready, Leni and the two boys, Stephan and 'Buddy' duly followed. Although the move to Switzerland was a financial risk, it later saved the Elias family's lives. For a few years after the Elias's move to Switzerland, Anne and

Margot lost touch with their cousins but got to see more of them from the mid-1930s when Anne and Margot (sometimes separately) were taken to visit their grandmother Alice Frank, Aunt Leni, Uncle Erich and the two boys. Although Buddy was nearer in age to Margot, he found her more serious and less on his fun-loving and mischievous wavelength than the younger sister.

By 7 October 1942, Anne is already in hiding and busy with writing her diary. On yet another interminable day in the claustrophobic annexe, her imagination flies off to a future post-war trip to stay with her cousins in Switzerland. She decides that her generous father will give her a sum of money to buy herself new clothes. She makes a long list of the clothes (and makeup!) she needs, including of course a skating dress and a pair of skates. Off she goes on the longed for shopping trip with none other than Bernd. Anne's last mention of Bernd in her diary is on 30 June 1944 when she mentions that they have heard from Basel that he has appeared in a play in the role of an innkeeper (he must have been heavily disguised as he was only 19 at the time). She notes that her mother comments 'Bernd has artistic leanings'. The Frank family's excitement about Bernd's acting was to be short-lived – five weeks later came their arrest.

In the book *Treasures from the Attic, the Extraordinary Story of the Frank Family*, Buddy describes the horror of learning the eventual fate of Anne, Edith and Margot, and why Otto was so driven when promoting his daughter's diary. 'It took time for the significance of the diary to become clear,' recalled Buddy:

> I think at first he felt he wanted to make it up to Anne. He felt bad that he had never really known her and thought he should have treated her differently. They had divided up the children – Anne was Otto's child and Margot was Edith's, not exactly but you know what I mean. You could tell from when Anne was very young. Margot was a wonderful girl, but very quiet and introverted. I always see her in my mind with a book in her hand, always. Anne, on the other hand, was a bit wild, funny and cheeky, as you can tell from her diary too.

After the war Buddy studied acting in Basel and Zurich and started a career down that road appearing in several plays. Then an opportunity arose to go back to his childhood love of ice skating. He became a professional ice dancer touring the world for ten years with a show called *Holiday on Ice*, first the British show, then the Danish version. How delighted Anne would have been – imagine her probing of her cousin each time they met as adults and when he returned from international tours. She would have giggled at his antics as one half of the skating and clowning duo 'Buddy and Baddy'. When ice dancing became too physically demanding, Buddy's complementary acting skills took over. He appeared on stage with some of the most famous actors in the German-speaking world, such as Maximilian Schell. In 1965 Buddy married Gertrude 'Gerti' Wiedner, a beautiful Austrian actress whom he had met in a production two years earlier. He fondly nicknamed her 'Bambi' and together they had two handsome boys, Patrick and Oliver, both of whom also became actors.

The first time I had met Buddy and Gerti in person was in 1995 when the Anne Frank Trust marked the fiftieth anniversary of Anne Frank's death with a memorial service at St Paul's Cathedral followed by a reception at the nearby Stationers' Hall, one of London's medieval merchant guildhalls. The dinner on the preceding evening was rather special. Around the table with them were Miep Gies, Fritzi Frank, Eva and Zvi Schloss, the film-maker Jon Blair and Bee and Sid Klug. It was as if the rest of the Frank family were palpably in the room with us. I went on to spend many wonderful times in the company of this devoted couple in London, Amsterdam and memorably on our trip to New York when Kofi Annan signed the Anne Frank Declaration at the United Nations headquarters.

In April 2005, Buddy and Gerti Elias, my husband Tony and I were sitting in a restaurant in Camden, north London having dinner. We had not seen Buddy and Gerti for well over a year, during which time they had suffered a shocking and traumatic experience, the memory of which, several months later, was still etched deeply in Buddy's face and demeanour. As an actor internationally known for his comic timing and skills, even in his late seventies Buddy Elias had continued to carry a youthful appearance, with his good looks and joviality defying his age. But on that evening in London we were shocked to see that he seemed to have aged at least ten years since we had last seen him – his eyes sunken and his skin pale. As our dinner progressed we learnt of the horrific trauma the couple had so recently been through, in which they had had to run for their lives over a distance of three miles. Despite Buddy's distance from the Holocaust's terrors by living in Switzerland, the vicissitudes of life were eventually to deal a terrible blow one day after Christmas of 2004.

Buddy and Gerti were spending an idyllic winter holiday in Sri Lanka. On the morning of 26 December, just a few minutes after breakfast and a pleasant conversation with a French woman staying at the hotel, Buddy and Gerti separated as Gerti had booked a reviving massage. This was the morning the Boxing Day tsunami hit the coast of Sri Lanka, having travelled across the Andaman Sea from Indonesia, the epicentre of the earthquake that caused it. Gerti was enjoying the spa and Buddy was in their room, when they heard frantic shouting and screaming. They were each, independently, ordered to run for their lives in the clothes they were wearing: Buddy in his bathing shorts and Gerti in a bathrobe. In the melee of terrified people running inland, it was in fact several hours before the couple were reunited, both believing each had been drowned. Buddy told us they had each run non-stop for three miles – an incredible feat for a man of nearly 80 and a woman of 71. They learned that their French woman companion at breakfast that morning had not been so lucky and had been swept away. Still without clothing, Buddy and Gerti were flown to safety in Colombo, where they were looked after by the Swiss Consulate, and despite the loss of their passports were repatriated to Switzerland.

I had been speaking to Buddy by phone at fairly regular intervals since 1991 (emails were not yet a way of communication then) as he and Gerti were members of the Board of the Anne Frank-Fonds. I recall one dramatic phone conversation with Buddy. He called me immediately after Jon Blair had given him and Gerti a private screening of the feature-length documentary *Anne Frank Remembered*. Buddy was so enthused he almost shouted down the phone, 'Gillian, everyone must see this film!!' He reiterated to me, 'They have to see this film!! It is wonderful.' He then thanked me for bringing the amazing talent of Jon Blair into the fold (I had initiated the documentary in 1994 and in 1996 had the thrill of joining Jon and Miep Gies at the Academy Awards ceremony in Hollywood).

Buddy and his brother Stephan had both joined the Board on the Fonds' inception by Otto Frank in 1963 and Otto was excited to have his nephews involved. In those early years Buddy's constant travelling precluded him from taking an active role, but his involvement grew as he got older. In August 1980 Stephan Elias died at the relatively young age of 58 from jaundice which had turned into a lethal sepsis. The Elias/Frank families were dealt a double blow as Stephan's death came just four days after that of Otto Frank.

In 1991, I was viewed by the Anne Frank-Fonds with a degree of suspicion – an unknown woman from a strange English place called Dorset who had allowed a set of T-shirts to be created with a logo that contained the words 'Anne Frank'. Unlike some of the notorious Anne Frank-branded goods that had been produced in the Far East, our T-shirts were not for any commercial gain. In July 1992 our fledgling charity had taken part in a charity walk to raise awareness and some much-needed funds. All the participating charities were invited to wear distinguishing clothing, i.e. a baseball cap or T-shirt, and we had printed the name Anne Frank Educational Trust and our eye catching yellow steps logo on the top right-hand side of the T-shirt. The President of the Anne Frank-Fonds in the early 1990s was a man called Vincent Frank-Steiner (no relation to the Frank family) and he was dogmatic in his view of the protection of Anne's name. I am not sure how our T-shirts (printed in a limited edition of ten items for the charity walkers) came to Vincent's attention, but a few days after the walk, I received a call from him. In no uncertain terms he instructed me to send EVERY single printed T-shirt to Switzerland immediately so they could be inspected. 'But Vincent,' I stuttered, 'They have been worn for a long summer walk – can I at least have a chance to wash them?' No, they must be packed up and sent that very day, came the further instruction. So ten sweaty T-shirts were duly packed into a padded envelope and sent off to Switzerland, where several days later Vincent Frank-Steiner appeared on Swiss TV displaying the T-shirts as an example of the misappropriation of Anne Frank's name! Buddy had no such irrational dogma, and though a great defender of the memory of his cousin Anne and Uncle Otto, years later we came to laugh about the story of the T-shirts. Vincent Frank-Steiner left the Anne Frank-Fonds in 1996 and Buddy appropriately took over as President. Like his Uncle Otto before him, Buddy's later life was devoted to spreading the ideals of Anne and Otto Frank, and combatting the evils of prejudice and hatred.

A call to Buddy in Switzerland usually involved Gerti taking part on an extension. I particularly recall one 'Elias conference call'. It was 1998 and Buddy had recently taken over his new role as President of the foundation. I had submitted an application for a grant from the Fonds to tour an Anne Frank exhibition to British university campuses. Optimistically, and I thought unrealistically, I had sent them a shopping list of the entire budget I would need to create, launch and keep the exhibition touring campuses for a full two years. The exhibition I planned would have an extra section on 'Students in the Third Reich,' with panels showing the persecution of Jewish and anti-Nazi professors and explaining how young German university students were often enthusiastic supporters of Nazism (seeing it as an exciting anti-bourgeois movement) and committers of the notorious book burnings. The ancillary exhibition, accompanying the story of Anne Frank, would remind students of their responsibility towards democracy.

I picked up the call to hear Buddy tell me that the Fonds would certainly fund the creation of the exhibition, for which I thanked him profusely. Then Gerti's voice informed me that they would also fund the launch of the new exhibition at University College London. Back to Buddy who told me they would fund the cost of bringing over a volunteer from the German volunteer organization Action Reconciliation Service for Peace to tour with and manage the exhibition for two years. And then to Gerti who told me they would fund the insurance, marketing and transportation of the exhibition. And thus it continued until the entire budget had been covered. The sum was not insignificant and they were as delighted as I was.

Buddy and Gerti were in London again in February 2011 for the British launch of the book *Treasures from the Attic*, a 400-page compilation of thousands of letters, photographs and memoirs of the Frank family dating back to Anne Frank's great-great-great-grandparents Juda Nathan and Gutta Cahn who lived in the Frankfurt Jewish ghetto in the eighteenth century. The cache was only discovered when Gerti was clearing the attic of the family house in Basel. Together with the German biographer of Anne Frank, Mirjam Pressler, Gerti edited and transcribed the documents over a period of over two years. What is so fascinating about this engrossing family saga recorded in the book is that it shows how Annelies Marie Frank actually came from a long line of family members who were descriptive and enthusiastic writers – and how much the skill of writing was in the young diarist's DNA.

At a London book festival, I chaired the session where Buddy and Gerti described the process of collating the material, as well of course of Buddy's memories of his two lost cousins. At the end of the session an elderly woman stood up from the audience and explained how she had been a school friend of Margot's until her own family were able to flee to England in the mid-1930s. Buddy and Gerti went over and made a great fuss of her.

The following year I saw Buddy again but this time it was not in the flesh. I was on holiday in Norway and was flicking through the TV channels looking for an English language station. A German language movie appeared and, before I had a chance to flick the channel over, a very familiar face appeared on screen. It was Buddy. I can't recall what the film was about, I think it may have been a murder mystery, but I was riveted nonetheless. I was also wondering how many people who saw the movie, or indeed had laughed out loud many years earlier at the crazy antics of the clowning on ice duo of 'Buddy and Baddy', had realized they were watching the beloved first cousin, playmate and hero of Anne Frank.

Chapter 18

Anne Frank and Daniel Pearl

Daniel Pearl was an idealistic young American journalist who was murdered by al-Qaeda in Pakistan in 2002. I was fortunate to know him. It was in January 1997 and he was researching a story for his newspaper, the *Wall Street Journal*. He called me early in the morning requesting an interview with me concerning a rumour he had heard regarding a dispute that erupted between the two Anne Frank organizations in the Netherlands and Switzerland over the use of trademarks. He was incredulous that the two Anne Frank organizations set up with such good intent by Otto Frank could not see eye-to-eye.

The young American man rang my doorbell on a dark January night in 1997. He parked his dripping umbrella considerately outside the front door, came inside, removed his navy blue preppy-style raincoat and sat himself down on my lounge sofa. He asked me to call him Danny and we spoke for an hour over coffee. I deflected his probing about the trademark issues that had blown up between the two Anne Frank organizations by speaking about Anne Frank's true legacy. He was intrigued by the educational work the Anne Frank Trust was doing in the name of a talented writer killed so tragically young and brutally. I shudder when I think that on that evening Danny was not to know that in just a few years there would be educational work done in his memory too.

Danny Pearl followed up our meeting with several phone calls to verify some of the things we had discussed. I also arranged for him to interview Eva Schloss at her home in London and Hans Westra, Director of the Anne Frank House, in Amsterdam. I subsequently read the article filed by Danny, and found it very fair, without sensationalizing what was a delicate situation.

I thought no more about this encounter until the publicity surrounding the shock execution of the young American Wall Street journalist Daniel Pearl in Pakistan in February 2002. The terrified young hostage whose photo was flashed around the world after his capture, sitting on the bare floor dressed in a pink shell suit with his wrists in handcuffs and a gun pointing at his head, bore so little resemblance to the affable, intellectual young man in a suit, tie and navy raincoat who had visited my London home that I didn't make any connection between the two. That was until I opened *The Times* newspaper the morning after the news broke of his murder.

The obituary photo showed a familiar face, with round glasses and in suit and tie. I then read that Daniel Pearl had worked for two years in London between 1996 and 1998 as *Wall Street Journal* Bureau Chief. In a frenzied mission I looked back through the Anne Frank Trust's press archive and found the piece – published on 30 January 1997, and filed by 'Staff Reporter Daniel Pearl.'

Following his posting in London, Danny had gone on to Mumbai as the *Wall Street Journal*'s South East Asia Bureau Chief. Five months after the 9/11 attacks, in February 2002, he went to Karachi in Pakistan to follow up a lead to an al-Qaeda suspect called Mubarak Ali Gulani, who was supposedly connected to the 'shoe bomber' Richard Reid. Danny never arrived at the meeting. On his way to the café rendezvous, he was abducted by a militant group.

Just two days before his abduction, Danny had learned that his Parisian-born wife Mariane was expecting a baby boy. Thrilled by this news, he told her of his choice of name for his son, Adam. In May 2002, three months after Danny's murder, Mariane Pearl gave birth to Adam. She went on to write a book about her husband, *A Mighty Heart*, which was turned into a movie starring Angelina Jolie as Mariane. Mariane channelled her intense grief into bringing up her son and tackling important causes through her journalism and writing, for which she has won many awards.

On 10 March 2007, Khalid Sheikh Mohammed, an alleged al-Qaeda operative who was reported to be third in command under Osama bin Laden, claimed responsibility for the murder of Daniel Pearl. In a confession read during his Tribunal hearing, Khalid Sheikh Mohammed said 'I decapitated with my blessed right hand the head of the American Jew Daniel Pearl, in the city of Karachi, Pakistan.'

Danny's parents Judea and Ruth Pearl set up a foundation in Los Angeles in their son's memory. The aims of the Daniel Pearl Foundation are to promote cross-cultural dialogue and understanding, to counter cultural and religious intolerance, to cultivate responsible and balanced journalism, and to inspire unity and friendship through music. My admiration for this family was huge, but I never suspected my path would cross again with the Pearl family, especially as Danny's parents were in LA and his widow Mariane and son were living in Barcelona.

In 2014, I attended the Global Conference on Sexual Violence against Women held in London. Angelina Jolie (soon to become a Dame) and our then Foreign Secretary William Hague were co-chairs of the conference and had kindly agreed to sign the Anne Frank Declaration together. When the Anne Frank Trust's chairman Daniel Mendoza and I entered the room where the signing was to take place, William and Angelina were already sitting at the table with the Anne Frank Declaration placed in front of them, beaming widely and with pens at the ready. The two clearly had a great rapport.

Angelina was as beautiful in real life as she is on the screen. I gave her a copy of the credit card-size version of the Declaration she had just signed, and asked her, as I do to all signers, to keep it in her wallet as a reminder of what she had just signed. She asked me for more copies for her six children and told me that as they were all being home-schooled, she would ensure they learned about Anne Frank.

At the end of our warm and friendly chat, I mentioned to Angelina that I had known Danny Pearl. 'But Mariane is here at this conference. I must get you two together,' she said. Angelina asked me for my business card, passed it to her assistant and within two hours Mariane had emailed me. Due to conflicting commitments on both our sides, Mariane and I didn't actually get to meet that week, but we spoke on the phone.

Seven months later Mariane Pearl and I did get to meet. Mariane was the worthy recipient of the 2015 Anne Frank Award for Moral Courage, presented to her at our annual lunch to mark Holocaust Memorial Day. She flew from Barcelona to London to receive it. In her acceptance speech, as well as speaking about Danny, Mariane Pearl, born Mariane van Neyenhoff, told the 600-strong audience how her family had their own 'Anne Frank experience'. Mariane's grandfather was a Dutch diamond merchant and she had only recently discovered that her aunt had also been hidden from the Nazis in Amsterdam.

I often think of the young man in the navy-blue raincoat who came to my home on that dark winter night. I think of his loneliness and fear in those days of captivity and his last moments, when he knew his imminent fate. Danny refused the sedative offered to him before these animals who masquerade as human beings took a knife to his throat. He read out to camera the propaganda statement written for him by his captors, giving clues to the world that this was obviously not written by him, but preceded this with the words, 'My name is Daniel Pearl. I'm a Jewish American from Encino, California, USA. On my father's side the family is Zionist. My father's Jewish, my mother's Jewish, I'm Jewish. My family follows Judaism. We've made numerous family visits to Israel.' Then his throat was cut and his head, with a brain brimming with intelligence, compassion, wisdom and talent, was cut from his body.

Chapter 19

The Anne Frank Declaration

The Anne Frank Declaration was a pledge to heal the world written by the Anne Frank Trust in 1998. Its creation and its reception is one of my proudest achievements with the Trust. The words of the Declaration remember and honour all children who were victims of wars, hatred and persecution in the twentieth century, motivating those who sign it to strive for a fairer and more just world for all our children in the coming century. It has been signed by many international statesmen, politicians and civic leaders, social activists, heads of organizations, academic and educational institutions, including Nelson Mandela, Bill Clinton, British Prime Ministers Tony Blair, Gordon Brown, Theresa May and David Cameron, the UN Secretary General Kofi Annan, and more. It has also been signed by some of our best known celebrities including Steven Spielberg, Angelina Jolie, Peter Gabriel, Nile Rodgers and others; but most importantly tens of thousands of young people. This is how it all came about.

For several centuries a horse chestnut tree had been growing in the small garden at the back of 263 Prinsengracht, a typical canalside house that was built by Dirk van Delft in 1635, and where 300 years later Anne Frank was hiding. In her diary, Anne mentions the tree during different seasons of the year and how glimpses of this deciduous tree, in its changes throughout the seasons, had given her comfort and hope. Even on a wintry February morning in 1944, when she and Peter van Pels had climbed the stairs up to the freezing attic, she recorded: 'The two of us looked out at the blue sky, the bare chestnut tree glistening with dew, the seagulls and other birds glinting with silver as they swooped through the air, and we were so moved and entranced that we couldn't speak.' Otto Frank also believed in the redemptive power of trees, once referring to his favourite saying as, 'If the world were to end tomorrow, I would still plant a tree today.'

In 1998, Anne's beloved chestnut tree was discovered to be diseased and withering. My colleague from the Anne Frank House Barry van Driel, who had first suggested and subsequently developed the concept of using the Anne Frank story for peer-to-peer education in the early 1990s, decided to live in London for a while. I was excited to be able to have his talent and skills for the Anne Frank Trust.

One morning Barry and I were sipping coffee in my home, both feeling in a positive and creative mood. Our train of thoughts and ideas were flowing and we soon came up with a plan. If Anne Frank's beloved tree was to die, then why couldn't we encourage the planting of symbolic trees to replace it? How wonderful it would be to walk past trees in city centres and parks which were dedicated to Anne Frank and all the children who had been killed in wars and conflicts in the brutal twentieth century. It would stop people in their tracks and, for a brief moment on their way to work or play, encourage them to think about a world that could be better.

Barry and I sat on my sofa and put together a tree-planting ceremony to accompany the physical act of putting a symbolic Anne Frank Tree into the ground. With his agreement, we included a poignant poem by the Children's Laureate, Michael Rosen, which he had written following a visit to the Anne Frank House and fortuitously entitled 'Anne Frank's Tree'. We added suggested pieces of music and relevant readings from Anne's diary, and even the wording for a plaque to be placed alongside the tree to explain its significance to passers-by. I then asked Barry if he could write a special pledge to be read out during the tree planting ceremony.

On 12 June 1998, the sixty-ninth anniversary of Anne Frank's birth, a group of people were gathered on the piazza of the British Library in central London for the planting of the very first Anne Frank Tree. The group included the Dutch Ambassador to the UK, Anne's cousin Buddy Elias, Eva Schloss, Jan Erik Dubbelman, our Patron the South African born actress Janet Suzman, TV presenter Diane Louise Jordan and many of the Anne Frank Trust's supporters.

Over the next twelve months, a further 500 Anne Frank Trees were planted in city centres, parks and schools all over the UK. One of the most poignant that I dedicated was sited at the Soham Village College, a school in an idyllic Cambridgeshire village. In August 2002, three years after their Anne Frank Tree was planted, the school suffered a terrible tragedy. Two of their pupils, 10-year-old best friends Holly Wells and Jessica Chapman, were abducted and murdered by the school's own caretaker. The Anne Frank Tree went on to provide a place of comfort and solace to the traumatized and grieving pupils, around which children could sit with their thoughts.

The Declaration we had written for the Anne Frank tree-planting ceremony then emerged from its place within the ceremony to follow its own independent trajectory. I often tell people that the Anne Frank Declaration was written on my sofa. I can't remember if it actually was, or if Barry wrote the lines upstairs in my teenage son's former bedroom (which had become Barry's temporary office), or even in Barry's own home. But I can say that it was definitely first read to me by Barry on my sofa and that he did so much creative writing and associated pen waving on our cream-coloured sofa that my husband Tony insisted we buy some sofa covers to protect it from the threat of Barry van Driel and his dangerously active pen.

When Barry had been considering the wording of the pledge, an image of a boy he had met in Bosnia and Herzegovina came floating into his mind. He had encountered the boy when he was working on Bernard Kops's play *Dreams of Anne Frank*, which he and his drama educator colleague Henrietta Seebohm had taken as a post-Bosnian war therapy programme to schools in Sarajevo. The play had been accompanied by the Anne Frank exhibition. The boy was called Adnan, a bright six-year-old child who lived in a neighbourhood called Hrasno, which had been heavily damaged by Serbian army shelling. Adnan was fluent in English. How could this be possible at such a young age? Well, it turns out that during the siege of Sarajevo, during the limited times when there was electricity, he had found respite from the incessant shelling and shooting by watching TV in the dark and damp cellar below his home. His choice of programmes was limited but he happened upon a channel which was in English only. So day and night there he was, sheltering from the terror of incessant bombing, but at the same time learning to speak English from the American Cartoon Network.

After he had shown me what he felt should be the wording of the Declaration, Barry shared with me Adnan's story. He related the horrific experience that had happened to the boy and his family on a day that should have been happy and special. So this was it, the event that Barry had been evoking when he sat and wrote the Anne Frank Declaration, the pledge to make the twenty-first century a better place for the world's children.

As he told me about that day in Sarajevo in 1995 as Adnan had described it to him, Barry's eyes glazed over as if it was happening right there in front of him and as if Adnan was in the room with us in peaceful north London. Barry described to me how Adnan, his family and neighbours, found themselves confronted with hundreds of hostile soldiers who then started to use their captives as human shields. 'On one such occasion', recalled Barry, 'Adnan's terrified family were brought outside their house. As they were standing there they came under fire. A mortar shell landed nearby and everybody ran for their lives in different directions. An hour or so later the family came together again back in their home. His 13-year-old cousin walked in the room with Adnan's older sister in her arms – dead. It was the day of her 8th birthday. I asked Adnan if he ever thought about this. He said, "Every day".'

Anne Frank's beloved chestnut tree in Amsterdam was eventually felled not by disease, but by a heavy storm that occurred on the night of 23 August 2010. Saplings from the tree have been planted around the world, including in the UK, enhancing our own symbolic tree-planting project.

Political activist Nic Careem heard that we were planning to get people to sign up to the Anne Frank Declaration. He became excited. He believed that all politicians should sign it and strive to abide by its wording. And so in June 1998, Nic organized a Declaration-signing event at the House of Commons. Three of the major political party leaders came along to speak and endorse it: William Hague (Conservative); Paddy, now Lord, Ashdown (Liberal Democrat) and Alex Salmond (Scottish Nationalist). Many other politicians came along to sign, including gold medal-winning Olympian Sebastian Coe, who went on to lead the organization of the 2012 London Olympics. Prime Minister Tony Blair then asked to sign it at 10 Downing Street.

The Anne Frank Declaration had started its own life as a tool for betterment. In 1998, the South African President Nelson Mandela arrived in London for a visit.

The South African Acting High Commissioner Mr Happy Malanghu arranged for Mr Mandela to sign the Declaration at the High Commission in Trafalgar Square. As one heroic Nelson looked down on us from his majestic plinth in the square, another heroic Nelson emerged from a car and walked into the building. Nic and I were delighted to get a friendly wave and beaming smile as Mr Mandela walked towards the building, and even more thrilled to think he was about to sign the Anne Frank Declaration. He looked alarmingly frail at that time in 1998, but remarkably this great fighter lived for a further fifteen years.

Encouraged by the response we had had to the Declaration so far, Nic's ambition did not stop there. Who better to represent the whole world than the Secretary General of the United Nations himself? It took some doing, but after many calls and faxes to New York, on 13 January 1999 a delegation left London headed to New York for the UN. The costs of our New York trip were kindly sponsored by Lord Sainsbury of Turville. Virgin Atlantic Airways, as directed by Richard Branson himself, arranged for all sixteen in our delegation to travel in the comfort of Upper Class. Virgin's CEO Steve Ridgway met us at Gatwick Airport and personally escorted us as honoured travellers to the plane. For such an auspicious occasion as the United Nations the Anne Frank Declaration needed to be suitably robed and protected for its long journey. An expensive leather goods emporium in London's exclusive Burlington Arcade very generously donated a rich dark-green leather folder, and a professional calligrapher meticulously hand scribed the words on thick vellum paper.

On the flight were myself and my husband Tony, Barry van Driel, Eva Schloss, Anne Frank's cousin Buddy Elias and his wife Gerti, John Bird (the charismatic founder of *The Big Issue* magazine), the footballer and UN Goodwill Ambassador John Fashanu, and several Members of Parliament. A three-man film crew was with us to capture the event. We were to be met at the United Nations by further additions to the delegation: Richard Branson; Carol Bellamy, the Executive Director of UNICEF; the UK Ambassador to the United Nations Sir Jeremy Greenstock; and our own Life President Bee Klug, who had been wintering in Florida. Bee was to be accompanied by her cousin and close friend Sharon Douglas, who subsequently became an active Board member of the Anne Frank Center USA. We were thrilled when we learnt that thanks to Nic's perseverance the leader of our delegation would be none other than Mo Mowlam, the ebullient Secretary of State for Northern Ireland who had recently successfully brokered the Good Friday Agreement for the British Labour government.

We awoke on the morning of 14 January to the alarming news that a severe ice storm had hit the eastern USA. All public transport was closed down and looking out of the hotel windows we saw that everything was either covered in a thick layer of white or was totally invisible. How could we get ourselves down to the United Nations building, let alone be joined by the other dignitaries? We knew that Richard Branson was flying in from Los Angeles to join us, would he make it?

After trying to flag down the few yellow cabs that were on the hazardous roads that morning, we were forced to concede defeat. Eventually a limousine company sent a large van to collect our anxious group. It was a slow, slippery and painstaking journey along the deserted New York streets and, knowing that in any weather conditions the Secretary General's diary would be still full, I wondered if our long trip across the Atlantic would be in vain, as we would miss our precious time slot. Thankfully, the multi-coloured line of international flags that signalled we were approaching the United Nations building finally came into view out of the whiteness. Bee Klug's dogged determination not to miss this historic occasion meant we also soon spotted her petite fur-clad figure battling towards the UN entrance, with her cousin Sharon holding her tightly to guide her way.

Richard Branson had indeed found himself stranded in Los Angeles due to the severity of the ice storm on the East Coast but sent instead Virgin's US Chief Executive David Tate. We then received the news that Mo Mowlam was going to be severely delayed and realistically we decided she was probably not going to make it.

Our group was shown into the Secretary General's ante chamber, to await the arrival of Mr Annan. Suddenly the heavy wooden double doors flew open and in her famously rumbustious manner, in strode Mo Mowlam, apologizing to one and all for her lateness. It appeared she had sent her classically ministerial navy blue woollen suit to the dry cleaners ready for the occasion but the weather conditions had delayed its return. 'Well folks', explained Her Majesty's Secretary of State for Northern Ireland, 'I had two choices. Wait for the suit to be returned or come here stark bollock naked.' Mo Mowlam certainly knew how to break the tension, a fact that Republican and Unionist representatives said had helped in the delicate peace talks the previous year. She then spotted her old friend John Bird among our group. 'What the f*** are you doing here?' she asked him as we anxiously awaited the arrival of the Secretary General.

Kofi Annan and his aides duly appeared and the event became serious, important and emotive. Mr Annan is a Ghanaian whose Swedish wife Nane Lagergren is the great-niece of Holocaust hero Raoul Wallenberg. I had the honour of introducing and explaining the Anne Frank Declaration to Mr Annan. When I had finished my speech, Anne's cousin Buddy Elias, an actor by profession, ceremoniously opened the green leather folder and slowly read the following words:

> Anne Frank is a symbol of the millions of children who have been victims of persecution. Anne's life shows us what can happen when prejudice and hatred go unchallenged. Because prejudice and discrimination harm us all, I declare that:
> I will stand up for what is right and speak out against what is unfair and wrong.
> I will try to defend those who cannot defend themselves.

I will strive for a world in which our differences will make no difference –
a world in which everyone is treated fairly and has an equal chance in life.

In response Secretary General Annan read his own welcoming statement which appropriately focused on the world's young. He started by saying, 'Anne Frank's eternal words have inspired people of all ages, religions and nationalities, but they resound most powerfully among the young. That is one reason why the United Nations has taken her message to heart. For whom does the United Nations exist if not for the oppressed and vulnerable children and youth of our world?' We nodded politely in agreement and I cast my mind back to the Trust's first Patron Audrey Hepburn, herself a child helped by the United Nations in its early incarnation after the Second World War.

Annan concluded with the words, 'If Anne Frank, in her living hell, could summon the will to imagine a better, more peaceful world, a future free of suffering and persecution, then surely we can summon the will to make that day come to pass. In that spirit I am pleased to add my name to those who have signed this Declaration.'

I looked over and smiled at Barry van Driel, who had written the words the Secretary General had just signed up to. Barry was deep in thought about the time he had been working in Bosnia, where, as a Dutchman, he had been accused by angry members of its Muslim community of the failings of the Dutch UN Peacekeeping force to stop the massacre in Srebrenica. Later that day Barry told me how he was feeling in the Secretary General's office, 'You know what, I felt that finally here in the United Nations there was a sense of recognition.'

After Mr Annan and his team left the room, and our group had shaken our heads in disbelief that this had really happened, Buddy, Eva, Nic and I were taken to the auditorium where United Nations press conferences are held and there we conducted our own Anne Frank Trust press conference to a group of waiting journalists. Then our entourage were taken on a private tour of the United Nations building. We had organized lunch in one of the large function rooms in the building. Joining us was the President of the Anne Frank Center USA, Bergen-Belsen survivor Jack Polak, whom I had got to know on several previous visits to New York. Jack had helped to set up the Anne Frank Center and remained a loyal supporter and the guiding light of the organization until his death at age 102 in 2015.

On that unforgettable morning at the United Nations, Mo Mowlam had apologized that she could not stay for the whole lunch as, due to the grounding of flights, a car was collecting her immediately after her speech. She was to be driven to Washington DC for an important White House meeting with President Clinton. I assumed it was connected to the Good Friday Agreement, but despite my curiosity I asked no questions. Mo was going to have her starter course, give her speech to our delegation and shoot straight off to DC.

We sat down at the long four-sided table with Mo and myself sitting next to each other at the head. After the empty plate of her starter course was taken away, she stood up and started her speech, during which time everyone else's main courses were served. In mid-sentence Mo looked down at my tranche of salmon which happened to be garnished with crisp thinly sliced fried onions. She abruptly stopped what she was saying about Anne Frank, and her story's relevance to her own mission in Northern Ireland, and instead I heard the words, 'Oh my god – please excuse me. I just can't resist crispy fried onions.' Mo's left hand came down from holding the pages of her speech, hovered above my plate and then a handful of my crispy onions disappeared into Mo's mouth. As if nothing unusual had happened she then continued her speech with the words, 'Bigotry and intolerance forced Anne Frank to live an extraordinary life and robbed the world of an individual of such great promise. Today her vision drives me in my work in Northern Ireland.'

Marjorie 'Mo' Mowlam was a larger-than-life character who cut through bullshit like a hot knife through butter. Despite her life-threatening brain tumour, which she insisted for many years was benign, she took on the seemingly intractable Northern Ireland situation with a combination of charm and force. Apparently during a particularly tough meeting, she once threw off her wig in frustration, exposing a scalp robbed of any hair by the courses of chemotherapy she was undergoing. A couple of weeks after the New York event I received a handwritten note on pale blue paper from her thanking me for the opportunity to be part of the Anne Frank Declaration. Mo Mowlam passed away in 2005 after finally admitting her brain tumour was malignant.

The Anne Frank Declaration continued on its journey. President Bill Clinton was next on Nic's hit list. Unfortunately, there was no time for the President to take part in a signing ceremony during his visit to Northern Ireland in 1999. However, later that year Clinton was waylaid by my supportive American cousin Sir Arthur Gilbert at a function in Los Angeles. Arthur, London-born and given an honorary knighthood in 2000 for his bequest of the Gilbert Collection of art treasures to London, was a serious funder of Clinton. The President could not refuse Arthur's request, and he agreed to endorse the Anne Frank Declaration, although the opportunity did not transpire for him to physically sign the actual document.

In his letter sent to the Anne Frank Trust, President Clinton wrote:

In the wake of the dark histories of this century, marred by abundant evidence of man's capacity for inhumanity, Anne Frank serves as a model of courage and hope. Her diary is an inspiration for young people and adults throughout the world.

On the eve of a new century, the remembrance of Anne Frank and the many children like her, so tragically lost to war, demands that we work together as one to overcome intolerance, prejudice and bigotry. I am honoured to associate myself with Anne Frank as well as this very worthy declaration.

As you can guess this letter, sent from the Oval Office of the White House, was proudly displayed on our office wall.

There were subsequent signing events at the European Parliament by the Presidents of the EU and of the European Parliament in Strasbourg, and by two successive Commonwealth General Secretaries, Nigerian Chief Emeka Anyaoku and New Zealander Sir Don McKinnon, at the Commonwealth headquarters at Marlborough House, the rather grand former home of Queen Mary in Pall Mall. Mr Anyaoku said about Anne Frank:

> Very few teenagers have left such powerful records of the human spirit's indomitable will in the face of adversity . . . I feel sure that, like all truly great people, she would have been astonished if anyone had told her that we should acknowledge and applaud the magnificent example of her triumph over evil . . . It is the prerogative of young people to be passionate and intense. Thank God for those who follow the example of Anne Frank and use these attributes with a view to changing things for the better.

In 2000, Education Secretary David Blunkett invited Michael Hussey, a Trustee and former Inspector of Schools, and myself into his ministerial office to sign the Declaration. Seizing the opportunity, I asked Mr Blunkett if his Education Department would kindly consider funding a teaching pack for schools about the Anne Frank Declaration and its role in human rights and citizenship. This was duly produced, beautifully written by Michael Hussey, and promoted in schools by the Department as a recommended resource to support the introduction of Citizenship as a new school curriculum subject.

A succession of British mayors soon followed, signing up to it on behalf of their city or town, including London mayors Ken Livingstone and Boris Johnson. On a visit to Chicago in 2013, the city's mayor Rahm Emanuel invited me, accompanied by my Chicago-based daughter-in-law and granddaughter, into City Hall to sign it on behalf of the city of Chicago. The Mayor was rather smitten with three-year-old Emily and the pair had a very intense and friendly chat, during which I am sure she put some of the city's pressing social issues to rights.

The Declaration has taken on different forms. The Trust's Head of Education Lucy Glennon came up with the idea of creating a credit card-sized version to leave behind with signers. Once they have signed the larger version, we ask them to keep the card in their wallets to constantly remind them of what they have signed up to. Lucy and I were once at a working lunch in an Islington restaurant when we spotted Lord Falconer, the Labour Government's Lord Chancellor, sitting at a table across the room. Lucy and I looked at each other, excused ourselves to our meeting hosts and rushed across to try to persuade him to sign up. He smiled, pulled out his wallet and said, 'But I already have. Look, I carry it in my wallet!'

In December 2014 Prime Minister David Cameron signed the Declaration at 10 Downing Street, sitting at the very table where he had hosted the last G8 summit. He signed his name and then casually pointed out to me the chairs where Barack Obama

170

and Vladimir Putin had sat. Two months before, Theresa May, in her role as UK Home Secretary, had agreed to sign our Declaration at the Conservative Party Conference in Birmingham. Siama Khan, our Communications Officer, and I arranged to meet her in the lobby of the Metropole Hotel, which throughout the conference was buzzing with throngs of delegates. Mrs May duly arrived, tall, imposing and as elegantly dressed as ever in a powder blue coat, black blouse and trousers.

I stepped forward and welcomed her. 'I have actually met you before,' I reminded her as I led her towards a quiet table where the Anne Frank Declaration was awaiting her signature. 'It was back in 2003, when you spent some time at the Anne Frank Trust's stand at the Conservative party conference that year.' The Home Secretary smiled so I continued in a chatty vein. 'I will always remember your beautiful shoes. They were leopard skin with an attractive kitten heel.' As I said the word 'shoes' my eyes automatically went downwards towards her feet. And there adorning her feet were a pair of adorable leopard skin kitten heel shoes.

The words came out of my mouth in an unstoppable and far too explosive way. 'Oh my god, you're wearing the same shoes!' With that Mrs May's eyes went downwards to the floor, as did those of Siama and Mrs May's Senior Advisor Liz Sanderson. 'I can assure you they are different shoes,' Mrs May firmly insisted. 'Of course, of course,' I spluttered. I am certain the Home Secretary would not be wearing the same shoes for some eleven years, and her fondness for the leopard skin design was well known. Siama would not let me forget this incident and each time Mrs May subsequently appeared on TV, we would discuss her shoes and the proportion of leopard skin contained in them.

Theresa May was the longest-serving Home Secretary for over 100 years with a reputation for being one of the toughest. She was also the first woman to take on this Cabinet position, and as I write is only our second female Prime Minister. Despite my faux pas about her shoes, Mrs May was very warm when she sat down and signed the Declaration, giving us time in her frenetic conference calendar to discuss the Anne Frank Trust's important work in some very divided British communities and how much she and the Home Office valued it. The following year the Home Secretary agreed to speak at the Trust's annual fundraising lunch to be held in January 2016. The Trust's lunch took place six months before the Brexit vote was to shake up British politics, paving the way for Mrs May's premiership. When she arrived at the London Hilton on Park Lane for our lunch, I escorted Mrs May around the 'green room' and introduced her to our most important guests. These were Daphne Schild, our long-time and very loyal lunch host, Holocaust survivors Eva Schloss, Leo Friedler and Lilian Levy, and some of our teenage Anne Frank Ambassadors. Even though many of our donors were jostling to catch Mrs May's eye, she was totally focused and generous with her time with those we had chosen for her to meet, as they, especially the teenagers, were the ones she really wished to hear from.

Mrs May's speech as Home Secretary to 600 business people in the room came at a time when the Home Office had seen hate crime dramatically increase by

18 per cent over the course of the previous year, and she described the upward trend of hate crime as very worrying. She praised the Trust's work in schools and communities and for 'raising awareness of prejudice and extremism of all kinds'. Referring to atrocities both in the UK and abroad, and stating that 'Sadly today this work could not be more pertinent or pressing', she added, 'We've seen an increase in anti-Semitic attacks, the like of which I thought we would never see again in Europe.' Later that year, following the Brexit vote to leave the EU, hate crimes in Britain spiked even further upwards.

Other well-known Anne Frank Declaration signers have included Dame Angelina Jolie in her role as UNHCR representative; the late Vidal Sassoon, who was a lifelong fighter against racism and anti-Semitism, legendary musicians Nile Rodgers and Peter Gabriel and actor Tim Robbins. Sir Paul McCartney has even endorsed it with a message of goodwill sent from the US. All these big names help to encourage others to sign up.

I realize of course that for many the signing of the Anne Frank Declaration, and the photograph of their signing, is the end rather than the means to the end. I know the words on the Declaration won't really stop the iniquities and injustices of this world, but the Declaration has proved to be a worthy door opener to gain access to the decision-makers and influencers who can help us continue our increasingly vital work. A faded and ghostly image of Anne Frank's smiling face stares out from the card version, her smile beseeching us to take the words seriously.

Most importantly, tens of thousands of children and young people have signed it online and at our exhibitions. And after all, they are the ones who will, or will not, make our world better, fairer and more equal.

Chapter 20

The Anne Frank Trust is Growing

How did the Anne Frank Trust grow from a one-man band to the successful and admired organization it is now? It was all about people, their belief in the power of Anne Frank's message and their contribution to perpetuating this. I will attempt to condense a quarter of a century of intense activity into a few thousand words about the significant milestones along the way and the people without whom it could not have happened.

After we had moved from Dorset in 1992, the Trust was run from my home in Hertfordshire, in no small part with the help of my husband Tony Bogush. A spiral staircase led from our living area up to a small bright room, which became the Trust's first official office. Our Trustee Board was growing to encompass people from the education and commercial worlds and we were holding our Board meetings at the West End offices of one of the Trustees, David Goldstein, a commercial real-estate agent. It was exciting to be attending Board meetings right in the heart of the West End, right opposite the headquarters of the BBC.

There was a new 'half' too. Ruth Allen was a lovely, caring woman who lived around the corner in Bushey. She was an old-style loyal, efficient and dedicated secretary, new technical innovations were not her interest, but she would not hesitate to help on all fronts, often collecting my children from school or activities. When we had a big mailout to get through, Ruth would be sitting round my dining-room table at weekends or late at night, often calling in her friends and family to help out.

A great status boost to the fledgling charity came in April 1994. The Dutch premiere of the movie *Schindler's List* was being held at one of Amsterdam's most iconic buildings, the lushly Art Deco style Theater Tuschinski. This was a poignantly appropriate venue as its visionary builder, the Polish immigrant Abraham Tuschinski, had been murdered with his family in the Holocaust. At the drinks reception prior to the movie, I had been introduced to the film's director, Steven Spielberg. Naturally, I found the same words spilling out of my mouth that had done so when I had met Audrey Hepburn in 1991. 'Would you agree to be a Patron of the Anne Frank Educational Trust?' I asked him. 'Of course,' came the reply from Mr Spielberg. To this day I wonder if he thought he was being asked to be a Patron of the Anne Frank House, but nonetheless his name went immediately on to our headed notepaper.

I have met Steven Spielberg several times subsequently and always found him to be a remarkably humble man. He was respectful of the fact that although he would have loved to have made his own movie about Anne Frank, he 'would not do anything to upset the Frank family'. By this he meant Otto Frank's nephew Buddy Elias, the President of the Anne Frank-Fonds, as the foundation had already sold the rights for a potential new movie elsewhere.

My continuing work with the Anne Frank travelling exhibition is covered separately, but while I was criss-crossing the country with the exhibition, other educational activities were simultaneously taking place. By 1994, the fiftieth anniversary of the death of Anne Frank and the end of the Second World War in May 1995 was getting to be a matter of months away. At that time the rights to publish Anne Frank's diary in the UK were held by Macmillan Books, who had held them since the 1950s. However, the CEO of Penguin Books, the publishing legend Peter Mayer, was desperate for his company to acquire the rights to publish Anne's diary in the UK; one of his staff described to me his tenacity in terms of 'I think he would even sell his own child to get it.' (Penguin did not succeed in getting the UK rights until 1997 when they published the full 'definitive' version of the diary. This edition had the one-third of the content that had been removed by Otto Frank and the original 1947 publishers, Contact, reinstated.) Despite not being able to publish a version of Anne's diary, Penguin was publishing two Anne Frank-related books to mark the fiftieth anniversary.

I arranged separate meetings with both companies, Macmillan and Penguin, to discuss how we could work together to mark the impending anniversary, and on receiving positive feedback from both of them, we finally all met together to talk about what could be a special and fitting commemoration. Then we heard that the Dean and Chapter of St Paul's Cathedral, its governing body, had agreed to host the Anne Frank exhibition throughout April 1995. Additionally, they would host a Memorial Service for Anne Frank, which for the first ever time in the cathedral's 300-year history, would use both Jewish and Christian liturgy. The service was sensitively written by the Deputy Director of the interfaith organization, the Council of Christians and Jews, a Catholic nun called Sister Margaret Shepherd.

Penguin and Macmillan offered to jointly fund the exhibition and the cost of poster advertising in central London Tube stations. The memorial service duly took place on 15 April 1995, the fiftieth anniversary of the liberation of Bergen-Belsen, in the OBE Chapel of St Paul's and in the presence of the Frank family's wartime helper, Miep Gies, who had come from Amsterdam; Fritzi Frank, Otto's widow, and Buddy Elias, Anne Frank's first cousin, who had both come over from Switzerland.

My spine still tingles when I recall that morning. The procession was led into the packed chapel by two esteemed and much-loved clergymen, Auschwitz survivor Rabbi Hugo Gryn (who was sadly to die the following year) and the Dean of St Paul's, the Very Reverend Eric Evans, who passed away just two months after Rabbi Gryn. Such was the significance of this ground-breaking and inclusive ceremony that it merited a whole item on the BBC's evening news programme and a full page of coverage in the *London Evening Standard*, as well as coverage in the next day's national papers.

The atmospheric crypt of St Paul's Cathedral housed the Anne Frank exhibition. Due to restoration works being carried out at that time on the main cathedral doorway, all visitors had to exit the cathedral via the crypt, thus ensuring that over the course of the month we were *in situ* approximately 100,000 people were exposed to all or some of the exhibition panels. The crowd waiting to make purchases at our Anne Frank bookshop was at times ten people deep. Ruth and the team of volunteers took the continuous crush of people in their stride, happily ringing up the cash machine.

In the months preceding the St Paul's exhibition in 1995, the Trust worked with Penguin Books to stage a national writing competition called 'Dear Anne Frank.' Children who were old enough to compose letters were invited to write a letter to the deceased Anne Frank, describing to 'her' their lives and hopes. The competition resulted in a lovely book of the best letters published to coincide with the opening of the St Paul's exhibition. Five winners were taken on a trip to the Anne Frank House, funded by Penguin Books, where they were fortunate enough to sit in Otto Frank's private office with Miep Gies present to answer their questions.

This was one of many wonderful writing campaigns and competitions the Trust has staged and the start of a long and fruitful association with Penguin Books and its team of publicists and editors. Sadly, Sally Gritten, who was the instigator of the competition in her position as Penguin Children's Books' Director of Marketing, and who became a dear friend, passed away in September 2102 after a long battle with leukaemia.

In the summer of 1996, we introduced a new educational event, to be known as 'Anne Frank Day'. On the anniversary of Anne Frank's birth, 12 June 1929, we would offer teachers an opportunity to reflect on the moral lessons of Anne's short life. We would provide teachers with specially written classroom materials and assemblies, suggesting they take a little time out from the usual curriculum demands to mark the day. This was still before we could send materials out by email and in the earliest days the Royal Mail would send a special van to our house to collect all the packs going out to British schools. Our Trustee Michael Hussey, a brilliant educator and former English inspector for London schools, set about writing a marvellous teaching pack for both primary and secondary schools, linking Anne's story across secondary level curriculum subjects. For the youngest pupils, who could not be exposed to the horrors of the Holocaust, Michael introduced accessible themes, such as the value of friendship and the importance of celebrating birthdays.

Michael Hussey had an intriguing life story. He had been born to an African mother and white father in colonial Rhodesia, and had been a freedom activist in both South Africa and pre-independence Rhodesia, now Zimbabwe. Michael had a natural warmth, charm and empathy as well as flair for creating beautifully-written teaching materials, and if I dare say it, was one of my favourite ever members of our Board of Trustees. He was forced to step down in 2000 after suffering a major stroke, which thankfully the dedication and determination of his former music teacher wife Margaret helped him to overcome.

For many years we continued to encourage Anne Frank Day school activities and created new assemblies with different themes for each year. If Anne Frank Day happened to fall on a Sunday, we would create a special service for churches and on one year we discovered our 'Anne Frank Sermon' had been used by many English cathedrals after being featured on the home page of the Church of England's own website. By that time Ruth Allen had retired and the administration team had grown by 100 per cent to two people. They manned the office while I was often away travelling around the country setting up new exhibitions, raising money or attending openings. In 1996, Tony and I had bought a new house in Highgate in a leafy and historic area of north London. My desk would be at one end of the L-shaped living area and an adjacent room became the administrative office.

By 2000, David Soetendorp had been our Founding Chairman for ten years and the time was coming for him to relinquish the reins to someone new. Our President Bee Klug and I remembered that in 1993 we had staged an Anne Frank exhibition at a venue owned and run by a dynamic and charismatic young man called Jack Morris. Like so many people we encountered over the years, there was already a connection to Bee. Jack's mother Gilda and Bee went back as friends a very long way and Bee often recounted that she had first met Jack before he had even been born. Jack Morris was the fifth son of Gilda and her late husband Sam, a visionary entrepreneur who had transformed a near-derelict Victorian livestock market building in Islington, known as the Royal Agricultural Halls, into a zinging modern exhibition and events centre, renamed the Business Design Centre. Bee and I paid Jack a visit in his office and within twenty minutes we had our new Chairman.

As well as his business skills, Jack was well-known and respected for his philanthropic life, and had a particular interest in education. He was the Chairman of the City and Islington College and was very involved in local charities. Jack brought a fresh enthusiasm to chairing the Board meetings, which met sometimes at the Business Design Centre, but oftentimes around my Highgate dining-room table. In 2001, we shortened the name of the charity, from the Anne Frank Educational Trust, to the Anne Frank Trust UK, while retaining its principal focus on education.

Jack soon set about introducing three of his good friends to his new cause. I duly went to meet with them: Sir David Michels, the CEO of the Hilton hotel group, Michael Hirst, the former Chairman and CEO of the Hilton group who was still very active in the hospitality industry, and Peter Galloway, a Mayfair-based accountant. David Michels was the son of a refugee from Nazism, who had actually been studying English in London when war broke out in 1939. David's father had been brought up in a wealthy family and the young student was so sheltered from a normal life that he sent his clothes back to Germany to be laundered every week. The family's cushioning wealth did not save David's grandfather from being murdered in the Holocaust.

David has summed up his long-time attachment to the Anne Frank Trust as, 'My history forces me to do it, and the people in the organization make me enjoy doing it.' Michael Hirst did not have such a close Holocaust connection but was drawn to the enduring personality of Anne Frank and her story. 'The Trust brought this to life and made it as relevant today as when Anne was writing her diary.' His initial feeling about the charity, not knowing much about it, was that if Jack Morris had invited him to get involved it had to be a cause worthy of support. However, fifteen years later he feels it is a charity he is immensely proud of and one it is almost a 'civil duty' to promote.

When I met Peter Galloway for an exploratory coffee he revealed to me that his interest in the Anne Frank story had been fired some time ago by his mother's cousin, whom he told me was passionate about the story. My ears pricked up at the possibility that his relative could be yet another potential recruit to help our charity. 'Her name's Bee Klug,' he continued, 'I wonder if you've ever encountered her.'

Jack, David, Michael and Peter started to meet on a regular basis and I have always referred to them since those days as 'Our Gang of Four'. Over early breakfast meetings at one or other of the London Hilton hotels they formulated a fundraising event aimed at London's business community that if successful could perhaps be staged annually. Working together with the very talented and creative owners of the Hype! communications company, we decided that our lunch would be held during the week of 27 January and by doing so would give it a special focus that would be hard for guests to decline.

On 27 January 2001 the UK had held its first-ever national Holocaust Memorial Day and thankfully it had seemed to capture the hearts and minds of the nation. As well as a major central London memorial ceremony, local commemorations had been staged around the country. A national Holocaust Memorial Day for Britain had originally been agreed at the Stockholm International Forum on the Holocaust held in January 2000, convened by the Swedish Prime Minister Göran Persson to plan how the Holocaust would be commemorated in countries around the world as we moved into the twenty-first century. To ensure that Holocaust remembrance and education continued to be taken seriously, out of this conference came an international 'task force', now known as the International Holocaust Remembrance Alliance (IHRA).

Leading up to the Stockholm conference, I had been a member of the Home Office's advisory committee to shape what our British Holocaust Memorial Day would look like. Our committee agreed that, as well as the Shoah against the Jews, the day would commemorate other more recent genocides such as in Cambodia, Rwanda and Srebrenica. The commemoration events would also offer an opportunity to reflect on racist and prejudicial attitudes to religious, racial and sexual difference, while not making equal comparison of attitudes with outright genocide.

Prime Minister Tony Blair and his Home Secretary Jack Straw wished to make a high-profile announcement that the UK would henceforth mark the date of the liberation of Auschwitz as Holocaust Memorial Day. Appropriately, they came to make the announcement at the 'Anne Frank, A History for Today' exhibition staged at Methodist Central Hall in Westminster. Holocaust Memorial Day, always marked around 27 January, has remained a significant fixture in the nation's calendar ever since. Events are supported by excellent planning and educational materials produced by the Holocaust Memorial Day Trust, which also organizes the main national ceremony in central London.

Our first 'Anne Frank Trust Lunch to mark Holocaust Memorial Day' was held at the Hilton Hotel in Paddington in January 2003 with the Right Honourable Paul Boateng MP as our speaker. Boateng, the Chief Secretary to the Treasury and as such Number 2 to Chancellor Gordon Brown, had been the first black politician appointed to the British Cabinet. He was also one of our founding Patrons, and had personally invited Opposition Leader Tony Blair to launch our new exhibition at Southwark Cathedral in January 1997. In January 2000, it was Boateng, when Home Office Minister, who had led the British delegation to the Stockholm Conference that had brought about Holocaust Memorial Day. The lunch committee all agreed that Paul Boateng would be an appropriate choice of speaker for the inaugural lunch.

The lunch sponsor was the entrepreneur Rolf Schild, a staunch Conservative supporter, but as a refugee from Nazi Germany who had lost virtually all his close family in the Holocaust, he was pragmatic about our choice of a prominent Labour speaker. During the course of the lunch I was happy to spot Messrs Schild and Boateng deep in animated conversation, I am sure debating their political differences, the economy and business opportunities.

I will always recall that day as an emotional roller coaster. Just before I was leaving for the wonderful event at the Hilton Hotel I had received a letter from the National Lottery, informing me that our application for funding to help create a new version of the Anne Frank exhibition had been declined. The disappointment was assuaged by an invitation to attend a meeting at the National Lottery's head office to discuss how we could make the next application successful (a process which duly came to a much happier conclusion the following year).

The high of the successful lunch continued well into that evening as I had been invited to attend the premiere of the movie *Catch Me If You Can*, directed by our Patron, Steven Spielberg. Spielberg had not been able to attend our lunch as he had previously committed to another Holocaust commemoration event, but the tickets for Tony, my daughter Tilly and myself to the premiere were offered as a token of compensation. It was a truly magical end to a memorable day, and at the after show party I found myself in conversation with our esteemed Patron, plus the film's leading actors, Tom Hanks and Leonardo di Caprio. Tilly got to meet the man whom the film was based upon, the one-time audacious fraudster Frank Abignale, who gave her a souvenir of his days as a bogus Pan Am pilot, a little Pan Am airplane pin badge. Pan Am by that time had actually ceased to exist as the company never recovered from the Lockerbie terrorist atrocity in 1988 and customer fears of terrorism flying with such an overtly American brand.

The first Anne Frank lunch had attracted over 200 paying guests and 'Our Gang of Four' decided it was definitely worth replicating. The lunch grew over the years, and since 2004 has been hosted continuously by Rolf Schild's widow, my close friend Daphne Schild. There have been some wonderful speakers, including former Foreign Secretary David Miliband, who told our audience of his Holocaust-related family background and how his aunt Nan Keen had been one of the first translators into English of Anne Frank's diary. When Miliband had told his aunt that he was to speak at the Anne Frank Trust's lunch, her face had lit up at the memory of her meetings with Otto Frank sixty years earlier.

In 2011 the former South African President F.W. De Klerk flew to London to address our lunch about his personal journey towards the dismantling of apartheid and in 2010 Judge Thomas Buergenthal, the American judge at the International Court of Justice flew from The Hague to speak to our audience. Buergenthal was one of the few survivors of both Auschwitz and an ensuing death march to Sachsenhausen camp, even more miraculous considering he was just 11-years-old. He was not reunited with his mother until two years after his liberation. In his distinguished legal career Judge Buergenthal was the recipient of many high-level awards for upholding international human rights.

Ours is a fundraising event with an unusual degree of depth and integrity, hence the loyalty to the event shown by our supporters. Each year we start the proceedings, setting a serious and emotive tone, by a candle-lighting ceremony. The imposing on stage candelabra is lit by a small group of Holocaust survivors, survivors of other genocides and those affected by recent atrocities or acts of prejudicial violence. As each candle is lit the lighter's story is explained to the audience. On each table around the room there is an individual candle centrepiece, and the table host is invited to light this ahead of a minute of silence to remember all victims of the Holocaust and other atrocities, historic and current.

We have been honoured to welcome some very special guests to the lunch, thanks to the help of PR consultant Richard Leon, who gives his time pro bono. Richard had a deeply-held respect for by-now elderly British war veterans who had given so much for their country. One year he invited his friend, the iconic wartime entertainer Dame Vera Lynn, to the lunch when she was already in her mid-90s. I had fully expected to see Dame Vera arrive in a wheelchair. Readying myself to welcome an frail elderly lady, I was amazed when she came striding into the women's cloakroom in full make-up, coiffed hair and mink coat. She looked as pretty as ever and her personality and warmth shone out of her sparkling eyes. One year Mr Henry Allingham, one of the last surviving veterans of the First World War, came from his home in Sussex and blatantly flirted with all the women gathered around him. Nearing the age of 113, he told me he was looking forward to being 'a teenager' again but sadly passed away soon after.

The first fundraising lunch that we held in January 2003 led in a noteworthy year for the Anne Frank Trust. The following month I was honoured by the social services charity Jewish Care at their fundraising lunch for the business community. I was to be the recipient of their annual award presented to someone they considered deserved public recognition. As I walked on stage at the London Hilton, collected the award and began to give my acceptance speech, unbeknown to me a young businessman in the room was responding to my words in a way that would have a long-term implication for the growth of our charity.

The young man was called Daniel Mendoza, a descendent of the famous eighteenth-century bare-knuckle boxer of the same name. Mendoza the boxer had helped transform the popular English stereotype of a weak defenceless Jew into someone deserving of respect. It was he who had changed the sport of boxing from the pugilists standing and delivering blows to each other, to one of balletic prancing, ducking and diving. The twenty-first-century Daniel Mendoza was the father of two young children and was at the stage in his life where he was making a good living from his commercial property business and wanted to give something back to society. Something I had said in my acceptance speech for my award lit a spark and he called me the following week wanting to know more about what the Anne Frank Trust did.

As Bee Klug and I had done to Jack Morris a couple of years earlier, Jack and I duly called Daniel to come for a meeting at the Business Design Centre. Jack immediately recognized the humanitarian impetus that was propelling Daniel as something he had also felt as a young father wanting to make the world better for his young children, and it was having my own children Joe and Tilly that had equally propelled me into the world of voluntary activism and then into the not for profit professional arena. It didn't take many minutes in Jack's office to sign up a new Trustee in the form of Daniel Mendoza.

Around that time too our full-time administrator was leaving and Ruth Allen, who by that time was part time, was planning to retire after eleven years with the Trust. I put an ad in a local paper for a new administrator (even by 2003 little was done digitally). One of the calls I received was from someone with a rather familiar voice – it was from a woman I had actually known since I was 11-years-old. My old school friend from Bournemouth, Marsha Selwyn, had seen the ad and although the position really interested her, her enquiry was tentative. 'Look Gilly, I realize that it might be difficult for you to be my boss when we have known each other for so long,' she started and then reminded me (although I needed no reminder) that our parents had been very friendly and our maternal grandmothers had actually remained the closest of friends well into old age. Marsha, who had just sold her partnership in a fitness club, certainly had all the right skills so I agreed she would be interviewed for the role, but with an open and frank discussion about how we could make this unusual relationship work. Well it seemed to work out because as

I write Marsha has been the office manager and company secretary, now with the title and responsibility of Director of Administration, for over fifteen years, and has played a huge role in the growth of the organization.

Throughout her first year Marsha and I worked hard together to bring about the inception of an educational programme for schools on the theme of moral courage. We planned that by highlighting Anne Frank's moral courage, and of course that of her helpers too, we could encourage an understanding of its value to the community and wider world. Our aim was to recognize those who were exemplars through making awards in Anne's memory.

But first came the materials. Although we had no in-house education team at that time, a teaching pack for schools and youth organizations called 'Moral Courage – Who's Got It?', accompanied by a VHS video, was funded by the Department for Education and created by a team of educators and civil servants we had previously worked with and trusted. Our planning meetings were held in the Department for Education's Westminster offices, leading up to the launch of our teaching materials, officially flagged by the Department as a recommended resource for their introduction of Citizenship as a new curriculum subject in September 2002.

We had started to develop a close working relationship with what was then called the Department of Education and Employment (it has changed name several times during the lifetime of the Anne Frank Trust) after one of its Education Secretaries, David, now Lord, Blunkett, had visited the Anne Frank exhibition in Westminster in January 2000. Two weeks later Michael Hussey and I visited his office where he duly signed the Anne Frank Declaration. A kind and empathetic man, Blunkett became a great endorser of our work. It was Blunkett in his next ministerial role as Home Secretary, who gave the Anne Frank Trust its first major Government grant of £50,000 in 2004 towards the creation of our planned new exhibition, 'Anne Frank + You'.

Life had not been easy for David Blunkett. Born blind due to a genetic disorder, when he was 12 his father died from a horrific work accident, after falling into a vat of boiling water. Compensation for the struggling family after this terrible tragedy was hard fought for as apparently David's father had been working beyond his official retirement age. Blunkett's own stellar political career, overturning all expectations for a blind man from such a tough background, was tragically felled in 2004 through his doomed affair with a married woman and a debilitating public battle for access to the son born of that relationship.

In the autumn of 2002, the Trust had taken a small exhibition stand at our first (of many to follow) party conferences. In this first instance it was at the conference of the then Labour government, held in the well-known seaside resort of choice for northern British working people, Blackpool – a highly appropriate destination for the Labour Party. Party conferences have always been an opportunity to capture all the strands of a charity's network under one roof, journalists, politicians and leaders of other NGOs. If you are prepared to throw yourself head-first into them, they can provide a great return on investment of time and expense. After only a day I realized that being at the conference was even more exhilarating than a ride on the town's famous Big Dipper – a never-ending round of important visitors to our stand, bumping into crucial government leaders and making sure a follow-up meeting ensued, running to fringe meetings and watching with undiluted glee as famous and usually serious politicians and journalists would make complete fools of themselves on the dance floor at the late night wind-down parties.

In 2003, Jack Morris stepped down as Chair of our charity, but continued to chair the lunch committee as both the event and the committee were growing. His role as our charity's Chair was taken over by one of the founding members of the Board, the South African-born publisher Dr Gillian Klein. Her company Trentham Books specialized in books and journals that promoted multicultural education in schools and universities. I guess it was somewhat confusing having a charity run by two women with the relatively uncommon first name of Gillian, and who both ran their companies from addresses in Highgate, but we managed well and collaboratively, even while chairman Gillian was undergoing exhausting treatment for breast cancer.

By the summer of 2003 we needed to ramp up the publicity for the Anne Frank Awards for Moral Courage, but had a limited PR budget. The Department for Education was getting the message out to schools and Penguin Books was helping too through their school book clubs. One morning I was travelling by Tube into central London and having nothing to read, started reading the advertisements on the train. An idea started forming in my mind and within a couple of weeks I was sitting in an office at the headquarters of the London Underground. Sadly, the name of the senior manager I met escapes me, but I detected he was very interested in the moral courage programme. 'If you were to give me a cheque today for £100,000 or offered to publicize the Anne Frank Awards for Moral Courage at every station on the Tube network,' I brazenly suggested, 'I would not hesitate in taking the latter.' And yet again the chutzpah seemed to work as that's exactly what happened. In July 2003, huge posters appeared on the platforms and escalator walls of nearly every station of the entire London Underground network, spotted from the outlying suburbs to the West End. They showed a Tube platform swarming with people and above it the headline, 'Sometimes it takes courage to stand out from the crowd'. The cost of the production of the posters, paid for by London Underground, plus the value of this prime advertising space, was inestimable.

That autumn saw Marsha and I busily preparing for the first Anne Frank Awards ceremony. In a room overlooking the Thames at Penguin Books' head office in London's famous Strand, the panel of judges, which included the Metropolitan Police Commissioner Sir John Stevens; Doreen Lawrence, the mother of murdered teenager Stephen, and actor Sir Ben Kingsley, deliberated over who would receive the awards.

The first Anne Frank Awards for Moral Courage ceremony took place a few weeks later at the Hilton Hotel in November 2003. Over the ensuing years there were so many recipients of these awards, children, educators and community activists whose stories were each worthy of a chapter to themselves, but sadly space precludes this. One recipient, Nicole Dryburgh, is described in my chapter on Miep Gies, as she was given the special Miep Gies Award in 2009. However, the winners of the Special Award at the first ceremony must be mentioned.

When a group of five well-dressed and smiling teenagers walked on to the podium to collect their award, none of the audience would have suspected the trauma those brave children had endured in their native country of Kosovo. The oldest, and their impassioned spokesman, was 16-year-old Saranda Bogujevci. She introduced her younger girl cousins Jehona and Lirie, and her boy cousins, Fatos, and the impish-looking youngest, Genc. None of these children had a living mother. The women of the two branches of the family had been murdered in 1999 in a notorious massacre of fourteen women and children by a vicious Serb paramilitary unit. The Scorpions, as the unit was known, had been sent to the Bogujevci family's home village of Podujevo on an ethnic cleansing mission.

Each of the children on the Hilton stage had nearly died of their gunshot wounds (Saranda had sixteen bullet wounds in her body) and Lirie, who was hit in the neck, had to be fed through her stomach for eight months. Their survival, evacuation to the UK for medical treatment and rehabilitation to a normal life of school in Manchester, would have been cause enough to merit the Moral Courage Awards, but there was more, which became the subject of a BBC documentary.

In the summer of 2003, Saranda and her cousins had flown from the safety of Manchester to the Serbian capital of Belgrade. There in turn they stood in a lonely witness box to testify in the court proceedings against Sasa Svjetan, the militia leader who had ordered and led the Podujevo massacre. They were forced to recall the details of the day they had been lined up against a wall in a neighbour's garden and robbed of their mothers, grandmother and siblings. It resulted in Svjetan's conviction and the maximum sentence of twenty years in prison. As the citation for the Special Anne Frank Award for Moral Courage was read out to our audience, there were gasps and subsequent sobs heard around the crowded room. We knew then that the Anne Frank Awards for Moral Courage had a meaning – passing on the baton of recognizing the spiritual courage and strength of Anne Frank to a new generation. And there was a rather odd coincidence in the three Bogujevci girls receiving these awards in memory of Anne Frank. When Marsha was planning the ceremony and had asked for the Bogujevci family's dates of birth Saranda told her, 'You may find this strange but we all three girls share the same birthday. It's 12th June.' June 12th is also the birth date of Anne Frank.

The Anne Frank Award for an outstanding teacher who brought moral courage issues into the classroom had been sponsored by the teaching union, the NASUWT (a much-needed acronym for the National Association of Schoolmasters and Union of Women Teachers). My first meeting at their London office had been with their General Secretary Eamonn O'Kane. Eamonn became seriously ill between our meeting and the first awards ceremony. Following his death in May 2004,

I suggested to our new colleagues at the union that the annual Anne Frank Award to a teacher could be made in his memory. Eamonn had been a well-known peace and workers' rights activist and they readily agreed. For several years Eamonn's widow Daphne would fly over from her home in Belfast to attend the Anne Frank Awards.

This was the start of the Anne Frank Trust's close collaboration with the NASUWT on many projects, and they have subsequently funded our educational programmes in several regions of the UK. After the Anne Frank Awards for Moral Courage programme ended in 2009, we continued to help judge the NASUWT's 'Anne Frank Poetry Prize', one of their annual Arts and Minds creative awards for schools in celebration of diversity. For the poetry prize we donated a bronze bust of Anne Frank that had been commissioned in 1995 by Bee and Sid Klug, which spends a year on display at the winning entrant's school, until the next award is made.

The Anne Frank Awards brought about some very valuable and long-lasting partnerships for the Trust, including with the NSPCC (the National Society for the Prevention of Cruelty to Children), the Prince's Trust and the Metropolitan Police. With any small and growing charity, collaborative partnerships across a diverse range of institutions and NGOs are critical, and if they also include warm and mutually admiring friendships, as ours often did, that is an added bonus.

The Trustees agreed we should bring in someone to run the Anne Frank Awards and that is how Lucy Glennon, who went on to head up our growing education team, came to join us in April 2004. Lucy had previously run the annual awards ceremony (also held at the London Hilton) for the mobile phone industry. She seemed a very bright young woman, had an engaging personality and loved Anne Frank. Around the same time, we decided that using an exhibitions company each time we put up or took down an exhibition was becoming too costly, so Doug Palfreeman, a freelance events and exhibitions manager, joined the organization to manage all the practicalities and logistics of the exhibition builds.

In 2006, Lucy successfully applied for the newly-created role of Head of Education. I suggested that perhaps she consider expanding her knowledge of the Holocaust, never intending that she would enrol for a Master's Degree in Holocaust Studies. Over the following four years she spent her days working on our education programmes, and her evenings and weekends immersed in her studies of the Holocaust. Once, on a study trip to Auschwitz-Birkenau, she was confined to bed with a nasty stomach bug, her hotel window directly overlooking the watchtower of the entrance to Birkenau camp.

Meanwhile our new Trustee Daniel Mendoza had been busy. He was so enthused by his new cause that he started speaking about the Trust at any opportunity – which included his business and social interactions. One of the property companies Daniel was doing business with was the Hampstead-based William Pears and Co, whose founders had built up one of the largest property portfolios in the UK. After his death in 1984 Clive Pears's three sons, Mark, Trevor and David, took over the company and in 1992 set up a charitable trust which the middle brother Trevor gradually took over running. When I was first introduced by Daniel to Trevor in 2003, he was still relatively new to the world of philanthropic management and was feeling his way. One often thinks it must be easy to distribute philanthropic funds when there are almost unlimited resources to give away but Trevor wanted to use the Pears funds wisely and with the widest and most profound effect.

Daniel took me to Trevor's office at the top of the Pears' company headquarters in north London. We talked about Otto Frank, his educational vision and our work around the UK to carry out this vision. Trevor expressed his surprise when I told him that it was all operated out of my home. After our meeting he set about doing some of his own research and contacted Stephen Smith, the founder – along with his parents and younger brother James – of the National Holocaust Centre in Nottinghamshire. Trevor had started to financially support the Smith family's centre and already felt he could trust Stephen's opinions in the Holocaust education arena. What were Stephen's thoughts about the Anne Frank Trust? What did he know of the woman who was running it? Stephen thankfully gave our organization, its work and me a glowing reference, because Trevor Pears came on board.

One afternoon I was sitting at my desk when Trevor called me. I will never forget what he said and have often quoted it when asked about critical turning points in our organization. He told me that with his new role and responsibility for the family's philanthropy he wanted to ensure that every penny donated meant something. 'Rather than give money widely and indiscriminately, I would prefer to invest in five or six small charities I believe in so as to help them flourish and grow. This I feel would have a real impact, and I think you should be one of them.'

Unusually for a philanthropist, Trevor was not so interested in putting his name to a number of sexy new projects but wished to invest longer-term into the core revenue costs needed to give charities a sound infrastructure for growth. This is music to a charity's ears as this is the area that is often the most difficult to get funded. In this respect Trevor was a visionary and a saint and in our case paid for two new much-needed full-time posts, a Director of Resources (i.e. operations manager) and a Head of Fundraising. In the early days of our relationship meetings were always held with Trevor himself, often attended by Daniel too. The Pears Foundation itself started to grow into a highly professionally-run operation employing a Director and team, and funding a very wide range of charities in the UK, Israel and Africa. A few years later Trevor Pears's philanthropy was deservedly recognized by being appointed a Companion of the Order of St Michael and St George, and in 2017, he became Sir Trevor Pears.

Always offering his candid views, in 2004 Trevor told Daniel and me that he wished to see the Anne Frank Trust move out of my Highgate house into proper offices. It was certainly getting towards that time. Sometimes lack of indoor space meant that if the weather was good enough staff members held meetings around my garden table. We also had a new team member, a trained lawyer who had worked for a very large City law firm and now wanted to work in the not-for-profit area. Emma couldn't shake off the habit of working very long hours and sometimes Tony and I would return home from an evening out to hear her still at work upstairs in the office. Much as I loved the very short commute to work, Tony and I agreed that we finally needed our home back.

A colleague suggested that I speak to Sir Sigmund Sternberg, a Holocaust refugee from Budapest who had built a business and property empire which had started from dabbling in scrap metal. Sir Sigmund, widely known as Siggie, had turned his energy to interfaith relations becoming President of the International Council of Christians and Jews and then setting up, along with his friends Reverend Marcus Braybrooke and Sheikh Zaki Badawi, the Three Faiths Forum. He had even been honoured by Pope John Paul II by being appointed a (Jewish!) papal knight, and the portrait of Siggie displayed in the National Portrait Gallery depicts him proudly in his uniform of the Papal Order of St Gregory the Great.

One of the properties Siggie owned was a 1960s office building in Kentish Town, which was mainly occupied by philanthropic organizations close to his heart. The ground floor contained his own Sternberg Foundation, the hub of his and his wife Hazel's interfaith activities. The second floor housed the Medical Foundation for the Victims of Torture, set up by a former nurse who had tended to victims of Bergen-Belsen, the much-admired Helen Bamber. The Medical Foundation was moving to larger premises and so the space had become available. It was perfect for the Trust's needs and offered us adequate room to expand.

So on 11 August 2004 the Anne Frank Trust moved into Star House where it is still located. We had 'nice neighbours', as we shared the second floor with the expanding Three Faiths Forum and its dynamic director Stephen Shashoua, who was busy creating a hub of interfaith charities. Once a year our joint organizations came together to stage a party to celebrate what we collaboratively termed 'Christnak-Eid' – Christmas, Chanukah, and when it fell reasonably near, Eid Mubarak.

As well as donors, there is no doubt that passionate and dedicated volunteers have played an invaluable role in our growth. Jack Morris's wife Susan organized several wonderfully successful fundraising events. Trevor Pears's wife Daniela pulled a group of her friends together to stage a sponsored cycle ride to Amsterdam, an event others have since replicated for the Trust. Lynn Winton has given us the benefit of her PR experience and we worked side-by-side on many ideas and projects. She also brought many of her friends into the fold. After Jack stepped down from chairing the Anne Frank Lunch committee, the responsibility was taken on by other fantastic people and thanks to them the event continues to flourish. In 2006, the social entrepreneur Dr Ann Limb brought her huge experience of building successful organizations (such as the Helena Kennedy Foundation and the e-learning initiative learndirect as well as many others) to chairing the Anne Frank Trust and guiding the next few years of growth. Daniel Mendoza took over as Chair in 2009.

Since the first days of Board meetings in David Goldstein's West End office, the Anne Frank Trust has had the benefit of the ideas and support of over forty different Trustees, bringing backgrounds and skills to reflect the diversity of our programmes and our beneficiaries. Robert Posner joined the Trust as Chief Operating Officer in 2009, we worked in close tandem with our complementary skills for seven years and in 2016 Robert succeeded me as the Trust's CEO. There have been changes too at the Anne Frank House, although because the work is such a vocation, most of the Anne Frank House team spoken of in this book continue in post doing their wonderful work. The Anne Frank House Director Hans Westra, the man who gave me his full confidence and trust in 1990 by appointing me as the Anne Frank House British Representative and then Anne Frank Educational Trust Executive Director, retired in 2011 after thirty years with the organization. He was succeeded as director by Ronald Leopold.

By the end of 2005, Tony and I were really enjoying the division of our work and home life. But then fate decided to deal a bitter blow. Tony, my beloved partner, was diagnosed with lung cancer. We received a tidal wave of love and support, including a handwritten note from Prime Minister Tony Blair telling us he and Cherie had been praying for Tony in church. Tony was blessed with an optimistic outlook and was determined that positive thinking would help him conquer the depressing odds of surviving a 3B size tumour on his lung.

But Tony did not make it. The end came very fast and he died at 7.00 a.m. on the morning of 24 August 2006. I was at his hospital bedside as he took his last laboured breaths. One hour after he left us, his daughter Susha and his new baby grandson, who Tony had been so excited about meeting, walked into his hospital room straight off a very early flight from their home in Spain.

Widowed at age 55, a new stage of my life was about to begin, which my real family, and my large surrogate family of the Anne Frank Trust and the Anne Frank House, undoubtedly helped me through.

Chapter 21

Who Betrayed the Frank Family?

On a warm bright summer morning, 4 August 1944, it is believed that a telephone call was made to the Gestapo headquarters in Amsterdam informing them that, despite it being over two years after the start of the round ups and deportations of Dutch Jews, there were 'Jews hiding on the Prinsengracht'. A Viennese Gestapo member, Oberscharführer Karl Josef Silberbauer, was attached to Sektion IV-B4, a unit recruited from Austrian and German police departments and which handled arrests of hidden Jews throughout the occupied Netherlands. Silberbauer, accompanied by three Dutch Nazi police officers, made their way immediately to Number 263 Prinsengracht, where Anne Frank, oblivious to what was about to unfold, was experiencing her 760th morning in hiding.

One floor below Miep Gies, Bep Voskuijl, Johannes Kleiman and Viktor Kugler were going about their daily office duties. At around 10.30 a.m. the door burst open and Otto Frank's trusted team found pistols being pointed directly at their heads. The intruders signalled towards the bookcase, and the office workers had no choice but to open it, revealing the staircase behind. The arresting party made their way stealthily up the steep stairs and into the main room of the hiding place, catching unawares first Otto, who was tutoring Peter van Pels, and then the other six people who had woken that morning to what they thought would be another tedious day of awaiting their liberation.

Over the past quarter of a century I have often been asked whom I thought had betrayed the Frank family. I cannot answer this question with any certainty as all those who know the truth are long dead. However, after twenty-six years of immersion in Anne Frank's story, spending much time in Amsterdam meeting people who were her contemporaries, hearing rumours and whispers from those who knew the family and their wartime circumstances, I will analyse the various theories that have been put forward as to the betrayer's identity, and describe the situation in Holland in 1944 that would have prompted the informant's actions and give my own view on whom I believe the betrayer could have been.

By August 1944, two months after D-Day and with the Allied troops slowly advancing across northern Europe, hopes were high that the eight people who had hidden themselves from the world for two years, would, against all odds, soon be able to walk downstairs, open the door concealed by a bookcase, and finally step out into the fresh air to resume their lives. However, it would be another nine months until victory over the Nazis was secured, and of the eight frightened captives taken that morning only Otto Frank would live to see it. After the war, it was estimated that only 5,000 of the 107,000 Jews deported from the Netherlands between 1942 and 1944 survived.

I have also been asked whether I thought the arresting officers ever subsequently discovered that one of the terrified Jews they took away that August day was actually Anne Frank. I don't know the identity of the Dutch officers but perhaps in their later years they would walk past the long queue outside the famous museum and tourist attraction on the Prinsengracht.

Karl Josef Silberbauer returned to Vienna in April 1945 and served a fourteen-month prison sentence for using excessive force against members of the Communist Party of Austria. After his release, he was recruited by the West German Federal Intelligence Service (BND), and spent ten years as an undercover operative, but in the mid-1950s went back to working for the Viennese police. His life was interrupted in 1963 when he was tracked down and exposed by the renowned Vienna-based Nazi hunter Simon Wiesenthal, who had been challenged by Austrian neo-Nazis to prove Anne Frank really had existed. When reporters descended upon Silberbauer's Vienna home, the policeman freely admitted that he had arrested Anne Frank. Asked about Anne Frank's diary, Silberbauer brazenly replied, 'I bought the little book last week to see if I am in it. But I am not.' Upon cynically being told by a reporter that he 'could have been the first to read it', Silberbauer chuckled and said, 'Maybe I should have picked it up off the floor.'

There have been several theories put forward as to who made that fateful telephone call in August 1944 that led Anne Frank and the other hiders on their journeys to death, and these point in different directions. In several books the betrayer has been referred to simply as a 'warehouseman' who worked for Opekta and had overheard noises from upstairs. In another theory it was one of the several opportunistic burglars who broke into the Opekta warehouse and offices during 1944, who had perhaps also heard something that aroused their interest while they were snooping around on the premises.

Opekta's warehouse manager Willem van Maaren has also been suspected, as according to Anne's diary the Annexe occupants 'did not trust him'. They had heard from the office staff that van Maaren seemed very inquisitive about whether anyone had been entering the stockroom after hours. He had also been laying his own traps to ascertain if there were nocturnal visitors to the warehouse, such as chalk on the floor and papers set on the corner of a desk. Anne talks about this in her diary entry of 25 April 1944. Van Maaren's inquisitiveness could have had an ulterior motive, as according to Anne Frank's German biographer Melissa Muller, he was also sheltering a fugitive at home. This was his own son, who had ignored the German occupiers' orders to report for either military or labour service. If there were indeed sheltering Jews above the warehouse van Maaren managed and they were discovered, as the building's warehouse manager this may have held dangerous implications for him and his fugitive son. Van Maaren died in 1971 without any conclusive proof that he was the betrayer.

In the 2001 American Broadcasting Company movie *Anne Frank, The Whole Story*, the person who makes the fatal call from a public telephone box is portrayed as a middle-aged woman, who simply says into the phone, 'There are Jews hiding in the Prinsengracht'. Based on Melissa Muller's book *Anne Frank, the Biography*, she is assumed to have been a cleaner called Lena Hartog who was working in the Opekta offices, whose suspicion was possibly aroused by hearing noises or seeing clues left when the hiders came downstairs in the night. Lena Hartog's husband also worked in the Opekta warehouse as van Maaren's assistant, and he had shared some of his suspicions with him. Muller is sure Hartog shared this with his wife, as she too started probing the young office assistant (and the hiders' helper) Bep Voskuijl.

I can definitively state that it was not the young burglar who broke in during 1943 as described in Anne's diary. I sat next to that very same 'burglar' at the lunch held after the official opening of the refurbished and enlarged Anne Frank House in 1999. My lunch companion's name was actually Hans Wijnberg, and he had lived a few doors along the Prinsengracht. As an adult he left his 'criminal activities' behind him and became a sea captain, eventually going to live in Malta. During our conversation, I asked if I should still call him 'The Burglar'. He laughed and explained he had been just a kid trying to find any money or items to sell as things were so hard in wartime Amsterdam. He did recall looking up at a window as he was scaling the wall of the courtyard of 263 Prinsengracht and seeing a young girl at the window of Otto Frank's office. He had not given the girl any thought at the time as she did not seem a threat to his nocturnal activities, but after the war, it became clear to him that this girl was most probably Anne Frank.

The dire situation for the Dutch people in the summer of 1944 helped stoke the number of betrayals. Enticing monetary rewards were offered to an exhausted and hungry population in return for turning in Jews to the authorities. Anne Frank Trust co-founder Eva Schloss, also in hiding in Amsterdam, was betrayed with her family on 13 May 1944, her 15th birthday. She has described to me the terror of that day, and the beating she endured from her captors, forever a terrible birthday memory.

In Carol Ann Lee's 2002 book, *The Hidden Life of Otto Frank*, an anti-Semitic Dutch Nazi and petty criminal called Tonny Ahlers, who had had 'business dealings' with Otto Frank before the family went into hiding, is identified as the potential culprit. According to Lee, Ahlers knew that at the start of the war Otto had continued to do business with the Wehrmacht (the pectin his firm Opekta produced was essential for the preservation of the German army's rations), a fact he would undoubtedly have wanted to remain secret. Otto Frank had also expressed his doubts about a German victory to an acquaintance he had run into, who then sent a letter to the Gestapo informing on him. Tonny Ahlers, who was active in the NSB (the Dutch Nazi Party) somehow got hold of this letter and blackmailed Otto for money in return for his silence. In her book, Lee maintains that Ahlers continued to blackmail Otto Frank with this until Frank's death in 1980. When this suggestion came into the public arena in 2002 through Lee's book, the British newspaper the *Daily Mail* published an extract from this chapter of the book covering a full three pages of the newspaper. It appeared in the Saturday edition, the thickest and most well-read edition of the week, with a headline splashed across the double-page spread boldly asking, 'Did Otto Frank Betray His Family?'. I recall I was walking round the peaceful grounds of the magnificent medieval Warwick Castle, when I received a frantic call from the Trust's President, Bee Klug. As a close friend and admirer of Otto Frank, she was beside herself with anger. 'Gillian Dear!' Bee always started her telephone conversations to me with the two words 'Gillian Dear', and the tone of these two words would give an immediate indication of whether what was to follow was good, bad or downright disgraceful. She went on: 'This is an outrage. Do you realize how many people will not bother to read the whole article but will remember those four words: OTTO FRANK. BETRAY. FAMILY.'

Bee was absolutely right and I was equally distressed. Of course if people read the three-page article to the end, they would also reach the conclusion that Otto Frank didn't betray his family. They were betrayed by an outsider. Thankfully, this was in the days when newspapers were published and read in print only, and could not whizz around the world by touching the Share and Enter computer keys. On the Monday morning I called the *Daily Mail* and asked for the office of the Editor, Paul Dacre. I explained what it was about and within an hour someone had called me back to inform me I would be receiving a visit in person by the paper's Executive Managing Editor, Robin Esser. This was good news – they were taking our concerns very seriously. Mr Esser came, met with myself and Bee and promised that if we wrote a letter of complaint it would be printed in the following Saturday's edition and would also be the featured letter on that day with a large photo of Anne Frank to attract people's attention to our letter. We were relieved that our letter of complaint would get an equally large readership as the offending headline.

In the event this did not actually happen. My letter was published in the less well-read Monday edition and was not the 'featured letter' of that day. Our next port of call was the Press Complaints Commission. Bee and I duly wrote to them with our worries, one of which was the field day that Holocaust deniers, and in particular those who continue to claim Anne's diary was a forgery written by her father to make money out of her death, would have with this misjudged headline to an explanatory article. This letter did not get the desired response either. Unknown to us at the time of writing it, the Chairman of the Press Complaints Commission's Editors' Code of Practice Committee was in fact none other than the *Daily Mail* editor Paul Dacre. The Press Complaints Commission was a self-regulating body and remained so until its closure in 2014 in the wake of the *News of the World* phone-hacking scandal and the Leveson Inquiry into the Culture, Practice and Ethics of the Press.

Carol Ann Lee has written several books about Anne Frank and her life, the most notable being *Roses from the Earth* (1999). Carol, who grew up in Cornwall, had an overwhelming passion for Anne Frank. As a girl she had even translated books word-by-word from the Dutch language using a Dutch-English dictionary, in order to increase her knowledge. I first met Carol in 1992 when she was 18, when I stayed overnight with her family during the time I was setting up the Anne Frank exhibition in Cornwall at Truro Cathedral. She has since become an acknowledged expert on the life of Anne Frank, and lived in Amsterdam for several years. She has told me that she was mortified that so much media attention for her 384-page biography covering the long life of Otto Frank had focused mainly on the relationship between him and Ahlers and her speculation that perhaps Otto had unwittingly given Ahlers a clue about his plans to take his family into hiding.

When I spoke to her in 2016, Carol Ann Lee remained convinced about the possibility that the betrayer was Ahlers or perhaps even his wife. But she was honest about her big regret at how she had presented this in her book on Otto Frank.

> It overshadowed what were for me much more important parts of the book – and Otto's own story. More than anything, I wrote the book because I thought Otto was such a remarkable and hugely courageous man, and that got hopelessly lost in all the kerfuffle about Ahlers, which was only ever a theory after all. I believe Ahlers is the most likely out of the suspects we have now, but I do wish that I had kept the information about him to one or two chapters, and not threaded his story throughout the book. I did that simply because I wanted to show the difference between Otto and someone like Ahlers, who typified how an ordinary young man could be drawn into the Nazi machine, but instead it read far more as if Ahlers was a huge part of Otto's story.

In 2015 a new book emerged written collaboratively by the Flemish journalist Jeroen de Bruyn and Joop van Wijk, the youngest son of Bep Voskuijl, one of the Frank family's helpers. Joop van Wijk pointed the finger within his own family, alleging that his aunt, Nelly Voskuijl, Bep's younger sister, may have been the person who betrayed Anne Frank's family. The authors found evidence that concluded that Nelly Voskuijl was a Nazi collaborator, and she also occasionally worked in the offices of 263 Prinsengracht. She could have picked up something herself or even overheard Bep, who held the hiders' secret for over two years, inadvertently saying something incriminating. Nelly died in 2001 without ever speaking about the events of August 1944, but to me this theory sounds the most convincing.

In 2016, there was another theory that came out of a study conducted by the Anne Frank House historians themselves. Could it have been that the officers who arrived at the Opekta offices on the morning of 4 August 1944 were there because of a tip-off about fraudulent food-ration cards and illegal employment happening there? The museum staff looked at the fact that the Nazi police unit who discovered the family usually investigated cases involving cash and securities, not Jews in hiding. During the course of looking through documents, could they have heard a sound from above, and by chance discovered that there were eight Jews hiding one floor above them?

So, in answer to my question 'Who betrayed the Frank family?' the answer is simply most probably someone who was around 263 Prinsengracht in the summer of 1944, but unless a cache of new incriminating documents happen to turn up or a person now in their mid-nineties suddenly recalls a crucial fact, none of the theories will ever be substantiated.

***

A footnote about Carol Ann Lee's Tonny Ahlers theory. In 2014, I was attending a meeting with the Prime Minister David Cameron's team at 10 Downing Street. At the entrance to Downing Street is an imposing iron security gate always manned by one or two police officers. As I walked through the gate a police officer politely asked me why I was coming to Number 10 today. I explained I was on Anne Frank Trust business. 'Oh, that's interesting,' he said. 'I have a sort of connection to the Anne Frank story.'

The officer went on to explain that he had a friend, who lived nearby, whose uncle was a man called Tonny Ahlers, who had once been accused of being the betrayer of the Frank family. I probed the officer further, who told me that according to his friend, his Uncle Ahlers was 'a real no good' and it wouldn't be at all surprising if Anne Frank's betrayer had been him. Standing there at the entrance to Downing Street, having this rather unexpected conversation, I again found myself explaining, this time to an officer of the Metropolitan Police, that we will never now know for certain.

Chapter 22

Anne Frank is Educating Millions

In 2006, the Anne Frank Trust's method of working with young people started to evolve into something rather different, which would have a profound effect on the way the educational charity carried out its mission. Instead of our primary focus on staging exhibitions in prominent city-centre locations for one month, smaller-sized versions of the Anne Frank exhibition would be taken directly into schools for two weeks at a time, accompanied by a range of educational workshops and activities. There would be no need to advertise for local volunteer exhibition guides, as we would train the school students themselves to be 'peer-to-peer educators'.

The Anne Frank House educator Barry van Driel, who was a seasoned trainer and academic and had a profound understanding of how to educate young people, was the first to present the concept of 'peer-to-peer educators' to his Dutch colleagues after he himself had encountered the methodology in the early 1990s while he was living in in California. This educational method had been used in the San Francisco Bay area as a way of spreading an urgently-needed educational method about HIV/AIDS as rapidly and effectively as the deadly disease it was trying to counter. Barry had met a health education expert called Jennifer Reinks and she explained to him about this inclusive new approach to teaching and learning. Instead of just being expected to listen and absorb information, the peer-to-peer method would give students an important role. As well as for HIV/AIDS and sex education, it was also being used to educate about drugs and health.

Barry decided to implement this method in the Watsonville community south of Santa Cruz where he was soon going to be working. 'This was then, and still is,' Barry recalled, 'a very Latino community with a high degree of poverty. There were many drive-by shootings there in the 1990s. The gang experts I brought in also mentioned peer education to reach the very troubled youth of Watsonville.'

After his time in California, Barry found himself deeply embedded in education programmes in areas of post-Communist Europe, as related in my chapter on the Balkan wars. In 1994, he was taking an Anne Frank education programme to Hungary. After Hungary emerged from Communism, the Dutch Ministry of Foreign Affairs started to invest funding to help the country in its transition to democracy. The process of coming to terms with Hungary's past would involve facing its own role in the Holocaust, where exactly fifty years earlier, in the weeks between 15 May and 9 July 1944, 440,000 Hungarian Jews had been murdered by the Nazis or helped in their deportation by Hungarian gendarmerie.

More recently, Hungary's own Roma community and its other minorities had been victims of persecution. The Anne Frank exhibition was invited to a 100 per cent Roma school in Pecs, a small town in southern Hungary. The Gandhi School was the only school in Europe preparing Roma children for university education, and was named after Mahatma Gandhi for two reasons. Firstly, it had a philosophy of non-violence, and secondly to recognize the Indian roots of the Roma people. It was a weekly boarding school as it was located in a particularly inaccessible mountainous region with notoriously dangerous roads, where the school's president and deputy president had both been killed in separate road accidents.

A group of ten 13- and 14-year-old students were trained to be Anne Frank exhibition peer guides and in the process learnt more about their community's own history, especially the destruction of the Roma community in the Holocaust, when 500,000 of their Roma people were murdered. Alongside the Anne Frank exhibition, the play *Dreams of Anne Frank* was presented with the students playing the roles.

The play went on to tour primary schools throughout Hungary, and the ten actors from the Gandhi School went with it. They became role models for Roma children who were minorities in other schools. It also broke down stereotypical attitudes among teachers towards the Roma community, one even being heard to mutter, 'I didn't believe Roma children could act.' Barry van Driel had taken a Dutch Surinamese colleague with him to Pecs. He remembers with a wry smile: 'The kids told my colleague, "We're considered black, but actually you're really black".'

The group even came to London at the invitation of Anna Sher, who had set up a renowned theatre school where many of our best-known young British TV actors had learnt the craft of acting. One of the most multicultural cities in the world, London was a real eye-opener for the Roma children. For the first time they felt they were not being treated differently because of the colour of their skin, which had been the case in predominantly fair-skinned Hungary. After their return from the London trip, two of the group, Sabina and Laszlo, continued their roles as peer-to-peer educators by giving after school lessons on sex education, as HIV was starting to gain ground in the area around their town of Pecs. In the years following the project, Barry discovered that many of the group had delayed having children to concentrate on their careers, unusual in the Roma community. One girl, Anna Ignasz, now lives in Bristol in south-west England where she teaches in a school for children with special needs.

After its success in the Latino community of Watsonville and its use to enhance the self-esteem of Roma children in Hungary, the new methodology for teaching the lessons from Anne Frank's life was discussed by Jan Erik Dubbelman and his International Department team. This could be a dramatically new way of working with the Anne Frank exhibition programme in other countries. Jan Erik saw the value of taking Anne Frank exhibitions directly into schools and training students in each participating school to be peer educators.

Surprisingly, the area chosen to pilot the new peer-education project in 2002 was as demographically far away from the culturally-diverse environments of Watsonville and Amsterdam as it was possible to find – the rural valleys of the Austrian Tirol. This was an unusual but carefully-considered choice of location. Unlike teeming metropolitan cities with excellent transport links enabling people to go wherever they choose, those who live surrounded by steep mountains have limited ability to travel. This creates strong feelings of community within each valley, something I also encountered when working with the Anne Frank project in the former mining communities of the Welsh valleys.

Amidst the towering pine trees and crystal streams of the Austrian Tirol, the exhibition 'Anne Frank, A History for Today' travelled from school to school along the winding valleys. Those children of the Tirolean valleys were not aware that they were the guinea pigs for an educational philosophy that would change lives and empower the next generation of teenagers around the world. Jan Erik's rationale was to take the learning experience of young people a step further into the realms of both teaching and learning. He explained, 'The biggest change-makers in our society are kids themselves. Young people can relate to complex issues of prejudice even better than adults.'

The Anne Frank House's educators Barry van Driel and Norbert Hinterleitner (whose surname coincidentally translates into English as 'those who lived on the back slope of a mountain') had the task of convincing schools in the hidden villages of the mountain valleys to take an Anne Frank exhibition and educational programme. This was far away from the high-profile government, embassy or corporate-funded international Anne Frank exhibition tours that the Anne Frank House had been accustomed to running. In the Austrian Tirol the participating schools were each encouraged to plan satellite events, such as lectures, discussions and film shows, for their own village community to take part in, while doing their own publicity and fundraising.

It proved easier than expected to convince the schools to take part. Schools in this sparsely-populated and inaccessible region of tall mountains and deep valleys were competing to attract students. The school principals each started to realize the value of showing that their school was thinking in a radically different way and engaging with the local community. Jan Erik explained, 'In these deep valleys you grow up looking out at mountains all around you. This creates a strong and cohesive community in each village. We wanted to pilot the peer-to-peer method where we knew there would be whole community involvement.' At the end of the Anne Frank exhibition's tour of the Tirolean villages, this new way of working was deemed to be fruitful and it was time to develop it further.

The Anne Frank Trust's Head of Education Lucy Glennon heard about the new methodology at an international education seminar she attended at the Anne Frank House in 2006. She came back to London enthused and wanted to discuss with me if somehow we could implement it in Britain. Happily, an interesting opportunity soon arose. Our Head of Fundraising Paul Tyack had a contact on Hackney

Council, an Anne Frank enthusiast called Nicola Baboneau who was working in the Community and Partnerships team. When Paul called Nicola, she liked the idea of bringing a small version of the exhibition 'Anne Frank, A History for Today' directly into secondary schools in the borough.

Hackney was an area of East London that had seen many waves of immigration. Its residents during the twentieth century had included my own Polish immigrant paternal grandparents. They had moved there just before the First World War from the grimy tenements of Whitechapel to an imposing new Edwardian house in what was then considered the leafy and quiet suburb of Hackney. I had spent much of my childhood visiting this Hackney house, but by then my cousins and I found ourselves playing in the street alongside other former grand houses that had been razed to the ground in the Blitz.

It was in Hackney in the mid-1950s that I vividly remember my first childhood experience of seeing a person whose skin wasn't the same colour as mine. We were driving towards the famous Ridley Road food market and a football rolled into the road in front of our car. My dad stopped the car and waved to a boy to retrieve his ball. The boy, roughly 8-years-old, ran and got his ball and gave my Dad a bright smile of thanks. Dad explained to my confused brother and me why the boy looked so different – that he and his Mum and Dad had come from a hot sunny place, and that's why his skin was dark to protect him from the hot sun. The first post-war wave of 492 immigrants from the West Indies had arrived in Britain on the ship the MV *Empire Windrush* only a few years earlier (ironically this vessel had originally been a German cruise ship during the 1930s) and maybe this boy's parents were among them.

As you can guess, with my childhood memories I didn't need much convincing that Hackney would be a great place to start our exciting new Anne Frank programme in 2006. This was an area of East London that still had a diverse population and many social problems, but parts of the borough were also becoming newly gentrified and affordable areas for young professionals. Nicola Baboneau was keen that as many secondary schools as possible in the borough should benefit from the Anne Frank programme, and so Lucy and Paul set about writing bids for funding for an anticipated year-long event. The Labour Government were supporting initiatives aimed at the Black and Minority Ethnic (BME) communities and we received funding from the Department for Education for half the salary of a project worker to deliver our work in the Hackney schools, plus a further two years in other London boroughs. The other 50 per cent for the first year came from the Prince's Trust, the foundation set up by the Prince of Wales in 1976 to help disadvantaged young people. Not only did the Prince's Trust agree to half fund the position of a Project Officer but our new project worker came through their ranks too.

In July 2006 we recruited a young man called Mukith Khalisadar who was on a Prince's Trust training programme. Mukith was 20-years-old, from the Bengali community in the inner city area of Tower Hamlets and this would be his first job.

Such was his inexperience in the working world that in his first week he popped his head around my office door and said to his Executive Director (i.e. me), 'Darlin' we are going for lunch now, are you comin'?' (we still laugh about this together). Little did we know that more than ten years later Mukith would, as a married father of a young son, still be leading our London Schools Project and considered by the Prince's Trust (and by the Anne Frank Trust too) as one of their greatest success stories. Mukith was so impressive and dedicated that for two full years his salary was funded by the investment bank Goldman Sachs.

As a Muslim man, the reasons for his dedicated work in educating about the Holocaust have sometimes been cynically questioned by teenage Muslim pupils and he has even been called a 'Jew Lover'. But he has always patiently and sensitively deflected these attacks, by explaining the importance and relevance of everyone knowing about what happened to Anne Frank and why. It has been difficult for him, as well as other members of our education team, working in schools during heightened conflicts between Israel and Palestine, and within our organization there are deep emotional ties towards both sides of the conflict. Our strategy is to explain that the history of the Middle East is complex, with grievances on both sides, whereas the history of Nazism and the Holocaust is black and white.

As well as Mukith, Jamie Arden was appointed in 2006 as London Schools Project Manager, to oversee the year-long Hackney project and the next two years. Jamie had come through the drama in education route and was a hugely engaging and charismatic educator for teenagers. The following year the tentacles of the UK's Anne Frank peer education project started to spread outward from London. Fiona Ranson, who worked in the Ethnic Minority and Travellers' Advisory Service at County Durham Council in the north-east of England, had heard about the project and called Lucy Glennon. She was enthusiastic about how it could be used in the former mining communities of County Durham and soon raised funding from an alliance of local trade unions and the local police. And so we took the new project northwards.

The Barcapel Foundation in Glasgow also heard about it via Jed Wilson who happened to be a Trustee of both our charities. The Barcapel Foundation had been set up by Jed's family from the sale of their successful pet food business, which had at one time captured 20 per cent of the UK market. Our work in challenging prejudice particularly chimed with one of their Trustees, a lawyer called Niall Scott, whose 16-year-old son Mark had been the innocent victim of the Protestant/ Catholic sectarian hatred that still blights parts of the United Kingdom. Walking with friends past a Protestant pub in his Celtic football scarf, Mark was attacked and stabbed in the neck by Jason Campbell, the son of a convicted Loyalist terrorist. Campbell served fifteen years for Mark's unprovoked murder.

Heather Boyce was employed in 2008 as our new Scotland Project Manager. Now based in York and married to our Fundraiser Paul Tyack (Anne Frank would love it that romance blossomed at her eponymous Trust), Heather is now responsible for the Trust's educational development.

ANNE FRANK IS EDUCATING MILLIONS

In 2009 we were invited to conduct a year-long education project in Addenbrooke's NHS Trust hospital in Cambridge to teach their 7,000-strong staff, from the venerated surgeons all the way through the staff chain to hospital porters, the value of treating their patients and staff colleagues with equality and dignity. Val Ross came on board to manage the project, and since its completion in 2010 remained as the Trust's East of England Project Manager. She has travelled extensively throughout this region (as a non-driver relying on often challenging public transport connections) bringing the peer education programme to schools in the predominantly rural eastern counties, from the county of Essex, immediately north-east of London, right up to the northern tip of East Anglia. Much of Val's work has been funded by local trade unions, including the NASUWT teaching union.

And so our peer education project continued to expand across Britain. The Department for Communities and Local Government have been supporting the project since 2007, and the consistently high externally conducted evaluations our work has received resulted in many other sources of funds, including a five-year major grant from the Big Lottery to expand the Anne Frank Ambassadors programme. To date we work intensively in seven regions of England and Scotland where our Anne Frank Trust teams are active week in and week out in schools, whilst building their own local relationships and networks of support. Sadly, I can't acknowledge every one of our expanding education team but I hereby put on record my immense pride in their work and huge appreciation of their dedication.

Even though it may appear that the peer-to-peer education programme is a very open style of presenting the Anne Frank story, there is a firm structure and ongoing evaluation lying beneath. The Trust implements the peer education programme in a school in the following way. Having visited the participating school several times, the Trust's Regional Manager or a member of his/her team installs the exhibition 'Anne Frank, A History for Today' in a designated area of the school. The installation usually takes place on a Monday morning and, as the exhibition stands and panels are flexible, durable and lightweight, two or three pairs of hands can get them set up in a couple of hours. The flexible structure means that they can be erected along a wall, or in different configurations around a central core, helpful when you are visiting a different busy and crowded school environment each couple of weeks.

Later that morning the team of young peer guides chosen for the task, anywhere between six and twenty in number, receive their training from the Trust's team member. Usually each peer educator has a responsibility for guiding visitors through a set of panels, learning a couple of different sets of panels in case they are called upon to substitute for an absent guide. The peer educators vary in age, but usually they are between the ages of 12 to 15. It isn't always the most obvious students – the quick learners, high achievers or good communicators – who are chosen by their teachers for the peer educator role. An astute teacher will often deliberately select a pupil who has had difficult issues to overcome – shyness, attention deficit or hyperactivity, a tough family background or has been the victim of bullying. Many of our peer educators have been from immigrant families, who have experienced difficulties of assimilation into their new school community, and some of our best educators have been refugees themselves from the wars in Kosovo, the Middle East and Africa. They have felt a particular affinity with Anne's story. In turn, their audience has come to a deeper understanding of their peer educator's own traumatic background.

During the week or two that the Anne Frank exhibition is in each school, the teachers have selected an enhancement programme from a range of accompanying workshops created and presented by the Trust's education team. These are on topics such as 'Rights and Responsibilities'; encouraging creative writing projects such as for our own year-long 'Generation Diary' online campaign; and addressing more current prejudices such as Islamophobia. In 2015, the Trust received a grant from the Department for Education to create a workshop and materials to help tackle homophobic, transphobic and biphobic bullying in schools, and was able to expand what it could offer to teachers even further. Where possible a Holocaust survivor, or survivor from a more recent genocide, will come to the school to tell their story.

But our programme does not end when the Anne Frank exhibition is taken down and moves on. Schools are then invited to sign up their peer educators for the 'Anne Frank Ambassadors' programme and twice a year the Trust conducts two-day training courses for new Ambassadors in each region. On this course the student will learn how to create social responsibility initiatives in their own community; or give a presentation on Anne Frank in their local primary schools; or create and run a campaign to tackle a local or national human rights issue. In many cases Anne Frank Ambassadors have used their skills to act as guides for the public at the large community exhibition held in their town, which since 2005 has been 'Anne Frank + You'. The Anne Frank Ambassadors are expected to carry their ambassadorial title with pride and this is certainly the case.

Since 2001 and the inception of the peer-to-peer methodology by the Anne Frank House there have been thousands of feedback responses from teachers and from the students themselves, gathered from all over the world. Both the Anne Frank House and the Anne Frank Trust UK regard all this feedback as accumulated learning, constantly helping to improve the training procedures and relevance to changing school systems. The Trust's attention to monitoring short-term responses and longer-term outcomes has resulted in the consistent renewal of Government grants supporting the programme and even expanding it to more regions of the UK.

Lucy Glennon echoed Jan Erik's views about tasking teenagers in this role, 'Whereas we as adults find ourselves talking in a rather self-conscious politically correct way about subjects like racial abuse, the children get straight to the point.' Mukith Khalidasar agrees.

> Peer education speaks the language of the audience. In my experience of working with young people when being taught about moral issues young people need to relate to the person talking to them. Teachers or adults, no

matter how in tune they are with the youth of today, will still be seen as an adult rather than one of them. This is why when you put a young person in front of their peers it cuts out the mentality of 'Oh it's just another adult telling us what to do'.

Over 1,000 Anne Frank peer educators are trained each year in England and Scotland and of those approximately half go on to the Anne Frank Ambassador training. However, in the same way that learning about Anne Frank creates an emotive connection with the destruction of millions of lives, relaying individual uplifting stories from some of the young people who have benefitted from being Anne Frank peer guides demonstrates the method's impact even better than statistics. I have heard many of these directly from the beneficiaries as well as their teachers.

The programme has been particularly successful in the former industrial towns and mining villages in the north-east of England. Despite it being a predominantly white monocultural region, high unemployment means many pockets are recruiting grounds for extremist organizations. When I visited the former mining town of Ferryhill, the Principal of the Business and Enterprise College explained to me the huge value he placed on having the Anne Frank programme. He told me that this was a community where there could be up to three generations of unemployed men in one family as the last coal mine had closed in 1968. He saw the Anne Frank programme as an insurance policy to help keep the next generation of adults away from extremist politics and had brought the programme into the school for four consecutive years. Faye, one of the peer guides who had become an Anne Frank Ambassador and was now about to leave school, told me she was a carer for her mother and that this was the best thing that had ever happened to her.

A consistent relationship with a school such as Ferryhill Business and Enterprise College gives us the luxury of a longer-term assessment of our theory of change. When we first interviewed Jordan Wilson as a newly-turned teenager and Anne Frank peer educator he told us in a pre-pubescent voice that there was racism in his area. He shrugged his shoulders; he didn't know how he could do anything about it. Interviewed again four years later, looking more a muscular adult, he said he felt much more confident to challenge racist remarks if he heard them. Jordan felt a strong responsibility to educate people about what he has learnt from working with Anne Frank and that this attitude affects everything he does. He even said 'I think Anne Frank would be happy as there are so many people preventing what she went through from happening again.'

Ferryhill's town councillors gave me one of my proudest moments at the Trust when, having rather furtively asked Jamie Arden for a copy of our charity's bright green and black logo, it suddenly appeared for a week prior to local elections in the form of a flag flying prominently above the town hall. The councillors saw the Anne Frank Trust flag as a symbol of defiance against extremist politics.

For one Anne Frank Ambassador training day, I visited the north-east city of Gateshead, where I met 14-year-old Joe. During the course of our chat he shared with me that his Mum had seen a transformation in his behaviour at home. Joe admitted that before he had become an Anne Frank educator he preferred his own company and to him family mealtimes were a social ordeal. But now he knew he was more communicative at home and actually enjoyed mealtime chat with his family. I thought that was a bold revelation from a 14-year-old boy.

Nathan was also a great exemplar from this region. He was a bullied autistic boy attending a special needs school, who had retired into his shell until he had become an Anne Frank Ambassador. His social transformation had been so great that it had allowed this young teenager to come on his first-ever visit to London (accompanied by his grandfather, who had also never before been to London), roll up at one of the city's most exclusive five-star hotels and stride confidently on to the ballroom stage, where he addressed 600 business people at our Anne Frank Trust lunch in 2016.

Looking around the packed room, he spoke without hesitation to tell them,

> I've faced prejudice because of my autism, and I have seen how people think differently of me because of it. There are people in my own community in County Durham who support racist groups, and if they knew the facts, rather than just the propaganda, they would change their minds. Doing the Anne Frank project has given me a completely different view than these kinds of groups. I'm now able to challenge prejudice when I'm confronted with it. I always try to help others who don't understand, and I challenge those who do understand, but spread hatred.

What Nathan stated so articulately echoes what we hear from young Anne Frank peer educators up and down our country, and if I tried to capture even a selection of the best responses this book would run to 5,000 pages.

Bradford in West Yorkshire is, conversely to the villages of County Durham, a very multicultural city with an Asian population making up nearly one quarter of the population. During the Industrial Revolution the woollen mills, fed by the soft waters of the nearby Yorkshire dales, had attracted first an Irish immigration and then German-Jewish merchants, who opened export businesses in a network of streets that became known as Little Germany. After the Second World War came Poles and Ukrainians, and then from the 1950s immigrants from India and Pakistan started arriving in the city to work in the woollen mills, which were in those days still flourishing.

The Metropolitan Council of Bradford have been hosting and funding an Anne Frank project over seven consecutive years. Jani Rashid, the former Head of Diversity & Cohesion for Bradford council's Education Department, crystallized why, by describing a change he had seen in one student. 'The project has been a real success for our students in terms of raising their self-esteem, aspiration and confidence. I could never have imagined that the pupil I saw three years ago, giggling through a Holocaust Memorial Day service, was going to be as committed as she is now to human rights issues and to making a difference.'

Jani Rashid has since retired and returned to his former home in Indonesia, but not before leaving his own rather unusual mark on his adopted city. Bradford's Victorian synagogue, one of the oldest in Britain, was falling into disrepair and its tiny remaining congregation were struggling to raise the funds for repair works. Jani mounted a fundraising campaign in his own local Muslim community, and as a gesture of appreciation from the synagogue he was invited to become one of their Board members. The first Muslim appointed to the Board of a British synagogue made national news headlines.

Bradford pupils themselves have come forward to openly share what the Anne Frank programme has meant to them. One boy, who was seemingly full of external confidence, found the courage to admit he was the victim of bullying so his teaching support officers could help him do something about it. He has since been a much happier person. One Asian teenage boy told us that he had come across boys in his community who were tempted to go to Syria to fight for Islamic State and this was an insurance policy against growth of those ideas. Uzma Zahid was a pupil at Laisterdyke Business and Enterprise College in 2009 when she first became an Anne Frank peer educator and then an Ambassador. Her grandfather had come to Bradford as a teenager from Pakistan to work in a woollen mill. Their family followed varying degrees of Muslim practice, some being more secular than others, but even those who were more secular still lived in a segregated community.

Uzma had never heard of Anne Frank when she was asked to be a peer guide. Once she had read the diary, she felt she shared some of Anne's sentiments but felt it hard to relate her own relatively easy life to a young girl who went through something so horrific and cruel. Uzma's initial nervousness about becoming a guide was helped by being one of a large group who were being trained together. She had attended an entirely Asian primary school, although her interaction with children from different backgrounds increased when she went to a different high school. Being an Anne Frank peer educator sparked a desire to go to university and she chose Royal Holloway College in Surrey, over 200 miles away from Bradford. It was only when she went to university that she realized what real diversity was. Although she had lived in such a multicultural city, Uzma had not realized how segregated her life had been.

When she had first become an Anne Frank guide for the Trust she had not fully discussed her role with her family, not realizing she was starting a relationship that she would describe as a 'lifelong one'.

I now feel this is a huge part of who I am so I have become more accustomed to telling people about this aspect of me. I have just been so lucky to be given so many opportunities: I have met Zlata Filipović, I have had the chance to be a witness to Holocaust testimonies, I have visited the Anne Frank House in Amsterdam, I have mentored younger ambassadors, and many more things. All of these encounters have helped me become someone who I hope my family, my friends, and members of the Anne Frank Trust, can be proud of.

Uzma went on to take a Master's Degree and her thesis explored the association of chemical imbalances in the brain with schizophrenia and memory impairment. Like so many of our Anne Frank Ambassadors, we are indeed proud of her.

Following the Anne Frank programme in a school, teachers have reported an increase in the number of students choosing to study History beyond 16 and as an A-level subject, as students' eyes have been opened to the impact history has upon our own lives. Another unforeseen by product of creating peer educators is that students themselves have told us they feel a greater respect and empathy towards their teachers, as being educators themselves has given them an understanding of the challenges teachers face in communicating knowledge.

Mukith cites the incident of a boy he was training in a West London school. During the guide training session, the boy was very engaged and answered all Mukith's questions, but Mukith felt it had been in a rather loud and overconfident way. At the end of the session, Mukith called him over and told him his knowledge was impressive but that he perhaps needed to curb his overenthusiasm. Mukith continued:

> I asked him how he knew so much about the subject, to which he answered that he was very interested in it and had learnt a lot outside of school. After the boy had left the room his teacher came over to me and asked me how I thought the training had gone. I mentioned that this particular young boy was a little disruptive but I was certainly impressed with his knowledge, even though it mainly revolved around the Nazis and Hitler. The teacher explained to me that there were reports that the community group this young boy belonged to were glorifying Nazism. The school did not have firm evidence and were scared of losing the boy to these extremist ideologies, so chose not to do anything radical, instead selecting him to be an Anne Frank peer educator.

Mukith continued:

> Keeping my conversation with the teacher to myself, the next day I tracked down the student before his first guiding session and told him that I wanted to go over the slides with him before his session. After a brief conversation, I asked him how he knew so much about the Nazis and Hitler in particular. He was vague but mentioned that in his culture there was a belief in a caste system which mirrored the Nazis' belief in a superior race. He explained that his community group did not have a violent approach but the similarities between the hierarchy of the Nazis'

race system and their own caste system made some in his community openly praise Hitler.

I sat with the boy and talked through some of the personal testimonies that I have been privileged to hear first-hand from Holocaust survivors and spoke extensively about the Nazi race laws and the meaning of racism. He slowly softened his stance and I asked him to research more about the Holocaust from reliable sources, giving him links to appropriate websites. The boy didn't show up for two out of the three guiding sessions he was supposed to give but I did see him on the last day, when he agreed to guide a class.

Afterwards he explained to me that he hadn't felt it was appropriate to guide classes around the exhibition while he held these beliefs but after researching more about the Holocaust, as I had suggested, he realized that what he had been taught in his community was not right – although he still believed a strong leader could be important. He admitted that pride in being part of a group should not mean treating others differently. I told him I was proud of him and really impressed by his bravery, not just for coming to guide the class around the exhibition but also for admitting something so personal, then challenging it and realizing it was wrong. I told him that if he could hold on to this bravery and continue being humble he would achieve some amazing things.

Uzma Zahid sums up why she feels the Anne Frank educational programme is so critical:

I think it's very apparent why we should learn about historical events, especially atrocities. It's also important to learn from personal accounts, to understand what an individual went through, to see events through the eyes of someone who lived through it really puts things into perspective. It is also necessary to draw comparisons between current and past atrocities, which can help put the events of today into perspective.

The Anne Frank Schools' Peer Guiding and Ambassadors programme received a huge boost in 2012, when its expansion was supported by the Trust's largest ever single grant, £836,000 from the UK's 'Big Lottery' released over five years. The programme was called 'Realizing Ambition' and was carried out in particular areas of deprivation, helping to divert young people from pathways into crime so that they can fulfil their true potential. A new Programme Delivery Manager, Shona Gibbs, joined the Trust and managed the Education team in its delivery. The Trust's work was scrupulously monitored and its impact assessed by independent agencies throughout the five years, and by the third year the Anne Frank Trust succeeded in receiving 'Gold Quality' standard. This led to further successful funding bids to other agencies. Shaun Whelan, a programme manager for 'Realizing Ambition', described why, 'Your [Anne Frank Trust's] commitment to the young people you work with has been amazing and your commitment to being challenged, to testing and improving the work you deliver, has been amazing too.'

The young people whose circumstances I have related reflect the impact on individuals of the peer education methodology. As well as the 'Realizing Ambition' continuous monitoring over five years, the Trust's work in schools has been academically evaluated by the Department of Social Psychology at the University of Kent. 80 per cent of teachers interviewed said that Anne Frank peer guides were more likely to challenge discriminatory behaviour and 90 per cent of teachers reported that peer guides are more confident after having taken part in the programme. We know that our work has a long term impact on the lives of young people, leaving them with a greater empathy and respect for others and a reduced negativity towards different groups.

The numbers are hugely encouraging but even more so are these beautiful words from an Anne Frank Ambassador at Lawnswood School in Leeds:

Did you know that when the world was invented, racism came afterwards? Racism was invented by people, and today, we as people have the power to eliminate racism. The colour of your skin does not define you in any way possible. Your appearance is only a cover, a cover which starts the most magical story ever, which is your life. Don't judge a book by its cover, because you don't know what the story holds.

Chapter 23

Inspired by Holocaust Survivors

Even though they may display a veneer of normality, survivors of wars and persecution rarely completely leave behind their profoundly affecting experiences. They are buried deep inside their psyche and come out to taunt them at night, or as they get older and find themselves with increased leisure time on their hands. However, despite the deep and long-lasting wounds they carry, it is a telling lesson for us all how they have readjusted to living in a civil society and in many cases given so much back.

I have been privileged to have spent time with many Holocaust survivors, as well as those from the Rwandan and Bosnian genocides and other terrible wars. I have learned that those have been fortunate to survive carry with them a wide range of experiences and stories. I would like to be able to relate the story of every survivor I have met, but that would make this chapter overwhelming in its length and content. I will therefore stick to those that have, for differing reasons, had a profound effect on me, in the hope that their stories also affect others.

The first Holocaust survivor I ever met was a Hungarian man called David Gold. A new exhibition about the Swedish Holocaust hero and rescuer Raoul Wallenberg was touring Britain and I had been invited on to the organizing committee to bring it to my home town of Bournemouth. In the summer of 1982, the exhibition in Wallenberg's honour was staged in a centrally-located Catholic church and we had invited a Hungarian Holocaust survivor called David Gold to come down from London to speak at the opening. This was the first full Holocaust testimony I heard first-hand, and like others when they first hear a Holocaust survivor describe their experiences, it remains with me to this day. The chairman of the local organizing committee was a charming and dapper émigré from Sweden called Mr Kay Mayer. Mr Mayer had a very special interest in keeping Raoul Wallenberg's memory alive.

Wallenberg, who had studied architecture as a young man at the University of Michigan, found on his return to Stockholm that his American qualification did not carry weight when seeking a job in his chosen field. He was compelled to earn a living in business and one of his associates was Kay Mayer. As I recall their company traded in men's neckties. In June 1944, after the German invasion of Hungary in March of that year, the international businessman Wallenberg had been recruited by the US War Refugee Board to go to Budapest on a clandestine mission for them.

Wallenberg was given the dangerous task of trying to assist and save Hungarian Jews. To help his cover he was given special diplomatic status by the Swedish legation. Together with the diplomat Per Anger, Wallenberg rented thirty-two safe houses that were designated neutral Swedish territory, and thus saved 10,000 people's lives. Through his clandestine operations this heroic young man, who had been trained as an architect and not as a spy nor a soldier, succeeded in saving an astonishing number of Jews from certain deportation and death. In January 1945 at the end of the war, and in one of the most distressing cases of the unfathomable injustice of life, this man of valour who had risked his own discovery and execution by the Nazis, was in fact captured and abducted by the Soviets as a presumed spy. Raoul Wallenberg spent the rest of his life, we know not how long, suffering in the dreaded Soviet Lubyanka prison. In October 2016, seventy-one years after his disappearance, he was officially declared dead by the Swedish government. It is believed that he was murdered by the Soviets in prison in 1947.

Speaking in Bournemouth in 1982, in the peace of a church in a picturesque seaside resort, David Gold's mind was reliving the German invasion of Hungary in 1944. The deportations of Hungarian Jews had come very late in the course of the Holocaust, during a period that had been short, piercing and deadly. In just six weeks during the summer of 1944, 400,000 Jews were deported to Poland. In Auschwitz-Birkenau the railway platform was lengthened to cope with the numbers of Hungarian arrivals, very few of whom avoided immediate gassing.

David Gold was not one of the deported. He and a group of men were taken down to the bank of the river Danube. There, in the centre of a European capital city, men, women and children were lined up facing the river and shot in the back one by one. As he saw the man next to him fall into the river and then heard the crack of the bullet destined for him, he somehow managed to time his own toppling into the river just before the deadly bullet hit his body. Following his split-second timing, his school swimming skills then came into play and he was able to play dead by remaining submerged for as long as possible. I can't remember what happened subsequently in David Gold's story but when I stood on the banks of the River Danube on a visit to Budapest in 2010 and walked amidst the poignant Holocaust memorial made up of hundreds of sculpted bronze shoes (they have been crafted in all shapes and sizes from toddler to adult), I thought again of David Gold and his speech to a shocked audience in a Bournemouth church in 1982.

My second memorable Holocaust-survivor encounter was with Leon Greenman. Unlike David Gold, Leon had a definite English accent. I met Leon in 1991 while I was working on one of the first Anne Frank exhibitions I had organized myself. It was staged at the Gunnersbury Park Museum in west London and one afternoon just before the opening, I was having coffee in the museum's café set in its beautiful garden. Opposite me was an elderly man who had introduced himself as Leon.

Born in the East End of London in 1910, and thus a British citizen, Leon happened to be living and working in Rotterdam when the Germans invaded in May 1940. He had considered returning to live in England in the 1930s, but after hearing Neville Chamberlain's 1938 promise of 'peace in our time' decided to stay in the Netherlands with his wife Esther and young son Barney. Leon expected that his British passport would mean the family would soon be repatriated back to England, but found to his horror that the British consulate in Rotterdam had immediately closed down. The Greenman family found themselves trapped.

As he continued to tell me his story amidst the usual coffee-shop backdrop of clattering coffee cups and trays, Leon pulled out from his jacket pocket photos of his young wife and angelic little curly haired toddler Barney, both of whom were gassed upon arrival in Auschwitz. I thought about the innocence of curly-haired Barney walking into a strange room clutching his mother's hand, and his painful struggle to breathe as the Zyklon B gas replaced oxygen in the packed room, or perhaps being trampled to death under hundreds of adult feet fighting for air. It is recorded that the screams before the silence in the chambers of death could last up to twenty minutes.

Leon endured slave labour, medical experiments and a death march. A small man of just over five foot, he had a fiery spirit, and felt he owed his survival to his physical fitness and the skills he could offer in the camp. Before the war he had trained as a boxer, became a professional barber and had loved singing songs from the operas, all of which skills came to be used in the camp.

Unlike most of the survivors I have subsequently met, Leon Greenman had begun speaking publically about the Holocaust not so long after the war. In fact, it was in 1962 after hearing a racist tirade by the leader of the British Neo-Nazis Colin Jordan. Leon became a very active anti-Fascist campaigner and in fact received his OBE in 1998 for 'Services against Racism'. To educators his talks to schools were always memorable, but sometimes deemed to be controversial as Leon admitted to me that he wished to see the pupils show their shock at his story by openly crying in the classroom. Leon Greenman died aged 97 in March 2008 and the permanent Holocaust exhibition at London's Jewish Museum is dedicated to his story.

As in the case of Leon, many of the survivors I have met have been rewarded by long lives and relative good health. Could this be explained through a combination of genes and strong will? Perhaps, but a Holocaust survivor, and even a rescuer, needed not one, not two, but many incidents of lucky escapes to evade the killing machine, often seizing opportunities that others were afraid of taking.

Otto Frank died at 91 and his wife Fritzi Geiringer-Frank at 94. Gena Turgel and Freda Wineman, both of whom survived the starvation and typhus of Bergen-Belsen, are in their 90s as I write. Rescuers Miep Gies and Sir Nicholas Winton were both over 100 when they died.

THE LEGACY OF ANNE FRANK

Sometimes just being in the presence of a survivor stops you in your tracks at the sheer miracle that they are actually standing in front of you. It is often hard to believe that this was the same physical entity that was living under the chimneys of Auschwitz, in the slave labour death pit of Mauthausen or in the squalor of Bergen-Belsen – you are looking into the very same eyes that saw these things. In Wakefield Cathedral in 2001 I sat listening to the by-then elderly writer and journalist Janina Bauman describing living in the Warsaw Ghetto. Throughout her talk I could not take my eyes off her feet. These are the very same feet, I was telling myself, that had walked through those foul-smelling cobbled streets of the ghetto, trying to avoid stepping on the desperate and the dying.

Concentration camp inmates, like those caught up in other wars, tried to hold on to their humanity and innate humanness whenever and wherever they could. Eva Clarke, who lives in Cambridge, has been involved with the Anne Frank Trust since I met her in 2000. She has been a great support to our team by enhancing the power of our work with her remarkable story, both in schools and prisons. Eva's mother Anka was a lively law student in Prague when the Germans invaded and she and her handsome new husband Bernd Nathan found themselves sent to Theresienstadt camp. The couple remained there for three years, and after several furtive visits to her husband in the men's barracks, Anka became pregnant. The baby boy, named Daniel, died of pneumonia just two months after his birth. Anka miraculously became pregnant again by her husband (Eva explains that despite being so weak from the privations, 'inmates sought human comfort whenever they could'). Early into Anka's pregnancy the couple were deported to Auschwitz; first Bernd was herded into the cattle truck and then one day later Anka, who volunteered to follow her beloved husband. The loving couple never saw each other again as Bernd was shot by the guards in January, three months before his daughter Eva was born.

Anka, by then heavily pregnant, was next transported on an open coal truck to Mauthausen in Austria, where, seeing the sign that showed she was about to enter the slave labour camp she had heard was even crueller to its inmates than Auschwitz, she went into sudden labour in the coal truck. Anka gave birth to a girl inside Mauthausen, just five days before its liberation, and miraculously Eva, who came into the world weighing just 3lbs (1.5kg), survived. Anka weighed 5 stone (31kg). Eva well understands that she owes her own existence to her older brother's death as, if Anka had arrived in Auschwitz with her baby boy in her arms, both mother and baby would have been immediately gassed.

Eva was born on 29 April and is also aware that if her mother had arrived in Mauthausen a couple of days earlier, while its gas chambers were still functioning, she would have died inside the body of her gassed mother. The new-born baby Eva was wrapped in newspaper and hidden until the camp's liberation on 5 May. After being nursed back to health, Anka remarried and the family moved to Cardiff. I saw Anka whenever I brought an Anne Frank exhibition or educational project to Cardiff. She remained a beautiful and strong woman into old age and a proud

'Cardiffian' (I am not sure if that word actually exists but my own mother who grew up in the city described herself as such). One time I had set up the Anne Frank exhibition at the new Welsh Assembly building and Anka and I were invited to sit in on that afternoon's parliamentary debate. As we sat listening to the session, Wales's First Minister, the late Rhodri Morgan, stood up to speak. Anka turned to me and with her twinkling blue eyes and mid-European accent, said with great pride, 'That's our Rhodri.'

Anka, whose young husband had not survived to see the birth of his beautiful daughter, lived to be 96 and was able to welcome into the world her three great-grandchildren. Mother and daughter remained extremely close and in her last years Anka moved to Cambridge to be with Eva. Eva's first public speaking engagement after Anka's death in July 2013 was seven months later at the February opening of the 'Anne Frank + You' exhibition at Ely Cathedral in Cambridgeshire. Eva had written out her speech, but before the proceedings began, she beckoned me over to where she was standing almost hidden behind one of the building's ancient Norman columns. I was quizzical about why she had beckoned me so furtively during the welcoming drinks reception. Her luminous green eyes stared straight into mine. 'Gillian, I may need your help. This is so emotional for me. It is the first time I'll be telling my parents' story since my mother's death. I just don't know if I'll be able to get through it.' I nodded sympathetically. And then she pointed to her notes and asked me, 'If I have to stop midway, will you take over?' I reassured her that of course she would be able to do it and what's more, in her customary brilliant way, but if she were to find herself overcome with emotion, then of course I would.

And that's what happened. Two-thirds into Eva's address as she was describing her mother's journey to Mauthausen, she stopped mid-sentence, looked at me and nodded. I walked towards the podium where she stood and, holding her close, I continued to read out her words. After this incident Eva regained her fortitude, and now retired from her work as administrator at Cambridgeshire Further Education College, she continues to speak in schools and other settings. The publication of a book *Born Survivors*, telling her story and those of two other babies born in the camps who now live in America, has opened up many new speaking opportunities. Eva well knows that, as she is perhaps one of the very youngest Holocaust camp survivors, even without the memories of those times being her own, the responsibility for educating new generations will fall to her for many more years.

Although we may believe that all camp inmates were no more than dehumanized tattooed numbers to their guards, I have heard first hand of the rare instances where there have been lightning flashes of empathy by guards with their prisoners. In 2009, I met Catherine Hill, who was in London for the launch of a book entitled *The Thoughtful Dresser*, a philosophical exploration of the importance of fashion by the journalist and writer Linda Grant. Catherine was featured in a chapter of the book.

Why was a Holocaust survivor being interviewed about a book on fashion? Well it transpired that her own desire to look pretty, even in Auschwitz, helped sustain her determination to survive. After her liberation from Auschwitz, Catherine moved to Canada, which in the post-war years had none of the creative and progressive drive of the large American cities. Starting her career as retail assistant on the shop floor of a major Montreal department store, Catherine's European flair for fashion saw her soon become appointed as the store's women's wear senior buyer. In the early 1970s and following divorce, she opened a boutique called 'Chez Catherine' where she gave women in Toronto their first experience of exciting young Italian designers such as Giorgio Armani, Gianni Versace and Gianfranco Ferre. Catherine Hill became a highly influential name in the growth of Canadian fashion, but not many of her followers may have been aware that her love of clothes could well have saved her life.

Having heard her speak at the book launch and then on BBC Radio 4's *Woman's Hour*, I wanted to spend more time with this glamorous and intriguing woman, so I invited her for lunch. She told me more about her time in Auschwitz as a teenager, just one of thousands around her earmarked for death. Her mother had been immediately gassed on arrival and her father died of typhus. When she arrived at the camp and her clothes were replaced by the dirty, ragged striped uniform still smelling of its murdered previous occupant, she knew she would have to do something to keep her spirits up. She tore a strip from the jacket and created a striped headband to cover her shaven head, reminding herself of the beauty of clothing and of life. Catherine could have been killed just for this act of defiance, but seeing the teenager's determination to be pretty in the face of death somehow generated a spark of humanity from a male guard. At the daily 5.00 a.m. roll call he had quickly spotted her covered head but chose to spare her life by sending her for kitchen duties instead of to the gas chamber. Catherine has carried that deep understanding of our need to be clothed and to look beautiful throughout her life, and when I recall her visit to London in 2009, I can still picture her sashaying into our lunch rendezvous in a sassy pink fur coat that drew approving smiles from all around the room.

French-born Freda Wineman, also a strikingly pretty woman, immaculately dressed and now in her nineties, survived the camps of Auschwitz, Bergen-Belsen, Raguhn, and finally Theresienstadt – but only just. Freda told me that in Auschwitz-Birkenau in September 1944 she is certain that she was held in the same barrack as Margot and Anne Frank, as all the women and girls who had arrived from France, Belgium and the Netherlands at that time were put together. Her own sister in law Janine was with Freda in the same barracks and when Anne Frank's diary started to become known, prompted Freda's memory by asking her, 'Don't you remember those two teenage sisters from Amsterdam who were with us in the barrack?'. Freda and Janine were moved on from Auschwitz to Bergen-Belsen, where they spent five months. When she speaks to schools, Freda describes the weeks in Bergen-Belsen without any substantial food, just a little watery soup, and only dirty water to slake her desperate thirst.

During a taxi ride in 2015 from north London to the predominantly Bengali area of Whitechapel to speak at our Anne Frank exhibition, Freda told me that she had only discovered in the 1980s how close she had come to being blown up along with hundreds of other women. She had long wondered why, in the last days of the war and so close to death from starvation, she had been transported away from Bergen-Belsen in northern Germany all the way south to Theresienstadt in Czechoslovakia. Once there, she met women who had been brought from camps all over Europe. Why had the Germans soldiers bothered with this final act of complex logistics, when they could already have gone home to their families?

Attending a lecture at the Imperial War Museum by a Russian army officer in the mid-1980s, Freda at last heard why. The Russian officer shocked the audience by what he revealed. Newly-discovered Russian archives had shown that the Nazi units had been directed by senior authorities to gather the remains of Europe's Jews in Theresienstadt. There they were planning to blow up the camp and all those inside in order to destroy evidence of their atrocities. This was to take place on 10 May. By a miracle, Theresienstadt camp, with Freda in it, was liberated by the Americans on 9 May.

Speaking to the audience at the Anne Frank exhibition launch, Freda told of another example of the persistence of the human capacity to love and dream of a future, even in the most hopeless of circumstances. Several members of the audience were seen wiping away a tear as she told them how her brother David had actually met his wife to be on the way to Auschwitz. In the same cattle car taking Freda and David and their family from the French internment camp of Drancy in the suburbs of Paris there was a pretty girl called Janine, who also came from their home region of Alsace. David and Janine's eyes had met in the frightened melee of people crushed together in the wagon over the three days of the journey.

Stepping out of the cattle truck into the blinding light at Auschwitz-Birkenau, the terrified and weakened people were confronted by SS guards, their whips and barking German Shepherd dogs. Freda's mother was ordered by an SS guard to take a baby from a young Dutch woman. Despite the young mother's imploring screams, Freda's mother had no choice but to take the baby. And because she was holding a baby and was with her own young son Marcel, Freda's mother and the children were sent to one side with other mothers, children and elderly. Freda tried to follow her mother but was ordered to stand in the other line, and told by the guard not to worry as her mother would be helping by looking after the children. In fact, Freda's mother and all those in her line were being sent immediately to the gas chamber.

Janine and Freda became close and supportive friends once they were in the crowded and uncomfortable women's barrack. It was there among the French,

Belgian and Dutch women crammed together on bare wooden bunks that Janine first remembered coming across Margot and Anne Frank, 'the two young sisters from Amsterdam'. Janine and Freda were set to work in the Kanada Kommando block alongside the crematorium sorting the still-warm clothes of murdered Jews. The two terrified young women formed a camaraderie, especially through the trauma of seeing three of the girls who worked alongside them being hanged for smuggling a few of the clothes back into the camp.

Janine confided in Freda that if she survived she wanted to spend her life with David. Her determination bore fruit. Janine and David were able to find each other again after liberation, they married and had four children. In 1950 Freda relocated to London and also fell in love. She married a discharged British soldier who had fought in the war. They had two children but when Freda's youngest child was six weeks old, her husband died of hepatitis, probably picked up during the war. Having to bring up two young children on her own and without the benefits of modern post traumatic counselling, Freda could not shake off the nightmares she endured. It was only after she gave her testimony to the British Library Sound Archive in the 1990s that Freda Wineman at last found herself more at peace.

When she speaks to schools Freda gives a powerful message to young people:

> They were terrible times. I sometimes wonder why it was that my friends and family were made to suffer in this way. It could happen again. The world has become much more fragmented and the prospect of suffering is very great indeed. It is certain that if you do nothing and say nothing this lets evil in. You should speak up for civilized behaviour . . . There are still people who deny that it happened. It was not a mistake by an otherwise good government. It was pure evil. It is vital that this message is not diluted. We all need to understand this.

Polish-born survivor Gena Turgel met her husband to be in the ruins of Bergen-Belsen. Norman Turgel was not another inmate but a liberating British soldier, attached to the British Intelligence Corps. He had been tasked with rounding up SS commanders.

Three days after they first spotted each other, Norman invited Gena to dinner with his commanding officer. Gena recalled,

> I walked in and saw beautiful decorated tables with white tablecloths and flowers, which I hadn't seen for six years. I said 'You must be expecting special visitors, what am I doing here?' Norman answered, 'You are the special guest. This is our engagement party'. I said 'Pardon?' All his colleagues said "Congratulations' too and I thought to myself: 'They must be mad'. But, you see, Norman had made up his mind when he first saw me in the hospital, in a white overall, that this was the woman he was going to marry.

Nowadays the impulsive determination shown by Norman Turgel and Freda's friend Janine would seem strange, but in the havoc of Europe at the end of that long and devastating war, people felt the need to grasp at any opportunity for happiness.

I first heard Gena's story in the 1980s when her memoir *I Light A Candle* had just been published. At a charity lunch in the host's beautifully furnished home, Gena politely made inconsequential conversation over white wine and canapés. Then she stood up in front of a group of fifty women and described seeing her sister Miriam shot in the back along with others who had been smuggling food. Gena had been forced to dig her own sister's grave. Dr Mengele had conducted one of his ghastly experiments on her other sister Hela, in which he had drained her blood and replaced it with petrol. Hela died in agony the next day. Gena was the only one of her parents' nine children to survive.

On that day back in the 1980s Gena did not choose to tell us another story about her time in the camps – one I would not hear for a further twenty years – that she and her mother had tried to comfort the dying Anne Frank in Bergen-Belsen. 'Anne's bed was around the corner from me. She was delirious, terrible, burning up. I gave her cold water to wash her down. We didn't know she would be special, but she was a lovely girl. I can still see her lying there with her face so red as she had caught typhus. And then she died.' At the time, there were outbreaks of both typhus and dysentery in the camp and when British soldiers came to liberate Bergen-Belsen, Gena reported to them that 'people are dying like flies'. Despite the nadir of existence she endured, as did her belief that 'The world is beautiful. But people are nasty.' Gena rebuilt her life through her happy fifty-year marriage to Norman resulting in thirteen great-grandchildren, whom she considers as a reward for all she suffered. Even now in her 90s, I have never seen Gena Turgel looking anything less than elegance personified, with her stylish blond hair and fashionable clothes. I accompanied a BBC television film crew to her home to interview her on the seventieth anniversary of the liberation of Bergen-Belsen, but we all had to wait while her visiting manicurist finished her nails.

Freddie Knoller is a nonagenarian survivor who is a very popular speaker with the Anne Frank exhibition in both schools and prisons. This is partly because his story is one of exciting escapes, daring do and eventual capture after a brave flight across western Europe. Freddie was born in Vienna and as a child was a talented violinist. Following the annexation of Austria by Germany in March 1938, anti-Semitism became even more virulent, causing Freddie and his brothers to leave Vienna. Freddie went first, and travelled illegally to Antwerp, Belgium. Freddie's mother and father, at 53 and 56, naively believed that they were too old for anything to happen to them, and so they stayed. They were deported to Theresienstadt and from there to Auschwitz-Birkenau, where they were murdered.

In May 1940, Freddie found himself in Belgium when Germany invaded. Freddie tried to escape to France but he was arrested at the border and detained as an enemy alien in an internment camp. He was able to escape in the middle of the night, and made it to Gaillac, in the unoccupied area of France, where his aunt, uncle and cousins lived. A city boy, Freddie quickly became bored with provincial Gaillac and decided to visit Paris, a city he had always dreamed of going to. While there, living in the heart of Pigalle with its famed Moulin Rouge nightclub, he became seduced by the exciting nightlife. He obtained false papers and earned money by taking German soldiers to the nightclubs, brothels and cabarets, where he earned a percentage of anything that they spent once inside. In May 1943, while plying his nighttime trade, he was apprehended by a Gestapo officer who bragged that he could 'easily identify Jews'. Despite this the officer did not remotely suspect that Freddie was Jewish and was using false papers. But he told him to stop working in Pigalle and that he should be working for the German Reich. Freddie knew that he could no longer risk staying in Paris and fled to Figeac in south-west France.

Through his contacts in Figeac, Freddie joined a French Resistance group. A broken love affair led to his vengeful betrayal by his spurned girlfriend and arrest by the Vichy Police. Under torture, and without giving away any details of his Resistance colleagues, Freddie Knoller finally admitted to being a Jew. He was sent to Drancy internment camp and then on to Auschwitz-Birkenau. During the horrific journey, he looked after a middle-aged Frenchman called Robert, who turned out to be a doctor. Robert went on to be put in charge of the camp hospital barracks, and in gratitude for Freddie helping him on the journey, he found him morsels of extra food every day, which Freddie believes was the reason for his survival.

Many British Holocaust survivors have been recognized with royal honours or honorary degrees for their contribution to our country. It is a happy irony that those who were considered 'Untermenschen' by their Nazi oppressors have been given this country's highest recognition for their voluntary work as educators, as distinguished entrepreneurs and as philanthropists. Educators honoured have included Mala Tribich and her brother Ben Helfgott, who came to Britain as teenage survivors in 1945. Just seven years later Ben represented his new country as a weight-lifter in the 1952 Olympics. Mala has described the shock of her childhood home town of Piotrkow-Trybunalski becoming a ghetto, in fact it was the first in Poland to have a ghetto.

> By the 1st of November 1939, all Jews were removed from their homes and herded into a small area of the town. This became very overcrowded and the inadequate sanitary conditions caused many epidemics. We were humiliated, subjected to beatings, shootings and deprived of the most basic human rights. The main deportation came in the autumn of 1942. I only managed to avoid it because my parents paid for me to stay with a Polish family, where I lived as a Christian. When it was safe for me to return, the ghetto had shrunk to less than 10 per cent of the original size and after a short time my mother and my sister Lusia, together with 560

other people, were taken away and brutally murdered in a local forest called Rakow.

My cousin Ann and I were among those to be deported, we were lined up in a column surrounded by soldiers with their rifles at the ready. When I spotted the officer in charge, I went up to him and told him that I had been separated from my father and brother, and asked if I could please go back to them. He looked shocked and a little surprised that I had the audacity or perhaps the courage to approach him but he smiled, called over a Jewish policeman and said 'take her back inside the ghetto'. I tried to take Ann with me but the policeman said she did not have permission. So I was faced with the dilemma of leaving Ann or missing the chance of being reunited with my father and Ben. However, I continued to argue and eventually he let me take Ann with me.

Towards the end of 1944 the final deportation took place. Although throughout the war conditions were constantly going downhill and at times we felt that they could not get any worse, somehow we managed to adapt. But when we arrived in Ravensbruck we felt that we would not survive. After we had queued up to have our details recorded we had to undress, everything was taken from us, our heads were shaved, we went through cold communal showers and were given the concentration camp garb, a striped skirt and jacket and a pair of clogs. When we emerged at the other end we couldn't recognize one another. Our identities, our personalities, our very souls had been taken from us. At this point we started to lose all hope. My aunt, Frania Klein, died within a few days of arrival, my best friend Pema died soon after that, people were just giving up. But little did we suspect what was to come.

From Ravensbruck Mala was sent to Bergen-Belsen where she encountered people who were walking skeletons. Somehow she managed to hold on to the end and liberation. She came to England in 1947 to be reunited with her brother Ben, her only surviving close relative. She learnt English, attended secretarial college and within a year was working in an office. Whilst her children were growing up, Mala studied and gained a degree in Sociology from the University of London.

Refugees who as youngsters fled Nazi Europe in the 1930s and came to Britain have also been great contributors to the country that gave them shelter. Many, such as the Labour peer Lord Alf Dubs, have publically spoken out in support of modern-day refugees fleeing oppression. Ian Karten MBE, who lost his father in Buchenwald and his sister on a death march, became successful in business and set up the Ian Karten Charitable Trust, which created 100 dedicated centres to teach computer skills to the disabled. With these inspirational lives, it is easy to forget the deeply-embedded scars that come out at night to haunt their living victims.

Lilian Levy, the wife of the Trust's long-time Principal Guide Herbert Levy, was liberated as a five-year-old orphan in Bergen-Belsen, and was brought over to England to live in the care of her aunt. Even though she was so little, Lilian can still remember the nauseating smell of the camp and lives with the fact that she survived because her mother had sacrificed her own precious morsels of food to save her daughter.

Survivor Ziggy Schipper has the demeanour of a warm, friendly and jolly man whose smile denotes he is always happy to see you. However, in a candid TV interview his wife has publicly described the difficult hours of the night when her husband's demons have come out to torment him.

Mala Tribich has summed up her life after the war by saying: 'Leading a normal life after living through the Holocaust is one of the biggest challenges, for the bleak shadow of that time penetrates deep. What we the survivors have been able to show is that the human capacity for resilience *can* prevail.'

Over the coming two decades, all those demons, along with the bodies of their physical owners, will be stilled. It will be up to us, who have been so privileged to have heard these stories first-hand, and those we have shared the stories with, to pass them onwards to future generations.

Between the completion and publication of this book, one more powerful survivor voice was silenced, that of Gena Turgel. Gena passed away in June 2018 at the age of 95. Her beauty, vibrancy and wisdom is much missed by all who knew, loved and admired her.

Chapter 24

Anne Frank and the Girl who was Kidnapped by Sardinian Bandits

'I could relate to Anne Frank. We were both teenagers in hiding, in danger and frightened and there was nowhere to escape.' Annabel Schild

As a young teenager in 1979, Annabel Schild was kidnapped by Sardinian bandits and held in captivity for many weeks. The Schild kidnapping case, as it unfolded, received a lot of media coverage in the UK. It had happened unusually, in the prevailing international climate of kidnappings, to a British family, so the British media were extremely interested. The Schild family went on to become great supporters of the Anne Frank Trust, for several profound reasons.

One of the highlights of the year for the Schild family was escaping London to stay at their villa in Sardinia. At that time Sardinia was not the tourist destination it is now, and the Schild family considered themselves pioneers in its discovery. In August 1979, the family arrived on the island for their summer break. Two weeks into the holiday, Rolf, Daphne and Annabel were returning to their villa after dinner when they were pounced on by a gang of waiting Sardinian bandits. The bandits threw the Schild family back into their own car and drove it up into the mountains. Kidnappings by Sardinian bandits were rife that summer, and over a dozen tourists had already fallen victim, most quickly released. After two weeks in captivity, Rolf was freed and instructed by the kidnappers to return to London to raise the ransom, believed to be several million pounds, which the bandits were demanding for the safe return of his wife and daughter.

Throughout the 1970s there had been several very high-profile kidnappings both for political and mercenary motives, carried out by gangs and terrorist groups such as the paramilitary Red Brigades in Italy, who murdered Italian Prime Minister Aldo Moro in 1978. Patty Hearst, the granddaughter of American newspaper magnate William Randolph Hearst, was abducted in 1974 and notoriously took part in violent robberies along with her own kidnappers. Sixteen-year-old John Paul Getty III, grandson of the billionaire J. Paul Getty, had his ear sliced off by his kidnappers to demonstrate their seriousness. Canadian politician and lawyer Pierre LaPorte was murdered by his kidnappers, the Front de Liberation du Quebec, in 1970.

Back in London, Rolf was able to raise £350,000, a huge sum in those days. After an appeal by Pope John Paul, Daphne was set free in mid-January 1980, but the 14-year-old Annabel was held on her own for a further two months. One can only imagine how her parents and older brothers Julian and David felt on every one of those remaining days, especially in the knowledge that Annabel had been born with a hearing disability. Upon her release on 21 March, Annabel told the media, 'After my mother was freed, I felt very lonely. I had no-one to talk to and no-one to speak English to.'

But Annabel felt she wasn't completely on her own and many years after the event she divulged to me the reason why.

> The first autobiography I read at the age of 13 was the diary of Anne Frank. To this day it certainly must be one of the most influential books I have ever read. I remember I was very interested in this book and it gave me a sense of real understanding of what my father and his family went through during the Nazi era. The following year at the age of 14, I was kidnapped from our family home in Sardinia with my parents. After both my father and mother were freed, I was left alone with the kidnappers for two months. I was locked up in a dirty and cramped loft without electricity, cleaning facilities and sanitation, not being able to hear without my hearing aids and sitting in total darkness with nothing to do. During that time, I was struck by how much I could relate to Anne Frank. We were both in hiding, in danger and frightened and with nowhere to escape. I found comfort in thinking if Anne Frank can do it so can I, and if I do not make it then at least I was brave like Anne Frank.

Daphne later told me: 'It was one of those situations you could not believe you were in.' Echoing what concentration camp survivors have told me, she went on, 'It was the isolation that was so frightening. No-one knowing where we were. Even the local solicitors were in cahoots with the bandits.'

I had been introduced to Rolf in 2002 by the MP for Luton, Kelvin Hopkins, as Kelvin thought Rolf could be interested in supporting the work of the Anne Frank Trust. Rolf's company was based in Kelvin's constituency so he knew him well. It was an auspicious meeting that resulted in many years of close association and friendship with the Schild family.

Rolf Schild was a handsome and engaging man, a born entrepreneur with strong views on free markets and capitalism. He came from Cologne to the UK as a 14-year-old boy in a group of 100 Jewish boys who were brought out of Germany by their teacher. Rolf was reunited with his older brother Walter, who had arrived in England earlier. After the war ended Rolf and Walter learnt that their parents, grandparents and wider family had been murdered by the Nazis. Rolf took his first job in 1943 as a machine operator in a Manchester company, while at the same time studying for his degree in engineering. After the war he moved to London and found work with a small medical instruments company, where he developed a phono-cardiograph to measure and record the sound of the heart, and a transducer device to measure pressure within the heart. His next career move came when he was approached by the aero engine manufacturer Rolls-Royce who needed a device to measure engine pressures. Rolf's view was that 'an engine is just a pump, similar to the heart', and that it was a matter only of adapting the medical technology. His boss thought the potential in the aviation industry too limited, and was not interested in diversifying, but Rolf had what he called 'fingerspitzengefuhl' (a feeling in his fingertips) about the new product.

He set up his own company with a business partner and they began assembling components in Rolf's Hampstead kitchen for manufacturers such as De Havilland. After winning a government contract to provide transducers for ballistic missiles, they took over a rented factory and the business took off. The company, SE Laboratories, went on to contribute to the development of the first heart and lung machine at Hammersmith Hospital, helping to advance open heart surgery. Rolf then went on to invest in Hymatic Engineering, a military equipment manufacturer, which became Huntleigh Technology in 1975. In 1954 he had met Daphne Scholtes, who was working at the BBC in Langham Place as an assistant to the Presentations Editor. They married and had three children, Julian, David and Annabel.

After the arrest of the Sardinian bandits who kidnapped the Schild family, it was reported that this uneducated group of men had actually mistaken the name Rolf Schild for Rothschild. That was one of the theories, another was that it was a case of mistaken identity, and that the gang had confused the Schild family with that of a famous football manager who lived in the next-door villa.

After these terrible and traumatic events, the family carried on their lives as best they could. On returning to school Annabel's head teacher had apparently told the pupils not to mention anything to Annabel, to treat her as though nothing had happened. It is difficult to know whether this was the wisest policy, although Annabel is a remarkably successful, down-to-earth and caring woman.

Rolf Schild was appointed OBE in 1997, and was also awarded the German Order of Merit for his contribution to Anglo-German relations. He also remained a practising engineer, both in the research department of Huntleigh Technology and as a hobby, and travelled widely in search of new ideas. In the final months of his life, he designed the 'air walker', an exercise device to help airline passengers avoid deep-vein thrombosis. He also became known for his charitable interests, and was the proud host of the very first Anne Frank Trust lunch in January 2003. Despite his great support of the Conservative Party, Rolf agreed to the speaker being the Labour government's Chief Secretary to the Treasury, Paul Boateng, and at the lunch they enjoyed a very lively conversation. Less than three months after hosting the lunch, Rolf died suddenly. Ironically, this man who had cheated murder by the Nazis and given so much to the medical industry, helping the lives of so many, died due to a medical misdiagnosis.

In August, when planning our second annual fundraising lunch, I called Daphne and suggested she may wish to host the lunch in honour and memory of Rolf. She readily agreed, and has generously hosted the lunch for the following fifteen years. Her children Julian, David and Annabel have all been wonderful supporters too. I once asked Daphne what was so appealing to her about the event. As well as the diversity of the guests that regularly attend, Daphne told me why Anne Frank had been so important to her and Annabel. During their lonely days of captivity together in the cold and isolated cave in Sardinia, they had often spoken about Anne Frank and her days hiding in the secret annexe. Anne had become part of their own life in captivity, and remained to this day very special to them.

Chapter 25

Anne Frank in the Far East

Anne in Japan

Anne Frank's diary was first published in Japan as early as 1952. Since its first Japanese-language edition, Anne has been portrayed in Japan as an enduring and recognizable symbol of the suffering of children, starting with those who had been killed or maimed by the atomic bombs dropped by the Americans on Hiroshima and Nagasaki at the end of the Second World War. 200,000 people died as a result of the two deadly bombs, and many were children whose bodies were found incinerated and covered in black carbon, looking much like the images we recall from the obliteration of Pompeii.

The first Japanese edition of Anne's diary sold a remarkable 116,000 copies in only five months, just seven years after the end of the war. What could be the reason for this remarkable interest in a Holocaust victim, by the people of a country that was allied with her persecutors?

Alain Lewkowicz is a French journalist who wrote an elaborate iPad application, 'Anne Frank in the Land of Manga', about his investigation of the Anne Frank phenomenon in Japan. 'She symbolizes the ultimate World War II victim,' said Lewkowicz. 'And that's how most Japanese consider their own country because of the atomic bombs – a victim, never a perpetrator.' Japan has seen the publication of at least four popular manga comic books about Anne Frank and three animated films. Rabbi Abraham Cooper, associate dean of the Los Angeles-based Simon Wiesenthal Centre, told the German broadcasting service Deutsche Welle why he believed Anne's story had so resonated with the Japanese people. 'The Japanese love children and this is a story of a child in a terrible situation, through no fault of her own. And she shows real honesty, opening up on so many different levels, including as a teenage girl. She talks about her first kiss, about her hopes for the future. Since she never expected anyone to read her diary, it has a particular sense of authenticity.' Rabbi Cooper ventured another possible reason, 'A lot of young Japanese people don't have much space or privacy, so there is also a parallel in [Anne's] struggle to find space for themselves.'

According to Anne Frank's and Otto Frank's biographer Carol Ann Lee, 'The marketing strategy in Japan had been to sell the diary as a protest against the great misfortunes brought by war. [Anne was] a young victim but one who inspired hope for the future rather than a sense of guilt for the past. Her sex further emphasised the stress on innocence.'

For many decades after the end of the war, guilt about the past wasn't on the Japanese agenda. The country's leaders did not use the term 'apologize' about the country's brutality in the Second World War until the fiftieth anniversary of the war's end, when in a speech on 15 August 1995, Prime Minister Tomiichi Muramaya finally used the Japanese word 'owabi', which is translated into English as 'heartfelt apology'.

Because Anne's diary was one of the first books to mention menstruation openly and her name had become so well-known, the word 'Anne's Day' became a euphemism in Japan for the female 'time of the month'. In the late 1960s, a manufacturer of feminine sanitary wear saw a commercial opportunity in the association between Anne and menstruation, by creating a branded 'Anne Frank' range of tampons. Production of these was stopped when it came to the notice of the Anne Frank-Fonds in Switzerland, who were understandably outraged.

The exhibition 'Anne Frank in the World' first visited Japan in 1987, and during this and subsequent tours, the exhibition was often located on the top floor of department stores. This is not unusual for cultural projects in the consumer-driven society of Japan (and actually in Britain too we have had several successful and busy exhibitions shown in shopping malls). From 2009 onwards, the focus changed from staging Anne Frank exhibitions for the wider community to that of educational establishments or cultural centres. Since then there have been over 100 different Anne Frank exhibition venues involving 300,000 participants.

Stefan Vervaecke is a Schools Improvement Officer in Amsterdam. He had become involved with the anti-racism work of the Anne Frank House back in the early 1970s, when tensions had erupted in Amsterdam over discrimination against the Surinamese community. Stefan, a graduate of Theology and Education, started his career working with Catholic schools in Amsterdam and over the years had developed good connections with Catholic missionaries throughout the Far East. In 2009 he received a call from the Anne Frank House. It was Jan Erik Dubbelman asking for some help. This was the time leading up to the 400th anniversary of the first formal trade relations established between the Netherlands and Japan in 1609, when the Dutch had been granted extensive trading rights. The Dutch had set up an East India Company outpost at Hirado to trade in exotic Asian goods such as spices, textiles, porcelain and silk. To mark the anniversary, the Prime Minister of the Netherlands, Jan Peter Balkenende, was due to attend a commemorative ceremony in Tokyo and the Anne Frank House had been invited to bring an exhibition on Anne Frank to mark the celebrations. A suitable venue quickly needed to be found.

Like many international Anne Frank projects, after Jan Erik had made the call to Stefan, a transcontinental thread of helpful connections quickly came into play. Stefan was doing some work in Hong Kong at that time, and through missionary friends in Taiwan, he was introduced to a Catholic school in the centre of Tokyo. This school was extremely happy to host an Anne Frank exhibition, and especially to mark such an auspicious occasion.

The exhibition opening took place at the Catholic school, garnering lots of positive publicity. Then the Anne Frank exhibition was invited, through Stefan's growing Catholic schools network, to visit others. Within two years, there was a clear need to take it even wider. A local Japanese based co-ordinator of the tour was urgently needed. Again, international networks came into play.

In the 1990s, Stefan had been one of the first people to encourage widespread use of computers in Amsterdam's schools. Some years later, in 2003, he had attended an educational conference and youth summit in Japan, where he was particularly impressed by a woman educator called Yoko Takagi. In the spring of 2011, the same Yoko received an email from Stefan Vervaecke asking for her help in co-ordinating an extended Japanese tour of the Anne Frank exhibition. Yoko had no hesitation in saying yes. She had read one of the first published editions of Anne's diary at junior high school back in the 1950s and, perhaps surprisingly for a girl from the Far East in those days, had found Anne's life to be 'not exactly outside my own world'.

Yoko's early childhood had been spent in the eastern Asian region of Manchuria, for a long time an area of dispute between China, Russia and Japan. Following an invasion of Manchuria by the Imperial Japanese Army in 1931, Japanese families had been encouraged to go and settle there. They did in large numbers, and swelled the local Chinese population more than threefold. Immediately after the Japanese defeat in the Second World War, the Soviet Union sent its army into Manchuria, ending the four years of peace between Japan and Russia during the Second World War (when the Soviet Union had been otherwise occupied defending its western borders against Nazi advances). During the nine months the Soviet army was in Manchuria, the Japanese community found themselves being regularly attacked and threatened by Soviet soldiers, often pointing guns directly at them. Yoko had a vivid memory of being five years old and threatened at gunpoint by a callous Soviet soldier. Even at such a young age, little Yoko had understood that Japanese children were being kidnapped and sold for a high price by the Soviet soldiers and that many Japanese adults were being killed. Yoko felt very fortunate that she and her family managed to survive until they were able to move back to Japan.

Yoko's early adult life in Japan was pretty conventional. She worked in a bank, married, raised children and then at the age of 35, decided she should learn English, which she went on to teach. But then, nearing the age of 50, she did something very unconventional. She had long held a dream of going to university, and leaving her husband at home in Osaka, she flew off across the Pacific to Hawaii State University to further her English studies.

Since Yoko received the invitation from Stefan Vervaecke in 2009 to help the Anne Frank House by finding suitable venues, she has taken the exhibition to eighty places, averaging ten a year, mostly high schools. One-third of a million people have seen an Anne Frank exhibition in Japan. Yoko also feels that the Japanese interest in Anne Frank has long been due to a connection to Anne's experience because of the suffering of children in the Hiroshima and Nagasaki atomic bombs. But she also proposed a more sensitive and controversial reason. 'Through looking at the genocide of the Holocaust, educators can see an important doorway into a very difficult time in Japanese history for young people to learn about – that of the cruelty of the Japanese occupying army. I hope that young people *will* make these connections. They know that the bombs dropped by the Americans on Hiroshima and Nagasaki were immensely cruel, but at the same time they need to learn that once wars start, human beings, and in our case the Japanese army, are capable of very cruel things,' said Yoko.

Today, Anne Frank's life story is taught in Japanese schools in tandem with that of Chiune Sugihara, the wartime diplomat who was the Japanese equivalent of Oskar Schindler and Raoul Wallenberg, in Sugihara's case saving the lives of 6,000 Lithuanian Jews. Yoko works with the practical side of taking the exhibition around schools and once it has been set up, she equips each school with a set of resources and suggested activities. Yoko organizes the tour from her home as a volunteer, and a grant initiated by the former Vice Education Minister covers the costs of the transport of the exhibition from school to school. She has an almost spiritual description for the practicalities of finding venues: 'When it's hard for me to find the next site for the exhibition, something happens and suddenly there is a new site waiting. I believe Anne is working with me!'

The Anne Frank Rose of Japan

> 'In the rose garden unless you retrace your steps, you'll find no way out.'
> Haiku by Tsuda Kiyoko (part of the text of 'Souvenir d'Anne Frank')

In 1960 a Belgian horticulturalist called Hippolyte Delforge created a fragrant orange blend floribunda rose he named 'Souvenir d'Anne Frank'. Symbolically the new rose was grafted together from one rose that had been created in 1929, the year of Anne's birth, and one created in the year of her death, 1945.

On reading Anne's diary at her school in Japan in the early 1970's, 15-year-old Michiko Otsuki became one of the thousands of young Japanese girls who were inspired to write to Otto Frank. The two corresponded for a while, during which time Otto sent Michiko a Christmas gift of a dozen of the 'Souvenir d'Anne Frank' rose bushes. All but one of the bushes died, and Michiko gave the last surviving rose bush to her uncle Ryuichi Yamamuro, a former teacher who in retirement had become an expert Bonsai grafter. Mr Yamamuro grafted the European rose onto Japanese stock, and then an idea struck him. He planted 'Souvenir d'Anne Frank' rose bushes in the Peace Gardens of Hiroshima and Nagasaki, and then set about sending the roses, along with a copy of Anne's diary, to schools in cities throughout the islands of Japan – from Hokkaido in the north to Okinawa in the south. Mr Yamamuro thought of the children he had taught long ago in the years before the Second World War and their sadness at being called up to fight an enemy.

Kenji Yamamuro, Ryuichi's son, continues the sacred work of his father to this day. One of the rose bushes grows in the gardens of a church in Nishinomiya City. The church is called the Anne's Rose Church, so named after consultation with Otto Frank. As far as it is known, it is the only church in the world named after Anne Frank.

In 2011, this remarkable story of the 'Souvenir d'Anne Frank' roses became the basis of a musical interpretation by the British-based Ensemble Theatre Group. The group's founder, the actress and singer Elizabeth Mansfield, had discovered an Anne Frank-inspired musical piece for piano, cello and violin entitled 'Het Achterhuis' (the Dutch name of Anne Frank's diary when published) written by the composer Colin Decio. Having been introduced to Colin at one of her performances, Elizabeth was thinking about putting Anne's own words to his music to create a new work for the Ensemble group. In the course of her research for this, she came upon the story of the 'Souvenir d'Anne Frank' rose which excited her.

Elizabeth described to me her particular motivation, 'I was interested in the correlation between Otto's return to life after his time in Auschwitz, through his discovery and publishing of Anne's diary, with Mr Yamamuro's passionate commitment to grafting "Souvenir d'Anne Frank" roses, and sending them to children in Japanese schools. From opposite sides of the world, and with vastly different personal experiences, both men were committed to inspiring young people to work for peace and against injustice and racism.' The Ensemble Theatre Group partnered with the Anne Frank Trust, who together applied for funding, and the production was launched alongside the Anne Frank exhibition at the Zion Arts Centre in Manchester. Elizabeth and her team also conducted educational workshops to further explore with students the themes of the story.

Nao Nagai was the lighting designer for Elizabeth's production, and as her name suggests, happened to be Japanese. Using dogged determination, Nao managed to track down Michiko Otsuki, the very girl who had written to Otto Frank all those years ago. Michiko was by now in her seventies, living in Nara City, not far from Nao's own home city of Kobe. Nao was then introduced to Kenji Yamamuro, Michiko's cousin and son of Ryuichi Yamamuro, the original creator of the 'Souvenir d'Anne Frank' rose. On a visit to Japan, Nao and Elizabeth were invited by Kenji to a special 'Souvenir d'Anne Frank' rose-grafting event at his house, attended by about fifty people. Over tea after the rose had been grafted, Kenji spoke about his father and how much the rose had meant to him. Elizabeth and Nao also visited Michiko Otsuki who showed them all her correspondence from Otto Frank from forty years ago, which he had typed on light blue gossamer-thin 'Par Avion' paper, typically used in those days for expensive overseas mail.

Looking back to 2011, Elizabeth Mansfield summed up what she saw as the legacy of the fascinating story of the 'Souvenir d'Anne Frank' rose and its musical interpretation. 'Anne's story is a complicated one. Within it lie important lessons for today and for all time. Man-made war is still with us, along with torture, genocide and persecution. People are still in flight from man-made horrors. And yet people also continue to do good for each other, and to fight against injustice and racism and for peace and understanding.'

Throughout Japan the 'Souvenir d'Anne Frank' roses continue to flourish. As does the Japanese people's love of Anne Frank.

The Vietnamese Anne Frank

The Vietnam War, or what the Vietnamese refer to as 'The American War', left over 58,000 Americans and millions of Vietnamese dead. It also left an indelible imprint on the national psyche of both countries.

One of those killed was a young, idealistically Communist North Vietnamese doctor, who became known after her death as the 'Anne Frank of Vietnam' – because of a diary that she had kept during the Vietnam War. The strange and circuitous route that enabled this young woman's wartime diary to come to the eyes of the world is a story well worth relating.

Fresh out of medical school in the late 1960s, Dang Thuy Trâm had headed down to South Vietnam to tend wounded Viet Cong soldiers. On 22 June 1970, Thuy Trâm was walking along a jungle path dressed in her regulation Viet Cong black pyjamas, when she came upon a group of American soldiers engaged in a gun battle with their Vietcong enemy. Several of her own patients had already been killed in the offensive, and she was caught in crossfire. She took a bullet in the head and died immediately.

It so happened that the original translator of Anne Frank's diary into Vietnamese was a woman called Dang Kim Trâm. In a twist of fate, Kim Trâm had no idea that her older sister Thuy Trâm, the very same young doctor who had been killed by the Americans, had also been keeping a wartime diary – one that would go on to sell more than 300,000 copies and would be translated into sixteen languages. When it was published, comparisons were drawn internationally between Thuy Trâm's writings and those of Anne Frank.

In June 1970, days before her death, Thuy Trâm had written of the American president, 'Nixon is foolish and crazy as he widens the war. How hateful it is! We are all humans, but some are so cruel as to want the blood of others to water their gold tree.' In another entry, she almost foretold her destiny writing, 'Death was so close as the bombing stripped the trees bare and tore houses to pieces'.

The country of Vietnam has had a complex history. It had managed to keep its independence from Chinese imperialism since AD 939. However, in 1859 the country's independence was eroded by colonialist France in a series of military conquests, after which the southern third of the country became a new French colony. By 1884, the entire country had come under French rule. This situation continued until almost the middle of the twentieth century.

Ho Chi Minh was a Communist revolutionary who was the leader of the Việt Minh independence movement from 1941 onward, founded originally to fight the Japanese. In 1945 Ho Chi Minh announced the establishment of the Communist-ruled Democratic Republic of Vietnam, and eight years of fighting the French followed. After the ferocious battle of Điện Biên Phủ, 10,000 starving French troops surrendered to the Viet Minh. The 1954 Geneva Accords was eventually agreed between France and the Viet Minh, allowing the latter's forces to regroup in the North whilst anti-communist groups settled in the South. Ho's Democratic Republic of Vietnam relocated to Hanoi and became the government of North Vietnam, a Communist one-party state.

South Vietnam meanwhile was ruled by a government led by Ngo Dinh Diem, who was a fiercely anti-Communist Catholic. His power base was significantly strengthened by 900,000 refugees, many of them Catholics, who had fled the communist North. In the early 1960s, the South was rocked by unrest, led by university students and Buddhist monks, several of whom shocked the world by setting fire to themselves in highly-publicized protests. In November 1963, a group of young generals staged a coup backed by the United States. It was planned that the unpopular South Vietnamese leader Diem would go into exile, but the generals got over-excited and Diem and his brother were killed. A succession of military rulers followed Diem but they continued his erratic policies.

With an era of political instability following, Ho Chi Minh's Communist National Liberation Front (NLF), which came to be known by the West as the Viet Cong, began to gain ground from the north. To support South Vietnam's struggle against this communist insurgency, the American government began increasing its number of military advisers over there. US forces became involved in ground combat operations in 1965. At their peak their forces on the ground numbered more than 500,000, backed up by a sustained aerial bombing campaign. Meanwhile, China and the Soviet Union provided North Vietnam with significant material aid and 15,000 combat advisers.

By the early 1970s, facing an increasing casualty count, rising domestic opposition to the war and growing international condemnation, the Americans began withdrawing. Saigon, the capital of South Vietnam, fell to the Communists on 30 April 1975 and the following year North and South Vietnam were merged, becoming the Socialist Republic of Vietnam.

During the preparations for the withdrawal from Vietnam, a young American military intelligence specialist called Fred Whitehurst had been passed the war diaries written by the young woman doctor Dang Thuy Trâm. Part of Whitehurst's brief was to destroy unwanted documents and, just about to burn one of the notebooks, was persuaded by his Vietnamese interpreter to save it. Whitehurst recalled that his interpreter had implored him, 'Fred, don't burn it, it already has fire in it.' Acting against orders, Whitehurst secretly posted the notebooks back to his home in North Carolina. For years afterwards Fred didn't know what to do with them, it was after all the personal diary of a dead young woman, and remarkably similar to Anne Frank's diary in the matters it discussed – ideals and convictions, love and life, as well as anger addressed at her persecutors, in this case the Americans and their president, Richard Nixon. So Whitehurst kept the tiny notebooks at his home for thirty-five years, holding on to the idea of one day perhaps returning them to Thuy Trâm's family.

Whitehurst's search for Thuy Trâm's family initially proved unsuccessful. After earning a Ph.D. in chemistry he joined the FBI, but was unable to get anyone from the Vietnamese embassy who could help. In March 2005, he met the photographer Ted Engelmann, another Vietnam veteran, who offered to look for the family during his next assignment to Vietnam. With the assistance of a staff member in the Hanoi office of the Quakers, Engelmann was finally able to locate Thuy Trâm's mother, Doan Ngoc Trâm, and through her, he also reached the rest of the family.

In July of that year, Thuy Trâm's diaries were published in Vietnam under the title *Nhật ký Đặng Thùy Trâm* (*Last Night I Dreamed Of Peace*), which quickly became a bestseller. In less than a year, the book sold more than 300,000 copies and was then translated into sixteen languages. 'She was my enemy but her words would break your heart,' Fred Whitehurst told the British *Independent* newspaper just after the book's publication. 'She is a Vietnamese Anne Frank. I know this diary will go everywhere on Planet Earth.'

Just as in Anne's diary there was a terrible poignancy in Trâm's final entries. She had written on 20 July 1970, 'No, I am not a child: I am grown up and already strong in the face of hardships, but at this minute why do I want so much a mother's hand to care for me, or really the hand of a close friend, or just that of a person I know who is all right? Please come to me and hold my hand when I am so lonely. Love me and give me strength to travel all the hard sections of the road ahead . . .' Two days later she was shot dead.

In December 2014, the Mayor of Amsterdam, Eberhard van der Laan, led a business delegation to Hanoi. As well as discussions about deeper co-operation on issues such as urban planning, water management, energy and waste treatment, a French-English language version of the Anne Frank exhibition was staged as a specially-linked cultural event. It opened at the Hanoi-Amsterdam High School and went on to tour international schools in Hanoi. At the opening Mayor Van der Laan talked with young students there on the heritage of Anne Frank's war diary and related Anne's message of peace to the story of Dr Dang Thuy Trâm.

In the autumn of the following year, the Anne Frank House received three very special visitors. Doan Ngoc Trâm, the 92-year-old mother of Thuy Trâm, had come to see the Anne Frank House along with her two surviving daughters Kim Trâm and Phuong Trâm. Kim Trâm was the woman who, years before her sister's diary had become known to the world, had translated Anne Frank's diary into Vietnamese.

Anne in Hong Kong

Hong Kong Island, off the south coast of China, had become a British colony under the Treaty of Nanjing, signed after the First Opium War in 1842. At that time, opium was a legal substance in Britain, used for pain relief before the discovery of aspirin, and so a key import alongside large quantities of Chinese tea.

On 8 December 1941, Hong Kong was invaded by the Imperial Japanese Army, just eight hours after their attack on American warships stationed at Pearl Harbor in Hawaii. The British colonial officials were forced to surrender to the invaders and three-and-a-half years of brutal occupation followed. Food was severely rationed and 10,000 civilians were killed.

In the 1950s and 1960s, the economy started to boom, partly due to skilled immigrants from mainland China who had fled Mao Zedong's Cultural Revolution. Hong Kong became a major industrial and manufacturing centre, and by the 1980s had become an international financial centre too as well as one of the world's top ten economies. In July 1997, Hong Kong was returned to China and the Union Jack was lowered for the last time, rolled up and handed to the British Governor of Hong Kong, former Conservative Minister Chris Patten. Now to be known as a 'A Special Administrative Region of the People's Republic of China', the new mother country promised that the former British colony would be run under the principle of 'One Country, Two Systems'.

In the summer of 2007, Jan Erik Dubbelman asked me to open the first Anne Frank exhibition in Hong Kong. It was only a year since I had lost my husband Tony, so this exciting project was a helpful distraction from my grief. An added bonus was that Jan Erik also invited our Head of Education Lucy Glennon to come with me to help train the volunteer guides.

China, already emerging from its Communist economy, seemed to be keeping its promise to treat the citizens of the dynamic business based community of Hong Kong with a degree of difference from the rest of its one billion people. Thus when Lucy and I arrived in November 2007, Hong Kong was certainly still a retail paradise. The first thing that struck me was a strange conundrum. The high-rise buildings soared into the clouds, each containing hundreds of tiny apartments, with what we were told were very compact living spaces. But everywhere, in malls or markets, Hong Kong's residents were seen to be buying new consumer products, always carrying smart apparel carrier bags or boxes containing the latest electronics.

Shani Brownstein was a Canadian expat who had lived and worked in Hong Kong since 1992. On a visit to Chicago in 2006 she encountered the Anne Frank travelling exhibition. The following train of events, which started as a whimsical idea, she describes as the 'highlight of my life'. It occurred to Shani when she was walking around the exhibition that here was something that could and should come to Hong Kong. She contacted the Anne Frank House and spoke with Barry van Driel and Jan Erik Dubbelman. When she realized that her first task was to find a venue she came close to aborting the project. Knowing that Hong Kong had a massive space problem (hence it is built upwards and not outwards), she also asked herself if there would indeed be an interest in anything so obviously not Chinese.

Shani saw the challenges she would encounter, explaining,

> There was a huge awareness in Hong Kong about the atrocities committed by the occupying Japanese, but an ignorance about the extent of Hitler's crimes in Europe. Hitler was perceived as a strong leader to be admired. A famous clothing chain had used images of Hitler in its marketing campaigns, with no real understanding of how offensive this was. When our expat European and American community objected, explaining that we would not revere a Japanese oppressor, they then understood and said they didn't realize that was the way the Nazis had behaved. There was clearly work to be done.

Shani worked on her plan to educate the children of Hong Kong about the Second World War in Europe. The board of trustees of Hong Kong's 100-year-old synagogue agreed to underwrite the costs of the exhibition. The organizing team were made up of members of the small Hong Kong Jewish community plus ex-pat British and Americans.

Shani, as the instigator, became 'team leader' and allocated tasks to the twelve equally enthusiastic committee members. Eventually a space for the exhibition was offered by the Government, a civic centre building in the bustling downtown area of Sheung Wan. The civic centre lobby was accessed through a ground-floor food market and after walking through surrounding stalls of pungent dried fish, one ascended in the lift to the fifth-floor exhibition space.

In November 2007, an English and Cantonese version of the exhibition 'Anne Frank, A History for Today' duly arrived in Hong Kong. Lucy and I spent our first evening in the city meeting the team over a memorable Cantonese dinner overlooking the harbour and the city's dazzling skyscrapers. Excitement reigned palpably over the city, but it was more to do with the filming that week of the Hollywood blockbuster *Batman, The Dark Knight*, as Anne Frank was yet to make her mark.

The following morning, when Lucy and I emerged from the lift at the community centre and inspected the exhibition space, we were a little disappointed. The room was small and stark with bare grey walls and linoleum flooring and none of the atmosphere we had come to expect when the exhibition is housed in a cathedral, museum or a busy educational establishment. Shani and her team had not let this deter them. One team member, Debbie Amias, had come up with the idea of creating a full-scale replica of Anne's bedroom. This was being completed by a local stage designer who was enjoying the task entrusted to him. Visitors would not be able to walk inside this space but instead would tantalisingly look through a window into Anne's recreated world. With a final flourish a richly-patterned rug was laid in the centre of 'Anne's bedroom', which turned out to be on temporary loan from Shani's own living room.

Shani also happened to have a friend who was a book publisher and thanks to the can-do attitude, availability and speed of Hong Kong manufacturers, facsimiles of Anne Frank's beloved red-checked lockable notebook were displayed in the bookshop ready for children to buy as a memento. In fact, at the close of the exhibition, the remainder of the stock was shipped over to London for the Anne Frank Trust and were hugely popular with British children too.

Eighteen months after Shani had first encountered 'Anne Frank, A History for Today' in Chicago, the Hong Kong launch day had finally arrived. That afternoon a local lighting engineer appeared and through his flair suddenly the entire room and the exhibition panels took on a sense of intense drama. The stage designer, who had built 'Anne's bedroom', also produced a symbolic wooden tree-shaped installation, the 'Leaves of Hope Tree' for children and adults to write down and attach their thoughts onto the leaves. The reflection of the oval-shaped leaves, bathed in a slowly-rotating bright green light, covered the bare linoleum floor. A visit to the Hong Kong Anne Frank exhibition was going to be a visceral and emotive experience.

Delighted with how the exhibition space was now looking, Lucy and I returned to our hotel to await the arrival from London of her fiancé Dan and my daughter Tilly. We took our newly-arrived family out to show them the streets of Hong Kong and tried to impress them with our knowledge of downtown Hong Kong. We started to walk our visitors across the busy rainy city to the venue in Sheung Wan, trying to convince them it would be a good way of refreshing themselves after their long flight and that it was only a fifteen-minute walk. Needless to say we lost ourselves in the maze of streets and umbrellas but eventually arrived twenty minutes into the reception, to the great relief of the worried organizers.

Prior to the pre-event volunteer training sessions, Lucy and I had discussed with the team how to make the content of the exhibition relevant to the local visitors. We knew that Hong Kong teenagers, especially girls, would relate to Anne Frank on a teenage level, but as the colony was now part of China, human rights and freedom of expression were an issue where one had to tread carefully. Shani explained that the grandparents of the schoolchildren would have lived cheek-by-jowl with Mao Zedong's aggressive Cultural Revolution.

We also spoke about relating the experience of Holocaust victims to those of the notorious 'Rape of Nanjing'. In December 1937, and for six following weeks, the occupying Imperial Japanese Army unleashed a wave of violence and cruelty on the people of Nanjing (then known as Nanking). It was thought to be in retaliation for the unexpectedly long campaign they had fought in the previous months against the Chinese in Shanghai. It has been estimated that up to 200,000 citizens of the Nanjing area may have been murdered.

As it happened, we didn't need to worry about the need for making explicit Chinese relevances. The people of Hong Kong supported the exhibition and 6,000 visitors, of which 4,500 were local and international students, made the journey up to the fifth floor of the Sheung Wan community centre. For many it was the first time that they had heard of Anne Frank and the Holocaust.

Midway through the event, watching Chinese children engage with the story, Shani came to a deep understanding of what Anne Frank represented to people. Having come to the Anne Frank story through her own personal connection to the Holocaust, Shani recalls that she suddenly experienced Anne Frank 'in a different way. In her diary Anne Frank talked about all people – and she herself speaks to all people.' According to a report in the *Jewish Times of Asia*, young people 'walked away forever changed from the experience.' Messages written on the 'Leaves of Hope Tree' included, 'Anne Frank is my hero', 'There should be no more hate', 'I wish I could have known her', 'We cannot kill people anymore just because they are different'.

After the end of the month-long exhibition, it was packed up and transported across the border, and thence 2,000km northward to the Chinese capital of Beijing. But as in so many countries of the globe, it had left something behind. There is now a Holocaust and Tolerance Centre in Hong Kong offering training for teachers within their own schools. It marks Holocaust Memorial Day each January by inviting survivors and other speakers, including the son of the heroic Japanese diplomat Chiune Sugihara.

Shani summed up: 'With the Anne Frank exhibition in 2007, we had created something. It's easy to talk about an idea, harder to make it happen. But we did make it happen.'

Anne in China

Like many visits of the Anne Frank exhibition to countries around the world, China came about through one person happening to mention it to another. In this case it was suggested by a local Chinese woman staff member at the Netherlands Embassy in Beijing who happened to have a friend who worked at the National Library of China. This chain resulted in the Anne Frank exhibition paying its first visit to China in December 2007. Opening first at the prestigious National Library, it was then shown in the Children's Library of Beijing. And now as I write plans are underway to take it back again to China with a different emphasis for a changing world.

Michael Liu is a Chinese academic whose field of interest is human rights related to criminal justice matters. In 2015 he founded the Chinese Initiative on International Law to engage and support communities in the Greater China Region to understand, critique, engage with, and eventually promote international law and justice. The organization has offices in both Beijing and The Hague as Michael believes that 'Any international justice without Chinese participation will not be a true global effort'.

In August of the same year Michael took a group of ten International Law students to the Anne Frank House where they met with Jan Erik and Stefan Vervaecke to learn more about the Anne Frank programmes in the Far East. Michael could immediately see a huge potential for the Anne Frank project in China, where a surprisingly large number of young people know Anne Frank's diary. For one of his own friends it was the first foreign language book she had read.

He described why he felt Anne Frank would have a future in China, 'It's not easy to sell international stories as there is usually politics in the background. Even talking about the recent experience of the teenage Malala Yousafzai, people would be asking about what would cause the Taliban to behave as they did. But because of the distance in both time and location, Anne Frank is seen to be non-threatening. Her story is primarily one of humanity.' Unlike in Hong Kong, there would be no connections made between individuals who suffered in the Holocaust and China's own history, such as the Cultural Revolution or the Nanjing Massacre, as these too were considered political stories.

In 2017, there was a new pilot Anne Frank project in China, starting at the Shanghai Jewish Refugee Museum. The city of Shanghai has its own Holocaust-related story. There is evidence that Jews have lived in China since the seventh century AD, often mistaken for Muslims by other Chinese. The Venetian explorer Marco Polo described the prominence of Jewish merchants in Beijing in the late thirteenth century, who had arrived in China through trade along the Silk Road. Over the centuries these Jews became very assimilated. Many Jewish White Russians also arrived in China following the Russian Revolution in 1917.

In the late 1930s, 18,000 German, Austrian and Polish Jewish refugees from the Nazis sought sanctuary in Shanghai, having been issued visas by Chinese diplomats. The Japanese diplomat Chiune Sugihara also helped them by issuing transit visas through Japan. By 1941, there were 20,000 Jewish refugees packed into a one-mile square area of Shanghai. Later in the war, the Nazis tried to pressure their Japanese allies who were controlling Shanghai to exterminate the city's Jewish refugees. Fortunately by this time the Japanese were becoming fearful of further provoking the anger of the Allies. After the war, and as Chinese Communism was taking hold, most Jews left Shanghai to make new lives in other countries. The Jewish Refugee Museum of Shanghai continues to tell their story.

Michael Liu felt that linking Anne's story to the refugee experience is a helpful entry point. 'She was a refugee', he said, 'schools are talking about the global refugee crisis caused by the war in Syria, and China has its own internal migration issues to look at. With Anne Frank we speak of human values, such as love, tolerance and humanity.'

***

Like the great explorers who journeyed along the Silk Road and the spice routes of the Far East, like the traders of the Dutch East India Company, Anne Frank has woven her silken thread from the north of Japan, westwards to South Korea, southwards through China and Hong Kong, through Vietnam, across the sea to the Philippines and all the way southwards to the former Dutch colony of Indonesia. With each community's diverse history and experience, Anne Frank has a unique relevance – but the work in her name continues to leave behind changed people.

Chapter 26

Anne Frank was a Real Person

Anne Frank has become so recognizable over the past seventy years that sometimes the reality of this child's life and death have become interwoven with myth or even parody. As if Anne Frank wasn't really real.

In Japan, the country that was allied with Nazi Germany during the war, an animated film, *Anne No Nikke*, was released in 1995 depicting Anne Frank as an angelic heroine. She had a likeness to Disney's animated Snow White, but Anne was clothed in mid-twentieth century costume. A dark-haired and pale-skinned girl is shown gambolling through flowered meadows, with birds and butterflies swirling around her. Accompanied by a score composed by the American Michael Nyman, the film was not well received in the West. On his 'Anime New Network' website, Justin Sevakis, an expert on the culture of animation, stated that he 'couldn't think of a worse way to experience the story than watching this film'.

A scene in the long-running British soap series *Eastenders* in 1999 showed a group of the fictional women characters going on a hen weekend in Amsterdam. The 'hen bride' was due to marry a rather unsympathetic character called Ian Beale. Prior to hitting the bars of Amsterdam, the young women stood alongside the canal on the Prinsengracht staring up at Anne's hiding place. A supposedly knowledgeable member of the group pondered on Anne having to hide from the Nazis, and another responded that 'surely that was a better fate than marrying Ian Beale'. Actually, it wasn't.

In November 2009, introducing a BBC radio comedy panel show called *The Unbelievable Truth*, the presenter David Mitchell started the show by stating that Anne Frank's last diary entry was, 'It's my birthday and my Dad bought me a drum kit.' It could be an amusing joke if we didn't understand Anne's daily terror of discovery. The BBC received almost fifty complaints about the comment, including my own on behalf of the Anne Frank Trust. The show's commissioning editor Caroline Raphael responded on the station's weekly *Feedback* show by apologizing to any people who had taken offence, but added that she did not regret the decision to broadcast the comment made on the show. She said:

> Personally I *did* find this funny. I don't think it was trivializing the Holocaust, the nature of her death or the situation they were in. For me it actually captures some of the extraordinary spirit of that remarkable girl,

Anne Frank, and there was a certain note of affection towards her. After all she was young, and if she was a teenager now she might have got a drum kit. It was satirizing the situation they were in.

David Mitchell defended the comment himself in an article in the *Observer* newspaper. He wrote that, despite not writing the joke himself, he found it 'funny' and that 'the tragic circumstances give it an edge and make the audience more likely to laugh, but that's not the same as finding the Holocaust funny'.

Both the above shows had warranted a letter from myself to the producer, explaining that Anne Frank still had living relatives and friends – some of whom were themselves Holocaust survivors – and who could find these references offensive. In each case I received an apology explaining there was certainly no offence intended, and of course I do believe that's the case. In 2015 I happened to bump into David Mitchell in a café and we discussed the joke in a very cordial way. Mitchell is a highly intelligent man. But these instances are indicative of Anne having gone beyond being thought of as a real person who lived in the twentieth century as a contemporary to the still-living elderly Holocaust survivors whom no-one would dream of joking about.

In 2012 the comedian Ricky Gervais was compelled, after a flood of criticism, to publicly defend his use of Anne Frank in a comedy routine he had been performing on stage for ten years. Writing in the *Jewish Chronicle* newspaper he said:

> It [the routine] is about the misunderstanding and ignorance of what is clearly a tragic and horrific situation. My comic persona is that of a man who speaks with great arrogance and authority but who, along the way, reveals his immense stupidity. In this particular routine, I envisage an almost slapstick version of the Nazis entering the home of Anne Frank on a daily basis and always failing to bother to 'look upstairs'.

Gervais continued to describe the scene he was portraying:

> The first Nazi says: 'What's that tapping sound?' – as I mime the tapping action of using an old-fashioned typewriter. Again the joke here is the supremely stupid assumption that Anne Frank obliviously and noisily typed her diary. The final layer of ignorance in the routine is that, instead of taking the obvious and correct stance that Nazis were disgusting, immoral and evil, I merely conclude that they were 'rubbish' because of their inability to find Anne Frank earlier – like it was all part of a big, mutually agreed game of hide-and-seek . . . I often get accused of finding comedy in places where no comedy is to be found. I feel you can make a joke about anything. It just depends on what the joke is.

Perhaps the most enduring Anne Frank joke has been deemed to be a true story and relates to a production of the stage play *The Diary of Anne Frank* being performed somewhere in the US, and attributed to the terrible acting skills of its leading lady. The joke goes that as the arresting officers came onto the stage for the tragic climax, a member of the audience, who had suffered two hours of the heroine's dreadful acting, shouted, 'She's in the attic'. I have heard the story many times on my travels, but it is apparently apocryphal and several different American actresses are the supposed targets.

'Fictional Anne Frank', the one who actually survived Bergen-Belsen and was supposedly rescued by the British and American liberating armies, exists in literature. There have been representations of her as a Holocaust survivor, such as in Philip Roth's 1979 book *The Ghost Writer*, wherein a woman author called Amy Bellette appears to believe she is actually Anne Frank. Reviewing the book in the *New York Times*, the critic Robert Towers noted, 'The account of Anne's survival of Auschwitz and Belsen and of her desperate adoption, after weeks of coma, of Amy Bellette's identity is packed with circumstantial detail of great vividness; her reactions to the reading of her own diary in its Dutch edition and her breakdown after seeing its dramatization on Broadway – these episodes are persuasively narrated.' It is surprising, and perhaps somewhat fearless, for Roth to write this post-Holocaust fantasy in 1979, just thirty-four years after the liberation of the camps, and a year after the American TV series 'Holocaust' opened the American public's eyes, albeit in a dramatic interpretation, to what had happened to the victims of the Nazis.

Shalom Auslander's satirical and acerbic first novel, *Hope, A Tragedy*, published in 2012, gives us the image of another post-war Anne Frank. This time she takes the form of an embittered old crone typing away in the attic of a New York State farmhouse. Auslander uses Anne Frank as a symbol not of hope, but of the futility of hope. This Anne powerfully negates the sentimentalized use of some of her writing and her iconic image. 'Me, I'm the sufferer,' Auslander's Anne finally says to a character called Kugel. 'I'm the dead girl. I'm Miss Holocaust, 1945. The prize is a crown of thorns and eternal victimhood. Jesus was a Jew, Mr. Kugel, but I'm the Jewish Jesus.'

Published in the US simultaneously with Auslander's novel, Nathan Englander's collection of short stories, *What We Talk About When We Talk About Anne Frank* uses her name as the title of the book even though Anne Frank features in a small, but nonetheless significant, section towards the end of the opening story. The focus here is not on Anne, but actually on the moral dilemma that the helpers of the persecuted Jews found themselves in. Through an imagination game, 'a thought experiment', presupposing a second Holocaust is taking place in contemporary south Florida (where the largest number of American Holocaust survivors actually live), the two couples think about which of their Gentile acquaintances would put their life on the line to save their Jewish neighbours. The four characters then turn their attention to each other. The characters are fictionalized but the moral dilemma is not, and the story also covers the premise that survivors have human failings like everyone else.

Over the decades, dramatic interpretations of life in the secret annexe have brought their own way of imagining the reality. The popular play *The Diary of*

Anne Frank, written by husband-and-wife team Albert Hackett and Frances Goodrich, reflected Otto Frank's wish to universalize the story to attract as wide an audience as possible. He envisaged the play being performed in cities throughout America where, in the 1950s pre-Civil Rights era, and despite knowledge of the Holocaust, cultural acceptance of difference was in short supply. The play's impact in the late 1950s was profound, but in recent years it has been accused of over sentimentality and two-dimensional characterisation.

Dr Shirli Gilbert, Karten Senior Lecturer in Jewish/non-Jewish relations at the University of Southampton, explored the de-Judaification of the Hackett and Goodrich play in a 2013 essay for the *Oxford Journal*.

> Several of Anne's entries focused on the Jews' specific fate and offered thoughtful observations about Jewish history and identity. These were excised in the stage version, and in some striking instances references to Jews were deliberately replaced with universal alternatives. On April 11, 1944, for example, Anne wrote: 'We've been strongly reminded of the fact that we're Jews in chains, chained to one spot, without any rights . . . We can never be just Dutch, or just English, or whatever, we will always be Jews as well.' In the American script, this passage was replaced with Anne's lament that, 'We're not the only people that've had to suffer. There've always been people that've had to—sometimes one race—sometimes another.'

In 1997 the American writer Wendy Kesselman gave the play a makeover, re-establishing Anne as a girl from a Jewish family, not baulking from making references to Zionism and the specific persecution of the Jews. Scenes gave the celebration of Chanukah and other manifestations of Anne's Jewishness more prominence.

In the first run on Broadway, Anne was played by 16-year-old Natalie Portman, who had actually been born in Jerusalem with the Hebrew name of Neta-Lee Hershlag. While playing the role of Anne each night, Portman was simultaneously studying for her public school exams in Syosset, Long Island. By casting a Jewish Israeli-born actor, this production was described as 'Anne Frank comes home.' In an interview on NBC's *Today* programme two days before the opening, Portman described how she had been connected to Anne Frank since the age of 12, as many of her own family had been killed in the Holocaust. 'I want to remind people of the wrongs of hatred and racism.' She went on to talk about this new version of Anne, and how it differed from previous representations of her. 'I wanted to present her as real. She was no saint, and it's wrong to present people's icons as saints, because they will feel they can't achieve that goodness. She was outgoing and hyper almost to an irritating point.'

The Kesselman play opened at the Music Box Theatre on Broadway in June 1997. I was present on the opening night along with Jack and Ina Polak, Dutch-born

Holocaust survivors of Bergen-Belsen, and Herbert and Lilian Levy, Herbert being the German-born Principal Guide of the Anne Frank exhibition in the UK and Lilian having been rescued as a five-year-old orphan from the same camp of Bergen-Belsen. Jack Polak had arrived in New York in 1951 with his wife Ina and two sons, had built a successful investment business and was a founder of the Anne Frank Center USA. All five of us, Herbert, Lilian, Jack, Ina and myself, were supremely protective of telling Anne's story as honestly as possible.

The Polaks and the Levys had met for the first time earlier that evening over drinks at Manhattan's legendary Algonquin Hotel and, partly due to their shared experiences but also their love of theatre, were by later in the evening firm friends. They all agreed that the size of the large Broadway theatre staging, and the consequent shouting of the characters across the stage, didn't leave any impression of the claustrophobic intensity of the small above-warehouse rooms and the need of the hiders to be oppressively quiet for most of the day. I had thought the same. At one point in the second act, I had found myself giving quiet instructions (actually whispered to myself) to the players, 'Please, please quieten down or you'll be discovered.' I still believe, having seen many different theatrical productions of Anne's story, from Broadway to local fringe theatres to school productions, that the dramatisation of life in the secret annexe works best in a small, intimate environment.

At the star-studded aftershow dinner, I approached the pretty young actress who had played 'Anne Frank' while juggling her school exams. She looked nervous and was carefully carrying her dinner plate over to her table. 'She looks a lovely girl, she was very good, it was her Broadway debut, so I am sure she will appreciate my encouragement,' I thought to myself as I walked towards her smiling. She thanked me with a sweet and polite smile when I told her supportively that I thought she would definitely go far in her acting career. Well, how was I to know that Miss Portman had already been cast as Padme Amidala in the *Star Wars* prequel trilogy?

In 2013, a new play was commissioned by the Anne Frank-Fonds in Basel. Simply entitled *Anne*, it was written by the Dutch husband-and-wife team Leon de Winter and Jessica Durlacher, and produced by the Tony Award winning Broadway producer Robin Levitan. It opened on 8 May 2014, the sixty-ninth anniversary of VE Day, in a purpose built theatre in Amsterdam's port area. The new theatre was lavish and impressive, and the glittering first night attended by the recently crowned King of the Netherlands, Willem Alexander (Queen Beatrix had abdicated in her son's favour the previous year), along with Dutch media and high society. I found myself sitting in the optimum seats between South African leisure mogul Sol Kerzner and British impresario Harvey Goldsmith, who was one of the play's producers, and after the performance having a brief chat to the new King to inform him about our flourishing Anne Frank organization in the UK.

Naturally the play was performed in Dutch, and foreign guests were handed out headsets with a rudimentary version of the script translated into English. After a few scenes I gave up on the audio, feeling that I was familiar enough with the narrative to watch the action played out in Dutch. Although the revolving sets were a staggering three storeys high, and certainly did not convey any sense of intimacy and claustrophobia, they, and the accompanying large-screen film footage and crashing sound effects, did give a heightened sense of the terrifying harsh reality beyond the secret annexe, most especially the penultimate scene showing Anne in a barren windswept Bergen-Belsen.

The first scene, which was an introduction to the stunning stage sets that would follow, is set in a post-war Paris café, where an imagined Anne is discussing the publication of her diary with a handsome young publisher. He then joins us as the audience is taken back to Anne's time in hiding. In an interview for CNN, the writer Leon De Winter explained the reason for using an imaginary post war Anne, 'It's all inspired by Anne's own writing,' he said. 'It's her dream to have this grand student bohemian life in Paris and London – and to become famous. We used these remarks to see glimpses of a life she never had.'

Peter van Pels, Anne's 'boyfriend' in the hiding place, has also had his life, words and thoughts subject to imagination. In 2010, the American writer Sharon Dogar's first novel *Annexed* looked at the Anne Frank story from Peter van Pels's viewpoint. Although the *Sunday Times* first criticized the novel for the 'sexing up' of the Anne Frank story, I was described by the *Guardian* newspaper as angry about fictionalizing someone who was until relatively recently a real person. 'I really don't understand why we have to fictionalize the Anne Frank story, when young people engage with it anyway,' I told the *Guardian*'s Richard Lea. 'To me it seems like exploitation. If this woman writer is such a good novelist, why doesn't she create characters from scratch?'

I was cynical too when Dogar explained in the same article her reason for writing the book, 'The problem is that a writer doesn't always choose what they write,' she said. 'The idea of this book plagued me for 15 years. I tried quite hard not to write it, mostly because I had similar concerns; I couldn't do it justice, I wasn't sure it was legitimate, I didn't believe I had the talent to portray the horror of the Holocaust. But sometimes stories just come and you can't stop them.'

The novel opens with Peter on the point of death in Mauthausen (in real life he tragically died just three days before it was liberated) and is told as a series of diary entries interspersed with the thoughts of the dying boy, charting the story of the time he spent hiding with the Frank family above 263 Prinsengracht, his discovery and arrest and then his time in the death camp. Regarding the part of the book that concerns Peter's teenage sexuality, I accused Dogar of putting twenty-first-century mores on to young people from a different era. Dogar rejected the accusation of anachronism, countering that,

> Whilst it's true to say that children of the war years lived according to different cultural mores and social strictures, it's also true that there are some fundamental and universal human feelings that are biological rather than social. The state of adolescence existed before 'teenagers' were invented. Adolescent hormones have always been in conflict with

social rulings. This is why some of Anne's thoughts remain as powerful and meaningful today as they were 60 years ago.

I found myself in conflict with Otto Frank's step-daughter and my Anne Frank Trust Co-founder Eva Schloss over my response, who concurred with Dogar that adolescents in the 1940s spent a lot of time thinking about sex. But although the *Guardian* article had made this the focal point of my critique, the sexual aspect wasn't really my prime concern. It was much more about taking real people, who were not around to correct the falsehoods, and making their thoughts and experiences not real. Especially in the light of neo-Nazi Holocaust denial.

John Boyne wrote the enormously popular but controversial novel *The Boy in the Striped Pyjamas*, which relates the story of two young boys, one the son of the camp commandant and the other a Jewish prisoner, who befriend each other on either side of the concentration camp's perimeter fence. It's a totally improbable scenario, but Boyne defended the role of children's fiction in dealing with subjects as charged as the Holocaust, on the grounds that novels can play a 'huge role' in educating young people. 'Children will switch off if they are lectured,' He continued, 'but tell them a good story with characters they can relate to and you're halfway there.'

Well, I actually believe, from working with Anne Frank's story and those of survivors of the Holocaust and other genocides, that the genuine stories of these people succeed in engaging young people and motivating them to make the world better. Moving forward, there will be a role for Holocaust fiction, but as there will soon be no more eyewitnesses to verify the facts and write their own memoirs, such novels must be based on historical truth.

The Anne Frank House itself has been featured in novels, such as Aidan Chambers's Carnegie Medal-winning 1999 novel set in the Netherlands, *Postcards from No Man's Land*. John Green's 2012 novel *The Fault in Our Stars* was about a couple of teenage cancer victims who fall in love. The terminally-ill young couple fly from their home town in Indiana to Amsterdam to meet a reclusive Dutch author whom the girl has long admired. While in the city they take the opportunity to visit the Anne Frank House and share their first kiss in the attic where Anne Frank and Peter van Pels had done so seventy years before (this memorable scene is a fictional premise as the attic is closed to the visiting public).

The British novelist and screenwriter Deborah Moggach approached Anne Frank with an honesty and a determination to be as accurate as possible. In 2008, the BBC commissioned a new TV drama series *The Diary of Anne Frank* to mark the eightieth anniversary of Anne's birth the following year. When Moggach was asked to write the screenplay for the series, she probed into the day-to-day privations of being in hiding for over two years. When Deborah came to visit the Anne Frank Trust office prior to the first screening in January 2009, she told me that she had wanted to depict a 'dirty Anne Frank', showing clothes that were not able to be washed, eight people who were squabbling over the use of the one bathroom basin, a toilet that could not be flushed in daytime hours, windows that had to be kept closed and covered even in the heat of summer, and many other daily miseries.

In an interview with the American Public Broadcasting Service's online magazine *Masterpiece*, Moggach said that the wardrobe department, 'had versions of the same clothes that the actors wore in practically every scene, but becoming shabbier; and in the case of the adults, bigger, because the adults were getting so thin; and in the case of the teenagers, smaller, because the teenagers were growing. That made it tragically real when I saw that.' Her honesty paid off. Moggach later said that Anne's cousin Buddy Elias described this dramatic interpretation as 'the most truthful he had ever seen'. Following its prime time BBC1 screening over five consecutive nights in January 2009, Moggach was regularly invited to speak about the challenges of creating such a truthful screenplay, and the Anne Frank Trust team and I became 'Deborah Groupies' following her around London to hear her, as what she revealed about the process and her thinking was so fascinating.

Over the years many musical productions of the story have appeared. One of my first experiences of this was in 1990 when I was a 'new player' in the Anne Frank educational arena. The New York writer Enid Futterman wrote a piece called *Yours Anne* with a score specially composed by Michael Cohen. The piece had its British premiere in Manchester and I went along to see it. I thought then, and still do, that this intimate production was one of the most truthful and moving ways of telling the story. Enid and I had lunch while she was in London and she described to me her personal connection to the persecution of Anne Frank. As a young girl in the Ukraine in the early years of the twentieth century, Enid's mother had seen the body of her murdered father during a pogrom in their village. The trauma of this event had filtered down through the years, causing Enid's mother to suffer from a lifelong sadness. As a child Enid had in turn suffered from her mother's inherent sadness – three generations had borne the trauma of this 100-year-old family tragedy. I often think of Enid's story when I see scenes of massacres and brutality on the present-day news and wonder how many future generations of the victims will go on to be affected.

James Whitbourn and Melanie Challenger's 'Anne Frank Oratorio', written in 1995, is a soaring and serious classical interpretation often performed in cathedrals and at significant memorial events. A Spanish musical version of the story was given the thumbs-down by the Anne Frank-Fonds and closed its doors after a few days. There has been no shortage of British composers, as well as dramatists, sending me their own 'unique' take on the Anne Frank story, believing they would be providing the definitive Anne Frank work. They were discouraged in their ambitions when I had to tell them they would need to seek the rights from the Anne Frank-Fonds in Basel. I am sure the flood will continue for many years. I hope it does and that Anne Frank will continue to inspire creativity, in all its varying degrees of merit.

Working in schools has shown that even children can give Anne Frank's character their own interpretation. Possibly attributable to one particularly famous line in her diary being taken out of context, children have often told us that the characteristic they most admire in Anne is her ability to forgive, and that they hope they would be as forgiving too in her circumstances.

The line refers to her own wonder that she hasn't abandoned all her ideals as in her view they seem so absurd and impractical. But she then decides to be positive, writing, 'Yet I cling to them because I still believe, in spite of everything, that people are truly good at heart.' Over the years this line has been isolated from its context and has served as creating an 'other-worldly' Anne, more forgiving and saintly than us. This sentence of twenty words in fact comes towards the end of one of Anne's longest entries, dated 15 July 1944, in which she rails against the loneliness of her situation, 'It's twice as hard for us young people to hold on to our opinions at a time when ideals are being shattered and destroyed, when the worst side of human nature predominates, when everyone has come to doubt truth, justice and God.' She hears, almost in a premonition of her fate, 'the distant thunder that will destroy us too'.

Giving the inaugural Anne Frank Lecture in London in January 2011, the cultural historian and writer Professor Simon Schama chose to analyse her smile:

> When we conjure up the features of Anne Frank's face, what do we remember first? Well surely the smile because it happens in the teeth of despair. Sometimes it's nothing more than elfin mischief, the knowing cheekiness that ignites every so often through her writing. At other times it's the full-on girly grin, so wide, artless and brilliant, that the rest of her countenance seems to arrange itself around it. And, as anyone who has ever written anything about Anne Frank has always noted, it is lit by an avidity for the life that was denied her in Bergen-Belsen.

Anne Frank, a fragile teenager who just wanted to grow up and live her life as an adult, a terrified girl who lived and laughed, who wanted to go back to school and hang out with her friends. Anne Frank, a frightened and vulnerable teenager, who was funny, cheeky, deeply driven, opinionated, bossy, happy with her hair and sometimes not, was as real as you or me.

Had she survived, Anne Frank may have returned to live in Amsterdam, or like Eva Schloss, who moved to London after the war, may have found it too hard to resume a normal life in a country where most of her non-Jewish peers could never really comprehend what Auschwitz was all about. She may have followed the dreams of her sister Margot and fled Europe for the Mediterranean climes of Israel, where in the early days of the fledgling state she would again have endured a lack of food, but I suspect she would have enjoyed the intellectual stimulation of Tel Aviv more than the rural life on a kibbutz. Or, like so many of the camp survivors, taken a ship across the Atlantic to America, where in the second half of the twentieth century she would have experienced the greatest prosperity in human history, tempered by the 1950s fears of nuclear war.

We can never speculate who Anne Frank would have been had she been able to hold on to the thread of life for just a few weeks longer to see the liberation of Bergen-Belsen. Because she was a real person and her post-war life would have guided her choices, we'll never know if she would have chosen to become a writer or journalist. She may have decided against this path, or tried and changed her mind and then chosen a completely different field. As it was not so usual in the 1950s for women to have careers, her pre-feminism yearning to 'do more than Mother ever did' may have not materialized and she may have spent her life as a wife, mother and homemaker.

All we know is that we will never know who or what she would have been or done or thought. Because Anne Frank was a real person and suffered and died as a real person.

Chapter 27

Anne Frank in the Indian Subcontinent

In her diary entry dated 27 February 1943, Anne happened to mention that Mahatma Gandhi 'the champion of Indian freedom' was on one of his umpteen hunger strikes. In her next entry, on 4 March, she follows this up with a rather sardonic four-word line: 'Gandhi is eating again.'

What would Anne Frank's response be if she knew that her diary was to be read and admired in India, and that seventy years after she wrote about Gandhi's freedom-fighting, an exhibition about her life was shown in Calcutta, Bangalore and Pondicherry, such exotic far-off places to a 1940s European girl? That the childhood photos of her family, her homes and her chosen friends and favourite clothes were gazed on by the children of India and her words avidly analysed across the Arabian Sea and the Bay of Bengal? That her writing has been published in Hindi, Assamese, Bengali, Marathi and Malayalam, five languages spoken in India that make up some of the seventy-three languages her words have been published and read in? That teachers in brightly-coloured saris have been learning and teaching about her life from her birth to the terrors of the camps? So what do you say, Anne?

India – the jewel in the crown of Queen Victoria's huge empire. A country of spirituality, gurus, ashrams and silent meditation, sanctuaries of calm which bear little relation to the tough daily struggles of the teeming masses of the poor. A country of 1.3 billion people still affected by the archaic mores of the caste system and where educated professional women need to protest against the prevalence of rape.

I had toured India in 2004, arriving just three days after the Boxing Day tsunami. The day-to-day exigencies of the poor, both in the cities and the countryside, is evident everywhere. From the teenage shoe polisher in downtown Delhi who furtively threw dog poop over my husband's shoes so he could run after him (pretending to be a Good Samaritan passer-by who had witnessed the unfortunate 'accident') and offer to clean them for a few rupees, to the beggar women proffering their deliberately-maimed babies for your compassion, to the children perilously chasing tourist taxis in dread of being beaten by their gang masters if they returned without money. It is hard to be inured in India from the harshness of the lives of millions.

The Anne Frank project in India was brought at the request of the Seagull Foundation for the Arts in Kolkata (the city Anne Frank would have known as Calcutta) and its special initiative called 'Peace Works'. Their team works with young people on issues of discrimination and human rights through the media of arts, theatre and video. The director of PeaceWorks had participated in a workshop run by our Anne Frank House colleague Barry van Driel in Turkey in 2013, and she expressed her interest in the two organizations working together.

As no Anne Frank educational project had ever taken place in India, a feasibility study was first carried out in Kolkata. The research discovered that Anne was well known in India through the popularity of her diary. It also found a very positive reaction to the idea of an Anne Frank exhibition coming to the city.

Two women from the Anne Frank House, Loes Singels and Priya Machado, led the Anne Frank project in India. They were both volunteers who were giving of their time and expertise and, above all, utmost passion. Loes had known Jan Erik Dubbelman since university days, where she trained as a cultural anthropologist, and had recently retired from her role as a policy maker for the Dutch Ministry of Health, Welfare and Sports. Priya, of Indian heritage, had trained in London as a teacher, and had moved to Amsterdam to join her Dutch partner. Her field of special interest was in education in rural India, where there is an alarming lack of school facilities. Whilst in London she had worked in several NGOs related to education and women's programmes: ActionAid, Christian Aid and in the Education Department of the Royal National Institute for the Blind. Both having a shared interest in India, Loes and Priya had been friends for many years, and decided to team up to see how they could bring the Anne Frank exhibition and related activities to India.

In early 2013, Priya had popped by the Anne Frank Trust office while in London to tell us about her plans. She told me that in India students read Anne Frank's diary in school but mostly it was not contextualized against the Holocaust, which was taught as a separate subject. The two were not always linked together. Anne's diary was studied in English literature class; the course focusing on the writing of a diary by a young girl. Students were encouraged to think about what made writing in a diary 'a strange experience' for Anne Frank (as she herself described it in one of her first entries) and why she would have wanted to keep a chronicle of her life. And then separately, and surprisingly in an Asian country of colonial heritage, students learn about the Holocaust, the Second World War and Hitler in their History syllabus through a dedicated 25-page section giving information on Hitler's rise to power and on the Nazis' world view.

In preparation for the visit of the 'Anne Frank, A History for Today' exhibition, a team of local teachers were trained by Priya, Loes and their colleague Aaron Peterer, who had come with them from Amsterdam. Training was then given to a group of teenage peer educators. As part of the Anne Frank House's programme, the Indian students were invited to film their own clips for a series of scenarios about human rights conundrums, to be part of a popular and long-running educational project called 'Free2Choose'. The topic they decided to focus on was censorship.

Priya told me that some of the students who were trained as peer educators openly referred to the Indian caste system and societal inequalities when talking about Anne Frank's situation. Some even mentioned that they felt that the less-privileged children should also get the opportunity to work with the exhibition, as they didn't get to see many of these kind of activities and important experiences. Priya admitted that for logistical reasons this initial programme had been restricted to more privileged English-speaking students, but 'These were in no way like Western rich kids who take everything for granted. They had an earnestness to learn and share what they had learnt for the good of their society.' Echoing the response from Anne Frank peer educators in so many other parts of the world, the Kolkata students felt that learning how to be a peer educator gave them more self-confidence to tackle issues of discrimination within their own community.

Take the case of one of the Kolkata peer educators, a young man called Tanuj Luthra. After the exhibition had finished, he was invited to attend an international conference hosted and organized by the Anne Frank House in Amsterdam in August 2014, an event which perpetuated Otto Frank's 1960s vision of international student conferences. The Anne Frank House had invited current and former exhibition peer guides from all over the world to exchange their experiences, discuss challenges and collect ideas for future activities in their respective countries. Tanuj was deemed 'the star of the Ambassadors programme' after he made a very impressive presentation at the closing ceremony.

When Tanuj returned to India, on a high from the experience in Amsterdam, he set about organizing a programme for local children with disabilities. He called it 'Pursuit of Happiness, Children's Right to be Happy'. Tanuj explained what had motivated the programme:

> Recently in 2014, an Indian man, Kailash Satyarthi, a children's rights and anti-child labour activist, won the Nobel Peace Prize [jointly with the Pakistani-born education activist Malala Yousafzai]. Inspired by him, a few friends of mine and I decided on creating a project that would help young children, particularly those with disabilities. We thought it was very relevant to Anne Frank's ideals as these children would be almost as old as Anne was when she went into hiding.

Urbi Chatterjee was another of the peer educators trained in Kolkata. She described reading Anne Frank's *Diary of a Young Girl* in primary school, and how she still sees the book as an important part of her childhood. However, the Peer Guide training workshop gave her the opportunity not only to learn more about one of her favourite characters from literature, but also the larger social, economic and political situation of Anne's era, 'such an important and infamous time in history'.

When I read Urbi's blog, and saw that she wrote very much in the spirit of Anne Frank, I emailed her to get to know more about her experience of the Anne Frank project. She did not disappoint.

Urbi had found it an empowering experience to be guiding and teaching the story to people much older than herself. She told me how relevant issues of racism and discrimination and the persecution of minority communities were in Indian society, especially in relation to religious fanaticism. She said that

> Every day one reads of violence perpetrated in the name of religion. India is notorious for virulent caste-based discrimination, and certain parts of the country seem to be constantly in near-warlike conditions, most prominently Kashmir. In today's world, especially a world where technological advancement has given humanity access to the worst kinds of weapons, I think Anne's story is highly relevant, and should demand in-depth study and reflection over how such atrocities affect and devastate individual human lives as well as entire societies.

Urbi felt that learning, and then teaching, about Anne Frank had made her think of social issues and problems more than ever before.

> This is probably one of the reasons why I have started making an effort to study my own society and the various problems that it suffers from. Most importantly though, the experience of the workshop and the exhibition made me realize how events set in different times and geographical locations and societies can still be similar in cause and consequence, and how the study of one can help in the resolving of issues in another. Although Anne Frank and I grew up in very different socio-political environments, at heart I could empathise with a lot of her thoughts and emotions. The family problems she faced, her teenage romances and heartbreaks, her experience of puberty and her changing body, the loss of friends, her daydreams and imaginary experiences, even her fascination with books and writing were all things that I could relate to.

In her blog post written immediately after her training as an Anne Frank peer educator, Urbi described the session in emotive terms:

> In every human being's life, there are ordinary forgettable days, and some days that stand out because something really unusual happens. And then there are days that get etched so deeply in one's heart, that whenever one closes one's eyes one gets transported back to those days, and relives it in its entirety. The details do not fade with time; if anything, they only become brighter and sharper, and one can think back to individual

incidents that made the days as incredible as they were. I can safely claim that 28th, 29th and 30th November were three such indelible days of my life, memories that I shall cherish forever.

Urbi's recollection of a particular cultural difference she encountered between India and the Netherlands on that training day is interesting.

> After we had all settled down, we were introduced to Mr Peterer, who had come from the Netherlands to conduct the training workshop. The first thing he told us was that he was not a teacher, and we should address him as Aaron, not Mr Peterer or Sir. I mention this as though it was a seemingly insignificant incident. I kept feeling distinctly uncomfortable addressing someone who was years my senior by his first name, since by Indian custom I usually refer to someone his age as kaku (uncle) or at least dada (elder brother)!

Many reports and reviews have been written by our Anne Frank educators about the reception by students to the training sessions, and many of these are written in a formal manner suitable for submission to sponsors and stakeholders. Urbi's blog described these events in Kolkata from her own point of view as a teenage participant.

> We discussed why Anne Frank should be called a history for today, and why our generation would do well to learn lessons from the past. Throughout the day we were given practical advice about being a good peer guide, and at one point were asked to make a poster and jot down all the qualities essential in a good guide. We were taught how to deal with 'obnoxious students' who made a point of disrupting the tour, and how to keep the audience engaged and interested. We also learnt that we should not simply lecture the audience about the panels in the exhibition, but rather ask them to participate by asking relevant questions and encouraging active discussions.

After describing the training sessions, Urbi also spoke about the excitement of the forthcoming opening event.

> The workshop had officially ended, but the exhibition was to be inaugurated the next day, at 5 o'clock in the evening. All the Modern High girls volunteered to come. Out of us, the Anne Frank House representatives randomly chose *me* to read out a passage from Anne's diary at the ceremony. I was supposed to be there by 4.30 pm, but like the certifiable dolt that I am, I managed to lose my way and reached the building twenty minutes late! Ms. Machado quickly showed me which

passage I would be reading out. I practised a couple of times, and then went to look for my classmates, who I found guiding our school's director Ms. Devi Kar around the exhibition. The inauguration started at around five thirty, and continued for about twenty minutes. I was called to read my part, and was greatly praised by many people. Afterwards there was a violin recital, and lots of tasty snacks. A boy from La Marts and I even had a glass of red wine each, much to the amusement of the adults present! The evening ended on a sweet note with me getting a picture clicked with Aaron, and one with Ms. Machado and Loes. The time had passed all too soon, and though I was happy, I felt more than a twinge of regret when I left the building for the last time.

Am I alone in thinking that Urbi writes her blog in the spirit that Anne wrote *her* 'blog' of seventy years before? Anne, described by her maths teacher Mr Keesing as 'An Incorrigible Chatterbox' and who by her own admission loved to chatter, and Ms Urbi Chatterjee, whose own childhood was so marked by Anne's writing. I believe that these two girls, Miss Chatterbox and Miss Chatterjee, living nearly a century apart and a world away, could have become the firmest of friends.

Thanks to the partnership with PeaceWorks, the Anne Frank exhibition has revisited Kolkata and also gone to Bangalore, Chennai and Pondicherry – leaving a legacy of sixty student peer guides and seventy-two trained teachers.

Priya, of Indian heritage, whose field of interest was education in rural India, was very proud to have been able to take the Anne Frank exhibition to her own home city of Bangalore, where she had first read Anne's diary as a child. The exhibition was held at the Bangalore International School and sponsored by the Consul General of Israel, Menachem Kanafi, who told the audience, 'We read [the diary] to remind ourselves that every teenager, every adult, every person has the right to grow, to learn, to develop in security as an individual – not as a faceless number who may be wiped out without any pang of conscience. Someone who looks you in the eye and says, "I am a person".'

He reminded the guests that in India, Jews were welcomed to its shores over 2,500 years ago, and since then had been a part of Indian life, as equals. Then, referring to Anne Frank and his own family's Holocaust experience, Mr Kanafi's tone changed: 'But not all countries of the world have been so welcoming. In many places the Jew has been seen as an outsider, subject to persecution, subject to be killed at a moment's notice.'

Despite the unusually benign experience of India's Jews, discrimination in India's society is still an alarming issue. Megha Malhotra, who ran the PeaceWorks initiative in Kolkata, summed up the strong connections young Indian students have themselves made to Anne Frank's experience. 'They see the relevance and compare it to the discrimination they see around them. The first thing that comes to their minds and their understanding is the word "ostracisation", or "differentiation" on the basis of caste, colour or creed. The students are aware of the atrocities still committed against the Dalits [lower castes]. Skin colour is a very big factor of discrimination in India – and they see that connection immediately.'

Anne in Sri Lanka

Sri Lanka, a beautiful teardrop-shaped island nation located approximately 32km off the coast of south-east India, a diverse and multicultural country, a home to many religions, ethnic groups and languages, has been scarred by a bloody thirty-year civil war. It ended in 2009 when the Sri Lankan military defeated the 'Tamil Tiger' rebels. It was actually the Tamil Tigers, ferocious in their cause, who had first introduced the concept of suicide bombing in 1980. Later they developed a unique suicide vest, which is now employed by terrorists around the world. This deadly tactic was carried out by a brutal armed unit known as 'Black Tigers', who terrorised the subcontinent by bombings and assassinations, including carrying out the assassination of Indian Prime Minister Rajiv Gandhi in 1991.

Sri Lanka's geographic location and deep harbours made it of great strategic importance from the time of the ancient Silk Road all the way through to the Second World War. The island was first colonized by the Portuguese in the year 1505. Over one hundred years later, during the reign of King Rajasinghe II, Dutch explorers arrived on the island. In 1638, the King signed a treaty with the Dutch East India Company to oust the Portuguese who ruled most of the coastal areas. In 1793, with concern about Napoleon's expanding empire, the British found no difficulty in occupying Sri Lanka's eastern coastline and eventually took over more and more of the island. The British called the island Ceylon and it remained known as this until 1972, twenty-four years after it achieved its independence.

In 1997, one week after the funeral of Princess Diana, my husband Tony and I had spent two weeks travelling around Sri Lanka. Due to the continuing civil war between the Lankans and the Tamil Tigers, we were not permitted to visit anywhere on either the northern or eastern parts of the island, including the reputedly beautiful coastal city of Trincomalee. Something that had particularly struck us driving round the island was the respect people gave to education. The Sri Lankan school uniform is almost always white. Even in the smallest and poorest villages, where domestic washing machines were an unthinkable luxury, we saw children walking to and from school, along dusty or muddy roads, with their white uniforms dazzlingly pristine.

It was tragic to see a country that had so much potential and inherent beauty so riven apart by internal conflict. Upon my return to the UK, I started a series of discussions with my colleagues, analysing the situation in Sri Lanka and trying to come up with an idea about how to take the Anne Frank exhibition to the wonderful people of Sri Lanka. Many years later, an opportunity finally arose.

The Sri Lankan Ambassador to the Netherlands made, as many dignitaries do, a visit to the Anne Frank House. While walking around, he was informed that the Anne Frank exhibition had recently been taken to India. The Sri Lankan Ambassador was now very keen on bringing the exhibition to his own country, so duly informed the Dutch Embassy in Colombo about this. It took just a few more meetings between the Dutch Embassy in Colombo and the Sri Lankan Ambassador to the Netherlands to find wider support for the idea of an Anne Frank project in Sri Lanka. Funding and logistical support was soon found.

So in 2015, 400 years after those first intrepid explorers, the Dutch arrived in Sri Lanka again. A team from the Anne Frank House arrived in the Sri Lankan capital of Colombo to set up a pilot project for future work. The Anne Frank House's goal was to stimulate engagement on issues of social cohesion and tolerance among students, teachers and the general public, but done in the context of Sri Lanka's recent past.

The Anne Frank exhibition visited the capital city of Colombo first and after a gap of a few months went on to Jaffna, one of the largest cities in Sri Lanka. The visit to Jaffna was not easy. As I had found on my holiday in 1997, during the years of the long civil war Jaffna and the north of the island, the stronghold of the Tamil Tigers, were out of bounds to foreign visitors. Even though the conflict was over, when the Anne Frank House's Aaron Peterer arrived in Sri Lanka to set up the exhibition in December 2015, he had to wait for several days in Colombo for travel restrictions to be lifted in order to travel up to the north.

Anne Frank in Colombo

The Colombo exhibition was opened at the Goethe Institute on 27 January, the international Holocaust Memorial Day that marks the anniversary of the liberation of Auschwitz.

The Anne Frank House's representatives Priya and Loes noticed that when delivering educational activities in Colombo the similarity between the war in Europe and the civil war in Sri Lanka had come up spontaneously on several occasions. For instance, a teacher in Colombo told them, 'It brings back memories, because our situation was the same as for people living in the war areas in the north. I say to myself every day, we are humans, respect differences and keep in mind that you can harm other people'. One of the teacher-training sessions was focused on personal identity. A brief introduction explained that understanding your own identity can be a key to understanding the world. The differences between people, such as ethnicity, origins, customs and lifestyle that are the causes of discrimination were looked at.

It was planned that there would be a surprising connection to the Anne Frank story at the Colombo exhibition launch event. But sadly due to ill health, the award-winning poet Anne Ranasinghe was unable to attend the event. Ranasinghe had actually been born Anneliese Katz in Essen in Germany into a Jewish family in 1926, sharing a first name and nationality with Anne Frank. In November 1938 her happy childhood was curtailed when she witnessed the Kristallnacht pogroms. The following year, at the age of 13, Anne Ranasinghe was sent by her parents to an aunt in England to escape the persecution. That year Germany and Britain declared war. After the war ended, Anne learned what had happened to her parents; they had been sent to the Lodz ghetto in Poland and later gassed in Chelmno death camp. All their relatives had also been murdered by the Nazis. As an only child, one can only imagine her feelings of isolation.

Anne Ranasinghe trained first as a nurse and then as a journalist. In 1949 she married a Sri Lankan medical professor she met in London and went with him back to his home country, where for the next forty years she had another form of isolation, as the only known Jewish woman living in Sri Lanka. Since the 1970s she has been writing powerful and unforgettable poetry and prose, which has been translated into seven languages. Ranasinghe has received many literary awards, including Germany's Order of Merit. On hearing of the forthcoming Anne Frank exhibition, Anne Ranasinghe explained how she identified with her German-born namesake, 'Both Anne Frank and I went to Jewish schools, wore the same kind of teenage fashion and had the same hairstyles. And we were both given identical diaries. Hers was in a lovely red cover – mine was in green. I still have it. She got hers on her 13th birthday; I got mine the night before I escaped to England on 26th January 1939. Diaries must have been a teenage speciality. Perhaps because they could be locked!'

Anne Frank in Jaffna

One of the most emblematic places the Anne Frank exhibition has been taken has to be the city of Jaffna, which had been so affected by the long civil war. The exhibition was on display at Jaffna Public Library for a week in December 2015. It was brought via a partnership with Shanthiham, the local Association of Health and Counselling, which provided psychological services for the war-weary community.

Teachers in Jaffna said they felt that the exhibition was especially valuable to them because of the connection with the hardship the people in the Northern Province had experienced in the civil war. It was described as an 'outlet for our emotions' and provided a catalyst for people to document their own experiences in the hope of creating a similar kind of exhibition for the future, with its content based on the Sri Lankan war. An anonymous exhibition visitor wrote, 'It has truly inspired us to be more sensitive and aware of discrimination that has existed, while at the same time appreciating the current intercultural society we live in.'

Priya and Loes described the pre-exhibition training they had given to Sri Lankan teachers, starting with the historical background to Anne Frank's life and writing. One aspect they discussed was how, as your situation gets tougher, your true character can be formed. As in India and Pakistan, Anne Frank's diary is taught in Sri Lankan schools. Former British Poet Laureate Sir Andrew Motion's five-stanza poem 'Anne Frank Huis' is on the syllabus in Literature classes, and the 'Life Competencies' syllabus also deals with Anne Frank and her experience, which teachers find useful for explaining about different ethnic groups in Sri Lanka.

Something that resonated with how Anne Frank's story is used in other parts of the world and in other recent conflict situations, was that Anne Frank provided a platform for children to speak about their past in an indirect and safe manner. I have heard this so many times over the years not only from educators, but also those in the political arena.

The Sri Lankan teachers felt that the Anne Frank project could create more understanding and empathy for other people and their past and teach them not to oppress others. One teacher pointed out that reading Anne Frank's writing helps young people to understand another person's state of mind. And conversely, it would show students how to act if they were ever faced with oppression.

Comments found in the exhibition's visitors' book included, 'I could identify myself and my people (Tamil) with the feelings of Anne Frank. We are also living with the same dreams, that the suffering of our people will pass away very soon.' Another visitor gave an indication of the Anne Frank exhibition's unique role in post-conflict regions by writing, 'Thanks for giving me this opportunity before I leave this world. It will be appreciated if this is provided to all who have undergone disasters in the past.'

Bangladesh

> *'When the civilization of mankind cries, a few brave people come to help. I feel Anne Frank was that inspiration.'* Visitor to 'A History for Today' in Dhaka

The recent history of Bangladesh, where the Anne Frank exhibition found itself in February 2015, is complicated and tragic. It is closely connected to the recent history of India, Pakistan and the UK – and even that of the Anne Frank Trust. So I will take a little extra time to explain the country's violent birth and upheavals.

After India was granted independence from British colonial rule in 1947, the All-India Muslim League arose demanding a separate State for India's Muslims, who were the majority in the north-western state of Punjab. Following the retributive genocide between the two religions, the former British Indian Empire was partitioned into two nations, the Union of India and the Dominion of Pakistan, the latter created as a separate homeland for Muslims. An estimated eleven million people eventually migrated between the Hindu and Muslim areas, with an estimated one million people killed in the inter-communal violence.

But there was a major challenge to be overcome in the new Pakistani nation, which was divided into two areas – East and West Pakistan. Normally one would expect East and West to be two adjacent zones of the same region of land but in the case of Pakistan, they were separated by nearly 1,000 miles of territory across northern India. From its outset, Pakistan was an unrealistic, and ultimately a dysfunctional, nation. Punjabi-dominated West Pakistan, although smaller in population than East Pakistan, had the larger share of the country's revenue allocation which led to greater industrial and civil development and control of the military.

In East Pakistan the traditional language was Bengali, but the Pakistani ruling elite subjugated the Bengalis politically, culturally and economically, even insisting on Urdu being the language spoken throughout the country. In Pakistan's national Parliamentary elections held in 1970, the Bengali nationalists, led by Sheikh Mujibur Rahman, won a landslide victory and his party, the Awami League, became the majority party of Pakistan as a whole. Thus, they should have been expected to form the new government. Rahman's victory was ignored by the defeated government and talks proved unsuccessful.

In early March 1971, Sheikh Rahman made a speech referring to 'our struggle is for freedom and independence'. This was seen as inflammatory; he was arrested but managed to pass on a hand-written note on which was written the 'Bangladesh Declaration of Independence'. Nine months of civil war followed in East Pakistan, in which an estimated three million people were killed and over 270,000 women raped. Killing fields were to be found in every town and village, and in the final days of the liberation war, local fundamentalist collaborators of the Pakistan Army abducted leading intellectuals – including writers, journalists, doctors, lawyers and engineers – blindfolded them, killed them and dumped them on the outskirts of the capital city of Dhaka. Afterwards the war was officially declared a genocide.

Finally, on 16 December 1971, 90,000 soldiers of the Pakistan Army surrendered, which was the largest capitulation since the Second World War. Independent Bangladesh was born amid high hopes of a new democratic and secular state. Sadly, a proper democracy was not to be restored until twenty years later, after successive periods of martial law where dissenters were jailed and executed. In 1981, the country's own president Ziaur Rahman was assassinated by a group of army officers. The population also suffered extreme poverty throughout these upheavals and natural disasters such as flood and famine.

For my generation the Bangladesh Liberation War is seared into our consciousness. This is partly due to the two 'Concerts for Bangladesh' held on the day and evening of 1 August 1971. They were the idea of former Beatle George Harrison and his close friend the renowned sitar maestro Ravi

Shankar, who had been born in Bengal. These were the first-ever concerts of such magnitude and included names such as Bob Dylan and Eric Clapton. The concerts, and then the following documentary feature and record, raised funds not only for the survivors of the genocide still taking place, but the victims of a devastating cyclone.

The impact of the Bangladesh liberation war is still felt in the UK through the immigration it triggered to London and to the northern and Midlands industrial cities of Britain. Significant numbers of ethnic Bengali people had actually come to Britain as early as the seventeenth century, mostly as seamen working on ships for the British East India Company and who settled in convenient port towns. One of the most famous early Bengali Muslim immigrants to Britain was a man called Sake Dean Mohamed, who had worked for the British East India Company. In 1810, he founded London's first Indian restaurant, the Hindoostane Coffee House near Portman Square in the West End, and he is also reputed as having introduced shampoo (from the Hindi word champo) and therapeutic massage to the United Kingdom.

Numbers also came in the 1950s and 1960s, and by 1970 Brick Lane in Tower Hamlets, and many nearby streets, had become predominantly Bengali. The former Jewish bakeries opened during the previous wave of immigration into the East End were turned into curry houses, the jewellery shops were turned into sari stores, and the synagogues into dress factories.

Following the Bangladesh Liberation War in 1971, and the subsequent turbulence and poverty, an even larger immigration to Britain took place. Throughout the 1970s, these new immigrants were to experience institutionalized racism and racist attacks by organized far-right groups such as the National Front and British National Party. A park in Whitechapel Road in London's East End is named after Altab Ali, a young Bangladeshi immigrant murdered on his way home from work in 1978 by three racially-motivated teenagers.

The decline in manufacturing businesses, especially in garment manufacturing which was a victim of the flourishing of the Far East, led to difficulties in finding employment among Bangladeshi workers. Instead they became cooks, waiters, taxi drivers and mechanics, often opening their own restaurants, but their progress up the social and economic ladder was a slow one for a long time.

This large-scale Bangladeshi immigration has left its mark on the Anne Frank Trust. Many of the young people we work with in East London schools and in the Midlands and north of England are the children of those very immigrants – and indeed the Trust's London Schools Project Manager Mukith Khalisadar is the son of Bangladeshi immigrants. It may take another generation for a fully successful integration as much of the Bangladeshi population still lives in insular communities, but the Anne Frank project in cities such as Bradford is helping to open second- and third-generation Bangladeshis' eyes to a wider world of opportunities.

In October 2014, the Bangladeshi Ambassador to the Netherlands, Sheikh Mohammed Belal, and the Minister for Cultural Affairs, Asaduzzaman

Noor, visited the Anne Frank House. Like the Sri Lankan Ambassador, and many dignitaries who are shown around Anne's hiding place, given special access to non-public areas and explained the educational philosophy of Otto Frank's vision, they left the Prinsengracht and returned to The Hague with their minds racing. They soon contacted the Anne Frank House with an offer of support to bring the Anne Frank exhibition to Dhaka.

The time frame they suggested was challenging as they were keen to have the exhibition launched as near as possible to the following 21 February, which is known as Mother Language Day. The commemoration honours a group of Bengali students killed on that very day in 1952 for campaigning for the freedom to use their mother language, Bengali, in post-partition East Pakistan. February also sees the month-long Amar Ekushey Book Fair in Dhaka, and this would acknowledge the great literary inheritance of Anne Frank's diary. The Minister of Cultural Affairs suggested the most suitable venue would be the National Museum in Dhaka, as he was its Chairman. Priya Machado and Loes Singels of the Anne Frank House, and their Indian tour partner, Megha Malhotra of PeaceWorks in Kolkata, were introduced to Ziauddin Tariq Ali of the Liberation War Museum and Tariq became their much-valued Dhaka-based partner in the urgently-needed planning and preparation.

The 'Anne Frank, A History for Today' exhibition was opened at the National Museum in February 2015 and shown for one week. It was the same English language copy of 'A History for Today' which had been touring India and was flown 300 miles across the India/Bangladesh border into Dhaka. A summary of the text in Bengali language was displayed alongside each panel, nonetheless there were requests for a full Bengali copy of the exhibition to be made and taken further afield – which is an understandable request for an exhibition that was launched to help mark Mother Language Day.

Some of the visitors' comments reflected a real interest in the Holocaust, but also connections were made to Bangladesh's difficult birth.

> I feel I'm a citizen of this global world. I feel human beings cannot be identified by their religion and race. It should be by their duty and deeds.
>
> I knew about Anne Frank but today I saw her for the first time. The exhibition is marvellous. I love it – and want it again.
>
> Anne Frank, I first read her when I was aged 15 and she made me feel how hard this world can be for a person who is born into a minority community. I felt a connection with her and that has been strengthened by this show.

It was agreed by the Dhaka organizers that, despite the fact that the exhibition was on show for only one week, the personal story of Anne Frank was an excellent way to explain the history of the Holocaust to young people who had not encountered it before, as well as issues that are relevant today, such as the importance of democracy, pluralism and human rights. Both the organizers and general public felt that the Anne Frank story had a place in explaining their own genocide of 1971.

In July 2016 Priya and Loes were due to fly to Dhaka to start plans for a return visit of the exhibition. But their plans were curtailed by a terrorist bombing of a café which killed twenty-eight people. This atrocity was not perpetrated by IS or al-Qaeda but by local militants. The democratic and secular state of Bangladesh, as envisioned in its founding declaration, continues to be riven by bloodshed. It is hoped for a return of the Anne Frank exhibition to tour beyond the city of Dhaka. It will still have some important work to do.

Malala Yousafzai – the Anne Frank of Pakistan
'One child, one teacher, one book and one pen can change the world'.
(Malala Yousafzai)

Malala Yousafzai, the 15-year-old daughter of a teacher, was living a normal life in the Swat Valley of Pakistan, when she was asked to write a blog for the BBC about girls being banned from school by the Taliban. Due to her international prominence as a critic of the ban on girls' education, she was targeted by the Taliban and shot in the neck by a masked gunman while travelling home on her school bus.

In January 2014 the Anne Frank Trust announced that our annual Anne Frank Award for Moral Courage would be given to Malala. We had recently created an entire panel about her heroic story at the 'Anne Frank + You' exhibition, which was attracting lots of attention. Malala's award would be presented at our next forthcoming fundraising lunch at London's Park Lane Hilton hotel.

Malala was about to sit for her school examinations so could not take valuable time out to come to London. This we understood – it would have been ironic for the world's most prominent campaigner for girls' education to miss out on her studies with crucial exams pending. Instead, her father Ziauddin Yousafzai came to accept the award on her behalf.

Following the citation read out by the actress Naomie Harris, Ziauddin Yousafzai strode purposefully to the stage amidst the applause ringing round the huge ballroom. When the award was handed to him, he clutched it tightly to his chest with one hand and with the other hand opened his handwritten notes. He then made a heartfelt appeal for understanding of the terror of life under the Taliban and how we in the West should do all we can to help those who were being so oppressed. His speech was a lot longer than we had anticipated, but as it drew to a close what he told the 600-strong audience elicited audible gasps from all around the vast Hilton ballroom.

'My daughter knew of Anne Frank in the Swat Valley,' he said. Prior to the shooting of Malala and their arrival in the UK, the Yousafzai family had lived in the commercial city of Mingora, in the Swat Valley area of the Khyber-Pakhtunkhura province of north-west Pakistan. Anne Frank, in the far and remote Swat Valley of north-west Pakistan? Mingora had been under the control of the Taliban, but Ziauddin, who ran the local school, continued to advocate for the education of girls including his daughter and her friends. He had after all named his own daughter after a nineteenth-century local Pashtun heroine, Malalai of Maiwand, who had lost her life at age 18 fighting against the British colonists.

Malala Yousafzai had come to the attention of Abdul Hai Kakkar, the local BBC Urdu-language correspondent, who approached her to write a blog about life under the Taliban. She later told the *Guardian* newspaper, 'He told me about Anne Frank, a 13-year-old Jewish girl who hid from the Nazis. It was very sad, as in the end, the family were betrayed.' Malala, at one time referred to in the media as the 'Anne Frank of Pakistan', has since cited Anne Frank's diary as the most inspiring book she has read, having been photographed proudly displaying her own copy to the world.

And in turn throughout the Indian subcontinent young people interacting with the Anne Frank educational programmes have been using Malala Yousafzai as their own inspiration. An ordinary but bright school girl from the Swat Valley who went on to become one of the world's most eloquent and fearless campaigners for education and winner of the Nobel Peace Prize.

Chapter 28

The Strange Circle of the House on Blaricummerweg

Life can sometimes throw up some very curious coincidences and unforeseen connections, the symbolism and outcome of which may not be realized for many years. The astonishing story of the house at 140 Blaricummerweg in Amsterdam links New York, Los Angeles and Amsterdam and spans over seventy years of secrets and deliberately, or accidentally, forgotten memories. It brings the consequences of a single act of proud defiance by a strong-willed young woman called Betty Polak into the present day, and tells us how, if not for this same young woman, the publication of Anne Frank's diary might never have happened.

In 2017 Jan Erik Dubbelman, the international director of the Anne Frank House, shared with me an incredible series of situations and coincidences that had connected his own birth in 1955, to Betty Polak's life and to Jan and Annie Romein, the couple who had been instrumental in helping Otto Frank to get Anne Frank's diary published. Jan Erik had first been introduced to Betty at her brother Jack and his wife's sixtieth wedding anniversary party in New York in 2006. With Jan Erik's insatiable interest in people's lives, Betty and he naturally started to chat about her wartime experiences in the Netherlands. She told him that she and her first husband Phillip Leeuw had both been active in the Dutch Resistance and that Phillip had been executed by the Nazis. Distraught and now fearing for her own life, Betty had been taken in as a domestic servant by a wealthy family in the town of Huizen; a way of Christian families acquiring additional domestic help and a sanctuary for a Jewish girl from almost certain death if she were deported.

During Betty's time working for this family, an expensive crystal glass happened to have been accidentally broken by the family's young son, and fearing punishment by their parents, he and his brother had both blamed their maid, Betty. On being confronted about something she hadn't done, Betty's youthful pride and indignation got the better of her. She immediately gave her notice to the family, packed her minimal belongings and ran out into the dark street. Not a wise thing to do for a Jewish girl seeking a safe haven from the threat of murder by the Nazis, but fortunately she found herself in a prosperous area of the town, populated by a liberal left-wing network of artists and intellectuals. To avoid being seen, she turned a corner into a quiet residential street and knocked on the door of number 140 of the street called Blaricummerweg.

It was opened by Jan Romein. Later on, Jan Romein and his author and historian wife Annie would come to play a crucial role in the publication of Anne's diary. Romein was shocked to see a trembling young girl on his doorstep clutching a brown leather suitcase. Instinctively he was going to shut the door in her face as there were so many desperate people begging for food and money during the war. But on that night in 1943, Jan Romein made a prompt and difficult decision, despite being aware that he could be jeopardizing his own life. Looking at this fragile, terrified girl, he realized this was not a beggar, but a Jewish girl who was running away from the Nazis. Jan beckoned the girl to come in, closed the front door and took Betty inside to meet his wife Annie. Betty remained living with the Romeins, feeling relatively safe again.

After the war, Jan Romein was the historian and literary critic who wrote an article for the Dutch newspaper *Het Parool*, insisting that Anne's diary be published and read by many. The article, which appeared on 3 April 1946, was entitled 'Kinderstem' ('The Voice of a Child') and focused on the pubescent innocence of the girl who was killed, while presenting the diary as a didactic tool to keep alive her memory. It was an anti-fascist call by the liberal-minded Romein to remind us to be vigilant against the enemies of humanity. Romein's article led to the diary being taken on and published in book form on 25 June 1947 by Contact, a small Catholic publishing house.

Jack Polak was the co-founder and Emeritus President of the Anne Frank Center USA. After he had made that first step of sharing his life story, Jack Polak spoke at hundreds of schools and civic events, and Anne Frank exhibition openings. Sometimes he would be joined by his sister Betty, and would usually end his talks with six key calls to action: Don't Discriminate; Don't Generalise; Don't Be a Bystander; Choose to Work for Peace; Appreciate your Life and, finally, Remember You Live in a Great Country.

After the war, Betty Polak and her brother Jack found themselves living thousands of miles apart, and even if they had not been siblings, their lives would be forever connected by the link to Anne Frank. Betty had owed her life to the goodwill of the couple who were to ensure the publication of Anne Frank's diary, and her brother, by coincidence, was to go on to be a founder of the Anne Frank Center in New York in the 1980s. But this story gets even more convoluted and astonishing.

On being told by Betty of where she had been hidden during the war, Jan Erik's mouth dropped open and he very nearly dropped the glass of white wine he was holding. He took another mouthful of wine and then these astonishing words came out of his mouth. 'Betty, I was actually born in that house on 30 March 1955', Jan Erik told her. 'Blaricummerweg 140 is the address of the house where I greeted the world.'

When in 2017 Jan Erik shared with me those incredible series of situations, he also revealed to me (some thirty years after our first meeting!) that he had actually been named after the Romeins' own son Jan Erik. 'I was born six weeks premature and my parents had not yet thought of a name for me. After my father had helped my mother give birth, he went upstairs to find a spare blanket to help keep me warm. Up in the attic, he came across some letters from the Romeins addressed to their son called Jan Erik. 'My father quickly spotted that Jan Erik Romein had also been born six weeks premature. He went downstairs to my exhausted mother to inform her that he could not find a blanket to swaddle me, but had instead found a name for me!'

Having discovered their incredible shared connection to the house in Huizen, Jan Erik and Betty decided it would be rather special to pay a visit to 140 Blaricummerweg together. Jan Erik had never been to the house before. He knew it only from its presence in the background of his own baby photos. So one evening in 2014, Jan Erik and Betty, accompanied by Jan Erik's father, his wife Dienke and son Robbie, drove east from Amsterdam.

On finding Blaricummerweg, Jan Erik asked a man standing in the street if he thought it would be OK for the party to ring the doorbell of number 140, replicating the action taken by the desperate Betty decades earlier. The man enquired politely as to why they wished to if they did not know the owners.

Jan Erik and Betty related their respective stories to the stranger, who turned out to be a local historian of the wartime period, a profession and specialism shared by Jan Erik's wife, Professor Dienke Hondius. The man told them about the area in which they were standing, which turned out to be a tiny pocket of humanitarian action that defied the comparatively poor record of the Dutch nation in helping its desperate Jews. The man then summoned the group into a small side street off the Blaricummerweg called Paviljoenweg. It was discovered only after the war had ended that six out of the seven houses in that one small street had sheltered Jews, and in all the lives of eleven Jews had been saved. The Dutch political leadership of that community had been pro-Nazi, not knowing what was happening right under their noses.

Jan Erik was curious as to why this one street had shown so much humanity, each house guarding its dangerous secret from its neighbour. He discovered that in the 1940s this area had been populated by intellectuals and artists who had previously numbered Jews among their friends, explaining a lot about how fundamental human connections, and the empathy and understanding this generates, saves lives.

On their drive back on that dark night to central Amsterdam, a glistening shard of memory from those distant post war days suddenly came back to Betty. She had never shared it with anyone before as it was one of those instances that can shape history but have no particular significance at the time it happened. The visit to Blaricummerweg had propelled it back to the forefront of her mind.

After the war ended, Betty had been working as a secretary for a civil servant whose government department controlled the distribution of paper, a valuable commodity immediately after the war as the limited amount available needed to be used wisely and productively. She told Jan Erik of a call she had received in

1947 from her wartime protector Annie Romein. Annie explained that a friend of hers had a manuscript that needed publication – it was the diary of his young daughter murdered in the Holocaust. After several rejections, they had at last found a company who wished to publish it, would she agree to supply the paper? Betty went to have a word with her boss, who agreed to supply Contact with the paper to publish 1,500 copies of *Het Achterhuis* – now known throughout the world as *Anne Frank – The Diary of A Young Girl*.

A phone call, a simple insignificant administrative action, and history is made. Jan Erik had found it perplexing that Betty, who in later life had been so interested and involved in her brother's educational work for the Anne Frank Center USA, had completely overlooked her important role in the chain of events that had brought Anne Frank's diary to the world.

The Love Story of Bergen-Belsen

In March 2017, I was staying for a few days in Los Angeles with Margrit Polak and her husband Harvey Shield, a London-born musician. Margrit is Jack Polak's daughter. Her mother, Catharina 'Ina' Soep Polak, had died in May 2014 at the age of 91, and unexpectedly her father Jack, who was a decade older, had outlived his beloved wife – but only by eight months, passing away in January 2015 at the age of 102.

I had heard a lot about Margrit from Jan Erik over the years, and although she and I had never met before the afternoon I walked through the door of her Victorian house in Echo Park, we connected immediately. We hugged, laughed and had fun over the following three days I stayed there.

One afternoon Margrit prepared tea and we sat at her table in a room surrounded by mementoes of her Dutch family. For the next two hours she opened up to me about the impact gradually learning the truth about her family story had had on her own life and more facts about her aunt Betty and the amazing love story of Jack and Ina.

Jack Polak and Ina Soep had fallen in love in Westerbork transit camp after their arrests in Amsterdam. They had first met at a birthday party of a mutual friend in 1943, and in Jack's case it was love at first sight. He was a struggling young accountant, already married, and Ina was the daughter of a wealthy diamond manufacturer. By the time he had met Ina, Jack's marriage to his flirtatious and vivacious wife Manja was in an increasingly unhappy state, and they had agreed to divorce should they both survive the war. Ina's fiancé Rudy Acohen had been arrested in a Nazi reprisal round-up of Jewish men in 1941, but she did not know at the time of the party that Rudy had been deported and was probably by then already dead.

Remarkably Jack found himself sharing Barrack 64 in Westerbork camp with both his wife Manja and his amour Ina, which he later sardonically described as 'not easy'. Ina was in a dilemma, feeling guilt about her missing fiancé but having more and more feelings for Jack. It was a very complex and bizarre situation, and on one occasion, when Ina got very sick, Manja gave up her own bread to save her. When it was difficult to meet, Jack and Ina started exchanging letters. 'I'm writing with a pencil stub. Darling, try to steal a pencil for me somewhere,' wrote Jack in one of his letters.

After their miraculous survival of Bergen-Belsen, and deeply in love with Ina, Jack divorced Manja, with whom he afterwards remained friends, and married Ina, who had returned to Amsterdam to the confirmation that her fiancé Rudy would never be coming back. Jack and Ina Polak emigrated to New York in 1951 with their two sons, Frederick, named after his murdered grandfather, and Anthony. Upon arrival in his new country, Jacob Polak, previously known to his Dutch family and friends as Jaap, Americanized his name to Jack. He got work as an accountant, they had a third child, a daughter called Margrit, and then he started to dabble in the stock market using his own and clients' funds. Jack's life as an investment counsellor started to take off.

In 1980, as a young adult, Margrit happened upon something that would change her life. She had been fascinated by a letter that her father kept in his study. It was in Dutch and apparently written to his beloved Ina during their time in the camps. One day, he casually told Margrit that there were 'probably more letters up in the attic'. As a teenager, and having learnt about her family's European history, she had experienced nightmares that there were both dreaded Nazis and the ghosts of murdered Jews living above them in their own New York attic. The attic of the Polak's large family home in New York was not a place that Margrit ever relished visiting. Summoning all her courage and buoyed by curiosity, she ventured up to the top of the house and after a good poke around found a bag within which was a folder containing a large collection of letters. They were in fact 130 passionate love letters from Jack to Ina, written in another time and a terrible place, where each day was thought to perhaps be their last. As Margrit had imagined, there had indeed been ghosts in the attic.

Margrit had suddenly found a cause and she set about working with her father to translate the letters into English. She convinced him that translating the letters together would help her to learn Dutch. Ina was still too traumatized by those years to take any part in the process, and even working with Jack took many months as Margrit adopted a patient and sensitive approach, working on just one letter at a time. She became so passionate about uncovering every aspect of her parents' lives that she even went over to Amsterdam to interview her father's first wife Manja. In 2000, the love letters became the basis of a book, *Steal A Pencil for Me*, and then a documentary film with the same title made by Michele Ohayon. The film was critically acclaimed and won several film festival awards, including the Yad Vashem Prize at the Jerusalem Film Festival. It continues to be used in schools throughout the US for Holocaust education. In 1992, Jack Polak was knighted by Queen Beatrix of the Netherlands for his work in Holocaust education.

Prompted by my curiosity to know more during my visit, Margrit and I spent time talking about her parents and their remarkable story. During her childhood there had been no mention of the Holocaust at home, but there were odd references made to the many family photos that adorned the walls. In answer to little Margrit's enquiries about the faces who stared down at her every day, there would be from her Mom, 'That's my cousin, she died in the war', or from her Dad, 'They were my parents, they didn't survive the war'. These were the only descriptions of her murdered family members that Margrit remembered. It was the same with her parents' Dutch survivor circle who would visit their home, elegantly-dressed Continental people who would drop their lively chatter during the evening to talk about 'certain things' in whispers.

One day in her early teens, Margit had been taken by her father to an amateur football game in the Bronx and so found herself with one to one time and the opportunity to probe further his early life in Europe. He quietly explained to his inquisitive American-raised daughter that his own parents had actually been murdered, he had had a difficult time in those years and talked briefly about his marriages to Manja and to Ina. But then the subject was closed down again.

Margrit only really found out about the Holocaust when she went to interview a local survivor called Jack Topolsky for her school magazine. At that stage she was trying to 'put the pieces together'. Margrit Polak finally learnt the truth about her own family's experiences through Topolsky's story. The terrible and incomprehensible truth about her parents' early lives affected Margrit's teenage years deeply. She was a sensitive and creative girl and started to read incessantly about the subject to find out more and more.

After school, she moved herself far away from New York to Kenyon College in Ohio, where she majored in drama (some years earlier their 'star pupil', one Paul Newman, had also studied the art of acting). After several years as an actress and then acting coach, Margrit opened a successful talent agency. Meanwhile she had married Harvey Shield, a musician who was a member of the London rock band that became Deep Purple, and had their daughter Sofia, known as Sofi.

For Margrit the stresses of the frenetic world of pitching clients around Hollywood are broken up by an early-morning walk of her dog around Echo Park Lake, a midday half-hour stop for a silent meditation session and her leisurely commute to work, which simply requires an enjoyable stroll down the path of her fragrant rear garden.

Margrit and Harvey's garden, with its lush trees, hot tub, barbeque and constantly blue sky, is firmly Californian, however the interior of the house is overtly European in its feel. Many of its contents help to keep the connection tangibly alive between Margrit, her daughter Sofi and their Dutch heritage. Sofi, who had been very close to her grandparents, had recently graduated from the University of Amsterdam with a Masters' Degree in Conflict Resolution and Government, while spending some of her time in the city as a volunteer at the Anne Frank House.

As we sat in her Los Angeles house, Margrit Polak wanted to tell me about the next project to share her family's history for posterity and to 'give life to those no longer there'. She and Sophie were planning to work on this together. Margrit pulled out a weathered album from beneath a pile of documents. It contained a series of black-and-white photographs that captured a summer's day in the Netherlands in 1941. A group of eight teenagers from Amsterdam had been on a cycling excursion in the countryside. One of them had recorded the laughter-filled day on camera, and the albums were distributed to all the eight. Ina's copy of the album had lain in her parents' Amsterdam home throughout the seizure of the house by the Nazis and had been found after liberation, along with half the family's valuable silver cutlery which had inexplicably been left behind.

The happy and carefree group of teenage cyclists included two Christians and six Jews, four of whom were to be killed within the next three years. There, amongst the group, was the pretty young Catharina Soep. Between that day of laughter and fun, and her death in New York in 2014 at age 91, the fortunes of Ina Catharina Soep Polak's life had turned like the wheels of her cycle.

Chapter 29

Anne Frank and her Fear

During her time in hiding, Anne often wrote about her fear of betrayal, arrest by the Nazis and its consequences. But this fear, as described from the relative safety of the hiding place on the Prinsengracht in the city of Amsterdam, would have been as nothing compared to the terror of the long train journey to Auschwitz, the separation from her adored and protective father, the strength and luck needed to get through each day, and the emptiness and despair knowing there were no rescuers in sight.

On 25 March 1944 Anne wrote a story entitled 'Fear'. She imagined not being in hiding, but nonetheless still trapped in war.

> It was eight thirty in the evening. The shooting had died down a bit and I was dozing fully dressed on the divan when we were suddenly startled by two horrendous booms. We all leapt to our feet as if we had been pricked with a pin and went to stand in the hall. Even Mother, who was normally so calm, looked pale. The booms were repeated at fairly regular intervals, and then all of a sudden there was a crash, followed by screams and the tinkle of broken glass. I began running as fast as my legs would carry me. Bundled up with warm clothes and with my rucksack on my back, I ran and ran away from the horrible mass of flames.

But Anne had an answer to the fear that had taken hold of her. She describes what happened next.

> I was in a field of grass, the moon was shining and the stars were gleaming overhead, the weather was wonderful, the night was chilly but not cold. Hearing no more noise, I sank exhausted to the ground, spread out the blanket I was still carrying and lay down. I gazed up at the sky and suddenly realized I was no longer afraid. On the contrary, I was quite calm. The odd thing was that I wasn't thinking of my family at all, nor did I long for them. I longed only for rest, and soon I fell fast asleep in the grass beneath the starry sky. When I awoke, the sun was just coming up. I instantly realized where I was. In the distance the morning light revealed a row of familiar houses on the outskirts of the city. I rubbed

my eyes and took a closer look around. There wasn't a soul around. The dandelions and the clover leaves in the grass were my only company. I lay back down on the blanket and thought about what I should do next, but my thoughts kept wandering back to the wondrous feeling that had come over me in the night, when I had sat all by myself in the grass and not been afraid. Later I found my parents and we all went to live in another city. Now that the war has long been over I know why my fear vanished beneath that spacious sky. You see, once I was alone with nature, I realized, without actually being aware of it, that fear doesn't help, it doesn't get you anywhere. Anyone who is as frightened as I was should look to nature and realize that God is much closer than people think. From that moment on, though countless bombs fell close by, I was never really truly afraid again.

This is just one of several stories Anne wrote where she describes herself after the war, reaching adulthood or even as a 16-year-old, the age she didn't reach. She writes in her diary too of the comfort she got from nature and the changing of the seasons, as displayed to her by the yearly stages of the deciduous chestnut tree she could see from the window.

In Bergen-Belsen camp, located on the barren and frozen Luneberg Heath in northern Germany, there was no chestnut tree, no verdant grass or dandelions to remind Anne of the wonder of nature. When Lien Brillesljper and her sister Jannie, who had described Anne and Margot's final days in harrowing detail to Otto Frank, last saw the girls they seemed beyond the fear of their first weeks in captivity and way beyond the hope that Bergen-Belsen could offer more of a chance of life than Auschwitz. Consumed by the fever of typhus and by delirium from lack of food, surrounded by the dead and dying, Annelies Marie Frank, the girl who just seven months earlier had written, 'I must hold on to my ideals, for perhaps the day will come when I will be able to realize them,' was accepting of the inevitable.

Having been involved with the stories of so many people who experienced and witnessed brutality, I often think about their terror in their final days, moments, seconds of their lives or their freedom, and wish that by thinking hard, I could somehow lessen that terror. I have heard their stories first hand and witnessed their determination to live as normal lives as possible. I think about 18-year-old Stephen Lawrence, waiting for a bus home, perhaps musing on how he will spend the following day and then seeing and hearing the knife-wielding mob surging towards him intent on harm. I think of Daniel Pearl, who refused sedation in his final moments before the knife slit his throat, instead defiantly declaring himself a proud Jew. I think of Nelson Mandela, a qualified lawyer and tribal prince, standing erect in the dock hearing that he will spend the next thirty years in a bare prison cell. I think of the mothers trying to shield their children from the bloodstained machetes of Rwanda, the rifles of the Einzatsgruppen killing squads, or the suffocation by poisonous fumes in the gas chambers, the despair and fear of a helpless mother or father. I think of those I personally know who experienced horror. I think of Eva Schloss, a fifteen-year-old believing she was alone in the world as her beloved mother had been gassed. I think of Zlata Filipović, now a successful documentary maker, trembling as a child in a cellar in Sarajevo while the bombs rained down, and Saranda Bogujevci, an artist and fundraiser for Manchester Aid to Kosovo, playing dead while her family really lay dead all around her. I think of Ahmad Nawaz, at 14-years-old lying in the agony of a bullet in his arm, being trampled by a gunman while having to play dead and then seeing his teacher burned alive.

No words of compassion or understanding can ever lessen the fears and agonies of those who have suffered these atrocities. All we can do is our tiny little bit to help make the world better.

Chapter 30

Anne Frank and the Future

This book has described a 'magical thread' that has circumnavigated the globe in the form of the Anne Frank travelling exhibition.

As this account of the impact of learning about Anne Frank over the past thirty years draws to a close, there seems to be no sign of interest in her life abating. Currently there is a stream of enquiries to the Anne Frank House to bring the exhibitions and educational programmes even further afield. But the time may come in the future that this fast moving world will no longer share the abiding passion for a teenage girl who died before the middle of the last century. If it is to continue, education about Anne Frank will need to adapt to the evolving demands and situations of our societies. Europe is currently threatened by the rise of a new type of Fascism, that of extremist ideology and cruelty conducted in the name of religion. It has spilled into Europe's major cities from its breeding ground in the Middle East and Indian sub-continent. People are also being drawn to the extreme right, which can erupt into the violence of Anders Behring Breivik, who murdered seventy-seven people, including sixty-nine teenage participants of a summer camp, in Norway in 2011, or Thomas Mair, who murdered the young mother and Member of Parliament Jo Cox in her own Yorkshire constituency in 2016. The belief by adherents in the righteousness and justification of the hatred fanned by both sets of views is as alarming as that of Hitler's massed worshippers' belief in their racial superiority.

Whereas the nightmares of Western children during the Cold War years were about a Soviet nuclear attack, young people now fear what could happen to them at a pop concert, football match or sight-seeing trip to a European capital city. Will a fear of crowded places generate more dependence on virtual communication with friends through social media? Will young people become as isolated from human contact in their social lives as Anne Frank was in her hiding place?

Since the economic crash of 2008, we have suffered a decade with negligible interest rates on savings and widely-fluctuating stock markets. We are currently educating a generation of youngsters who do not understand the age-old concept that money, if it is wisely saved, can actually grow, so it's no surprise that saving money for the future is not on the agenda. And then there is the planet itself. When I was a child and learnt that we stay rooted on the ground through gravity and centrifugal force, I started to have nightmares that the

Earth would slowly stop spinning and we would all be thrown into space. Then my childhood fears changed to the threat of huge meteors hurtling towards us from the stratosphere, not to mention an invasion by aliens. In hindsight it was fanciful, unlike the reality of the long-term and profound effects of climate change and global warming that are facing children now. These are scary and unpredictable times in which to try to engender hope and aspiration for the future in teenagers.

With this in mind, I asked several of the educators whose work has been featured in these pages for their thoughts about Anne Frank's role as the world moves further away from the middle of the twentieth century, and towards the time when the last first-hand witnesses of those times are no longer living, breathing or speaking. I will start with two women who have worked for many years with the Anne Frank projects in Latin America: Mariela Chyrikins and Joelke Offringa. Mariela is based in Amsterdam and Buenos Aires, but has worked on Anne Frank projects throughout the Spanish speaking countries of the South American continent. Mariela believes that the story of Anne Frank will continue to provide unique insights into human nature, especially into the more negative aspects of 'homo socius'. However, she knows that it will be more challenging as time passes to convince young people of the importance of this history to their own personal lives and their community. Mariela also feels that this will be the case even in those countries directly affected by the Holocaust, let alone in places where there is no direct link. Nonetheless, she believes from her experience that Anne Frank's diary is still one of the most powerful tools that can be used to engage young people in reflection about the Holocaust and related issues, despite the fact that Anne wrote the diary before being arrested and experiencing the horrors of the death camps herself.

Joelke Offringa runs the Anne Frank programmes in the huge Portuguese-speaking country of Brazil, through the NGO she set up called the Instituto Plataforma Brasil. Climate change is already having a noticeable consequence on the country's vast but perilously shrinking rainforests, which affect the entire world's ecosystem. In Brazil you will find extreme wealth and poverty living, but not co-existing, in surprisingly close proximity. Joelke and her team at the Instituto Plataforma Brasil believe there is a need for Brazilian young people to work closely together, hand-in-hand with all the other sectors of society, to create a better environment and tackle climate change at the grass-roots level. By doing so they will be taking their future lives into their own hands.

Through this process of co-creating, a new Anne Frank educational project titled 'From Ego to Eco' has already been developed in the municipality of Cabreúva in the vast state of São Paulo. Youngsters have been working together from across differing community sectors with the joint aim of creating a just and sustainable society. As a result of this educational programme, the 'All for Cabreúva Movement' has emerged, an organized active community initiative that unites young people, local government and civil society. And there, at the core of this exciting new initiative thousands of miles away from her Amsterdam hiding place, is Anne Frank. The young Brazilian participants are motivated into action by learning about Anne Frank's life and views through an exhibition entitled 'Let Me Be Myself', the most recent travelling exhibition created by the Anne Frank House. Anne Frank's plea to adults – those living with her and those unknown who persecuted her – sparked the exhibition's poignant title and her voice is strongly reflected in a youth-driven Brazilian movement for future change.

By using this exhibition and Anne's plea as the starting point, the Instituto Plataforma Brasil believe that a culture of peace is first created based on the understanding of the importance of good relations: with yourself, with the other, with your environment and with the spaces of decision. The youngsters involved go through a process of empowerment, receiving ongoing training and preparation as guides, and then by producing and utilising their own videos as triggers for reflection on Human Rights dilemmas in daily life. Joelke and her team strongly believe in Brazilian youth as the solution rather than the problem. Their ultimate aim for their country is the future implementation of a permanent youth forum and other community projects where young people are drivers for improvement to their multiracial society, one which comprises the descendants of original Native Brazilians and Portuguese colonizers, as well as the waves of Black African, European, Arab, and Japanese immigrants. The demography of the country has been changing and in the past decade, black and mixed-race Brazilians now outnumber whites. As Joelke explains, 'Our plans involve a deep process of learning how to respect individual identities and, progressively, will embrace the power of diversity to safeguard our shared future, uniting governments, civil society and youth to build a new dynamic society together'. In order to carry out and grow her vision of widespread youth civic and political engagement in a country thirteen times the size of France, Joelke will be relying heavily on the use of communication technologies. She firmly believes that Anne Frank's role cannot be underestimated in a truly forward-looking project that encourages young people to reflect on the dangers of discrimination, racism and social exclusion, and reinforces the importance of freedom, equal rights, democracy, and respect for diversity. And perhaps Anne Frank, who wrote so movingly about her love of nature, could even have a hand in the reversal of our planet's ecological catastrophe.

Back across the Atlantic in northern Europe, Norbert Hinterleitner, Head of Education at the Anne Frank House, described a project he had undertaken a decade earlier that could have future implications for divisive communities that straddle national borders. Between 2005 and 2009, Norbert and his colleague Peter Hörburger from the Anne Frank Verein (Association) based in Vienna, ran a project they called 'Crossing Borders' along the Austrian-Slovenian border. Schools from the regions Carinthia and Styria, lying on both sides of the border, participated. These regions have both Austrian and Slovenian names; the region we call Carinthia in English is called Kärnten (German) and Koroška (Slovene), and Styria is called Steiermark (German) and Štajerska (Slovene). As in many other communities where groups from a different ethnic heritage live side by side, freedom to use one's language can become a matter of great significance. Jörg Haider, the leader of the populist right wing Freedom Party and Governor of Carinthia from 1989–91 and 1999–2008, was against bilingualism in the Austrian region of southern Carinthia, despite the fact that an indigenous Slovene community had lived there for generations. In 2001, the Austrian Constitutional Court had ruled that road signs in areas of Carinthia which had Slovene-speaking inhabitants, should be written in both the languages of German and Slovene. Haider hatched a cynical plan to outwit this by moving the German signs a few metres to outside the jurisdiction of the court's ruling. This triggered a wave of protest among the local Slovene minority, including some acts of civil disobedience.

Here was an inflammatory situation in a border region between two nations where the language issue was playing a significant role. The local inhabitants approached the Anne Frank Verein in Vienna, who, as well as taking the Anne Frank exhibition to the area, facilitated open and safe discussion in schools within the community. The aim of the 'Crossing Borders' project was to enable exchange between the young people of Austria and Slovenia to give them new insights into each other's lives – their interests, their understanding of history and their ideas about the future. In schools on both sides of the border, Peter Hörburger led debates on the language issue, whilst a professional film-maker interviewed one of the official representatives of the Slovenian Minority in Carinthia, which was spoken in German and subtitled in Slovenian.

In Britain, the Anne Frank Trust continues to garner plaudits and empirical proof of the success of its peer education methods. Mukith Khalisadar, who arrived at the Anne Frank Trust as a young project assistant in 2006 and went on to manage the Trust's London Schools Project, is one who also believes that Anne Frank's story is a timeless way of educating about the dangers of prejudice. He feels that her teenage writing defies time because her emotions of love, anger and frustration are what every young person feels at that age. He says that 'Anne's way of communicating her message in her diary will always be relevant. Although most young people don't keep diaries now, they have Facebook and Instagram and other social media platforms to communicate their message.'

Mukith insists that in ten or twenty years' time, Anne Frank's life will still be relevant and her story won't stop needing to be told. 'I could be naïve and say that in the coming decades time her story won't be relevant as there will be equality everywhere, but I have to be realistic. There will continue to be injustice in the world until people can accept that there will always be difference between people, and until people start to realize and respect that fact there will never be equality.' The Anne Frank project's ability to help bring about honest discussion on painful topics can be summed up by one London teenager who was motivated by learning Anne's story to speak out. He told his peer group in a facilitated discussion on stereotyping, 'It's not a good feeling when people see me just as a black boy. They're missing a lot of other things about me.' Sadly, Mukith was right, Anne's story will continue to be needed.

In a lecture given in San Francisco in 2017, Ronald Leopold, the Director of the Anne Frank House, explored the moral dilemmas surrounding Anne Frank's continued iconic status in the world, even referring to her as 'a queen among icons'. Covering many of the issues that have occupied the minds of the educators, researchers and guardians of Holocaust memory who have been featured in this book, he asked,

> Must she be protected against those who would use her as a tool for their own present-day political ends? Must she be protected against comparisons between then and now? Must she be protected against those who would wish to de-Judaify her? Must she be protected against those who would prefer to ignore their own roles as perpetrators? Must she be protected against those who shared her fate, the survivors who suffered just as she did, and who look upon the 'personality cult' surrounding her with abhorrence and pain? Do we have to demystify her and make her an ordinary girl again (which is anything but what she wanted to be)? . . . And if we answer just some of these questions in the affirmative, who should do the protecting?

He went on,

> For a long time, the Anne Frank House has felt and expressed the responsibility to counteract the misuse and abuse of the memory of Anne Frank. There were also good reasons for this: after all, what is at stake is a vulnerable legacy that is threatened from all sides. Firstly, of course, from neo-Nazi circles who have regularly denied the authenticity of the diary of Anne Frank, often as a component of Holocaust denial in general. Secondly, her memory is threatened by the pressure to commercially exploit it. Examples of Anne Frank merchandising constantly crop up, from roses and tulips bearing her name to T-shirts, caps, underwear and Anne Frank snacks on Amsterdam canal boats. This marketing does not necessarily have to lead to a devaluation of her legacy, but it does pave the way for increasing superficiality. Thirdly, the remembrance of Anne Frank is threatened by appropriations that simply have to be called into question.

Referring to the responsibility of the Anne Frank House's central and worldwide role in the remembrance of this girl's life and death, he pondered on whether what could be considered 'undesirable appropriations' should be stopped. His conclusion, for several reasons, was that they should not. Ronald was looking to the future when he came to this conclusion. He reasoned that,

> More than seventy years after the end of the Second World War, the greatest threat to the remembrance of the life story of Anne Frank and the history of her time is that *no* appropriations will be made of them at all. In other words: that this history is in danger of becoming ever less relevant to current and future generations. It is precisely the fact that Anne Frank remains a source of inspiration, in whatever context, that her life story does not lose relevance, even if we might raise our eyebrows at the ways in which the connection with today's world is made.

A contentious issue, particularly among academics in the field of Holocaust studies, has been using Holocaust history for tackling social issues such as bullying in school, and more recently online. Ronald felt that even though the Anne Frank House were not proponents of using the life story of Anne Frank for anti-bullying programmes, citing the big difference between bullying on the one hand and persecution on the other, he did understand the reasons for doing this, and that this could even 'add more colour to the palette of the remembrance of Anne Frank'.

In saying so, he was, however, adamant that in order to diversify the use of Anne Frank's story as a vehicle for addressing social issues, the history must be reliably and authentically presented. He pledged that the Anne Frank House would never relinquish its role in taking a stand against attacks on the authenticity of the diary of Anne Frank and attempts at Holocaust denial.

Professor Tony Kushner of the Department of History at the University of Southampton, and one of the Anne Frank Trust's first board members, reflected on how Holocaust education had moved on over the past three decades since the Trust had been set up. 'Even just twenty years ago we were fighting tough battles to get the Holocaust taught, but now it's so established, it's easy.' He compared the Conservative government's plan for a new Westminster-sited Holocaust memorial for Britain, and its £50,000,000 cost, to the unsuccessful campaign to get a similar memorial for slavery, which in fact had a closer connection to several British cities such as Liverpool, Manchester and Bristol.

Tony felt there was a great future in education about Anne Frank but there was however a danger of complacency because the Holocaust is currently considered such a safe topic. After the non–existence of Holocaust education until the 1990s, and then its growth up to now, he felt that the third stage moving forward should be more reflection about what we can improve. Referring to his own area of expertise, that of Britain and the Holocaust, he noted that the Kindertransports (the children's rescue transports of the late 1930s) were looked upon positively as

Britain welcoming endangered children. 'But in fact the parents should have been allowed to come too.'

He was optimistic that the work of the Anne Frank Trust would ensure that complacency doesn't happen. Echoing Ronald Leopold's insistence on imparting sound historical knowledge, Tony made clear his view that, 'Connections should be made, and will be made, between then and now, but a good knowledge of what happened then and what is actually happening now can help avoid crass comparisons. For example, the homosexual community was persecuted but very few gay people were killed in the camps, rather they were arrested and held in police cells.'

Tony expressed another concern. 'You know, I'm very aware of the dangers of Anne Frank falling into the wrong hands. Her story can so easily be made into schmaltz. But it is a story that is so powerful, especially as now we take the story right into Bergen-Belsen.' And then this distinguished academic and renowned historian surprised me by letting his emotion guide his thoughts, 'The seven seconds of moving footage of Anne Frank, used to such powerful effect in the final scene of Jon Blair's film "Anne Frank Remembered", still has an amazing power to get to me. Anne was a messy, incredibly bright person and seeing her alive brings home the loss, not just of her, but all the others.'

The Anne Frank House's International Director Jan Erik Dubbelman, after over thirty years of travelling the world with the Anne Frank exhibitions, has a pragmatic view about Holocaust education, 'Even the Holocaust with a big "H" doesn't move the general public now like it did our generation.' However, referring to the peer-to-peer educative approach he expanded, 'But the idea to engage young people and give them responsibility for teaching others, be it in Sri Lanka, Brazil or Argentina, the same magic seems to apply. It is not an exclusively European or Christian concept. Young people learn when they explore, less so when they listen.'

The Anne Frank House and the Anne Frank Trust UK are now harnessing the power of social media to let young people spread Anne's message themselves. 'Switch Off Prejudice' is a British government-funded innovative new programme that the Anne Frank Trust have designed for young people to help them understand the dangers of prejudice and discrimination that they can encounter in the digital world, where they are being increasingly exposed to hate speech. The programme examines prejudice and discrimination both from a historical perspective, and in the modern world, encouraging young people to question and challenge what they see online, and nurturing their development as responsible digital citizens.

The Trust's teenage 'Anne Frank Ambassadors' who participate in the programme will learn how to make their own social media campaigns to share Anne's powerful message, how to research information needed to support their campaigns, and how to use the different online social media platforms. They are being taught how to distinguish between fact and opinion in this challenging digital area, and how to become safer, more responsible, competent, confident and creative users of social media and other technologies.

***

Personally, I have had a long-held dream to see a real thread joining up the legions of young people around the world who have been motivated into positive thoughts and actions by learning about Anne Frank. I have often referred to this idea by my own term of 'Anne's Army' – creating the physical embodiment of the force for good that Otto Frank envisaged when he dedicated his life to his daughter's diary. Along these lines, in 2017, the Anne Frank House started developing a project called the 'Anne Frank Youth Network'. This will be an expanding global network of young people aged between 15 and 20 trained to challenge discrimination, racism and anti-Semitism through peer education and volunteering in their communities. The Anne Frank House will work with its locally-based partners in fifty different countries a year, encouraging and equipping around 6,000 young people to play an active role in shaping society. The young participants will have online access to specially created learning resources and social media contact with each other. The Anne Frank Youth Network aims to trigger a global movement of youth activists who will play an active role in creating positive change in their local communities. The Anne Frank Youth Network could maybe play their part in creating a world free from hatred, a world where all humans are treated with dignity and where people aren't indifferent to the suffering of others. In return, members of the Anne Frank Youth Network will feel valued, motivated and empowered.

As I write, there are plans to take the Anne Frank exhibition and accompanying education programmes to South Korea, Taiwan, and Myanmar. The pilot projects held in Vietnam, India, Sri Lanka and Bangladesh are being expanded. Thailand and the Philippines have expressed interest in showing the exhibition. In the continent of Africa, the South African tour continues and there have been expressions of interest in the exhibition from Tanzania and Rwanda, and in the 'Free To Choose' human rights workshops from Morocco and even Egypt. In Brazil, as well as the community programmes in São Paulo, a chain of Brazilian supermarkets is considering bringing the Anne Frank exhibition to all of its ninety-one shopping malls in the country. The extensive education programmes in Argentina and Uruguay, and the exhibition tours in Peru, Colombia and Venezuela may be extended into Paraguay. In the Caribbean, programmes are scheduled for the islands of the Dutch Antilles, Trinidad and Tobago and Surinam, and across the Pacific in Polynesia, Hawaii hosted its first-ever Anne Frank exhibition in December 2017.

On 15 July 1944, Anne wrote about how hard it was to hold on to her ideals when she could feel the suffering of millions and see the 'approaching thunder that one day will destroy us too'. And then she remembers the comfort she got from looking up at the sky (something we take for granted, but she could only do on the rare occasions she climbed the steep ladder steps to the attic above the hiding place). She finishes her entry by writing, 'And yet, when I look up at the sky, I somehow feel that everything will change for the better, that this cruelty too will end, that peace and tranquillity will return once more. In the meantime, I must hold on to my ideals. Perhaps the day will come when I'll be able to realize them!'

That day never came. But through her father's mission, through determined educators, through community activists and thousands upon thousands of young people around the world, Anne Frank's ideals are being realized.

References

Author's note

Most of the content of this book has been my own recollections and interviews - many of them thanks to Skype - with colleagues who are credited within the pages. Historical dates and facts were cross checked using several online references in each case. Hence this list of references may appear somewhat short as I have only listed books and media that I have taken direct quotes from. Books and media referenced, but not quoted from, have been listed in the Index.

Chapter 5: 'Eva's Story' Eva Schloss, W H Allen, 1988

'The Promise' Eva Schloss, Puffin Books, 2004

'After Auschwitz' Eva Schloss and Karen Bartlett, 2013

Chapter 7: 'Reflections in Rhyme' Bertha Klug 1972, self-published

Chapter 8: Robert Cox, former editor of the Buenos Aires Herald writing in The Guardian, 1999

Chapter 9: 'Audrey Hepburn, An Elegant Spirit' Sean Hepburn Ferrer, Atria Books, 2003

Chapter 10: 'Voices from the Past' Herbert Levy, Book Guild Publishing, 1995

Chapter 11: 'Zlata Filipovic, whose journal was Sarajevo's answer to Anne Frank's diary, tells of her fears for Bosnia today' Harriet Alexander, Daily Telegraph, 2012

Chapter 13: 'We Are Stones: Anne Frank, The Diary and The Play' Len Rudner Published on Linked In 2015

'Anne Frank, The Biography' Melissa Müller, Bloomsbury Publishing, 1999

Chapter 14: 'Speaking with conviction, how an 85-year-old survivor reduced high-security prisoners to tears' Rosa Doherty, Jewish Chronicle, 2014

'Shut in: relating to Anne Frank' Jackie Cosh Times Educational Supplement, 2012

Chapter 17: 'Anne Frank, The Biography' Melissa Müller, Bloomsbury Publishing, 1999

'Treasures from the Attic, The Extraordinary Story of Anne Frank's Family' Mirjam Pressler with Gertrude Elias, Weidenfeld & Nicolson, 2011

Chapter 19: 'The Anne Frank Declaration', Barry van Driel for the Anne Frank Educational Trust, 1998

Chapter 21: 'The Hidden Life of Otto Frank' Carol Ann Lee, Viking, 2002

Chapter 25: 'Anne Frank in the Land of Manga' Alain Lewkowicz, iPad application and book Arte Editions, 2013

'Diary of a Vietcong doctor: The Anne Frank of Vietnam' David McNeill, The Independent, 2005

'Last Night I Dreamed of Peace, The Diary of Dang Thuy Tram' first published in Vietnam, 2005. Paperback edition, Penguin Random House, 2008

Chapter 26: 'Why it's kosher to joke about Anne Frank' Ricky Gervais, Jewish Chronicle, 2012

'The Ghost Writer' Philip Roth, Farrar, Straus & Giroux, 1979

'The Lesson of the Master' Robert Towers, New York Times Book Review, 1979

'Hope, A Tragedy' Shalom Auslander, Penguin, 2012

'What We Talk About When We Talk About Anne Frank' Nathan Englander, Weidenfeld & Nicolson, 2012

Dr Shirli Gilbert, Essay for the Oxford Journal, 2013

'The Fate of the Idea of Toleration' Professor Simon Schama, Inaugural Anne Frank Lecture, Anne Frank Trust UK with the Pears Institute for the Study of Antisemitism, sponsored by the Nirman Foundation, 2011

Chapter 29: 'Fear' a story from 'Anne Frank's Tales from the Secret Annexe' Halban Publishers, 2010

Exhibitions and Educational Resources referenced in this book:

'Anne Frank in the World 1929 – 1945', a travelling photographic exhibition that toured from 1985 – 1996. © Anne Frank House

'Anne Frank, A History for Today', a travelling photographic exhibition launched in 1997 and which is still touring internationally in various formats © Anne Frank House

'Anne Frank + You', a travelling photographic exhibition launched in 2005 and which is still touring. UK only. © Anne Frank House and Anne Frank Trust UK

'Let Me Be Myself' a travelling photographic exhibition launched in 2015 designed for peer education use. © Anne Frank House

'Switch Off Prejudice' workshops which aim to give students an in-depth insight into the dangers of prejudice and discrimination, looking at examples from the real world and online. UK only © Anne Frank Trust UK

International Anne Frank organizations:

Anne Frank House www.annefrank.org

Anne Frank-Fonds www.annefrank.ch

Anne Frank Trust UK www.annefrank.org.uk

Anne Frank Center for Mutual Respect, USA www.annefrank.com

Anne Frank Zentrum Germany www.annefrank.de

Centro Ana Frank Argentina www.centroanafrank.com.ar

International linked organizations:

South African Holocaust and Genocide Foundation www.ctholocaust.co.za

Instituto Plataforma Brasil www.ipbrasil.org

Seagull Foundation for the Arts, India www.seagullindia.com

Russian Research and Educational Holocaust Center (English site) http://en.holocf.ru

Gedenkdienst, Austrian volunteer organization www.gedenkdienst.at

Action Reconciliation Service for Peace, German volunteer organization www.actionreconciliation.org

Index

This index is of those people, places and resources that are integral to this story. Where a person or place has been mentioned in passing, I have not included the name in this index. I have not included in the indexing Anne Frank, Otto Frank, Anne's diary, the Anne Frank House nor Anne Frank Trust UK as they form the threads that run throughout the entire book.

Ahlers, Tonny 190-3
Ahmad, Nawaz 150
Allen, Ruth 112-14, 173, 176, 180
Altman, Dr Ilya 59-60, 62-4
Amnesty International 42
And Then They Came For Me 49-50, 66
Annan, Kofi 166-7
Anne Frank + You exhibition 104-5, 181-2, 260
Anne Frank Ambassadors 200-205
Anne Frank Awards for Moral Courage 43, 180-4, 260
Anne Frank Children to Children Appeal Bosnia 97, 110-15
Anne Frank Day 175-76
Anne Frank Declaration 50, 163-72
Anne Frank in the World exhibition 31-40, 45-7, 75, 83, 103, 120, 151, 224
Anne Frank Lecture 245
Anne Frank Remembered, documentary feature 24, 104, 136, 153, 158, 278
Anne Frank Remembered, memoir by Miep Gies 23
Anne Frank Trees 164
Anne Frank Verein 274-75

Anne Frank, A History for Today exhibition 30, 67, 79, 83, 85, 100, 103, 108, 147, 196, 233, 248
Anne Frank, The Diary of a Young Girl 24, 28, 74, 121, 249, 265
Arden, Jamie 198, 201
Argentina 80-6
Association Mutual Israelite Argentina (AMIA) 82-3
Auschwitz-Birkenau concentration camp 15, 17, 22-3, 45-7, 74, 140, 210, 212
Auslander, Shalom 239

Baboneau, Nicola 197
Bangladesh 256-60
Bartz, Immanuel 109
Bauman, Janina 210
Belzec concentration camp 8, 24
Bergen-Belsen concentration camp 15-7, 23, 59, 241-2, 246, 265-6, 270, 278
Bergman, Anka 210-11
Beslan massacre 62-3
Blair, Jon 24, 104, 128, 136, 153, 157-8, 278
Blair, Tony 178

Blitz, Sientje 128-9
Blunkett, Lord David 170, 181
Boateng, Lord Paul 178
Bogujevci, Saranda 183, 271
Bogujevci, Jehona 183
Bogujevci, Fatos 183
Bogujevci, Lirie 183
Bogujevci, Genc 183
Bogush, Tony 97, 111, 123-4, 157, 164, 166, 173, 176, 178, 186-7, 253
Bolkestein, Gerrit (Dutch wartime minister) 11
Bosnia Herzegovina 110-19, 164-5
Boyce, Heather 198
Boyce, John 243
Brazil 86-90
Brilleslijper, Jannie and Lientje 17, 270
Broekhuizen, Kleis 40
Brownstein, Shani 232-34
Buergenthal, Judge Thomas 179

Cameron, Rt Hon David 172
Careem, Nic 50, 104, 138, 165-6
Centro Ana Frank Argentina 81-2, 85-6
Challenger, Melanie 244
Chatterjee, Urbi 249-52
Chelmno concentration camp 8
Chile 78-80
China 234-6
Chinchilla, Erika del Carmen Mendez 91-2
Chyrikins, Mariela 78, 80, 82-6, 93-4, 273
Clarke, Eva 210-11
Clinton, President William J (Bill) 169
Collins, Richard 152-3
Contact Publishers 24, 174, 263, 265
Cooper, Rabbi Abraham 223

Dang, Thuy Tram 228-31
Dang, Kim Tram 228-31
Davidowicz, Monica 135

Davies, Ellen 103
de Bruyn, Jeroen 192
De Klerk, President FW 179
De Winter, Leon 241
De Winter, Rootje 'Rosa' 47
Delaney, Jonny 149
Delaney, Nellie 149
Delforge, Hippolyte 226
Doan, Ngoc Tram 230-1
Dogar, Sharon 242
Donda, Victoria 81
Donovan, Julia 102
Douglas, Sharon 77, 166-7
Dreams of Anne Frank, play by Bernard Kops 118, 164, 195
Dryburgh, Nicole 133
Dubbelman, Jan Erik 33-4, 36-7, 39-40, 55-8, 75, 78-9, 84, 86, 126, 164, 195-6, 200, 224-5, 231-2, 235, 248, 262-4, 278
Dubs, Lord Alf 217

Einzatsgruppen killing squads 61, 65
Elias, Bernd 'Buddy' 3-4, 12, 155-9, 164, 166-8, 174, 244
Elias, Helene 'Leni' 19, 155-6
Elias, Erich 4, 155-6
Elias, Stephan 3, 155-6, 158
Elias, Gertrude 'Gerti' 12, 156-9, 166
Englander, Nathan 239

Filipovic, Zlata 115-7, 271
Frank, Alice 3, 6, 19, 156
Frank-Hollander, Edith 2-4, 7-8, 10, 15, 17, 20-1, 23, 32, 46-7, 51-2, 129-132, 156
Frank, Herbert 19
Frank, Margot 1-5, 7, 11, 15-8, 20-1, 23, 33, 46, 52, 82, 130, 155-6, 159, 212, 214, 245, 270
Frank, Michael 19-20, 155
Frank, Robert 19

Frank Geiringer, Elfriede 'Fritzi' 24-5, 28-30, 40, 46, 49, 51-3, 73, 95, 98, 157, 174, 209
Futterman, Enid 244

Gadd, Steve 141-3
Galloway, Peter 176-7
Gandhi, Mahatma 247
Gedenkdienst Austrian Holocaust Memorial Service 69
Geiringer, Erich 45, 49, 51, 53
Geiringer, Heinz 45-6, 49, 52-3
Genieva, Ekatarina 58-9
Gervais, Ricky 238
Gibbs, Shona 205
Gies, Miep 9-10, 13-4, 18, 21, 23-4, 52, 74, 128-36, 157-8, 174-5, 183, 188, 209
Gies, Jan 14, 52, 129-31
Gilbert, Dr Shirli 240
Glennon, Lucy 170, 184, 196-8, 200, 231-3
Gold, David 207-8
Goldstein, David 173, 186
Goodrich, Frances 29, 240
Gorbachev, Mikhail 42, 43, 54
Goslar, Hannah 'Hanneli' 5-7, 15-7, 51, 102
Green, John 243
Greenman, Leon 208
Grootendoorst, Cor 135
Grootendoorst, Truus 135
Guatemala 91

Hackett, Albert 29, 240
Hartog, Lena 190
Helfgott, Ben 216
Hepburn, Audrey 95-8
Hill, Catherine 211-12
Hinterleitner, Norbert 64, 66-9, 196, 274
Hirst, Michael 176-7, 180
HMP Belmarsh 142

HMP Durham 138-9
HMP Holloway 142
HMP Reading 137-8
HMP Redditch 144
HMP Wakefield 141
HMP Wormwood Scrubs 48, 137, 139-40, 142-3
Hollander, Rosa 'Grannie' 3
Holocaust Educational Trust 36, 40
Holocaust Memorial Day 177, 202
Holocaust, American TV mini-series 41
Hondius, Dienke 32-3, 37-40, 76, 264
Horburger, Peter 274-5
Hussey, Michael 170, 175-6
Hyman, Mavis 149-50
Hyman, Esther 149

India 247-53
Instituto Plataforma Brasil 86, 273-4

Japan 223-8, 237
Jolie, Angelina 161, 172

Kanafi, Menachem 252
Karten, Ian 217
Kazakhstan 55, 70-2
Keen, Nan 24, 179
Kesselman, Wendy 240
KGB 63, 65
Khalisadar, Mukith 197, 200, 204-5, 258, 275-6
Kindertransport, children's rescue mission 21, 103, 106, 134, 277
Kindertransport, play by Diane Samuels 111
Kinsella, Ben 149
Kirill, Archbishop Vladimir 59
Kleiman, Johannes 7-9, 11, 13-4, 129-30, 188
Klein, Gillian 182
Klug, Bertha 'Bee' 38, 40, 73-77, 113, 133, 166-7, 176-7, 180, 191

Knoller, Freddie 140, 215
Kops, Bernard 118, 164, 195
Kugler, Victor 7-9, 11, 13-4, 129-30, 179, 188
Kulchevych, Sergiy 71-2
Kushner, Professor Tony 36, 40, 277-8

Lancaster, Sophie 149
Latvia 55, 66
Lawlor, Eddie 151
Lawrence, Stephen 43, 145-8, 270
Lawrence, Baroness Doreen 145, 148, 182
Lawrence, Neville 146-8
Leader, Nick 137-8
Ledermann, Susanne 'Sanne' 4-5, 7, 51
Lee, Carol Ann 190-3, 223
Leopold, Ronald 34, 187, 276-87
Let Me Be Myself exhibition 274
Levin, Meyer 29
Levy, Herbert 105-9, 138, 140-1, 147, 218, 241
Levy, Lilian 106-8, 218, 241
Lewis, Helen 153
Lewkowicz, Alain 223
Limb, Ann 186
Lithuania 55, 63
Liu, Michael 234-6
Livingstone, Ken 46-7
Luthra, Tanuj 249
Lynn, Dame Vera 179

Machado, Priya 247-9, 254-5, 259-60
Majdanek concentration camp 27
Malhotra, Megha 252-3, 259
Mandela, Nelson 120-22, 127, 165-6, 270
Mansfield, Elizabeth 227-8
Mauthausen concentration camp 17, 52-3, 210-11, 242
May, Rt Hon Theresa 171-2
Mayer, Peter 174
Mayer, Kay 207

Mbeki, Govan 121-2
McKinnon, Sir Don 170
Men, Alexander 58
Mendoza, Daniel 161, 180, 184
Merwedeplein 4-5, 8-9, 16, 21, 48, 50
Michels, Sir David 101, 176-7
Miliband, David 24, 179
Miliband, Ed 24
Mitchell, David 237-8
Mizen, Jimmy 149
Moggach, Deborah 243-4
Montessori School 4-7
Morris, Jack 176-7, 182, 186
Moscow 54-9
Mowlam, Marjorie 'Mo' 166-9
Mr Keesing, Anne's teacher 252
Muller, Melissa 136, 155, 189-90

Nagai, Nao 227-8
NASUWT 77, 183
Nawaz, Ahmad 271
Netherlands Institute for War Documentation 29
Neuengamme concentration camp 17

Offringa, Joelke 86-90, 273
O'Kane, Eamonn 183-4
Oliveira, Marceo Camargo 88
Opekta 4, 7-8, 18-129, 155, 189-90, 192
Osrin, Myra 122-3, 125-6
Otsuki, Michiko 226, 228

Pakistan 260-1
Palfreeman, Doug 105, 184
Pearl, Daniel 160-2
Pearl, Mariane 161-2
Pears, Sir Trevor 184-5
Pectacon 4, 7, 9
Peru 91-3
Peterer, Aaron 126-7, 248, 251, 254
Pfeffer, Fritz 9-10, 17, 129, 134
Pinochet, Augusto 78-80

Pisar, Samuel 41
Polak, Ina 241, 265-8
Polak, Jack 168, 240-1, 263, 265-7
Polak, Betty 262-4
Polak, Margrit 265-7
Portman, Natalie 240-1
Puisyte, Ruta 63-4

Ranasinghe, Anne 254-5
Rashid, Jani 202
Redhouse, David 137, 142-3
Refuseniks 42-3, 64-5
Remembering for the Future
    conference 36
Robinson, President Mary 124, 152
Roma 59, 92, 107, 195
Romein, Jan 24, 262-4
Romein, Annie 262-5
Rosen, Michael 164
Ross, Val 199
Roth, Philip 239
Rudner, Len 135-6
Russian Research & Educational
    Holocaust Centre 62

Savakis, Justin 237
Sayid, Ruki 113
Schama, Simon 245
Schild, Annabel 219-22
Schild, Daphne 179, 219-22
Schild OBE, Rolf 178, 219-22
Schipper, Ziggy 218
Schloss, Zvi 45, 48, 50, 73
Schloss Geiringer, Eva 39, 45-6, 49-51,
    53, 66, 73, 95-7, 138-40, 142, 160,
    164, 166, 168, 190, 243, 245, 271
Schuitema, Berend 28
Seagull Foundation for the Arts,
    Kolkata 247, 252, 259
Selwyn, Marsha 180-1
Serious Road Trip 113-4
Shvetsova, Yelena 70, 72

Silberbauer, Karl Josef 13, 130, 188-9
Silverberg, Ed 'Hello' 49
Simmons-Richner, Edith 97-8, 113-4
Singels, Loes 247-8, 254-5, 259-60
Sinti 92
Soetendorp, Rabbi Avraham 27, 55
Soetendorp, Rabbi David 24-5, 36,
    38-40, 43, 55, 76, 176
Soetendorp, Rabbi Jacob 24, 27, 38
South Africa 120-7
South African Holocaust and Genocide
    Centre 53
Spielberg, Steven 173-4, 178
Sri Lanka 253-6
Stanfield, Millie 21
Sternberg, Sir Sigmund 186
Suijk, Cornelius 24, 38, 76
Suzman, Dame Helen 124-5
Swerdlow, Michael 25-7
Szulman, Mauricio 80-2

Takagi, Yoko 225-6
Thatcher, Margaret 34, 54
The Black Book 60
The Diary of Anne Frank, feature film
    243-4
The Diary of Anne Frank,
    play 238-9
*The Promise: A Holocaust Tale of Love
    and Hope* 53
Theresenstadt concentration camp 17,
    133, 153, 210, 212-3, 215
Tito, Josip Brod 109
Treasures from the Attic, Gerti Elias
    and Mirjam Pressler 12, 156, 159
Tribich, Mala 216-8
Turgel, Gena 209, 214-5
Turgel, Norman 214-5
Tyack, Paul 196-8

Ukraine 54-5, 59-61
UNICEF 111, 116

Vallentine Mitchell, publisher 24
van Driel, Barry 78, 80, 93-4, 111,
   117-9, 163-4, 168, 194-6, 232
van Houte, Hans 28
van Kooten, Jan 85-6
van Maaren, Willem 189
van Maarsen, Jacqueline 51
van Marxveldt, Cissy 8
van Pels, Auguste 9-11, 16-17,
   130, 132-3
van Pels, Hermann 9-11, 17,
   129-30
van Pels, Peter 9, 11, 14, 17, 21-2, 130,
   163, 188, 242-3
van Wijk, Joop 192
Verhagen, Maxime 87-8
Vervaecke, Stefan 224-6, 235
Vierya, Magdalena 91-2
Vietnam 228-31
Vinakur, Clara 61
Voskuijl, Bep 9, 11, 13, 129, 188,
   190, 192
Voskuijl, Johannes 9
Voskuijl, Nelly 192

Waldheim, Kurt 68
Walker, Anthony 149
Wallenberg, Raoul 167, 207-8
Walnes, Joe 42
Walnes, Tilly 42, 178, 233
Westra, Hans 34, 39, 40, 56, 160, 187
Whelan, Shaun 206
Whitbourn, James 244
Whitehurst, Fred 229-30
Wijnberg, Hans 190
Wilson, Jed 198
Wilson, Jordan 201
Wineman, Freda 209, 212-14
Winton, Sir Nicholas 134-5, 209-10,
   212, 214-5, 217

Yacovitz, Elena 55-7, 62
Yamamuro, Riuchi 226-7
Yamamuro, Kenji 227
Yousafzai, Malala 249, 260-1
Yousafzai, Ziauddin 260-1

Zahid, Uzma 203-05
Zlata's Diary: A Child's Life 117